ALSO BY NANCY J. ALTMAN

The Battle for Social Security:
From FDR's Vision to Bush's Gamble
(Hoboken, NJ: John Wiley & Sons, 2005)

Social Security Works!
Why Social Security Isn't Going Broke and How
Expanding It Will Help Us All
(New York, NY: The New Press, 2015)
(with Eric R. Kingson)

THE TRUTH ABOUT SOCIAL SECURITY:

The Founders' Words Refute Revisionist History, Zombie Lies, and Common Misunderstandings

Nancy J. Altman

WASHINGTON D.C.

Published in the United States by Strong Arm Press, 2018

www.strongarmpress.com

Book design and Composition by Strong Arm Press.

Cover Art by Ebonie Land

Pictured on the Cover: President Franklin Roosevelt (left), Frances Perkins (center), and Arthur Altmeyer (right)

ISBN-13: 978-1-947492-12-7
ISBN: 1-947492-12-8

DEDICATION

Dedicated to my grandchildren, Ezekiel Jackson, Kylie Conner-Sax, Beatrice Jackson, and Sadie David-Sax, and to my grandnephews, Luke and Jake Trepanier, and Ryan and Jax Irwin. You and your peers are our most precious and valuable assets. You are the future.

SUMMARY OF CONTENTS

CONTENTS

CHAPTER ONE: THE FOUNDERS' VISION

President Franklin D. Roosevelt and the others who created Social Security understood the value of what they had accomplished. Frances Perkins was President Roosevelt's close advisor, his Secretary of Labor, and the chair of the Committee on Economic Security, his interagency task force that developed the Social Security legislation. In her memoir, *The Roosevelt I Knew*, she wrote that President Roosevelt "always regarded the Social Security Act as the cornerstone of his administration and, I think, took greater satisfaction from it than from anything else he achieved on the domestic front."[1]

Now more than eight decades old, our Social Security system has stood the test of time. Social Security insures wages against their loss in the event of disability, death, or old age. Its benefits are the most significant and, often, the only retirement annuities, life insurance, and disability insurance that America's working families have. It is most Americans' largest asset.

Social Security is not often described as an asset, yet it is. Though the exact value varies with age and other important factors, it is an extremely valuable one. In fact, it is among working families' most valuable assets. Take the case of a family of four consisting of a 30-year-old worker earning around $35,000, two young children, and a spouse, at home caring for the children. If that worker were killed in a highway accident, the family's Social Security's life insurance protection would provide monthly benefits with a present value of more than $674,000.[2]

If that worker did not die, but instead was so severely injured that future work was impossible, Social Security would provide worker and family benefits with a present value of more than $703,000.[3] Let's instead assume that the worker were neither killed nor disabled, but instead reaches age 65, earning $48,000. The married couple's Social Security retirement benefits have a present value of more than $527,000.[4]

Moreover, like the assets of trusts generally, Social Security benefits cannot be taken or garnished by private-sector creditors to satisfy debts. (In 1996, the law was changed to allow the federal government to garnish Social Security for outstanding student loans or other debts owed to the government.) The inability of creditors to get at Social Security adds immeasurably to its value.

Social Security Works

In addition to being an extremely valuable asset, Social Security works tremendously well. Today, over sixty million Social Security beneficiaries receive guaranteed monthly payments replacing lost wages. Unlike savings, this is income that cannot be outlived.

Social Security's guaranteed benefits are much more secure than retirement savings, which can be lost as the result of a market downturn or simply poor or unlucky investment decisions. They are also much more secure than employer-sponsored traditional pensions and much more secure, as well, than the life insurance, disability insurance, and retirement annuities sold by private insurance companies. Unlike private sector pensions and insurance products, Social Security is sponsored by the federal government, which is permanent, and so will not go out of business. All risks are spread nationwide, not concentrated on single employers, insurance companies, or worse, individual workers.

Furthermore, Social Security, unlike traditional pension plans, is easily and completely portable from employer to employer, and imposes fewer administrative costs on those employers. It is carried from job to job; records are kept seamlessly by the Social Security Administration through the use of Social Security numbers. Wages from all covered employment are automatically recorded by the

Social Security Administration and used in the calculation of benefits.

Moreover, Social Security includes features that are not found in private sector alternatives. For example, private sector annuities and defined benefit pensions reduce the annuity amount of the primary insured, if a spouse is added. In contrast, Social Security's annuities automatically include add-on benefits for the joint and survivor portion of the annuity without reducing by a penny the life annuity portion of married workers.

If the worker has been divorced after having been married ten years, there are add-on spouse and widow(er) benefits for every ex-spouse. Again, those add-on benefits don't reduce the worker's retirement, disability, and family benefits by a penny. Importantly, those divorced spouse and widow(er) benefits are the ex-spouse's as a matter of right. The parties to the divorce are spared the burden of having to negotiate or go to court to secure their benefits.

Though most probably don't realize it, Social Security is the nation's largest children's program.[5] Social Security provides benefits to children when adults supporting them lose wages as the result of death, disability, or old age. Like spousal benefits, these too are add-on benefits, not reducing by even a penny the primary insured's benefits.

Importantly, all benefits are annually increased to offset the effects of inflation. Social Security provides inflation protection without limit, regardless of the rate of that inflation. Consequently, unlike traditional private pension benefits which erode over time, Social Security maintains its purchasing power. (The measure of inflation is in need of updating, but the availability of uncapped inflation protection is one of Social Security's most valuable attributes.)

And the administration of our Social Security system is extremely efficient. Less than a penny of every Social Security dollar is spent on administration. The rest – more than 99 cents of every dollar – is paid in benefits. No private sector arrangement offers those features and that efficiency. Social Security's wage insurance can provide all of these benefits so efficiently because it is sponsored by the federal government.

Social Security's one shortcoming is that its benefits are woefully inadequate. Workers, earning around $50,000, who retire at age 62, will receive only around 30 percent of their pay or about $15,000 a year.[6] Lower-income workers, earning around $22,000, will receive around 40 percent of their pay, but that is only about $9,000 a year.[7] Those percentages are not nearly enough to maintain one's standard of living.

Nevertheless, though Social Security's benefits are modest, they are vitally important. Those benefits account for more than half the income of four out of five people receiving disability insurance,[8] and two out of three seniors receiving retirement benefits. They account for virtually all of the income of one-third of senior and disability beneficiaries.[9] Moreover, the children who receive Social Security live in families with considerably fewer resources, on average, than other families with children.[10]

Social Security was created to allow workers to maintain their standards of living once wages are lost. As a byproduct of that goal, it is our nation's most effective anti-poverty program. Indeed, it lifts over 20 million Americans – including over a million children – out of poverty, and lessens the depth of poverty for millions more.[11]

Furthermore, Social Security benefits are projected to be even more important to future generations of beneficiaries, as a result of the disappearance of private sector traditional pensions, which, even at their height, never covered more than about half the workforce. Even in cases where employers do not simply end their traditional plans but replace them with so-called 401(k) savings plans, the replacements have proven wholly inadequate for anyone but the already wealthy.[12] As a result of these and other factors, many analysts are documenting a looming retirement income crisis, where most workers will be unable to cease work without a drastic reduction in their standards of living, and will be even more dependent on Social Security in the future.[13]

At base, Social Security protects us against the economic consequences of risks to which all of us are vulnerable. Rich or poor, any of us can suffer a devastating, disabling accident or illness. Rich or poor, any of us can die prematurely, leaving young children behind. Rich or poor, all of us hope to grow old. When we do, if we are to have a dignified and independent retirement, we need a guaranteed steady income which we cannot and will not outlive. Social Security recognizes that the best way to protect ourselves and our families against the economic consequences of those risks is to

4

join together and pool them, sharing both our risks and our responsibilities.

Social Security addresses universal economic risks that have always been with us and always will be. That explains why more than 170 countries today have some form of social security. It also explains Social Security's deep and longstanding popularity in our country. In a survey conducted in 1936 – one year after the enactment of Social Security, before a penny of benefits was expended – 68 percent of those surveyed expressed approval for the new and untested program. By 1944, that percentage was a nearly unanimous 96 percent. That high level of support has been consistent throughout the last eighty years.[14]

Today's Misunderstandings and Willful Refusals to Understand

Despite Social Security's more than eighty-year history, some elites either do not understand Social Security or willfully refuse to understand it. They talk about providing benefits to those who need them, as if the program were government largesse, which it is not. Rather, Social Security is insurance that is earned through work and paid for with premiums regularly deducted from workers' pay. Others seem to think it is forced savings, though it is not. Again, as discussed at length in chapter two, it is insurance.

In addition, elites often speak as if the trust funds were some kind of gimmick, somehow less real than private pension trust funds. Perhaps most absurd are those who claim that what the creators of Social Security intended is not the program we now have.

Indeed, today's discussions of Social Security are replete with revisionist history – statements made today about what was or was not intended by its original creators and champions. Some of today's revisionist statements are zombie lies: Claims made and refuted again and again over the last eighty years; claims that refuse to die. Some misunderstandings even come from Social Security supporters, who don't realize their mistake.

The purpose of this book is to set the record straight. The architects of Social Security, men and women at the heights of their careers, mentored a number of younger colleagues who carried on their work. In turn, those younger colleagues, at the peaks of their careers and expertise, mentored the next generation. My colleagues and I are products of that training; we are now mentoring the next generation. Consequently, the Social Security vision forms a seamless, continuous thread. Those who have been involved in policymaking have always taken that vision as a guiding beacon towards which all incremental changes are pointed and against which all proposed changes are evaluated.

But you don't have to rely on this form of oral history. The founders left a rich written record. This book quotes the words of those who created and built Social Security. Some of the statements are from well-known figures from history; others are the words of civil servants, advisors, and others whose names were not even well known during their lifetimes. All had instrumental roles to play in the creation and development of Social Security.

The Far-Reaching Vision of the Founders

It is customary to read commentary today about the intentions of the founders. Most of it is wrong. Former Senator Alan Simpson (R-WY), for example, has stated that Social Security "was never intended as a retirement program. It was set up in '37 and '38 to take care of people who were in distress—ditch diggers, wage earners...."[15] Nationally syndicated columnist George Will claims, "People forget Social Security was advocated ... in the 1930s, as a way of getting people to quit working, because they thought we were confined to a permanent scarcity of jobs in this country."[16]

Syndicated columnist Robert Samuelson in a column entitled, "Would Roosevelt recognize today's Social Security?" even claims, "Social Security has evolved into something he never intended and actively opposed."[17] In that statement, Samuelson is referring to a narrow question about how the program is financed – a matter addressed in chapter three. Nevertheless, on both the specific point and the general point of what Roosevelt intended, Samuelson, Will, Simpson, and the other revisionist historians are wrong. Indeed, to state it bluntly, those modern-day statements are all nonsense.

Roosevelt's and the other founders' words and actions make clear that they envisioned Social Security to be a permanent part of the economy, once the Great Depression was history. They knew that the nation would return to full employment. When we did, the goal was to have in place Social Security and other programs that improved the economic security of all Americans and prevented, as much as possible, the human cost imposed by the ups and downs of all modern economies. In particular, Social Security was not designed to alleviate the suffering of people caught in the immediate distress of the Great Depression, nor to get people to quit their jobs. Rather, it was set up as wage insurance that people earned.

This should be obvious to anyone with even a superficial knowledge of Social Security's history. Because the architects knew that it would take time and work to earn Social Security's benefits, the Social Security Act of 1935 was written so that not a single penny of those earned monthly retirement benefits was payable for six years!

But the absurdity of those revisionist historians goes much further than simply being wrong on the facts. They seek to expunge the far-sighted and noble vision of Social Security's founders. President Roosevelt and those around him had a sweeping vision that still has yet to be fully realized.

When Roosevelt signed the Social Security Act of 1935 into law, he described it as "a cornerstone in a structure which is being built but is by no means complete." He and his colleagues were anything but short-sighted. They were not simply and solely focused on the immediate distress caused by the Great Depression, as the revisionists would have us believe. Rather, they saw Social Security as a "cornerstone," a beginning on which to build.

Their vision, of which Social Security was a first step, was never far from Roosevelt's mind. Even in the midst of World War II, during the height of America's participation, Roosevelt was thinking about it. He succinctly but powerfully articulated this vision in his 1944 State of the Union Message to Congress, reprinted, in part, below.[18]

****

Franklin Delano Roosevelt
State of the Union Message to Congress
January 11, 1944

To the Congress:

This Nation in the past two years has become an active partner in the world's greatest war against human slavery.

We have joined with like-minded people in order to defend ourselves in a world that has been gravely threatened with gangster rule.

But I do not think that any of us Americans can be content with mere survival. Sacrifices that we and our allies are making impose upon us all a sacred obligation to see to it that out of this war we and our children will gain something better than mere survival.
…
The one supreme objective for the future… can be summed up in one word: Security.

And that means not only physical security which provides safety from attacks by aggressors. It means also economic security, social security, moral security…
…
It is our duty now to begin to lay the plans and determine the strategy for the winning of a lasting peace and the establishment of an American standard of living higher than ever before known. We cannot be content, no matter how high that general standard of living may be, if some fraction of our people—whether it be one-third or one-fifth or one-tenth—is ill-fed, ill-clothed, ill housed, and insecure.

This Republic had its beginning, and grew to its present strength, under the protection of certain inalienable political rights—among them the right of free speech, free press, free worship, trial by jury, freedom from unreasonable searches and seizures. They were our rights to life and liberty.

As our Nation has grown in size and stature, however—as our industrial economy expanded—these political rights proved inadequate to assure us equality in the pursuit of happiness.

We have come to a clear realization of the fact that true individual freedom cannot exist without economic security and independence. "Necessitous men are not free men." People who are hungry and out of a job are the stuff of which dictatorships are made.

In our day, these economic truths have become accepted as self-evident. We have accepted, so to speak, a second Bill of Rights under which a new basis of security and prosperity can be established for all regardless of station, race, or creed.

Among these are:

The right to a useful and remunerative job in the industries or shops or farms or mines of the Nation;

The right to earn enough to provide adequate food and clothing and recreation;

The right of every farmer to raise and sell his products at a return which will give him and his family a decent living;

The right of every businessman, large and small, to trade in an atmosphere of freedom from unfair competition and domination by monopolies at home or abroad;

The right of every family to a decent home;

The right to adequate medical care and the opportunity to achieve and enjoy good health;

The right to adequate protection from the economic fears of old age, sickness, accident, and unemployment;

The right to a good education.

All of these rights spell security. And after this war is won we must be prepared to move forward, in the implementation of these rights, to new goals of human happiness and well-being.

America's own rightful place in the world depends in large part upon how fully these and similar rights have been carried into practice for our citizens. For unless there is security here at home there cannot be lasting peace in the world.

■■

Arthur Altmeyer, nicknamed "Mr. Social Security" by President Franklin Roosevelt, was unquestionably the most important individual responsible for the creation, implementation, and development of Social Security over its first twenty years. When Social Security was enacted, Roosevelt nominated and the Senate confirmed him to serve on the three-member Social Security Board. When the Board was replaced by a single Social Security Commissioner in 1946, Truman appointed him to that position, where he served until 1953. In a 1965 speech at a banquet honoring his protégé Wilbur Cohen, Altmeyer gave concrete examples of Roosevelt's commitment to achieving that sweeping vision:[19]

****

Arthur J. Altmeyer
Address Presented at the 10th Anniversary Award Banquet,
NASW, Honoring Wilbur J. Cohen
Under Secretary, HEW
Washington-Hilton Hotel
December 9, 1965

SOCIAL SECURITY—YESTERDAY AND TOMORROW

[B]efore the war broke out, it was possible to secure amendments to the Social Security Act which converted the federal old-age insurance system into an old-age and survivors insurance system,

providing widows' and orphans' benefits as well as benefits for aged beneficiaries and their dependents....

The Social Security Board was kept rather busy putting into effect the 1939 changes in the Social Security Act. But, nevertheless, it did recommend to the President in 1941, just before Pearl Harbor, that a comprehensive social insurance system be established, including not only old-age and survivors' insurance, but also temporary and permanent disability benefits, unemployment insurance and cash hospitalization benefits. The Board also recommended federal grants for public assistance to all needy persons. It is interesting to note that, although President Roosevelt said at his first press conference following Pearl Harbor that "old Dr. New Deal" had to be replaced by "Dr. Win-the-war", he included in his January 1942 Budget Message all of the recommendations the Board had made except federal aid for all needy persons.

....

The President did continue to show his interest in a comprehensive social security program. Thus, in October 1944 he called for an Economic Bill of Rights....

In his last Message on the State of the Union in January 1945, he again urged an expanded social security program and health and education programs, saying, "I shall communicate further with the Congress on these matters at a later date." But he died three months later.

■■■

As Altmeyer's comments make clear, Roosevelt's far-reaching vision was in his thoughts during World War II even when victory was by no means assured. The excerpted section of his 1943 State of the Union message, printed below, is another expression of that broad vision, which Roosevelt and his colleagues saw extending "from the cradle to the grave."[20]

****

Franklin Delano Roosevelt
State of the Union Message to Congress
January 7, 1943

....

Two years ago, I spoke in my Annual Message of four freedoms. The blessings of two of them—freedom of speech and freedom of religion—are an essential part of the very life of this Nation; and we hope that these blessings will be granted to all men everywhere.

The people at home, and the people at the front, are wondering a little about the third freedom—freedom from want. To them it means that when they are mustered out, when war production is converted to the economy of peace, they will have the right to expect full employment—full employment for themselves and for all able-bodied men and women in America who want to work.

They expect the opportunity to work, to run their farms, their stores, to earn decent wages. They are eager to face the risks inherent in our system of free enterprise.

They do not want a postwar America which suffers from undernourishment or slums—or the dole. They want no get-rich-quick era of bogus "prosperity" which will end for them in selling apples on a street corner, as happened after the bursting of the boom in 1929.

When you talk with our young men and our young women, you will find they want to work for themselves and for their families; they consider that they have the right to work; and they know that after the last war their fathers did not gain that right.

When you talk with our young men and women, you will find that with the opportunity for employment they want assurance against the evils of all major economic hazards—assurance that will extend from the cradle to the grave. And this great Government can and must provide this assurance.

....

In this war of survival, we must keep before our minds not only the evil things we fight against but the good things we are fighting for. We fight to retain a great past—and we fight to gain a greater future.

■■

This breadth of vision was not just in the mind of President Roosevelt. It was shared by those around him who were involved in the development of Social Security. With a guaranteed right to employment, unemployment insurance could be a temporary bridge. Universal health care was originally intended to be part of Social Security, but was dropped when opposition from the medical establishment became so intense that the president feared it would doom his entire Social Security legislation. Nevertheless, he and his advisors continued to work towards its eventual passage. In short, the vision was for economic security that extended, in Roosevelt's words, "from the cradle to the grave."

Mary ("Molly") W. Dewson was an activist who was prominent in the women's suffrage movement and a longtime official in the Democratic Party. In 1934, President Roosevelt appointed her to the council advising the Committee on Economic Security, the interagency working group developing the Social Security legislation. Then, in 1937, the legislation now enacted, the president nominated and the Senate confirmed her to serve on the three-member Social Security Board, where Altmeyer also served. In 1938, she gave a speech about Social Security to the Women's City Club of Boston. The speech, reprinted in large part below, provides another articulation of the sweeping vision the creators of Social Security had in mind.[21]

****

Mary W. Dewson
Member, Social Security Board
Address Before the Women's City Club of Boston
February 17, 1938

THIS SOCIAL SECURITY—WHAT IS IT?

I am one of those heretics who believe that nine-tenths of an audience goes away from a talk with an impression, but few facts—and that the few facts, because they are scrappy and disassociated, roll off to some little-used corner of the mind and are lost. Therefore, today I am drawing you a picture. I hope it will associate your ideas on social security and get them into relationship, so that they will mean something you don't have to remember, but can't forget.

The picture shows what government—that is, all of us—is doing to give each of us a firm footing on which to fight for a living.

Rugged individualism is grand if the odds aren't insuperable. But in high-powered, mass-production industry, with its great rhythmic fluctuations of employment and unemployment, the odds are insuperable for a staggering number of men and women. Under such conditions rugged individualism is a losing fight unless all of us get together to provide protection and insurance against certain risks. England, Sweden, and other foreign countries recognized this truth some 30 or 40 years ago. It's a three-volume novel why we didn't. But now we have.

Stripped down to bare terms, what does "social security" mean? Just that the inevitable hazards of life shall not be allowed to take their uttermost toll of the defenseless.

Life being what it is, it seems to me a little silly to fear, as some people seem to, that we shall ever have too much security. Insecurity is the lot of rich and poor. Babies of the rich die. Their children could be better educated, better equipped to make their own way in the world. Sickness and accident spare none. Wives lose their husbands and children their parents, whatever their economic status. Many of the well-to-do are unable to find work for which they are fitted. And in the end, the portion of the fortunate who live is old age; but, this again has hazards for all, the bitter hazards of declining power and decreasing independence.

Little by little—actually, during the past century, with amazing speed—medicine and science, education and training, invention and industry have made life easier and at least potentially more secure. But the great hazards of life remain. For the big man and the little man, for the rich and the poor, there is no absolute security, today or any day, past, present or future.

Yet the effect of these disasters that are the common lot of man can be mitigated to a certain extent. Today as in the past, men of substance may be able to weather most storms alone, as long as their cash or credit holds out. But I know, and you know, that these relatively self-sufficient ones are a mighty small part of our people. The vast majority has never at any time in our history had enough reserves to with-stand single-handed "the slings and arrows of outrageous fortune." In pioneer times the wind was tempered to the shorn lambs by neighbors, relatives, and friends—except in individual cases where prejudice was stronger than sympathy. Today neighbors have practically disappeared; and family and friends are often powerless to help because they, too, have no margin between earnings and necessities. Of all those insured under the Federal old-age insurance law who died in 1937, a full half left not one penny.

Before the great depression, private philanthropy relieved the misfortunes of a few and satisfied the instincts of the good and charitable. But it left the many to endure their hardships as best they might, until in the last extremity the "poor laws" were invoked to preserve the so-called decencies of civilization. The widespread anguish following the economic collapse of 1929 blew away the rosy fog which we had permitted to obscure these unpalatable realities. And practical plans began to take shape for a minimum of protection against certain major hazards.

None of these plans we lump together as social security is new. Some, like workmen's compensation, were already pretty well established by the end of the 1920's. Others, like provisions for children and for the aged, have been developing piecemeal for 25 years. Today they are being carried out in fresh and more effective ways, and much more inclusively. Still others, like unemployment compensation, after lingering in the doldrums of discussion for a generation, have at last become a reality. And a final group, including basic essentials like minimum-wage legislation for both men and women, and health insurance, have not yet emerged from the era of high-powered talk which has preceded every piece of social legislation on record.

All these plans have one common purpose—to enable every man and woman in this country to come to terms with life according to his own initiative and industry and capacity and courage. They represent only a minimum; they do not—and are not intended to— measure up to an abundant life. Their purpose is simply to give the worker a fair chance, with the cards no longer stacked against him in advance. This much security all of us would surely have for each of us.

I like to compare these social provisions for individual security to a platform—a firm footing for the worker. And now I want you to examine with me, for a few minutes, the strengths and weaknesses of this platform as it stands before you. You will see that it is built out of separate planks. The ones in black are still lacking; the others are already in place. But the fact that any particular piece is in place does not necessarily mean that it is a stout 2-inch plank, capable of carrying its full share of the load. Legislatures are constantly replacing timbers too weak to stand the strain, or full of knot holes.

I want to make it clear, too, that the relative size allotted to these planks, or segments of security, in this picture is not statistically significant. It represents simply the value that I, personally, set on each of these sectors in the worker's security platform.

Wholesome Childhood

It may be trite to say that its children are a nation's best assets. But it is true. And on the whole, Americans have done pretty well by their children, though not as well as they should. One of the important things about the Social Security Act is that it has recognized this national responsibility for the well-being of children. Through the four cooperative Federal-State children's programs established by the Act, more children than in the past will have a chance to grow up with healthy bodies and in wholesome homes.

....

... Though a lot of work remains to be done, this is a substantial beginning in building these children's planks into a Nation-wide social security structure.

....

Education

Public education was the first labor law. A certain amount of schooling is a prerequisite to every kind of work except the most unskilled. Education helps a man to get a job and to hold a job. This tie-up between school and job has been more and more clearly recognized, and today in some States the school gives working papers to young people, in order to make sure that they have fulfilled minimum educational requirements.

Public responsibility for education has so long been taken for granted, particularly here in New England, that we may forget how generally it was once viewed with alarm. Only a hundred years ago, a "public-spirited citizen" could say of public schools that "a more pernicious notion could not prevail. It has given (the people) a premium for idleness.... The education of their children is the first and most obvious duty of every parent. Is it the friends of the poor who absolve them from what Nature, what God Himself has made their first and most sacred duty?"

That has a strangely familiar ring. More recent orators have worked similar arguments overtime in protesting against child labor legislation. Who knows but what Americans may live to see the time when child labor provisions will be as respectable as educational provisions are today?

Meantime the Federal Government has recognized the advantages of training in relation to work....

A Job

The first, last, and main thing people want and have a right to is a job. Good health, education and training help to get a job and to keep it. But whether or no, a man must work to live.

Individual initiative today, as in the past, is the one most important factor in getting a job. But with conditions of employment—or perhaps one should say of unemployment—what modern industry has made them, a man's opportunity of selling his services in the market place is limited. Such markets as there are may be scattered and inaccessible; there may be no market at all for particular skills; and if so, new and strange kinds of work must be hunted up and tried out. These problems exist quite independently of the major issue of mass unemployment, with which we have become all too familiar in recent years.

...

Paying compensation when a man loses his job is one part of the picture; helping him find another job is the other, and even more essential, part.

At Least a Health and Decency Wage

Next in importance to the dire necessity of a job, any kind of a job, is earning enough to live on in health and decency. Workers are forced to take whatever they can get, and will under-cut anyone rather than go without work. Nothing but minimum wage legislation can prevent the chiseling minority of employers in unorganized industry from paying substandard wages. Labor unions can and do prevent substandard wages in organized industry. But up to now their membership has included only a comparatively small percentage of the Nation's workers, and in the main their emphasis has been on bargaining for increasingly adequate pay for this relatively small group. Important as their efforts are, they have not touched the problem of setting a basic level below which wages cannot fall for the great mass of working people.

Minimum wage and hour legislation is, after the job itself, the most important of all the planks in the social security platform. Yet it is still in the future for men workers in every State in the Union, and even for women and children, except in 22 states, the District of Columbia and Puerto Rico.

Housing

Decency and health demand not only a wage to live on but a fit place to live in. Americans have done a conspicuously poor job in recent years at "keeping the home fires burning"; and today housing is one of the major problems confronting us as a Nation and as individual families. Even before the depression at least 11 million families— and that means some 45 million men and women and children were living in homes that endangered their physical safety, their health and their morals. ...

Housing is a public menace and a public responsibility.... Through Federal housing and home-financing legislation we have made a significant beginning. But it is only a beginning....

Unemployment, Sickness and Old-Age Insurance

With health, training, a job that pays a living wage and a chance to live in decent surroundings, most of the people most of the time will manage to get along without further help. With that much of a footing to stand on, they can and will look out for themselves and their families—most of the time.

Except in a depression, periods of unemployment for the undefeated are comparatively brief and infrequent. Except for those cut down by accident or slowly going under with disease, spells of sickness are comparatively rare. Yet in a nation of 130,000,000 "comparatively" is a large and elastic word, and even for the fortunate, unemployment or illness will nick the work year. During the prosperous 1920's there were never less than a million-and-a-half workers out of a job, and the number now unemployed is anybody's guess from 7 to 10 millions. Estimates indicate that on an average day at least 2 1/2 million people are incapacitated for work because of sickness, and that in an average year over 10 million suffer accidents of one sort or another. When "comparatively few" means millions, protection becomes a national concern.

There is another and still more cogent reason for recognizing protection against these hazards as a national concern. Actual catastrophes—when the individual worker is knocked out by unemployment, accident, or sickness—may be relatively few and far between. But the risk—the chance that the blow may fall—is universal. The only practical method of protection against widespread hazards is to pool the risk. And the only agency big enough to administer mutual protection for all the people is the government. This is the what and why of social insurance.

…

Unemployment Insurance is one of the new planks in social security established by the Social Security Act. …

Because unemployment compensation is new and because in this early stage its administration looks complicated, it looms large in the public eye. As a matter of fact it is only a relatively narrow plank in the worker's platform. It offers no panacea for unemployment. All it is intended to do is to bridge the gap between jobs.

...

Unemployment compensation is essential, and the beginnings already made will no doubt be extended and strengthened. But when you come right down to it, the basic insurance against losing a job is health. And maintaining health is one of the first responsibilities of the individual and of the Nation. I heartily agree, and I think you do too, with Surgeon General Parran, in believing that we must accept as a major premise that our citizens should have an equal opportunity to health, as an inherent right co-equal with the right to life and liberty. Yet today, except for the tiny proportion of illness due to industrial causes and so covered by workmen's compensation, the American people have no adequate protection against this universal risk.

The place where adequate health protection ought to be—and isn't —is, after a health and decency wage, the biggest gap remaining in the security platform. At this point two separate planks are missing. One of these is sickness compensation against loss of earning power during temporary or permanent disability. .... The other is adequate medical care, including whatever medicines, treatment, and hospitalization are needed—a far more expensive proposition but one of the most profound importance. ... Adequate health protection may still be mostly pious hope. But it is not a vain hope; both of these measures are already on the horizon.

Supposing, now, our worker has cleared all these hurdles; there is still one before him and that the least escapable of all. For the only way to avoid coming up against old age is to die beforehand. Most of those who outlive their capacity to work and support themselves have not been able to lay by enough to eke out an existence, much less to enjoy their new leisure. And the only way to provide any kind of old-age security for the bulk of the people is through social insurance.

Old-age insurance established by the Security Act and administered by the Social Security Board, is a national program through which young and middle aged workers can build up, by their own and their employers contribution, benefit rights which will give them something to live on when they are old and stop working. ... This means that the present and future generations of industrial wage earners will be spared much of the humiliation and suffering that has too often been the lot of old age. With a regular monthly payment— even a small one—they will not be resourceless, forced to become a dead weight upon their families, who more than likely are already stretching every penny, or—worse yet—to seek private or public charity....

Social insurance, like private insurance, has limitations. You can't, for example, insure people who are already old against old-age dependency, any more than you can insure your car against property damages after you have had a smash-up. Yet some provision has to be made for this non-insurable need. Nobody knows exactly how many of those now old are without sufficient resources for their own support. Surveys made some years ago in Massachusetts, Connecticut, and other States showed that anywhere from 40 to 50 percent of the people over 65 had an income of less than $300 a year. And $300 a year is the modest minimum which, the American people seem to think, is essential for health and decency. To take care of such old people, the Social Security Act adds another provision—for assistance on the basis of need. With Federal grants to match State funds, the States are now providing cash allowances for well over a million-and-a-half needy old people. As time goes on, however, more people will be covered by the old-age insurance system, particularly when, as we hope, it is extended to include practically all wage earners.

Assistance and Relief

Freely admitting this and other limitations, I still contend that these things are the basis of social security—wholesome childhood, education, a job, a living wage, decent housing, and social insurance against major risks. With these the worker's platform is complete— or would be if some planks weren't still lacking and others in need of strengthening. As long as there are gaps and weak spots in the platform, a lot of people are going to fall through—through into destitution and misery. And as long as these gaps and weak spots remain, some fairly extensive—and very expensive—life net will have to be stretched underneath to catch these often needless casualties before they quite strike rock bottom. That, I take it, is the function of relief. ... I am no visionary. I know that the need for relief will be with us in the future as in the past. And I hope that we shall be prepared to meet it more adequately than in the past.

Toward Firmer Footing

The point I am emphasizing is that it is incomparably better to assure the worker a firm footing—to close the gaps and strengthen the weak spots, insofar as we possibly can—rather than continue depending on the tragically wasteful business of picking up the pieces—pieces of human lives that might, but for our patchwork building, have remained whole and self-sufficient.

I believe that these gaps—child labor, minimum wage, health insurance and others—will be closed, maybe not today or tomorrow but sometime in the not unforeseeable future. All the signs of the times point that way. In the last 3 years we have done more building —and better building—on this social security platform than in the preceding half-century. There is no reason to think that the passage of the Social Security Act marked the finish of social legislation in the United States. Rather, there is every reason to think, and to hope, that it marked a new and clearer-headed awareness of what this security really is, and a new and vastly more determined effort to get the kind of security Americans want, the kind of security that assures every man and woman a chance to stand on his own two feet, and to make a winning fight to support himself and his children in the good old American way.

■■■

Dewson's statement captures the vision of the creators of Social Security. Today, people think of Social Security as referring simply to what was Title II of the Social Security Act of 1935–old age insurance. That is a limited view, not shared by its creators. In that same 1965 speech quoted above, Altmeyer provided some perspective on the phrase, "Social Security":

> The Cabinet Committee created to develop a legislative program …was called the Committee on Economic Security, not Committee on Social Security. …But, during the course of the legislative hearings, the term "social security" was used by a number of witnesses and the Ways and Means Committee used this term in reporting out a bill.

> The term social security captured the public imagination not only in this country, but throughout the world. In the course of time the term came to be used in other countries in an expansive sense as a synonym for the Good Life.

> …However, gradually the term social security in this country, instead of being used in a more expansive sense, has been used in a more limited sense to refer only to the Old Age, Survivors, and Disability System. I consider this extremely unfortunate…

Significant Step Toward the Still
Not Yet Fully-Attained Vision

It is ludicrous to claim that Roosevelt would not "recognize" today's Social Security system, as a Washington Post headline of a Robert J. Samuelson opinion piece proclaimed. Indeed, if President Roosevelt and his colleagues were alive today, they would likely be shocked that so little progress has been made since their important start.

Over a half century ago, in 1965, founder Arthur Altmeyer reflected on how much still remained to be achieved. In the same address excerpted earlier in this chapter, Altmeyer concluded:

> Upon the basis of this brief chronological discussion of the development of the Social Security Act, let me attempt a brief appraisal of the extent to which we have achieved the dream of President Roosevelt of "assurance against the evils of all major economic hazards—assurance that will extend from the cradle to the grave."

There is no question that President Roosevelt wanted this assurance to consist primarily of contributory social insurance. We do have a nation-wide old-age, survivors' and disability system and also a nation-wide unemployment insurance system. However, the benefits provided are far from being adequate and they do not protect all workers.

....

The great gap in our present Social Security Act is its failure to include two forms of social insurance which are found in the social security systems of practically all other industrialized countries: insurance to cover wage loss resulting from temporary disability and insurance to cover the cost of medical care for all workers. I believe both of these forms of social insurance should be included under the Federal Old-Age Survivors' and Disability Insurance System.

President Roosevelt knew that the progress made during his administration was a significant first step but fell short of his far-sighted vision. In August 1938, on the third anniversary of the enactment of Social Security, the President took stock of the newly enacted legislation. He understood the work still left to do. The accomplishments of the Social Security Act of 1935, he remarked, are "impressive," but cautioned that "we should not be unduly proud of them." He explains why in the following transcript of his 1938 radio address:[22]

****

Franklin Delano Roosevelt
Radio Address on the
Third Anniversary of the Social Security Act
August 15, 1938

A SOCIAL SECURITY PROGRAM MUST INCLUDE ALL THOSE WHO NEED ITS PROTECTION

You, my friends, in every walk of life and in every part of the Nation, who are active believers in Social Security:

The Social Security Act is three years old today. This is a good vantage point from which to take a long look backward to its beginnings, to cast an appraising eye over what it has accomplished so far, and to survey its possibilities of future growth.

Five years ago the term "social security" was new to American ears. Today it has significance for more than forty million men and women workers whose applications for old-age insurance accounts have been received; this system is designed to assure them an income for life after old age retires them from their jobs.

It has significance for more than twenty-seven and a half million men and women wage earners who have earned credits under State unemployment insurance laws which provide half wages to help bridge the gap between jobs.

It has significance for the needy men, women and children receiving assistance and for their families—at least two million three hundred thousand all told; with this cash assistance one million seven hundred thousand old folks are spending their last years in surroundings they know and with people they love; more than six hundred thousand dependent children are being taken care of by their own families; and about forty thousand blind people are assured of peace and security among familiar voices.

It has significance for the families and communities to whom expanded public health and child welfare services have brought added protection. And it has significance for all of us who, as citizens, have at heart the Security and the well-being of this great democracy.

These accomplishments of three years are impressive, yet we should not be unduly proud of them. Our Government, in fulfilling an obvious obligation to the citizens of the country, has been doing so only because the citizens require action from their Representatives. If the people, during these years, had chosen a reactionary Administration or a "do nothing" Congress, Social Security would still be in the conversational stage—a beautiful dream which might come true in the dim distant future.

But the underlying desire for personal and family security was nothing new. In the early days of colonization and through the long years following, the worker, the farmer, the merchant, the man of property, the preacher and the idealist came here to build, each for himself, a stronghold for the things he loved. The stronghold was his home; the things he loved and wished to protect were his family, his material and spiritual possessions.

His security, then as now, was bound to that of his friends and his neighbors.

But as the Nation has developed, as invention, industry and commerce have grown more complex, the hazards of life have become more complex. Among an increasing host of fellow citizens, among the often intangible forces of giant industry, man has discovered that his individual strength and wits were no longer enough. This was true not only of the worker at shop bench or ledger; it was true also of the merchant or manufacturer who employed him. Where heretofore men had turned to neighbors for help and advice, they now turned to Government.

Now this is interesting to consider. The first to turn to Government, the first to receive protection from Government, were not the poor and the lowly—those who had no resources other than their daily earnings—but the rich and the strong. Beginning in the nineteenth century, the United States passed protective laws designed, in the main, to give security to property owners, to industrialists, to merchants and to bankers. True, the little man often profited by this type of legislation; but that was a by-product rather than a motive.

Taking a generous view of the situation, I think it was not that Government deliberately ignored the working man but that the working man was not sufficiently articulate to make his needs and his problems known. The powerful in industry and commerce had powerful voices, both individually and as a group. And whenever they saw their possessions threatened, they raised their voices in appeals for government protection.

It was not until workers became more articulate through organization that protective labor legislation was passed. While such laws raised the standards of life, they still gave no assurance of economic security. Strength or skill of arm or brain did not guarantee a man a job; it did not guarantee him a roof; it did not guarantee him the ability to provide for those dependent upon him or to take care of himself when he was too old to work.

Long before the economic blight of the depression descended on the Nation, millions of our people were living in wastelands of want and fear. Men and women too old and infirm to work either depended on those who had but little to share, or spent their remaining years within the walls of a poorhouse. Fatherless children early learned the meaning of being a burden to relatives or to the community. Men and women, still strong, still young, but discarded as gainful workers, were drained of self-confidence and self-respect.

The millions of today want, and have a right to, the same security their forefathers sought—the assurance that with health and the willingness to work they will find a place for themselves in the social and economic system of the time.

Because it has become increasingly difficult for individuals to build their own security single-handed, Government must now step in and help them lay the foundation stones, just as Government in the past has helped lay the foundation of business and industry. We must face the fact that in this country we have a rich man's security and a poor man's security and that the Government owes equal obligations to both. National security is not a half and half manner: it is all or none.

The Social Security Act offers to all our citizens a workable and working method of meeting urgent present needs and of forestalling future need. It utilizes the familiar machinery of our Federal-State government to promote the common welfare and the economic stability of the Nation.

....

What we are doing is good. But it is not good enough. To be truly national, a social security program must include all those who need its protection. Today many of our citizens are still excluded from old-age insurance and unemployment compensation because of the nature of their employment. This must be set aright; and it will be.

Some time ago I directed the Social Security Board to give attention to the development of a plan for liberalizing and extending the old-age insurance system to provide benefits for wives, widows and orphans. More recently, a National Health Conference was held at my suggestion to consider ways and means of extending to the people of this country more adequate health and medical services and also to afford the people of this country some protection against the economic losses arising out of ill health.

I am hopeful that on the basis of studies and investigations now under way, the Congress will improve and extend the law. I am also confident that each year will bring further development in Federal and State social security legislation—and that is as it should be.

....

We have come a long way. But we still have a long way to go. There is still today a frontier that remains unconquered—an America unclaimed.

This is the great, the nationwide frontier of insecurity, of human want and fear. This is the frontier—the America—we have set ourselves to reclaim.

∎∎

As this chapter makes clear, the vision of the founders was extremely far-sighted. Even eight decades later, their vision remains largely aspirational. We are much wealthier as a nation than we were when Roosevelt was president. It is time to move further in making the founders' vision a reality. But to do so, we must first see clearly.

The founders wanted to establish something that would last. As a consequence, they were extremely careful in what they constructed, focusing intently on the details of what they were creating. As chapters two and three explain, the basic structure they created was ingenious. It is the same one in use today.

Some say the program of insurance against the loss of wages in the event of old age, disability, or death – what today we call "Social Security" – needs to be modernized, but nothing could be further from the truth. The structure, which is as sound now as it was when enacted, continues to address extremely well a modern challenge: providing some measure of economic security in a modern, wage-based economy.

Chapter two explains what the basic structure is, and responds to decades of efforts to mischaracterize that structure. Chapter three focuses on the sound and thoughtful financing of Social Security, and responds to efforts, starting shortly after enactment and continuing to this day, to sow confusion and undermine confidence in Social Security's financing.

While the vision was broad and the structure ingenious and sound, the founders were practical. They knew that their vision could only be achieved incrementally. Chapter four highlights that incremental growth, completely consistent with the original intent – again despite claims to the contrary that somehow today's Social Security would be foreign to the founders.

Despite these clear facts, there have been a small group – Republican President Dwight D. Eisenhower described them as "a tiny splinter group" whose "number is negligible" – who have always hated the idea of Social Security.[23] Though "a tiny splinter group," they are wealthy with oversized access and influence. Through the decades, they have propagated misinformation and confusion about our Social Security system, much of which has become today's conventional "wisdom." Chapter five traces the unbroken chain that unites the efforts over the decades and is still with us today.

Those efforts to spread confusion and misinformation are likely to be with us for as long as we have a Social Security system. Chapter six explains the need to be vigilant. It also reminds us, though, that despite the money and power arrayed against our Social Security, the American people have always understood its importance and have supported it. Armed with the information contained in these pages, the American people will prevail against the attacks. We will prevail not just in protecting Social Security. We will prevail in expanding Social Security, as the founders envisioned us doing.

CHAPTER TWO: SOCIAL SECURITY'S UNCHANGING STRUCTURE

In 1934, President Roosevelt proclaimed, "Among our objectives I place the security of the men, women and children of the Nation first."[1] Ten years later, at the height of World War II, he reiterated even more succinctly that his "supreme objective...can be summed up in one word: Security." He defined that "supreme objective" as "not only physical security," but "also economic security, social security, moral security."[2]

In articulating this vision of security, Roosevelt spoke forcefully about achieving "freedom from want." That freedom included, in his view, the guarantee of "full employment...for all...men and women in America who want to work." It held out the promise of "decent wages." It was freedom from an "America which suffers from undernourishment or slums." And the vision included "assurance against the evils of all major economic hazards— assurance that will extend from the cradle to the grave."[3]

Establishing the Basic Structure on Which to Build

Roosevelt's vision remains to this day a shining beacon, by no means fully achieved. He and his advisers recognized that the various elements of what he labeled a second Bill of Rights would have to be created carefully and incrementally.

To achieve "The right to earn enough to provide adequate food and clothing and recreation;" Roosevelt proposed minimum wage and maximum hour legislation, which was enacted at the federal level in 1938. Unfortunately, current leaders have allowed that bold start to languish, by failing to enact increases to the federal minimum wage so that it keeps pace with inflation and productivity.

Another part of the Economic Bill of Rights, "The right to adequate protection from the economic fears of old age, sickness, accident, and unemployment;" received an important start in 1935, with the enactment of two forms of wage insurance: old age insurance – insurance against the loss of wages in the event of retirement (what we today call "Social Security"); and unemployment insurance – insurance against the loss of wages in the event of unemployment.

Another important incremental step was taken in 1939, when Social Security's wage insurance protection was expanded to include survivors' or life insurance – insurance against the loss of wages in the event of death. In addition, Social Security's old age insurance was expanded to provide not just life annuities, but joint and survivor annuities for married couples. In 1956, another important step toward Roosevelt's vision was the addition of long-term disability insurance. As a major first step toward "The right to adequate medical care and the opportunity to achieve and enjoy good health," Medicare was enacted in 1965 for people aged 65 and older. In 1972, Medicare was expanded to cover people with disabilities.

Short-term disability insurance, including paid sick leave and paid parental leave, has not been added yet, despite the comprehensive vision of the original architects. Nor has universal health insurance – Medicare for All.

Today's Social Security rests on the conceptual underpinning that Roosevelt envisioned so clearly. Its growth, incremental in nature and by no means complete, built on the basic structure, the "cornerstone," laid down in 1935.

Prior to the enactment of that cornerstone, soon after the legislation was starting to be considered by Congress, Roosevelt's Secretary of Labor, in a 1935 radio address, explained the need to proceed carefully and incrementally:[4]

****

Frances Perkins
National Radio Address
February 25, 1935

SOCIAL INSURANCE FOR U.S.

I have been asked to speak to you tonight on the administration's program for economic security which is now, as you know, before Congress. It seems to me that few legislative proposals have had as careful study, as thorough and conscientious deliberation as went into the preparation of these measures. The program now under consideration represents, I believe, a most significant step in our National development, a milestone in our progress toward the better-ordered society.

As I look back on the tragic years since 1929, it seems to me that we as a Nation, not unlike some individuals, have been able to pass through a bitter experience to emerge with a newfound insight and maturity. We have had the courage to face our problems and find a way out. The heedless optimism of the boom years is past. We now stand ready to build the future with sanity and wisdom.

The process of recovery is not a simple one. We cannot be satisfied merely with makeshift arrangements which will tide us over the present emergencies. We must devise plans that will not merely alleviate the ills of today, but will prevent, as far as it is humanly possible to do so, their recurrence in the future. The task of recovery is inseparable from the fundamental task of social reconstruction.

Among the objectives of that reconstruction, President Roosevelt in his message of June 8, 1934, to the Congress placed "the security of the men, women and children of the Nation first." He went on to suggest the social insurances with which European countries have had a long and favorable experience as one means of providing safeguards against "misfortunes which cannot be wholly eliminated in this man-made world of ours."

Subsequent to this message he created the Committee on Economic Security, of which I have the honor to be the chairman, to make recommendations to him with regard to these problems. The recommendations of that committee are embodied in the economic security bill, now pending in Congress.

The measures we propose do not by any means provide a complete and permanent solution of our difficulties. If put into effect, however, they will provide a greater degree of security for the American citizen and his family than he has heretofore known. The bill is, I believe, a sound beginning on which we can build by degrees to our ultimate goal.

We cannot hope to accomplish all in one bold stroke. To begin too ambitiously in the program of social security might very well result in errors which would entirely discredit this very necessary type of legislation.... [Emphasis added.]

• •

Despite today's revisionists, the structure and size of today's Social Security program is completely consistent and harmonious with what Roosevelt began. Medicare is consistent with a first step toward the vision of universal health insurance.

The revisionists are wrong when they claim that Roosevelt would not recognize today's Social Security and Medicare. He would be surprised that more progress hadn't been made, but he would absolutely recognize how those who came later built on what he envisioned and began.

Misunderstanding Social Security's Basic Structure

To attain, in Roosevelt's words, "assurance against the evils of all major economic hazards—assurance that will extend from the cradle to the grave,"[5] insurance is what the architects intended to create and, indeed, what they did create. Nevertheless, from the beginning, Social Security was mischaracterized by its opponents as forced savings, not insurance. More recently, Social Security has been mischaracterized by its opponents as welfare or in the language of Roosevelt, the dole, rather than insurance.

Both of these mischaracterizations may be made out of ignorance or simply the failure to think hard about what Social Security is and is not. Those who view Social Security simply as a government transfer program, financed by a tax like any other tax, may fail to recognize that it is insurance, as opposed to savings or welfare.

Opponents of Social Security, though, have an incentive to mischaracterize the program as forced savings or welfare. As explained below, labeling Social Security as forced savings or welfare allows for straw-man arguments against the insurance program. In contrast, understood as the insurance that it is, Social Security's striking superiority and essential role in our modern economy becomes crystal clear.

Social Security Is Wage Insurance, Not Retirement Savings

In 1936, just the year after the Social Security Act of 1935 had been enacted, Alf Landon, the Republican presidential standard bearer that year, made Social Security's repeal a central theme of his campaign. Landon mis-described Social Security as "compulsory saving," in the lead-up to the election. In a speech delivered in Milwaukee, Wisconsin on September 26, 1936, five weeks before the election, he inaccurately explained it as follows:[6]

> Now in broad terms there are two ways to approach the development of a program of economic security. **One is** to assume that human beings are improvident - that it is necessary to have the stern management of a paternal government to force them to provide for themselves - that it is proper **for the government to force them to save for their old age**. The other approach is to recognize that in an industrialized nation some people are unable to provide for

their old age-- that it is a responsibility of society to take care of them.

The act passed by the present administration is based upon the first of these approaches. It assumes that Americans are irresponsible. It assumes that old age pensions are necessary because Americans lack the foresight to provide for their old age. [Emphasis added.]

In fairness to Landon, he may not have thought through the difference between insurance and savings. Nine times in the speech, he referred to Social Security as savings and to workers being forced to save for a lifetime. But, in the same speech, he referred to Social Security as compulsory insurance five times and once referred to workers who qualify for benefits, as "insured."

More recently, when President George W. Bush and others have advocated allowing people to divert their Social Security contributions to private accounts, the implication is that they are comparable forms of protection. Despite Landon's apparent confusion and today's opponents simply ignoring the distinction, there is a stark difference between insurance and savings. Insurance, not savings, is what the founders intended and what they, indeed, created.

Insurance involves the pooling of risk. People faced with the possibility of a loss can protect themselves against the financial consequences of that loss, if it were to occur, by joining with others who face the same risk. The members of the group contribute an amount of money related to the average likelihood that the loss will occur. If and when the loss occurs, the group member or members experiencing the loss are paid from the group fund. Each group member is protected from a large possible loss by making a smaller but certain contribution.

This financial exchange is the essence of insurance, and it is the essence of Social Security. Like other group insurance, Social Security involves making periodic payments and sharing the financial risk of particular, defined losses. In the case of Social Security, the risk is the loss of wages to support oneself and one's family in the event of disability, death, or old age.

The payments are the periodic payments mandated by the Federal Insurance Contributions Act ("FICA"). These FICA payments are paid by employers and workers, generally as deductions from pay checks, and held in trust for the sole purpose of paying Social Security benefits and related expenses. Those FICA payments are today commonly referred to as payroll taxes, but that is a misnomer in two respects. First, workers, who pay FICA, do not have payrolls; they have wages. More importantly, those payments are better understood as mandatory insurance contributions or insurance premiums, rather than mere taxes.

In that regard, it is instructive to pause and note that the acronym for the Social Security payment is "FICA," which, as just stated, stands for the "Federal Insurance Contributions Act," the legislation authorizing these payments. It is noteworthy that FICA was enacted in the 1930s. It is only relatively recently that policymakers have adopted the practice of naming legislation in the manner of Madison Avenue advertising—titles like the No Child Left Behind Act, the USA PATRIOT Act, the Defense of Marriage Act, and the Repealing the Job Killing Health Care Law Act.

In stark contrast, Franklin Roosevelt named his legislative proposals plainly and straightforwardly. His tax bills were labeled Revenue Acts; his legislation to ensure the right of workers to unionize, the National Labor Relations Act; and his Federal Insurance Contributions Act specifies the contributions or, in more modern parlance, premiums that workers and their employers pay for Social Security wage insurance.

Why, though, if insurance was the intention from the start, was FICA not enacted until 1939? The answer is the Supreme Court. The designers of Social Security intended that the monies collected– the premiums – should be used, just as they are in private insurance– to cover the cost of the benefits and the associated administrative costs. But there was a problem. The architects were concerned that the Supreme Court would find that the federal government lacked the power to enact this kind of broad-based wage insurance and would hold that the legislation was unconstitutional.

The Constitution gives Congress the power to impose taxes and the power to spend for the general welfare. What was in doubt in 1935, though, was whether Congress had the power to enact compulsory wage insurance. For that reason, the Administration lawyers wanted to blur the connection between Social Security's income and outgo, hoping in that way to uphold the arrangement by denying potential plaintiffs standing to sue. (Taxpayers generally have no standing in court to challenge spending. Since monthly benefits were not to be paid for a number of years, it was not clear who could successfully sue right away, if the Administration could convince the courts that the income and outgo were unrelated.)

The creators always referred to Social Security as insurance. But, to satisfy the lawyers, the 1935 drafters did not call Social Security insurance, nor the taxes, insurance contributions or premiums, because the lawyers were worried that the insurance language would make Social Security more vulnerable to constitutional attack and make more likely that the Supreme Court would find it unconstitutional.

In addition to avoiding calling Social Security the insurance it is, the drafters separated the income and outgo into two separate titles. Title II of the Social Security Act created "an account in the Treasury of the United States to be known as the 'Old-Age Reserve Account.'" Title VIII of the Social Security Act imposed taxes on employers and employees. Looking at the legislation comprehensively made clear that this was simply a contrivance. The taxes imposed by Title VIII were paid into the general fund, but the legislation authorized an automatic annual appropriation from the general fund to the Old-Age Reserve Account in the exact amount as the proceeds from the Title VIII tax.

Thomas H. Eliot served as Counsel for the Committee on Economic Security, the 1934 interagency task force that developed the Social Security Act of 1935. He described the constitutional concern, and the clumsy attempts to circumvent those concerns, in a speech he delivered at a general staff meeting at the Social Security Administration headquarters in Baltimore in 1961:[7]

****

Thomas H. Eliot
Speech Delivered at a General Staff Meeting at Social Security
Administration Headquarters, Baltimore, Maryland
February 3, 1961

THE LEGAL BACKGROUND OF THE
SOCIAL SECURITY ACT

OLD-AGE INSURANCE

...Nobody knew, when the Committee started its work in the summer of 1934, what kind of a program, beyond old-age assistance, there might be....What you had to do was provide something the people would get as a matter of right, and how are you going to do it? Could you do it by State laws as the Democratic platform had promised? On this the research staff headed by Witte promptly said "no." People move too much during a lifetime. It couldn't be done on a State-by-State basis, if you're going to do it actuarially.

From the beginning, it was assumed that it was going to be an actuarially sound insurance program. That could only be done on a national basis....

....

DOUBTFUL CONSTITUTIONALITY OF OLD-AGE
INSURANCE PLAN

...There was a great fear, which became more acute a little later, that this didn't have a chance, constitutionally speaking....

...A special tax, in effect, on employers and employees and the payment of benefits to the employees made possible by the proceeds of that tax. Now we did all we could in the drafting of the bill to make a difference. We separated the tax title and the benefits title— one was title II of the bill and the other was title VIII. Nobody was being fooled by this. The idea was to give Justices, who might want some kind of an out, a legal peg to hang their hats on by saying, "Look, this is a tax over here and these are benefits over there and never the twain shall meet."

The difficulty with this fiction was that if you looked at the taxing titles of the law and the benefit titles, all the definitions were exactly the same. The fact that the tax was certainly tied in with the benefit program could not be missed nor did we expect it to be missed.

■■

Not surprisingly, supporters and opponents of Social Security alike doubted whether these obvious attempts would keep the courts from finding Social Security to be unconstitutional. On the vote to report the bill to the House Floor, every Republican member of the Ways and Means Committee voted against the bill. In the report accompanying the bill, the Republicans called out the obvious effort to hide that Social Security was insurance:[8]

****

Committee on Ways and Means
U.S. House of Representatives
Report To Accompany H.R. 7260
The Social Security Bill Report No. 615
74ᵗʰ Congress, 1ˢᵗ Session (April 5, 1935)

MINORITY VIEWS

We, the undersigned members of the minority, submit the following statement showing in brief our attitude toward this proposed legislation, which is known as "the economic security bill":

I

The bill is separated into several titles, which readily and naturally segregate themselves into two categories:

(1) Those which spring from the desire of the Federal Government to provide economic assistance to those who need and deserve it.

(2) Those which are based upon the principle of compulsory insurance.

....

We favor the enactment of [those in the first group], which in our opinion should have been incorporated in a separate bill.

II

In the group of titles which are based upon the principle of compulsory insurance are title II, with its related title, VIII....

COMPULSORY OLD-AGE ANNUITIES

Title II provides for compulsory old-age annuities, and title VIII provides the method by which the money is to be raised to meet the expense thereof.

These two titles are interdependent, and neither is of any consequence without the other. Neither of them has relation to any other substantive title of the bill. Neither is constitutional. Therein lies one of the reasons for our opposition to them.

The Federal Government has no power to impose this system upon private industry.

The best legal talent that the Attorney General's office and the Brain Trust could marshal has for weeks applied itself to the task of trying to bring these titles within constitutional limitations. Their best effort is only a plain circumvention. They have separated the proposition into two titles. This separation is a separation in words only. There is no separation in spirit or intent. These two titles must stand or fall together.

The learned brief submitted by the Attorney General's Office contains in its summation the following weak, apologetic language:

> There may also be taken into consideration the strong presumption which exists in favor of the constitutionality of an act of the Congress, in the light of which and of the foregoing discussion it is reasonably safe to assume that the social security bill, if enacted into law, will probably be upheld as constitutional.

■■■

The Republicans' minority views pointed out what everyone knew, but hoped the courts would not pierce through. The subterfuge was not very subtle, but it was the best the lawyers could do.

There was, of course, real reason to expect that the Supreme Court was going to find Social Security unconstitutional. Between January 1935 and May 1936—a period of less than a year and a half—the Supreme Court invalidated eleven pieces of federal legislation, including two that were integral parts of Roosevelt's New Deal program to restore the country to economic health.

Indeed, one of the enactments held unconstitutional was the Railroad Retirement Act, which created a national pension system for railroad workers. Because the Social Security Act was so similar in both subject matter and structure, the danger of the Court invalidating it too loomed especially large. The Railroad Retirement case was supposed to be the easier for the government, because railroads, unlike manufacturing, had long been held to be instrumentalities of interstate commerce and already were highly regulated by Congress.

The many bills held unconstitutional in such a short period of time contrasted with the first 140 years of U.S. history, during which the Supreme Court invalidated an average of one federal statute every other year. The district courts, taking their direction from the signals sent by the Supreme Court, issued 1,600 injunctions against federal officials seeking to carry out New Deal laws, during the same short period of time.

Surprising court watchers, the Supreme Court abruptly reversed course in the spring of 1937, and found constitutional a number of important New Deal enactments. This was after Roosevelt unveiled his threatened, highly controversial court-packing scheme.

Supreme Court deliberations are kept secret, so no one can know for certain what caused the Court's seemingly abrupt reversal—dubbed by pundits "the switch in time that saved the Nine."[9] Most people assumed the switch was in direct response to Roosevelt's attempt to pack the Court.

After retiring from the bench, though, Justice Owen Roberts wrote a memorandum on the matter. It was published posthumously in 1955. As it turned out, the Court voted to uphold a Washington state minimum wage law on December 19, well before the president proposed his legislation to pack the Court, though the decision was not announced publicly until March 29. (Roberts' reversal—the deciding vote—surprised the other justices, causing one to remark, "What is the matter with Roberts?")

Whether the Supreme Court reversed course because of Roosevelt's landslide re-election victory in 1936, the threatened court packing of 1937, or for some other reason, the decision on the Washington minimum wage was the first signal of a reversal of course that became a cascade. Sure enough, on May 24, 1937, the liberal jurist Benjamin N. Cardozo delivered the Court's opinion in the case of Helvering v. Davis.[10] The Court had found Social Security constitutional.

Once the Supreme Court held Social Security constitutional, Roosevelt and Congress could, without concern, accurately call Social Security what it is – insurance. When Congress amended Social Security in 1939, the language was clarified. The word "insurance" appears 101 times and the phrase "insured individual" appears fourteen times in Title II of the Social Security Act Amendments of 1939.[11]

Title II itself was renamed, "Federal Old-Age, Survivors *Insurance* Benefits." [Emphasis added.] The 1939 Act also placed what had been Title VIII into the Internal Revenue Code. Since it made no sense to now call it Title VIII, the section was renamed the Federal *Insurance Contributions* Act of 1939 ("FICA"). [Emphasis added.]

The Stark and Fundamental Difference Between Insurance and Savings

As just explained, Social Security's wage insurance, and indeed all insurance, involves the pooling of risk. Those who are insured seek to manage an identified financial risk by trading the possibility of a larger, perhaps devastating loss for a smaller, certain payment. The arrangement requires the use of statistical data and mathematical methods to assess the probabilities of various contingent future events and the attendant costs of those contingencies. Assumption of the risk of those future events is then exchanged for a share of the attendant costs. In contrast, savings are the straightforward accumulation of assets.

Unless so wealthy that one can essentially self-insure, insurance requires a group or, at least, individuals organized by the insurer. Though savings can be pooled, it is at base an individual venture. Insurance, not simply savings, is what is needed for a secure retirement.

It is easy to confuse wage insurance in the event of old age and retirement savings. Both are focused on protection in old age, a state virtually all of us hope to reach and most of us will. Adding to the confusion, some insurance products have savings components. So-called whole life insurance, for example, generally refers to insurance that is combined with an investment fund. Moreover, most bank deposit savings are insured through the Federal Deposit Insurance Corporation ("FDIC").

At base, though, insurance and savings are fundamentally different, despite these overlaps. Indeed, Social Security has been described as "pure" insurance because, unlike private insurance products such as whole life insurance, it lacks any element of savings.

Insurance, not savings, is what is needed to prepare for the possibility of substantial financial losses which are predictable for groups but unpredictable for individuals – like living to age 110, or becoming disabled, or dying prematurely, leaving dependent children. Social Security protects against all those risks.

Although achieving old age is probable, it is not certain. None of us can predict, at the start of our adult lives, how long we will live, how high our future wages and future standards of living will be, whether we will face periods of no wages as the result of unemployment, planned departures from the labor force for life cycle events such as the birth of a child, or other circumstances. It is impossible to predict whether we will have intervening expenses, such as medical costs resulting from serious illness or injury, costs associated with the presence of dependents, educational expenses, or other conditions that require us to draw on our savings.

Even if and when we reach old age, there is the uncertainty of how long we will live and therefore need wages replaced—the so-called longevity risk. The language is jarring—most people would not describe a long life as a "risk," but it is, in financial terms. It may be easier to think of longevity as a chance, like winning the lottery, which is the mirror image of a risk. It is noteworthy that when actuaries at the Social Security Administration and elsewhere calculate mortality rates in projecting future costs of Social Security or private annuities, they consider increases in life expectancy, a "pessimistic" assumption, because it increases the cost of the insurance product.

Retirement savings are, at best, poor substitutes for Social Security's wage insurance. Most workers in this country find that they have insufficient savings even for short-term needs, but even if workers were willing and able to sacrifice current consumption in order to maintain their standards of living in retirement, they would confront unanswerable questions. How much savings is enough? How much is too little? How much is more than necessary? If too little is saved, one risks destitution if wages are lost. Even if complete destitution is avoided, saving too little may force people to sell their homes, move from their neighborhoods, and cut all expenses drastically. If too much is saved, one needlessly reduces one's standard of living decades in advance of the contingent event, which may never occur.

Most experts believe that around seventy percent of pre-retirement wages is necessary for average-waged workers to maintain their standards of living in retirement, once wages are gone. Higher percentages are needed for low-paid workers, somewhat lower for the highest paid. Less than one hundred percent is needed, because people no longer have work expenses and, instead of saving, start to spend their savings.

But how does seventy percent of final pay translate into annual savings over the available years before retirement? Workers who want to save over their working lives the precise amount needed to replace seventy percent of pre-retirement wages each and every year until their deaths must know all sorts of eventualities that actuaries know for groups, but no one knows for an individual. As just mentioned, those worker-savers have to know in their late teens or twenties, at the start of their working lives, what their wages will be at the time of their retirements decades away. They have to know at what age they will retire and whether they will have worked and saved every year until that retirement date or whether they will have had periods of no wages or even periods of dis-saving for more immediate expenses, such as child care, medical costs, and other necessities.

They also have to know their rate of spending in retirement. Extensive medical costs or the need for long-term care can result in the rapid drawdown of savings. Those saving for retirement also have to know how long they will live, for if they do not live until retirement, they will not need to save anything for that eventuality. On the other hand, if they will be fortunate enough to live to the age of 105, they will have to save substantial amounts—20 more years of support than they will need if they die, for example, at age 85.

Worker-savers could avoid the risk of outliving savings that accompanies the uncertainty of how long beyond retirement they will live, by buying insurance—a life annuity or, to protect a spouse, a joint and survivor annuity—but that can be a costly purchase. Moreover, waiting until retirement creates its own uncertainties and risks. They will need to know what return, in real terms, minus inflation, they will receive on their savings prior to the purchase of the annuity. If they plan to invest their retirement savings in equities, they will have to know how their stocks are performing at the time they will be purchasing the annuity, decades away.

Unlike savings, insurance pools all of these various risks. Wage insurance like Social Security, where the benefit is explicitly designed to replace wages, is precisely geared to the goal and, in the case of Social Security, protects in the event of death or disability before reaching retirement.

As insurance against lost earnings, Social Security pays identical monthly benefits, pegged to earnings, to workers with identical earnings. In contrast, retirement-savings plans provide whatever savings have accumulated by the time of retirement. The amount can vary drastically as the result of market fluctuations alone. Individuals might have to retire, at great financial loss, during a market downturn. They bear all investment risks. Gary Burtless, a senior fellow in economic studies at The Brookings Institution, has calculated that workers with identical forty-year careers, identical wages, all retiring at age 62, "who follow an identical investment strategy but who retire a few years apart can receive pensions that are startlingly unequal."[12]

Historically, equities have had an overall higher rate of return than bonds and are a better hedge against inflation than bonds, but equities provide no protection of principal, which can be completely lost. Placing savings in interest-bearing bonds preserves the underlying principal, but that is only if the issuer of the bond remains in business and remains able to repay the borrowed amount. Moreover, the return may be quite low.

If the money is held in a savings account, the federal government, through the Federal Deposit Insurance Corporation ("FDIC"), insures those savings as long as they are held in insured banks and do not exceed a maximum amount. Currently, the maximum amount insured by the FDIC is $250,000 for each account. Even low-income workers, who somehow managed to accumulate that amount during their working lives and withdrew carefully once retired, would likely outlive the amount well before death, if that were all they had to live on. Savings can be outlived, but not Social Security and other annuities that are payable until death.

Also, retirement savings frequently are spent before old age. While savings plans could restrict preretirement withdrawals, they generally don't. People understandably believe that they should have access to their own savings, especially in emergencies. Because Social Security is insurance, people understand that it is only payable when the insured event—retirement, disability, or death—occurs. Moreover, those worker-savers have no protection if they become permanently and seriously disabled or die leaving dependent children or spouses, before reaching retirement age.

In short, to manage the risk of the financial loss associated with the loss of a home as the result of fire, homeowners purchase fire insurance; they do not simply save for the contingency. Similarly, car owners have car insurance, not car-accident savings accounts. And to manage the risk of lost income as the result of disability, death, or old age, wage insurance like that provided by Social Security is necessary, not retirement savings. To be economically secure, everyone who works for wages needs wage insurance in the form of Social Security and unemployment insurance.

The founders of Social Security understood extremely well why insurance, not savings, is what is needed. The Committee on Economic Security, the task force that developed the 1935 legislation, had a large staff of experts divided into working groups. The group working on old age security was chaired by Barbara Nachtrieb Armstrong, the first female law professor in the United States and a PhD economist. Also on the working group were J. Douglas Brown, an economics professor at Princeton, and Murray Latimer, a private pension expert and Chairman of the Railroad Retirement Board. They were assisted by several actuaries. The working group's staff report, published in 1937, explained:[13]

****

Committee on Economic Security
Social Security in America
Published by the Social Security Board (1937)
(Drawn from unpublished staff reports)

Part II

OLD-AGE SECURITY

Chapter VII

THE ECONOMIC PROBLEMS OF OLD AGE

For a given individual the problem of old-age dependency may begin when he is 60 or 65 years old and may last until he is 80 or 90. His health or that of his family may or may not complicate the problem. Moreover, his economic, occupational, marital, or family status may each contribute in turn to make his situation different from that of his neighbor. Hence the date and conditions of the ultimate interruption of his earning power, when the head of a family or a single person must face the fact that he is no longer able to earn a living, is unpredictable for an individual. For a large enough group of wage earners, however, calculations can reveal with reasonable accuracy the number who will survive to old age and the amount of weekly, monthly, or annual contribution on behalf of each member of the group which will provide a given retirement income for each. It is, therefore, possible and practicable through social insurance to provide a safe, adequate income for the period when the individual will be no longer able to earn a living.

When he has the assurance that each day's work builds up an investment for his old age, permitting independence of the charity of the community or financial aid from sons and daughters already overburdened by the cost of maintaining their own families, much of the wage earner's haunting fear of insecurity is removed.

The increase in the proportion of older persons in the population of the United States, the mounting ratio of dependency in old age, and the difficulties which an older worker meets in his attempt to find and hold employment make it imperative that legislative and collective action be taken in this country to avoid ever-mounting costs of relief to the aged and the humiliation of subsistence upon charity.

■■■

Everyone should save, if they possibly can. Everyone should also have adequate insurance. Savings are necessary for short-term emergencies and expenses; insurance, for large losses that are predictable for groups, but not individuals. Both are needed for economic security. Savings have their own strengths, but those strengths are not marks of their superiority to insurance. Savings are different from, but not superior to, Social Security or other insurance.

Why Opponents Willfully Refuse to See Social Security as Insurance and Not Savings

Throughout Social Security's history, there have been those who – willfully or not – fail to acknowledge the difference between Social Security and retirement savings. In bootstrap fashion, politicians and others confusing the two have argued that private savings arrangements are superior to "saving" through Social Security. To show the supposed superiority, they make straw man arguments supposedly proving their point.

Former President George W. Bush and others who favor substituting mandatory savings in private accounts for Social Security's guaranteed monthly benefit argue, for example, that, if individuals could save on their own rather than through Social Security, they could get higher rates of return. Campaigning in 1964 for Republican presidential nominee Barry Goldwater, then G.E. pitchman Ronald Reagan asked, "[C]an't we introduce voluntary features [into Social Security] that would permit a citizen who can do better on his own to be excused upon presentation of evidence that he had made provision for the non-earning years?"[14]

This is a classic straw-man argument. Social Security's benefits are not determined – nor, as insurance, should they be – by investment returns, but are defined by statute and guaranteed. Investment return should not determine the size of benefits. As the previous section explains in detail, Social Security is insurance, not savings. As wage insurance, Social Security benefits are appropriately pegged to wages, not to investment returns.

It is important to recognize that the higher rates of return that can be obtained through investment in equities could easily be obtained, on a collective basis, through Social Security, without affecting its basic structure of specified, guaranteed benefits, if that is what the American people favored.

Indeed, the fundamental rule of virtually every investment strategy is a diversified portfolio. Almost all public and private pension funds invest in both stocks and bonds. Public funds in the United States that invest in the stock market include the Federal Railroad Retirement Plan, the Federal Reserve Board pension plan, and the plan covering the Tennessee Valley Authority employees. Moreover, Canada's Social Security program, modeled after ours, now invests some of its reserve in equities, as well.

Unlike these plans, Social Security continues to be restricted by law to investment in United States' obligations or in entities whose principal and interest are guaranteed by the United States. The funds are restricted in this manner because our government wants American workers' money invested in the safest investment on Earth. Investors the world over recognize that the most secure investments are Treasury bonds and other obligations backed by the full faith and credit of the United States. (All of this is discussed at greater length in chapter three.)

The law could be changed and the funds could be invested in equities. To provide the safest investments and avoid the government's involvement in picking winners and losers among private companies, those investments could easily be limited to a broadly diversified, indexed equity fund or funds. In addition, a variety of other safeguards could be imposed to ensure no interference with the market or with the entities in which the funds are invested.

Having Social Security diversify its portfolio is starkly different from individuals who invest retirement funds in the stock market. When individuals do so, they take a substantial risk. They bear the entire risk of poor investment performance. In addition, they have the risk of being forced to sell when the market is down. They ordinarily will have to cash in their investments at or near the time of retirement and, if they are to protect themselves from running out of money before they die, will need to purchase annuities, which makes the saver unable to recoup investment losses. In other words, individual investors have limited time horizons. Their retirements may not time well with the ups and downs of the stock market, as Burtless's research, referenced above, shows so dramatically.

In contrast, a well-managed, diversified Social Security portfolio would never be in a position of having to reduce net assets at any particular time and so could ride the market's ups and downs. Investment risks would be spread over the entire population and be independent of the time a worker filed for benefits. Retirement income would continue to be based on earnings records, not the vagaries of the stock market

Social Security's accumulated reserves could be diversified. They could be invested partly in private equities, not just government obligations, in order to achieve the higher returns that equities have enjoyed over bonds historically. Or the reserves could continue to be restricted to investment in government obligations. Both are consistent with Social Security's mission of providing basic economic security in the form of wage insurance.

The point is that it is a straw-man argument that working families could do better investing on their own. The higher investment return could be achieved through Social Security as currently structured. But, as insurance, its benefits are not based on investment return. Those making the argument fail to recognize Social Security for the insurance that it is. They fail to acknowledge that, as insurance, Social Security's benefits are specified and guaranteed. In contrast, the return on savings invested in the stock market is not guaranteed, but subject to the vagaries of the performance of those investments.

Another straw man is that private savings are superior to Social Security, because private savings are under the saver's control and can be spent and bequeathed in ways that Social Security cannot. As far back as 1978, George W. Bush, in an unsuccessful run for Congress, predicted that Social Security "will be bust in 10 years unless there are some changes," adding, "The ideal solution would be for...people [to be] given the chance to invest the money the way they feel."[15] Fast forward to Bush's 2005 State of the Union address. There, he made those and other straw man arguments to sell his Social Security privatization plan:[16]

> Right now, a set portion of the money you earn is taken out of your paycheck to pay for the Social Security benefits of today's retirees. If you're a younger worker, I believe you should be able to set aside part of that money in your own retirement account, so you can build a nest egg for your own future.
>
> Here's why the personal accounts are a better deal. Your money will grow, over time, at a greater rate than anything the current system can deliver—and your account will provide money for retirement over and above the check you will receive from Social Security. In addition, you'll be able to pass along the money that accumulates in your personal account, if you wish, to your children and—or grandchildren.

The two paragraphs contain a variety of straw-man arguments: If the goal is to have a steady predictable source of income that cannot be outlived, bearing the investment risk where money can grow at a faster rate but also can be lost, is not a virtue. Moreover, controlling savings, so they can be diverted for immediate needs and wants, means that they are unavailable if and when wages must be replaced in the event of death, disability, or old age. This advantage of savings – the ability to withdraw or borrow against money held in retirement accounts before retirement – is a disadvantage with respect to Social Security's insurance, which is always there if and when the insured event occurs.

Similarly, if the goal is to replace wages in the event of disability, death, or old age, the ability to bequeath funds to adult children, nonrelatives, or charities is a disadvantage. Insurance allows the greatest concentration of the funds for the specified purpose. In the case of Social Security, benefits are only available in the event of death, disability, or old age.

Moreover, even in the event of death, the benefits are not paid to adult children who can support themselves or to other non-qualifying heirs, but instead are limited to spouses, divorced spouses, children who are eighteen or younger (nineteen in the event still in high school), or children who are adults but became disabled before age twenty-two. These limitations provide more precise targeting and, therefore, greater efficiency and effectiveness in achieving the intended goal.

Robert J. Myers, who was a staff member of the 1934 Committee on Economic Security, the interagency task force that developed the 1935 Social Security legislation, explained in his memoir why all of the arguments that people are not getting their money's worth and can do better on their own are so completely wrong:

****

Robert J. Myers
Within the System: My Half Century in Social Security
(Winstead, CT: ACTEX Publications, 1992)

We pay for insurance protection on our homes, our cars, and our lives. If the house doesn't burn down, the car doesn't get wrecked, or we don't die, the insurance company doesn't pay any money, and what we paid in premiums we don't get back.

Consider the hypothetical case of two workers who have been employed at the same salaries for their entire careers and have been paying Social Security taxes all that time. One dies at his desk on his 65th birthday and leaves no eligible survivors. He paid all that money in for all those years and got nothing back. Not a dime.

But the other guy retires at 65 and lives to be 100. He will get back far more than he paid in, even after you compute the interest he could have collected on the money that was taken from him by the payroll tax. He got a good deal.

These are individual cases. If we project this to a national scale, we get a better view of how the system works.

Take the people who are now 20 years old. Roughly 80 percent of them can expect to be alive on their 65th birthday, and they will then live beyond that, on the average, for 18 years. That means some of them may die the next day, while others live another 35 years or even longer.

All of them collect something. Even the 25 percent who died before retiring got something for their money. Their surviving spouses and dependents are eligible to collect, and on top of that during their working lives they were insured against the calamity of becoming disabled.

▪▪▪

Social Security has been mischaracterized as forced savings from the beginning. Opponents of the program have used that mischaracterization to argue that Social Security is inferior to saving on one's own.

Starting decades after its enactment, opponents started mischaracterizing Social Security's wage insurance as welfare, and making similar bootstrap arguments against it. But the founders knew the difference. They were very clear about what they were creating.

Social Security Is Insurance, Not Welfare

The late Senator Barry Goldwater (R-AZ), often called the father of the modern conservative movement, was one of those who refused to see that Social Security is wage insurance, not welfare. In

1960, he released a highly influential book, *Conscience of a Conservative*, ghostwritten by National Review editor and speechwriter L. Brent Bozell.[17]

In a chapter entitled "The Welfare State," Goldwater lumped together, undifferentiated, Social Security and public assistance. He claimed that "collectivists" had been unsuccessful in bringing about "Nationalization," or "a State-owned and operated economy." But, he warned, "The collectivists have not abandoned their ultimate goal—to subordinate the individual to the State—but their strategy has changed. They have learned that Socialism can be achieved through Welfarism quite as well as through Nationalization."

His bottom line was that Social Security and welfare should be provided by the private sector or, if government involvement was absolutely necessary, by state and local governments, but under no circumstances by the federal government.

Social Security and welfare programs, he claimed, inevitably lead to "unlimited political and economic power...as absolute...as any oriental despot." The beneficiaries of Social Security and recipients of means-tested federal programs, according to Goldwater, are transformed "into a dependent animal creature."

Campaigning for Goldwater, then-actor Ronald Reagan, went further. He not only wrongly claimed that Social Security was welfare, not insurance; he accused the government of systematically and deliberately lying to the American people about it. In a speech that was to launch his political career, Reagan asserted that "we're against those entrusted with [Social Security] when they practice deception," charging, "They only use the term 'insurance' to sell it to the people."[18]

Despite Reagan's accusation, those who developed Social Security did not just claim it was insurance. Rather, that is how they designed it. Just as Social Security is insurance, not forced savings, it is also not welfare. Like savings and insurance, welfare and insurance are fundamentally different. Viewing Social Security simply as a government-transfer program, as it commonly is in today's dominant policy frame, blurs this essential distinction. A careful analysis reveals, though, that Social Security and means-tested welfare are intrinsically different, having developed from two very different and distinct historical roots.

Humans have always sought security from life's dangers. Generally, the most effective actions against life's insecurities have been collective in nature. Collective action to enhance physical security has taken the form of armies, police forces, and militias. Collective action to enhance economic security has taken two separate forms, welfare and insurance – each quite distinct from the other.

The antecedents to modern welfare programs can be traced from biblical prescriptions, such as the command that "thou shalt not wholly reap the corners of thy field, neither shalt thou gather the gleanings of thy harvest. And thou shalt not glean thy vineyard . . .; thou shalt leave them for the poor . . . ."[19] In England, the practice of voluntary tithing to the church to help the poor evolved into compulsory tithing, and then into the English poor laws. They, in turn, were transplanted from England by the colonists, and transformed into America's welfare laws. Those early American welfare arrangements evolved into today's welfare programs.

In contrast, a second, equally rich but fundamentally different tradition – wage insurance – developed where workers dependent on wages sought to protect themselves and their families from the loss of earnings by banding together and pooling their risk. At least as far back as the Middle Ages in England and Europe, individuals who had a common trade or craft joined together to form mutual aid societies or guilds, which, in addition to regulating the craft, provided a variety of wage-replacement benefits to their members. Similarly, in the mining districts of central Europe as early as the sixteenth century, workers formed customary funds, which provided benefits for sickness and accidents.

Building on these models, Chancellor Otto von Bismarck was the first to provide compulsory, nationwide, universal social insurance, and the concept spread quickly around the world. It spread to the United States in the form of Social Security through a number of experts, including Barbara Armstrong who chaired President Roosevelt's working group which developed the old age insurance part of the Social Security Act of 1935. Indeed, Armstrong was among the leading experts on social insurance. Prior to her work on Social Security, she had authored *Insuring the Essentials*, a landmark treatise that exhaustively surveyed social insurance programs throughout the world.

As its historical origins make clear, welfare programs involve arrangements among financially unequal parties – those materially better off providing assistance to those less advantaged. Eligibility for welfare is based on need and is determined by an examination of potential recipients' incomes and assets to ensure that they are really in need. Welfare benefits are generally an amount designed to provide the recipient with enough simply to get by, to subsist, as judged by the provider.

In contrast, insurance programs involve arrangements among equals who are pooling their risks. Eligibility for insurance is based on achieving insured status, irrespective of need. Benefits result from experiencing the event covered by the insurance. They are paid irrespective of need.

The Stark and Fundamental Difference Between Insurance and Welfare

Welfare programs are essential as long as there is poverty, but they have inescapable, inherent weaknesses not found in insurance arrangements. The necessity of determining need has the potential of discouraging work and savings. If potential recipients are capable of earning enough to get by, as defined by those providing the assistance, they, by definition, are not in need of the community's help. Conversely, those who are incapable of earning more than the designated welfare amount have no financial incentive to work.

Moreover, those who have savings upon which to draw are also not in need of the assistance of others. As a result, because only those with no or limited savings receive benefits, thrift is penalized. Those who have been thrifty in the past generally must exhaust their savings before they are eligible to receive welfare.

Insurance has none of these shortcomings. Indeed, if the insurance is wage insurance, where work is a condition of reaching insured status and the insurance benefit is higher as a result of higher wages and more years of work, the arrangement rewards increased work effort. Unlike welfare, savings do not disqualify a person from the receipt of insurance benefits. Rather, savings provide an additional source of income from which to draw, and so are encouraged.

A comparison of Social Security to the Supplemental Security Income program ("SSI"), illuminates the stark differences between the two forms of arrangements. Like Social Security, SSI provides benefits to people who are old and people with disabilities, but unlike Social Security, eligibility for benefits is based on need, not achieving insured status. Under Social Security, both work and savings are encouraged. Under SSI, both work and savings are disincentivized.

Under Social Security, the higher one's earnings that are insured and the longer one works, the larger the dollar amount of the benefit received. In contrast, both earned and unearned income reduce SSI's already modest payments: In 2018, SSI provides a maximum monthly federal benefit to individuals of just $750. Nonwage income, such as Social Security benefits, reduces a recipient's monthly SSI benefit dollar-for-dollar, with the exception of a disregard of the first $20 of income. That is, for every dollar that SSI recipients receive in Social Security benefits or other nonwage income, they lose a dollar of their SSI payment, with the exception of the first $20. For every dollar in a month they earn in excess of $65, their SSI benefit is reduced by fifty cents.

To alleviate the inherent work disincentives of welfare, SSI allows recipients to earn $65 a month without reduction of their SSI and lose 50 cents on the dollar, rather than a dollar-for-dollar reduction, on earnings higher than $65. The program allows them to keep $20 of unearned income, before they experience a dollar-for-dollar reduction above the $20.

Think about how harsh that is: The dollar-for-dollar reduction of unearned income above the $20 disregard constitutes conceptually a 100 percent tax. Losing 50¢ for every dollar earned above the disregard is equivalent to a 50 percent tax rate, a higher rate of taxation than the top marginal rate of the federal income tax code!

Past work is irrelevant unless it has resulted in savings of more than $2,000; savings of that amount disqualify an individual from receiving SSI. Indeed, if resources are given away or sold, not only by a potential recipient but also by the recipient's spouse or co-owner, for less than fair market value, the potential recipient may be ineligible for SSI for up to thirty-six months.

In contrast, savings are immaterial to the determination of Social Security benefits. Because Social Security's benefits are too low to allow most workers to maintain their standards of living in retirement, savings are implicitly encouraged. In recognition of the desirability of supplementing Social Security's modest benefits, the Internal Revenue Code provides preferential tax treatment for those who save for retirement.

Those who take advantage of the preferential tax treatment will receive their full Social Security benefits, but will be ineligible for SSI if the savings, together with other countable assets, are in excess of $2,000. Even if the retirement savings account is below the threshold for eligibility for SSI, the withdrawals from it will be offset dollar-for-dollar, once the twenty-dollar monthly disregard of income is reached.

In order to ensure that the income and assets limitations are not exceeded, SSI recipients are required to regularly report numerous details of their lives. Every month, for example, they must take or mail all pay stubs to the Social Security Administration. They must report any changes to the income of spouses, if living together, as well as changes in assets, including those of their spouses.

They must report, within ten days, changes in living arrangements, such as a change in the number of people in the household. SSI recipients who receive help with food, utilities, or housing costs must report that and suffer a reduction in their benefits. If recipients live with their children and do not reimburse them totally for the cost of food and shelter, their SSI benefits may be reduced by up to one-third.

In contrast, Social Security beneficiaries are not required to file burdensome and intrusive reports about the details of their lives. Their children may provide them with help without any impact on their benefits.

The different way that assets and income are treated in the determination of benefits results directly from the inherent difference between welfare and insurance programs like Social Security. Welfare is designed by those financially better off for people who are already poor; insurance is designed by equals to prevent members of the group from becoming poor in the first place. Welfare discourages work; wage insurance encourages it. Welfare discourages savings; wage insurance is indifferent to savings and actually encourages workers to save to the extent it simply provides a floor of protection.

In short, to qualify for and continue to receive welfare, recipients must prove something negative about themselves—that they do not have enough to get along on their own. In contrast, beneficiaries of Social Security must prove something positive— that they have worked and contributed long enough to qualify for benefits.

Founders' Recognition That Insurance, Not Welfare, is Optimal for the Long Run

Insurance, not welfare, was President Roosevelt's clear vision. He was committed to structuring Social Security as insurance, not welfare. This was a deeply held goal that President Roosevelt embraced well before becoming president. When he had been governor of New York, the state enacted means-tested welfare, in response to the problem of insecurity in old age. Although an improvement over poor houses, the legislation was not what Roosevelt believed to be optimal. In his message to the New York legislature, delivered on January 7, 1931, he explained:[20]

> In 1929 I recommended to the Legislature a commission to report on Old-Age Security against want. The report of this commission resulted in the passage of the Old-Age Security bill, by the last Legislature, and actual payments under the new law went into effect on January first of this year. I have many times stated that I am not satisfied with the provisions of this law. Its present form, although objectionable as providing for a gratuity, may be justified only as a means intended to replace to a large extent the existing methods of poor-house and poor-farm relief. Any great enlargement of the theory of this law, would, however, smack of the practices of a dole. Our American aged do not want charity, but rather old age comforts to which they are rightfully entitled by their own thrift and foresight in the form of

insurance. It is, therefore, my judgment that the next step to be taken should be based on the theory of insurance by a system of contributions commencing at an early age. In this way all men and women will, on arriving at a period when work is no longer practicable, be assured not merely of a roof over head and enough food, to keep body and soul together, but also enough income to maintain life during the balance of their days in accordance with the American standard of living.

Roosevelt's strong commitment to structuring Social Security as insurance, not welfare, may have resulted in part from his own personal experience. Having suffered the ravages of polio, he understood what it meant to be dependent. Frances Perkins, President Roosevelt's Secretary of Labor and long-time associate, witnessed Roosevelt undergo "a spiritual transformation during the years of his illness....The man emerged completely warmhearted, with humility of spirit and with a deeper philosophy. Having been in the depths of trouble, he understood the problems of people in trouble."[21]

His own experience perhaps taught him on a visceral level that people would be uplifted in spirit if they worked hard and joined together to provide a common pool of funds from which to draw when working days were over. His dependence resulting from his polio perhaps illuminated for him, on a personal level, how demeaning it was for people to have to prove to some other person that they could not support themselves without help, and how crippling in spirit to feel oneself to be helpless.

Roosevelt recognized that to get immediate assistance to people in need – to alleviate the immediate suffering caused by the Depression – there was no alternative to welfare. But for the long term – once the Depression was history and the economic health of the country was restored – the President wanted a system of insurance in place to guarantee for posterity that people would have a reliable, stable source of income from which they could draw in old-age. Acutely conscious of the debilitating quality of fear, he wanted all workers to have the peace of mind, the security, of knowing that they would be insured against the loss of their wages.

The Social Security Act of 1935 consisted of eleven titles, but only Titles II and VIII created the program commonly referred to today as "Social Security." Titles I, IV, and X provided grants to the states for means-tested, welfare programs of old-age assistance, aid to dependent children, and aid to the blind, respectively. These had immediate effective dates.

In stark contrast to the welfare titles, which began paying benefits right away, the two titles comprising Social Security were designed to start paying monthly benefits only in 1942. Although enacted at the height of the Great Depression, those two titles were not designed to alleviate the immediate conditions of the Depression. Rather the first monthly benefits were not to be paid until more than six years after the program's enactment, and more than twelve years after the Depression's start.

Those who designed the legislation recognized that welfare was all that could be implemented quickly to alleviate the poverty and hardship caused by the Depression. Consequently, the 1935 Act authorized immediate appropriations for the several new welfare programs. For the long term, however, Social Security's creators believed that a better solution — one that prevented poverty in the first place — should be created.

In an economy where most are dependent on wage income, the better solution was and remains Social Security's insurance against the loss of wages. Insurance, paid for during working years, allows workers and their families to maintain their standards of living and prevents poverty if and when those insurable events occur and wages are lost.

The Report to the President from the Committee on Economic Security, the interagency task force that developed Social Security, explained this specifically:[22]

> Only non-contributory old-age pensions will meet the situation of those who are now old and have no means of support. Laws for the payment of old-age pensions on a needs basis are in force in more than half of all States and should be enacted everywhere....

The satisfactory way of providing for the old age of those now young is a contributory system of old-age annuities. This will enable younger workers, with matching contributions from their employers, to build up a more adequate old-age protection than it is possible to achieve with non-contributory pensions based upon a means test.

In a fireside chat explaining his plan for Social Security, President Roosevelt observed that Social Security would be self-help, where Americans were "to use the agencies of government to assist in the establishment of means to provide sound and adequate protection against the vicissitudes of modern life—in other words, social insurance." Perhaps to emphasize that Social Security, unlike welfare, is a program among equals, he reminded those listening, "We remain, as John Marshall said a century ago, 'emphatically and truly, a government of the people.'"[23]

In his 1935 State of the Union Address, in explaining the legislation that would become the Social Security Act of 1935, President Roosevelt made clear why he preferred insurance as a permanent solution:[24]

The lessons of history, confirmed by the evidence immediately before me, show conclusively that continued dependence upon relief induces a spiritual disintegration fundamentally destructive to the national fibre. To dole out relief in this way is to administer a narcotic, a subtle destroyer of the human spirit.

As described above, supporters of Social Security in 1935 had to be careful in their language for fear that they would be giving ammunition to the program's opponents in the inevitable constitutional challenge that was coming to the courts. Nevertheless, the Ways and Means Committee Report made clear that they were setting up two programs: One would be a federal-state system of welfare (or gratuitous old age pensions, as they were then called) for seniors, as Title I of the Social Security Act of 1935; the other would be a program of wage replacement, today known as Social Security, when people reached old age, as Title II of the Social Security Act of 1935. Here is what the Report says:[25]

> The provisions for Federal aid, included in title I, are designed for the support of people now old and dependent. They do not, however, furnish a completely satisfactory solution of the problem of old age support, considered from a long time point of view. If no other provisions are made, the cost of gratuitous old age pensions is bound to increase very rapidly, due to the growing number of the aged and the probable increasing rate of dependency....

> To keep the cost of Federal aided State pensions under title I from becoming extremely burdensome in future years, and to assure support for the aged as a right rather than as public charity, and in amounts which will insure not merely subsistence but some of the comforts of life, title II of the bill establishes a system of old age benefits, paid out of the Federal Treasury, and administered directly by the Federal Government. The benefits provided for workers who have been employed during substantially all their working life, will probably be considerably larger than any Federal aided State pensions could be. The benefits to be paid are related to the wages earned....

Consistent with the intention of creating insurance as the permanent solution, but welfare to meet the immediate need, it is instructive to repeat here a part of Founder Mary Dewson's 1938 address:

****

Mary W. Dewson
Member, Social Security Board
Address Before the Women's City Club of Boston
February 17, 1938

THIS SOCIAL SECURITY - WHAT IS IT?

....

Social insurance, like private insurance, has limitations. You can't, for example, insure people who are already old against old-age dependency, any more than you can insure your car against property damages after you have had a smash-up. Yet some provision has to be made for this non-insurable need. Nobody knows exactly how many of those now old are without sufficient resources for their own support. Surveys made some years ago in Massachusetts, Connecticut, and other States showed that anywhere from 40 to 50 percent of the people over 65 had an income of less than $300 a year. And $300 a year is the modest minimum which, the American people seem to think, is essential for health and decency. To take care of such old people, the Social Security Act adds another provision—for assistance on the basis of need. ... As time goes on, however, more people will be covered by the old-age insurance system, particularly when, as we hope, it is extended to include practically all wage earners.

Assistance and Relief

... As long as there are gaps and weak spots in the platform, a lot of people are going to fall through—through into destitution and misery. And as long as these gaps and weak spots remain, some fairly extensive—and very expensive—life net will have to be stretched underneath to catch these often needless casualties before they quite strike rock bottom. That, I take it, is the function of relief. ... I am no visionary. I know that the need for relief will be with us in the future as in the past. And I hope that we shall be prepared to meet it more adequately than in the past.

Toward Firmer Footing

The point I am emphasizing is that it is incomparably better to assure the worker a firm footing—to close the gaps and strengthen the weak spots, insofar as we possibly can—rather than continue depending on the tragically wasteful business of picking up the pieces—pieces of human lives that might, but for our patchwork building, have remained whole and self-sufficient.

■■■

Today, people often describe Social Security as a "safety net." It is not. As Founder Mary Dewson explained, it is a foundation, a platform on which to stand. As Dewson so clearly understood, safety net programs – that is, welfare – are designed to alleviate poverty. Social Security and other types of insurance are designed to prevent poverty and destitution in the first place. This distinction – prevention versus alleviation – is a subtle but essential difference.

Alleviation of Poverty is a Byproduct of Social Security

Part of the confusion between Social Security and welfare stems from the fact that Social Security is an incredibly effective anti-poverty program. Indeed, it is the nation's most effective anti-poverty program. It currently lifts over 22 million Americans – including a million children – out of poverty and reduces the depth of poverty for millions more. Without Social Security, almost half of all seniors would have incomes below the poverty line.[26]

From the start, Social Security's benefit formula has provided higher-earning workers benefits that are larger in absolute dollars, but are smaller in proportionate terms, than those received by lower paid workers. For example, workers who earn around $80,000 a year and claim Social Security benefits starting at age 62 receive Social Security benefits of around 25 percent of their wages, while workers earning around $22,000 a year receive annual benefits starting at age 62 of around 40 percent of their salaries.[27]

Some incorrectly think that Social Security's explicitly redistributive benefit formula makes Social Security welfare, but it does not. Redistribution is not a feature unique to welfare. All group insurance redistributes. Life insurance redistributes from those who live beyond average life expectancies to those who die prematurely. Old age annuities do the opposite, redistributing from those who die prematurely to those who live beyond their average life expectancies. Disability insurance redistributes from those who do not become disabled to those who do.

In recognition that those with lower wages or periods of unemployment have less discretionary income and are likely to need a higher proportion of their pre-retirement wages to maintain their standards of living, the designers of Social Security created Social Security's benefit formula to redistribute from those with higher wages over their careers to those with lower wages. That design is perfectly consistent with the idea of group insurance and pooled risk.

Looking forward, at the start of working life, even people with careers that promise high remuneration do not know whether they will, at the end of their lives, have had a lifetime of high wages. They might have had to take time off from those careers as the result of illness or accident, for example, or might experience other intervening events that change the trajectory of their earnings. Social Security, which is often referred to as "social" insurance, redistributes in this and other ways that are not generally found in private group insurance but are socially beneficial. Nevertheless, Social Security, including its progressive benefit formula and all of its other attributes, is completely consistent with the concept of insurance and completely inconsistent with the concept of welfare.

Social Security's efficacy in fighting poverty is a byproduct. Social Security was designed not as a welfare program, alleviating poverty, but as insurance, preventing people from falling into poverty in the first place. Its goal is much more expansive than simply the alleviation of poverty, or even its prevention. Its goal is to replace sufficient wages to allow people to maintain their standards of living if and when they are no longer receiving wages as the result of retirement, disability or death.

Why Opponents Willfully Refuse to See Social Security as Insurance and Not Welfare

Those determined to dismantle Social Security brick by brick, and others who unwittingly adopt the language of opponents' propaganda, fail to recognize what the founders of Social Security created. Over eight decades later, the basic structure remains the same, to this day: wage insurance. The mischaracterization by some may be the product of ignorance, but the mischaracterization by others appears to be willful.

The false characterization appears to be an effort to undermine support for the program. Talking about Social Security as a safety net and entitlement, as opposed to a platform, an earned benefit, and insurance implies that Social Security is welfare, not insurance. These shifts in language did not occur by accident, but by the efforts of determined foes of the program, as chapter five explains in detail.

Welfare is likely to be with us as long as there is poverty. It would be wonderful if Americans generously supported welfare willingly and compassionately. But that has never been our history. Welfare programs have trouble winning majority support. When they are enacted, they tend to incorporate harsh and punitive measures.

Those who claim that Social Security is welfare, just like those who claim it is forced savings, routinely generate straw man arguments to criticize Social Security as poorly designed welfare.

Those who mischaracterize Social Security as welfare or what is pejoratively referred to as a government "handout," often falsely claim that it results in dependency. Speaker of the House Paul Ryan (R-WI), who has led the effort to dismantle Social Security, talks about "makers" and "takers."[28] He has warned that Social Security and the nation's other supposed safety nets were in danger of turning into hammocks – implying that those who receive these benefits would inexorably be lulled into slothful and lazy "takers." Though the language is new, the complaint that Social Security creates dependency is not.

How far back does the argument about dependency go? Even at the time of the enactment of Social Security, the charge that government programs created dependency was not a new claim.

Frank Bane, executive director of the Social Security Board (the predecessor of the Social Security Administration and single commissioner) addressed the issue in a 1938 article, which was based in part on a speech he delivered on May 6, 1938:[29]

****

Frank Bane
Social Security Bulletin, Vol. 1, No. 8 (August, 1938)

A NEW AMERICAN REALITY

The majority of the American people have always regarded their democratic ideals with realism. The rapidity with which the social security program has been woven into the fabric of our lives shows that the vast majority see it as a realistic expression of those ideals—a method of safeguarding our people and our economic system by extending those well-known protections which government has always thrown around the property of some men— their farms, their homes, their stocks and bonds—to include the only property of many more men—their opportunity for a normal childhood, their ability to work, their jobs, and their chance for a tranquil old age. Throughout our history we have exercised democratic political control to promote individual initiative in some areas and at some times, and joint action through government in other areas and at other times, depending upon which seemed most likely, under given conditions, to serve the common welfare. Yet whenever changing circumstances have compelled us to ask government to lend a hand in what were once private responsibilities, there have always been some to cry that our cherished institutions and our time-honored traditions would immediately be overthrown.

Let me quote from one of these viewers-with-alarm: "Among these strange notions.... there is one which has lately seized the minds of men, that all things must be done for them by the government, and that they are to do nothing for themselves. The government is not only to attend to the great concerns which are its province, but it must step in and ease individuals of their natural and moral obligations. A more pernicious notion cannot prevail. Look at that ragged fellow staggering from the whiskey shop, and see that slattern who has gone there to reclaim him; where are their children? Running about ragged, idle, ignorant, fit candidates for the penitentiary. Why is all this so? Ask the man and he will tell you, 'Oh, the government has undertaken to educate our children for us. It has given us a premium for idleness . . .' The education of their children is the first and most obvious duty of every parent. Is it the friends of the poor who absolve them from what Nature, what God himself has made their first and most sacred duty?"

That is what John Randolph, of Virginia, thought and said in 1829 about the then "revolutionary" institution of public education. It parallels what a few people thought and said in 1935 about the social security program. Yet in these 3 years that program, like public education, has become an accepted and practical reality. Building on their past, but looking at the present and toward the future, the Federal Government, the States, and the localities stand shoulder to shoulder to promote individual and national security.

▪▪▪

Social Security is part of workers' compensation packages. It creates no more dependency than cash wages and salaries. Speaker Ryan's salary is paid for from our tax dollars. I doubt he would call himself and his colleagues "takers" because they are dependent on payments by the federal government. Nor should that be the label applied to those who receive earned Social Security benefits.

Those who mischaracterize Social Security as welfare, a government handout, not only argue that it creates dependency. Another one of their straw man arguments is that Social Security is not well targeted because it goes to middle class and wealthier workers who don't "need" its benefits. Today's leaders in the Republican Party and their allies in conservative think tanks propose a variety of measures in response to these straw man arguments. Some have proposed scaling back the benefits of middle class workers while increasing somewhat the benefits of those of lowest income. As chapter five explains, that would convert Social Security into the proposal the Republican Party campaigned on in 1936. Others have proposed subjecting Social Security to a means test, which would transform it from insurance to welfare, with all the attendant disadvantages.

Limiting Social Security to those who are determined by some objective criteria to "need" it does not make it more efficient. Its benefits appropriately are pegged to replacing wages. Scaling back the benefits of those who are middle class or wealthier simply makes it less adequate for those whose benefits are reduced or eliminated.

Indeed, such a change would make Social Security less efficient. Social Security currently pays more than 99 cents of every dollar on benefits. Less than a penny goes to administration. That would change with a means test.

Currently, contributors need only provide their Social Security numbers and proof of the insured event to receive benefits. Means testing Social Security, which would convert it from insurance to welfare, would require an intrusive examination of income and assets. If there were a means test, people would presumably have to disclose income tax returns and valuations of assets to prove that their incomes were within the specified means.

More fundamentally and conceptually, Social Security insurance requires the proof of something positive: that a worker has earned and contributed enough to qualify for benefits. If a means test were added to Social Security, people would have to prove something negative: that their means are low enough to qualify for benefits. When Social Security is clearly seen as the wage insurance it is, these arguments that Social Security is, in effect, poor welfare, are clearly seen as the straw men that they are.

Key Elements of Social Security

Social Security is an earned benefit. Not only are the benefits earned, the insured workers also pay part of the cost, generally through regular deductions from current pay. Social Security premiums are matched, dollar-for-dollar, by employers and transferred to the Old Age, Survivors and Disability Insurance Trust Funds, where, like premiums paid to private insurance companies, they are kept in reserve and invested until they are needed to pay Social Security benefits and related expenses.

Social Security requires that workers work and contribute long enough to achieve insured status as a prerequisite to receiving benefits.[30] Not only is Social Security not a giveaway, as critics imply, it requires many years of work and premium payments to be eligible to receive even a penny of benefits.

Despite confusion even by supporters of Social Security, the program is insurance. It is not welfare; it is not forced savings. This was well-understood from the very beginning, throughout most of the program's history. In the same article quoted above, Frank Bane, executive director of the Social Security Board, explained:

> The idea of joining forces for mutual protection has been a habit of ours throughout our history. Mutual cooperation has long been accepted as good business; and, practical men that they are, American businessmen have been its apostles. The pooling of risks through insurance is considered the epitome of economic respectability by those who can afford it. Social insurance simply extends this kind of protection to those who need it most and have been least able to obtain it.

President Dwight Eisenhower eloquently explained the concept of self-help, underlying our Social Security system, in a message to Congress proposing its expansion:[31]

****

President Dwight Eisenhower
Special Message to the Congress Transmitting Proposed
Changes in the Social Security Program
August 1, 1953

To the Congress of the United States:

In my message to the Congress on the State of the Union, I pointed out that there is urgent need for making our social security programs more effective.

I stated that the provisions of the Old Age and Survivor's Insurance law should cover millions of our citizens who thus far have been excluded from participation in the social security program.

Retirement systems, by which individuals contribute to their own security according to their own respective abilities, have become an essential part of our economic and social life. These systems are but a reflection of the American heritage of sturdy self-reliance which has made our country strong and kept it free; the self-reliance without which we would have had no Pilgrim Fathers, no hardship-defying pioneers, and no eagerness today to push to ever widening horizons in every aspect of our national life.

The Social Security program furnishes, on a national scale, the opportunity for our citizens, through that same self-reliance, to build the foundation for their security. We are resolved to extend that opportunity to millions of our citizens who heretofore have been unable to avail themselves of it.

...

There are two points about these proposals which I cannot stress too strongly. One is my belief that they would add immeasurably to the peace of mind and security of the individual citizens who would be covered for the first time under this plan; the second is my belief that they would add greatly to the national sense of domestic security....

■■■

Social Security's basic structure is unchanged from its enactment, over eight decades ago. It has stood the test of time. The National Commission on Social Security Reform, popularly known as the Greenspan Commission, developed recommendations that became the Social Security Amendments of 1983.[32] Its very first recommendation, which Congress followed, states:

> The members of the National Commission believe that the Congress, in its deliberations on financing proposals, should not alter the fundamental structure of the Social Security program or undermine its fundamental principles.

So what is that fundamental structure and those fundamental principles? To understand them, it is necessary to see clearly that Social Security is wage insurance.

Universal Earned Insurance, No Means Test

Insurance is most cost-efficient and reliable when the risks can be spread across as broad a population as possible and when no one can purchase the insurance only when personal risk factors increase – a practice known as adverse selection. The only entity that has the power and ability to establish a nationwide risk pool, one that covers all workers and avoids adverse selection by making the insurance mandatory, is the federal government.

Consistent with the goals of providing insurance as effectively as possible, with a risk pool covering all workers and their families, it was the founders' intention for Social Security to be universal and mandatory. As chapter four explains in detail, the view, sometimes expressed today, that the founders limited the coverage initially out of racist reasons is not borne out by any of the available evidence. Quite the contrary, the intent, from the beginning, was coverage of all. Today, 94 percent of the workforce is covered by Social Security.

Because Social Security is insurance, it has no means test. Benefits are based on achieving insured status, which requires working and contributing long enough to reach that status, and experiencing the insured event – disability, death or retirement.[33] Need is immaterial. In other words, benefits are earned, rather than based on need. They are payable as a matter of earned right.

Social Security, as the insurance that it is, did not have in 1935, and never has had, wealth as a restriction on receipt of benefits. Imposing a means test would fundamentally change the nature of Social Security. No one would ever say that wealthy people with fire insurance should not be permitted to collect under the policy, if the insured property burns down, simply because they are wealthy and do not need the insurance proceeds. Similarly, Social Security has from its inception been designed to be payable to anyone who is insured, when an insured event occurs.

Means tests are extremely expensive to administer, because administrators must continually determine that the recipient's means have not changed. Moreover, that determination is extremely burdensome on and invasive of recipients.

Social Security's nearly universal coverage and earned benefits, payable as a matter of right, without a test of means, allows its administrative costs to be so extremely low. Social Security spends less than a penny of every dollar on administration, efficiency unachievable with private sector insurance and pensions. More than 99 cents are returned in benefits. Because Social Security is insurance, its beneficiaries receive their earned benefits without burdensome, invasive prying into their finances.

Replacement of Worker's Highest Average Pay

As insurance against the loss of wages, benefits are related to those wages. From the start, if a worker was insured and the insured event occurred, the level of benefits a worker qualified for was related to the wage level on which contributions were made.

The benefit formula is designed to replace a certain percentage of final pay, as many private sector, employer-sponsored traditional pensions do, in order to allow the insureds to maintain their standards of living once wages are no longer being earned.

Simply replacing a percentage of final pay is tricky, though, when the plan sponsor is the federal government, not workers' employers. A plan based on final earnings may inadvertently penalize those who are laid off late in life and can only find work at much lower wages. In addition, final pay can be manipulated by employers and employees interested in gaming the system.

As the actuaries of the Social Security Administration explain:[34]

> In the context of national pensions, career earnings patterns of individuals vary widely. Many individuals have earnings patterns that differ markedly from the patterns of individuals with stable careers and high compensation...or who have long careers at one company...

Social Security uses an ingenious method of calculating benefits that avoids those problems, while basing benefits on an extremely close approximation of final pay. The method is technical, but the intent is clear. The late Robert J. Myers, an actuary who began his Social Security career as an employee of the Committee on Economic Security, the Roosevelt task force that designed Social Security, wrote a comprehensive treatise on Social Security, which he updated several times. In it, he describes this intent:[35]

> ...[T]he manner in which [Social Security] benefits were adjusted in the past...and the manner in which they will be adjusted automatically...in the future, produced about the same results as if a final-average basis had been used....In other words, using a career-average wage and dynamic benefit factors can produce about the same result as using a final-average wage and static benefit factors.

Recently, Social Security's actuaries compared the results produced by the formula to actual earnings records of beneficiaries. They looked at the records of over 200,000 recent retirees and compared their benefits to their pre-retirement earnings. As Myers predicted, they found that Social Security produces results that are "consistent with a 'late career' or 'final-earnings' approach to replacement rates for steady, consistent earners."[36]

Another advantage of Social Security's method of calculating benefits is that it replaces the same percentage of wages regardless of when similarly situated working families experience an insured event. In determining benefits, wages are indexed to ensure that the same percentage of wages are replaced, no matter the year one begins to receive benefits. Prior to wage-indexing, the percentage of wages replaced would decline over time, as a result of increased standards of living and inflation. The only way to restore the value was an act of Congress updating benefits. Now, that happens automatically.

Recognizing that those who have had higher earnings require a smaller percentage of wages to be replaced than those with lower earnings, the formula provides larger benefits, as an absolute dollar amount, to those who have earned and contributed more, but larger benefits, as a proportion of past earnings, to those who have experienced lower average wages over their working years. These results are achieved through the use of a weighted benefit formula, which replaces a higher percentage of first dollars earned.

That was the structure of benefits in the original enactment in 1935, and it has been the structure ever since. The founders designed the benefit formula to be fair: They recognized that those who earn and contribute more should receive larger benefits, but those who earn less generally have less discretionary income and so need a larger percentage replaced.

As mentioned above, most experts believe workers need to receive, on average, about seventy percent of wages to maintain standards of living. Higher income workers who have had more discretionary income, can maintain their standards of living with a somewhat smaller percentage, while those of lower income require slightly more.

Social Security falls far short of that goal. For workers earning around $50,000 at the ends of their careers and retiring at age 62, Social Security replaces around 30 percent of those wages. Those earning less have a larger percentage replaced; those earning more, a lower percentage replaced.[37]

It is common today to hear the claim that the founders never intended Social Security to be fully adequate, without the need of supplementation. As chapter four explains in detail, that is wrong. Indeed, those who opposed Social Security initially feared that it would crowd out private plans. Rather than a conscious decision to keep Social Security's benefits inadequate, benefits may have begun lower than fully adequate as an incremental first step.

Primarily Financed From Employer and Employee Premiums

The 1935 enactment, just like today's program, required workers and employers to contribute an equal amount to finance benefits. This remains the primary source of Social Security's financing.

All of Social Security's three sources of revenue, discussed in chapter three, are dedicated: They can only be used to pay Social Security benefits and related administrative costs. Just as private pension plans' assets are held in trust, Social Security's assets are held in trust. When Social Security has a surplus, those funds are invested.

There is much confusion and willful misunderstanding around Social Security's funding and investments. Those elements of Social Security's basic structure, established at the program's start, will be discussed in detail in the next chapter.

The Founders' Descriptions of Social Security's Basic Structure

The basic structure of Social Security today, described in this chapter and the next, is the same as the structure enacted in 1935. At least two founders have articulated what that basic structure was and is. One of those founders is J. Douglas Brown, mentioned earlier in this chapter. He was a key member of the old age working group of the Committee on Economic Security, the interagency task force that developed the 1935 legislation. The chair of the group was Barbara Nachtrieb Armstrong, but she was not the first one asked.

In 1934, Brown, an economics professor at Princeton University, was invited to head the working group. Although Brown declined the offer, explaining that the position was incompatible with his responsibilities at Princeton, he agreed to serve as a consultant to the working group. He was an integral member, spending a few days every week in Washington until the project was complete.

Though Brown never said so, he may have declined the offer to chair the group because the president of the university, Harold Willis Dodds, a staunch Republican who hated Roosevelt, may have refused to give Brown a leave of absence. Dodds once famously said, "Each one of us requires the spur of insecurity to force us to do our best," and may have not wanted to be a party, even indirectly, to efforts to increase the security of workers.

Brown, who died in 1986 at age 87, was involved in Social Security policymaking until his death. His contributions included serving on numerous Social Security advisory councils. Indeed, he chaired the very first Social Security advisory council, whose recommendations were largely enacted as the Social Security Act Amendments of 1939. The recommendations of the 1937-38 Social Security Advisory Council and the resulting legislation were the first expansion of Social Security, consistent with the founders' vision.

Twenty-two years after Social Security was enacted, Brown, by then Dean at Princeton, outlined what he considered five essential attributes of Social Security:[38]

****

J. Douglas Brown
Dean of the Faculty Princeton University
Address Before a General Staff Meeting of the Bureau of Old-Age and Survivors Insurance, Baltimore, MD
November 7, 1957

THE IDEA OF SOCIAL SECURITY

....

I am going to list five basic elements of the philosophy of social insurance. The first and the foremost element in our philosophy of social insurance I have already suggested. Without that element, social insurance would not exist. It is that the system must provide protection as a *matter of right* and not as benevolence of a Government, nor of an institution, nor of an employer. It is a matter of right and not of benevolence.

In establishing social insurance, Federal and State governments reversed the previous presumption that the payment of a benefit to an individual is a generous act of mercy. That had always been the concept in olden times, that the sovereign was generous to the individual and held him in his hand. Rather, a benefit was to be a matter of right on the part of the individual, rather than the result of a generous act.

The change in presumption was that such a payment under social insurance was the honest fulfillment of a contract, of a contract between the citizen and the state; that the right of the eligible beneficiary was protected, in general — and this is important — by the conscience of the electorate, and in particular by an established appeals machinery. This is the approach of contract, not of benevolence.

This concept of individual right under social insurance is to my mind peculiarly compatible to the American way of life. We fought for our rights more than once and our ancestors came here, most of them, to preserve them. We are not given to the acceptance of wholesale assurances. We deeply prefer individual rights. We may crowd into great halls for concerts and into stadia for football games, but we prefer to hold our individual tickets.

The second major element in our philosophy of social insurance, I believe, came into our legislation almost without conscious recognition or debate. It was one of those things we weren't fighting for, yet it was mighty important. Sometimes the most important things are the accepted things, not the issues. It is that *all citizens, should be eligible to coverage under a system regardless of class or level of income, and that, in principle, exceptions to coverage were to be made only for constitutional or administrative reasons.*

Unlike European systems, American programs have arisen in a classless society in which the individual's economic status, with its social position, was in a constant state of flux. The wage earner of yesterday is the manager of today; and if luck falls, the unemployed worker of tomorrow. Why should not the first segment of his earnings be covered, first as a wage earner, then as a manager?

So we had the development of the concept in this country, almost automatically, almost without question, that every individual should if he wanted—and most did—enjoy the advantage of this individual contract of security under a universal system. That is to me another one of the amazing things, to see the way our coverage, which was fought inch by inch at first, has now become almost universal.

This concept of citizen-wide coverage under the Social Security system has been a powerful factor in the expansion of our Old-Age and Survivors Insurance. It has, of course, been reinforced by the obvious fact that all men grow old or die; even though they may avoid unemployment. The concept has influenced the removal of constitutional obstacles by legal devices in the case of state employees. It has had sufficient vitality to have overcome in large measure the difficulties of administration. A tough and unyielding barrier has been set up by a small but vocal group who have made independence of government in their economic activity a political religion reminiscent of our Victorian grandfathers.

A third element in our philosophy of social insurance again arises out of the essential individualism of the American people. Our approach is that, *within limits, the individual worker establishes the level to his protection by his individual contribution to our economy.* I want to emphasize the distinction, "to our economy," not "to the system." Not to the Treasury of the United States but to our economy.

The limits to this principle are important, but the concept is simple; benefits by and large in the American system are firmly related to the wage system. Differentials in wages resulting from the efforts of the worker are reflected to a degree in differentials in benefits. The relative continuity of earnings under the wage system is also reflected to some degree in the level of protection.

The simple device of averaging wages over a period in the determination of benefits has important significance in adding a factor related to contribution through time to that of the economic worth of such contribution in a single period of time.

Some of these things look almost obvious, but have basic, theoretical importance. The concept of differential benefits related to wages and the duration of earnings is essentially a conservative element in our social insurance philosophy. We still believe in America that a man should be rewarded according to his own efforts. Established differentials in one's earning and living standards is a precious asset. Don't doubt it for a moment; it is a precious asset not only to the individual himself, but to society in its progress toward a better world.

...

A fourth element in our philosophy of social insurance is...the concept of protection of the family unit, as such, by social insurance against all hazards which that unit might face.

...

Now we come to the last element in the American philosophy of social insurance....This is *the concept of joint contributions by both employer and employee.*

In the development of our Old-Age and Survivors Insurance, this concept was adopted almost without debate. That's a remarkable thing. Speaking for the AFL, Mr. Green said, "Of course we will go along on the fifty-fifty-contribution in old-age insurance..."

...

The soundness of the concept of joint contributions in the American system of social insurance does not arise out of economics. It stems out of our political and social traditions. Of course, arguments can be made about shifting and incidence, as with all taxes or costs, but the fact remains that the first incidence of any contribution to Government or to any other recipient, church, family or trade union, is of great psychological importance. Out of such incidence, political influences arise. Loyalty and responsibility are encouraged. Personal satisfaction and dignity are gained. Why does a church prefer contributions from the many to the largesse of the few, if it did not realize the tremendous psychological value of contribution as a stimulus to individual responsibility and dignity?

One of the most interesting things about social insurance is that it runs across several disciplines—that is, political science, economics, sociology, social psychology—at least those. At times we are dealing with social psychology because we are dealing with great masses of people, the reactions of individuals and the reactions of great groups.

Social insurance systems, it seems to me, must be within the state but separate from the state; to be strong, responsible and alive, they must have the interest and attention of the citizen not as a voter alone, but as contributor and beneficiary.

In America we have a wholesome suspicion of big government. Now we have given the Government the tremendous task of providing for our individual security. I, for one, would feel more certain that our leaders in Government would continue to respect the sanctity of the trust we have imposed upon them if every potential beneficiary who is gainfully employed were both a voter and a contributor to all our social insurance systems.

■■■

The basic principles underlying Social Security have been carefully articulated, as well, by the late Robert M. Ball. He began his Social Security work on January 1, 1939, as a field assistant in a Newark, New Jersey Social Security field office. He began his Social Security career in the lowest-level job at the lowest pay given an employee with a college degree. Over the next few decades, he rose steadily through the ranks and, ultimately, became the head of the Social Security Administration. Indeed, he remains the longest serving commissioner in the history of the program.

He worked tirelessly on Social Security for seven decades, until his death in 2008. Though technically not a founder himself, he worked closely with many of the founders and was a key player in Social Security's development over most of its history. He had a major impact on every single Social Security enactment after he began his Social Security work in 1939. At the time he wrote the following excerpt, just a decade before his death, Ball was the world's foremost expert on Social Security. In the essay, he discusses the basic principles underlying Social Security:[39]

****

Robert M. Ball

THE NINE GUIDING PRINCIPLES OF SOCIAL SECURITY: WHERE THEY CAME FROM, WHAT THEY ACCOMPLISH

Reprinted with the generous permission of The Century Foundation, from Robert M. Ball, *Straight Talk about Social Security: An Analysis of the Issues in the Current Debate*. Copyright © 1998 by The Century Foundation, Inc.

In the midst of the Great Depression, the founders of today's Social Security system took the bold step of establishing a new institution that they expected to be slow-growing but permanent. They wanted to make a decent retirement attainable for millions of Americans who would otherwise become dependent on their families or on public assistance when they grew too old to work or could no longer find employment. They wanted to protect workers' dependents by providing insurance to make the death of a breadwinner financially manageable. They wanted to put an end to the poorhouse by distributing program income so as to provide at least a minimally adequate benefit for everyone regularly contributing. And, foreseeing the inevitability of change – including the eventual need to insure against other major risks, such as disability and illness – they sought to design an institution based on sustainable principles.

Accordingly, they took the long view. They gave major emphasis to estimating program income and expenses over a much longer period than was customarily done in other countries, and this is still true today. The time frame of 75 years that is now used for Social Security is much longer than that used in almost all other contexts, from foreign social insurance programs to federal budgeting. The point, then and now, was not to try to pretend that anyone could really know precisely what would be happening in 75 or even 25 years; the point was that the planners of Social Security, in making exceptionally long-term commitments, wanted always to be looking far enough ahead to anticipate necessary improvements and make needed changes in ample time to preserve the integrity of the program.

That approach has served well. The legislation of 1935 and 1939 created the basic design of Social Security, and all major legislation since then can be seen as building on that design: extending coverage to more and more workers, improving the level of protection, adding protection against loss of income from long-term and total disability, providing protection for the elderly and disabled against the increasingly unmanageable cost of medical care, protecting against the erosion of income by inflation, and abolishing all statutory differences in the treatment of men and women.

These and many other accomplishments and adjustments have taken place within a framework consisting of nine major principles. Social Security is *universal; an earned right; wage-related; contributory and self-financed; redistributive; not means-tested; wage-indexed; inflation-protected; and compulsory.* As with any framework, the stability of the entire structure depends on the contribution made by each part, so it is useful to review these principles and how they work together.

1. Universal: Social Security coverage has been gradually extended over the years to the point where 96 out of 100 jobs in paid employment are now covered, with more than 142 million working Americans making contributions in

1997. The goal of complete universality can be reached by gradually covering those remaining state and local government positions that are not now covered.

2. Earned right: Social Security is more than a statutory right; it is an earned right, with eligibility for benefits and the benefit rate based on an individual's past earnings. This principal sharply distinguishes Social Security from welfare and links the program, appropriately, to other earned rights such as wages, fringe benefits, and private pensions.

3. Wage-related: Social Security benefits are related to earnings, thus reinforcing the concept of benefits as an earned right and recognizing that there is a relationship between one's standard of living while working and the benefit level needed to achieve income security in retirement. Under Social Security, higher-paid earners get higher benefits; the lower-paid get more for what they pay in.

4. Contributory and self-financed: The fact that workers pay earmarked contributions from their wages into the system also reinforces the concept of an earned right and gives contributors a moral claim on future benefits above and beyond statutory obligations. And, unlike many foreign plans, Social Security is entirely financed by dedicated taxes, principally those deducted from workers' earnings matched by employers, with the self-employed paying comparable amounts. The entire cost of benefits plus administrative expenses (less than one percent of income) is met without support from general government revenues. This self-financing approach has several advantages. It helps protect the program against having to compete against other programs in the annual general federal budget— which is appropriate, because this is a uniquely long-term program. It imposes fiscal discipline, because the total earmarked income for Social Security must be sufficient to cover the entire cost of the program. And it guards against

excessive liberalization: contributors oppose major benefit cuts because they have a right to benefits and are paying for them, but they also oppose excessive increases in benefits because they understand that every increase must be paid for by increased contributions. Thus a semi-automatic balance is achieved between wanting more protection versus not wanting to pay more for it.

5. Redistributive: One of Social Security's most important goals is to pay at least a minimally adequate benefit to workers who are regularly covered and contributing, regardless of how low-paid they may be. This is accomplished through a redistributional formula that pays comparatively higher benefits to lower-paid earners. The formula makes good sense. If the system paid back to low-wage workers only the benefit that they could be expected to pay for from their own wages, millions of retirees would end up on welfare even though they had been paying into Social Security throughout their working lives. This would make the years of contributing to Social Security worse than pointless, since earnings deductions would have reduced their income throughout their working years without providing in retirement any income greater than what would be available from welfare. The redistributional formula solves this dilemma.

6. Not means-tested: In contrast to welfare, eligibility for Social Security is not determined by the beneficiary's current income and assets, nor is the amount of the benefit. This is a crucial principle. It is the absence of a means test that makes it possible for people to add to their savings and to establish private pension plans, secure in the knowledge that they will not then be penalized by having their Social Security benefits cut back as a result of having arranged for additional retirement income. The absence of a means test makes it possible for Social Security to provide a stable role in anchoring a multitier retirement system in which private

pensions and personal savings can be built on top of Social Security's basic, defined protection.

7. Wage-indexed: Social Security is portable, following the worker from job to job, and the protection provided before retirement increases as wages rise. Benefits at the time of initial receipt are brought up to date with recent wages, reflecting improvements in productivity and thus in the general standard of living. Without this principle, Social Security would soon provide benefits that did not reflect previously attained levels of living.

8. Inflation-protected: Once they begin, Social Security benefits are protected against inflation by periodic Cost-of-Living Adjustments (COLAs) linked to the Consumer Price Index. Inflation protection is one of Social Security's greatest strengths, and one that distinguishes it from other (except federal) retirement plans: no private pension plan provides guaranteed protection against inflation, and inflation protection under state and local plans, where it exists at all, is capped. Without COLAs, the real value of Social Security benefits would steadily erode over time, as is the case with unadjusted private pension benefits. Although a provision for automatic adjustment was not part of the original legislation, the importance of protecting benefits against inflation was recognized, and over the years the system was financed to allow for periodic adjustment to bring benefits up to date. But this updating was done only after a lag. Provision for automatic adjustment was added in 1972.

9. Compulsory: Social Security compels all of us to contribute to our own future security. A voluntary system simply would not work. Some of us would save scrupulously, some would save sporadically, and some would postpone the day of reckoning forever, leaving the community as a whole to pay through a much less desirable safety-net system. With a compulsory program, the problem of adverse selection—

individuals deciding when and to what extent they want to participate, depending on whether their individual circumstances seem favorable—is avoided (as is the problem of obtaining adequate funding for a large safety-net program serving a constituency with limited political influence).

***

In the midst of the Great Depression it took courage to enact a system based on these principles. The Great Depression was a time of enormous and immediate needs, but Social Security was designed to be a slow-growing tree, one that could not provide much shelter in the near term. The point, however, was that, once grown, it would be strong enough to weather bad times as well as good.

A contributory retirement system takes a long time to develop, since by definition those who are already retired are not eligible for benefits. Fifteen years after the program was set up, only 21 percent of the elderly were receiving benefits, and it was not until the 1950s that politicians began to see much advantage in championing improvements in Social Security. And it was only in the 1960s, three decades after enactment, that Social Security began having a major impact, paying benefits that were high enough and universal enough to significantly reduce poverty among the elderly, the disabled, and the survivors of beneficiaries. After the amendments of 1972 further increased benefits substantially and provided for automatic inflation protection, Social Security fully assumed the role planned for it as the all-important base of a multitier retirement system in which private pensions and individual savings are added to Social Security's defined protection.

The importance of that role would be difficult to exaggerate: today, Social Security is the only organized retirement plan – the only assured source of retirement income – for at least half of the total workforce. And it is the base upon which all who are able to do so can build the supplementary protection of pensions and individual savings.

Social Security has become and continues to be the most popular and successful social program in America's history because its guiding principles enable it to work exactly as intended: as America's family protection plan.

■■■

The basic structure of Social Security, described in the founders' essays, remains unchanged today. This chapter examined all of the attributes articulated by Founders Brown and Ball except the program's financing. That is a subject that needs its own chapter, because so much misinformation and such a strong willful refusal to understand has surrounded it. The next chapter discusses this broad and important subject in great detail, referencing, once again, the founders' own words.

CHAPTER THREE: SOCIAL SECURITY'S SOUND AND SECURE FINANCING

As chapter two discusses in detail, Social Security is insurance. It only pays claims on behalf of those who are insured. Workers achieve insured status by working and paying premiums for the requisite amount of time. Claims are paid to insured workers and their families, if and when the insured condition of death, old age, or serious and permanent disability occurs.

Overview of Social Security's Prudent and Responsible Financing and Management

To satisfy claims, Social Security must have sufficient revenue not only to cover every penny of the claimed benefits, but also the costs of field offices, personnel and all other expenses associated with the administration of those insured benefits. Even though the plan sponsor is the federal government, Social Security must pay all of its own costs out of its dedicated revenue. It has no borrowing authority and therefore lacks the ability to deficit-spend to meet its obligations. To make sure that it has sufficient revenue to meet all claims, it maintains a reserve, as all responsible insurers do.

For sound reasons, the law requires that private employers who sponsor pension plans keep plan reserves segregated from the company's general operating fund. Those reserves are held in trust on behalf of the employer's current workers, beneficiaries, and former workers who are vested and will receive benefits in the future.

For the same sound policy reasons, the law requires that Social Security's income and assets be kept segregated from the general operating fund of its plan sponsor, the federal government. Like employer-sponsored pension plans, those reserves are held in trust on behalf of its beneficiaries, who are virtually all of us.

The predominant source of Social Security's revenue has always been premiums (also known as insurance contributions, "FICA," or payroll taxes), paid by workers and matched dollar-for-dollar by their employers. All of Social Security's revenue is dedicated to the sole purpose of paying Social Security benefits and the associated costs.

As would be expected, all excess revenue, which is held in reserve, in trust, is invested until it is needed to pay claims and associated costs. As of December 31, 2016, Social Security had excess revenue from current and past surpluses of about $2.848 trillion, up from about $2.813 trillion at the end of 2015, thanks to a surplus in 2016 of about $35.2 billion.[1]

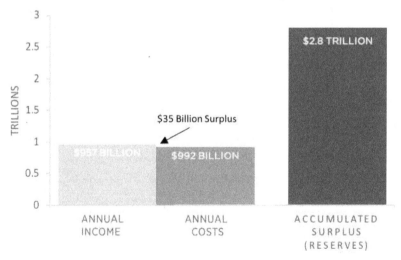

SOCIAL SECURITY RESERVES, COSTS, AND ACCUMULATED SURPLUSES, 2016

Source: Social Security Administration, "Office of the Chief Actuary, "Old Age, Survivors, and Disability Insurance Funds, 1957-2016," accessed April 24, 2017.

From the start, Congress has wanted the monies that workers and their employers have entrusted to Social Security to be invested prudently and conservatively. Consequently, the trustees are required to invest Social Security's trust funds in interest-bearing Treasury obligations or in entities whose principal and interest are guaranteed by the United States. Those are the safest, most secure investments on Earth.

Congress does not permit Social Security's reserve to be invested in equities; the investments are limited to bonds. While stocks can provide higher returns, they are also at risk of losing their value. Rather, Congress requires the reserves to be invested only in bonds that pay fixed interest. Those bonds cannot be corporate bonds, or even state or municipal bonds. Rather, the law requires that they must be bonds backed by the full faith and credit of the United States.

There are several dozen civil service employees involved in issuing these bonds, redeeming them, and keeping track of the associated interest. The maturity dates of the bonds range from next June 30th all the way to long-term bonds with maturities fifteen years into the future. The interest rates are fair market rates, ranging from 1.375 percent for those bonds purchased recently, to 5.25 percent for bonds purchased years ago when interest rates were higher.

Every year, Social Security's Board of Trustees is required by law to report to Congress about the financial status of Social Security. Included in each report are tables listing all of the bonds and certificates of indebtedness, together with their maturity dates, interest rates, and par values (the value printed on the face of the bond, which is also the amount payable when redeemed). Certificates of indebtedness mature on the June 30th following the date of issue; bonds generally have maturity dates ranging from one to fifteen years.

Here are all the holdings as of the end of the prior two calendar years, carefully accounted for in the 2017 Trustees Report:[2]

OASI Trust Fund Asset Reserves, End of Calendar Years 2015 and 2016
[In thousands]

Certificates of Indebtedness:	December 31, 2015	December 31, 2016
2.125 percent, 2016	$38,935,438	—
2.375 percent, 2017	—	$50,383,106

Bonds:	December 31, 2015	December 31, 2016
1.375 percent, 2017	6,693,020	—
1.375 percent, 2018-25	53,544,160	53,544,160
1.375 percent, 2026	6,693,019	6,693,019
1.375 percent, 2027	173,240,401	173,240,401
1.750 percent, 2017	4,908,186	—
1.750 percent, 2018	4,908,186	4,908,186
1.750 percent, 2019-25	34,357,295	34,357,295
1.750 percent, 2026-27	9,816,372	9,816,372
1.750 percent, 2028	178,148,587	178,148,587
1.875 percent, 2018-19	—	4,641,910
1.875 percent, 2020-27	—	18,567,648
1.875 percent, 2028-30	—	6,962,865
1.875 percent, 2031	—	188,111,583
2.000 percent, 2017	3,655,629	—
2.000 percent, 2018-19	7,311,258	7,311,258
2.000 percent, 2020-25	21,933,768	21,933,768
2.000 percent, 2026-29	14,622,516	14,622,516
2.000 percent, 2030	185,790,628	185,790,628
2.250 percent, 2017	3,986,412	—
2.250 percent, 2018	3,986,412	3,986,412
2.250 percent, 2019-25	27,904,891	27,904,891
2.250 percent, 2026-28	11,959,236	11,959,236
2.250 percent, 2029	182,134,999	182,134,999
2.500 percent, 2017	5,971,788	—
2.500 percent, 2018-25	47,774,296	47,774,296
2.500 percent, 2026	166,547,382	166,547,382
2.875 percent, 2017	7,264,432	—
2.875 percent, 2018-24	50,851,024	50,851,024
2.875 percent, 2025	160,575,595	160,575,595
3.250 percent, 2017	10,628,270	—
3.250 percent, 2018-23	63,769,620	63,769,620
3.250 percent, 2024	153,311,163	153,311,163

OASI Trust Fund Asset Reserves, End of Calendar Years 2015 and 2016 (cont'd)
[In thousands]

Bonds:	December 31, 2015	December 31, 2016
3.500 percent, 2017	9,513,752	—
3.500 percent, 2018	86,900,994	86,900,994
4.000 percent, 2017	12,075,192	—
4.000 percent, 2018-22	60,375,960	60,375,960
4.000 percent, 2023	142,682,893	142,682,893
4.125 percent, 2016	9,936,522	—
4.125 percent, 2017	10,516,946	6,883,312
4.125 percent, 2018-19	21,033,892	21,033,892
4.125 percent, 2020	106,585,700	106,585,700
4.625 percent, 2016	9,167,663	—
4.625 percent, 2017-18	18,335,326	18,335,326
4.625 percent, 2019	96,068,657	96,068,657
5.000 percent, 2016	12,454,232	—
5.000 percent, 2017-21	62,271,160	62,271,160
5.000 percent, 2022	130,607,701	130,607,701
5.125 percent, 2016	11,567,866	—
5.125 percent, 2017-19	34,703,598	34,703,598
5.125 percent, 2020	11,567,769	11,567,769
5.125 percent, 2021	118,153,469	118,153,469
5.250 percent, 2016	$9,235,911	—
5.250 percent, 2017	77,387,242	77,387,242
5.625 percent, 2016	68,151,331	—
Total Investments	2,760,517,758	2,801,405,593
Undisbursed Balances	19,733,589	-56,915
Total Asset Reserves	2,780,251,347	2,801,348,678

Source: Table VI.A4, 2017 Annual Report of the Board of Trustees of the Federal Old-Age and Survivors Insurance and. Federal Disability Insurance Trust Funds

[a] A negative amount for each year represents a situation where actual program cash expenditures exceeded the amount of invested securities of the OASI Trust Fund that were redeemed to pay for such expenditures. In this situation, future redemption of additional invested securities will be required to pay for this shortfall. For 2015 and other calendar years where January 3 of the following year is a Sunday, a positive amount is shown on a liability basis for benefits scheduled to be paid on January 3 of the following year that were, by law, actually paid on the preceding December 31.

Note: Amounts of special issues are at par value. The trust fund purchases and redeems special issues at par value. The table groups equal amounts that mature in two or more years at a given interest rate.

DI Trust Fund Asset Reserves, End of Calendar Years 2015 and 2016
[In thousands]

Certificates of Indebtedness:	December 31, 2015	December 31, 2016
.375 percent, 2017	—	$8,437,206
Bonds:	**December 31, 2015**	**December 31, 2016**
.875 percent, 2018	—	180,001
.875 percent, 2019-22	—	12,045,560
.000 percent, 2023	14,675,554	$14,675,554
.000 percent, 2022	11,425,890	11,142,596
Total investments	26,101,444	46,480,917
Undisbursed balances[a]	6,157,191	-143,066
Total asset reserves	32,258,635	46,337,851

Source: Table VI.A5, 2017 Annual Report of the Board of Trustees of the Federal Old-Age and Survivors Insurance and Federal Disability Insurance Trust Funds
[a] A negative amount for a given year represents a situation where actual program cash expenditures exceeded the amount of invested securities of the DI Trust Fund that were redeemed to pay for such expenditures. In this situation, future redemption of additional invested securities will be required to pay for this shortfall. For 2015 and other calendar years where January 3 of the following year is a Sunday, a positive amount is shown on a liability basis for benefits scheduled to be paid on January 3 of the following year that were, by law, actually paid on the preceding December 31.
Note: Amounts of special issues are at par value. The trust fund purchases and redeems special issues at par value. The table groups equal amounts that mature in two or more years at a given interest rate.

Although these government obligations are sometimes pejoratively referred to as "IOUs", they are legal obligations. These are not casual promises to pay. Not promises made by schoolchildren, shouting, "IOU!" These are, to repeat, legal instruments backed by the full faith and credit of the United States. These legal instruments are as solid as those the federal government issues publicly to willing buyers. They have the same legal status as bonds bought by you, me, a foreign government, or any other person or entity that invests in U.S. Treasuries.

Here is a facsimile of one of the Treasury bonds:

The sale and purchase of bonds are straightforward transactions, well understood by anyone with the slightest understanding of financial and business arrangements. States, municipalities, and corporations all issue bonds as one way of raising money. Those who purchase the bonds are guaranteed that they will be repaid the principal amount loaned, plus interest. Bondholders hope the funds are used prudently, but the way the funds are used is immaterial. Bondholders simply want their monies paid back, with interest. The bond gives the investor a legal claim for repayment.

Misunderstandings and Zombie Lies

Despite the straightforwardness, security, and value of these investments, however, some either don't understand or willfully misunderstand them when the investor is our Social Security system. Despite Social Security's careful, transparent recordkeeping, those seeking to undermine confidence in – and therefore support for – Social Security, derogatorily label the legal obligations issued by the Treasury Department as "IOUs." They claim that the trust funds are not "real." And they seek to undermine confidence by pointing out the obvious and unremarkable point that Social Security monies that have been invested in Treasury bonds have been spent. They, of course, never point out that monies of private pension plans, individuals, and foreign nations invested in Treasury bonds have already been spent, as well!

In addition, they claim that, despite the dedicated nature of Social Security's revenue, the program is a drain on the general funds of the United States. In contradictory fashion, they also claim that Social Security is going broke, because it is limited to its own dedicated revenue. These two claims are in direct contradiction. Social Security can't do both – draw from general funds and be in crisis. The truth, of course, is that it is neither a drain nor in crisis.

All of these are zombie lies. Though they have been answered by numerous experts many times throughout the more than eighty-year history of Social Security, they refuse to die. Using those very explanations of founders and subsequent experts, this chapter makes one more effort to expose these misunderstandings and zombie lies for what they are.

Let's start with the claim that the Treasury bonds, in which Social Security's reserves are invested, are somehow worthless IOUs, that they are accounting gimmicks, where the government simply owes itself money. In 2005, when President George W. Bush tried to sell his Social Security privatization scheme to the nation, he sought to convince the American people that Social Security's investments in Treasury bonds were worthless. Indeed, he staged a photo-op in Parkersburg, West Virginia, where the Social Security bonds are kept. There he said:[3]

> There is no "trust fund," just IOUs that I saw firsthand... The office here in Parkersburg stores those IOUs. They're stacked in a filing cabinet. Imagine—the retirement security for future generations is sitting in a filing cabinet.

An irony of President Bush's photo-op is that one could argue that the paper Treasury bonds purchased by our Social Security system are more "real" than other Treasury bonds purchased by investors throughout the world. Generally, when governments, pension plans, and other investors from around the world purchase Treasury bonds today, the transaction is done electronically, with no paper record. When Treasury was changing from the issuance of paper bonds to simply electronic transactions, the late Robert J. Myers, the longest-serving Chief Actuary in Social Security's history, wanted to have Treasury continue to produce and issue paper bonds to Social Security.

Myers was among the program's founders, a young actuary in 1934 working on the staff of the interagency task force that developed Social Security. He continued to work on Social Security until his death in 2010. As he aged, he became increasingly concerned that young people especially were losing confidence in the future of Social Security because of all the zombie lies. Fighting for paper bonds was one small way to fight back.

Consistent with Myers's desire, Congress included Section 301 in 1994 legislation, which established Social Security as an independent agency. Section 301 provides:[4]

SEC. 301. ISSUANCE OF PHYSICAL DOCUMENTS IN THE FORM OF BONDS, NOTES, OR CERTIFICATES TO THE SOCIAL SECURITY TRUST FUNDS

(a) REQUIREMENT THAT OBLIGATIONS ISSUED TO THE OASDI TRUST FUNDS BE EVIDENCED BY PAPER INSTRUMENTS IN THE FORM OF BONDS, NOTES, OR CERTIFICATES OF INDEBTEDNESS SETTING FORTH THEIR TERMS.—

(b) Section 201(d) of the Social Security Act (42 U.S.C. 401(d)) is amended by inserting after the fifth sentence the following new sentence: Each obligation issued for purchase by the Trust Funds under this subsection shall be evidenced by a paper instrument in the form of a bond, note, or certificate of indebtedness issued by the Secretary of the Treasury setting forth the principal amount, date of maturity, and interest rate of the obligation, and **stating on its face** that the obligation shall be incontestable in the hands of the Trust Fund to which it is issued, **that the obligation is supported by the full faith and credit of the United States, and that the United States is pledged to the payment of**

the obligation with respect to both principal and interest. [Emphasis added.]

But reassurance, careful explanation, and even actions, like the issuance of paper bonds, have never stopped the accusations. These are zombie lies which refuse to die. Bush was not the first to label Treasury bonds backed by the full faith and credit of the United States, as IOUs, simply because they are purchased by Social Security. Indeed, that bit of shade dates from the beginning of the program.

Social Security was a major issue in the presidential election of 1936, despite the fact that Social Security had just been enacted, and not a single premium had been collected nor an insurance claim paid. The Republican standard bearer, Alf Landon, made numerous charges about Social Security. These included the security of its financing. In a major speech in Milwaukee, Wisconsin, delivered on September 27, 1936, he raised doubts about Social Security and mocked:[5]

Under the compulsory insurance plan of the present law, none of our old people will get any pension at all until 1942...

But, meanwhile, beginning on January 1 of next year, 26 million working people begin paying taxes to provide these pensions. Beginning next January employers must start deducting these taxes from the pay envelopes of their employees and turn them over to the government.

Beginning next January employers must, in addition, begin paying taxes on the pay rolls out of which your wages are to come. This is the largest tax bill in history. And to call it "Social Security" is a fraud on the workingman.

...

According to this plan, our workers are forced to save for a lifetime. What happens to their savings? The administration's theory is that they go into a reserve fund—that they will be invested at interest, and that in due time this interest will help pay the pensions. The people who drew this law understand nothing of government finance.

Let us trace the process step by step. The worker's cash comes into the Treasury. What is done with it? The law requires the treasury to buy government bonds. What happens when the treasury buys government bonds: well, at present, when there is a deficit, the treasury gives some nice new bonds in exchange for the cash which the treasury gives the treasury. Now what happens to the cash that the treasury gives the treasury? The answer is painfully simple. We have good spenders at Washington and they spend the cash that the treasury gives the treasury.

Now I know all this sounds silly, but it happens to be an accurate recital of what this administration has been foolish enough to enact into law.

Let me explain it in another way, in the simple terms of the family budget. The father of the family is a kindly man, so kindly that he borrows all he can to add to the family's pleasure. At the same time he impresses upon his sons and daughters the necessity of saving for their old age. Every month they bring 6 per cent of their wages to him so he may act as trustee and invest their savings for their old age.

The father decides that the best investment is his own IOU. So every month he puts aside in a box his IOU carefully executed, and, moreover, bearing interest at 3 per cent. And every month he spends the money that his children bring him, partly in meeting his regular expenses, and the rest in various experiments that fascinate him. Years pass—the children grow old—the day comes when they have to open their father's box. What do they find? Roll after roll of neatly executed IOU's.

I am not exaggerating the folly of this legislation. The saving it forces on our workers is a cruel hoax.

…

…The workers asked for a pension and all they have received is just another tax.

Founders' Efforts to Set the Record Straight

As far back as 1938, an advisory council, jointly convened by the Senate Finance Committee and the Social Security Board (the predecessor of today's Social Security Administration), sought to reassure the public in the aftermath of Landon's charges. The members of the Advisory Council consisted of representatives of business, labor, and the general public. A number of members of the Council had been instrumental in the development of Social Security.

The Advisory Council issued its report on December 10, 1938, but issued a special, unanimously agreed-to statement on the April before. The Council explained that it "deems it advisable to make a public statement at this time to allay unwarranted fears. This relates to the method of handling the funds collected for old-age insurance purposes." Just as this book is seeking to correct the record and clarify the truth here, the statement reads:[6]

****

Report of the Advisory Council on Social Security
Appendix
December 10, 1938

On April 29, 1938, the Council unanimously approved the following statement concerning the financing of the old-age insurance system:

The Advisory Council on Social Security has been giving much attention to the problem of financing the old age insurance system. The Council recognizes that there are other ways of financing the old-age insurance system which upon further study may prove to have greater advantages than the present system. The entire subject, however, is so complex that the Council is not yet prepared to express a final judgment as to the method of financing which would be most desirable from a social and economic standpoint.

Upon one aspect of the general problem the Advisory Council deems it advisable to make a public statement at this time to allay unwarranted fears. This relates to the method of handling the funds collected for old-age insurance purposes.

…

The special securities issued to the old-age reserve account are general obligations of the United States Government, which differ from other securities of the Government only in the higher rate of interest they bear and in the fact that they are not sold in the open market. The issuance of such special securities is not only expressly authorized by law, but is required by the provision of the Social Security Act that the old-age reserve funds are to be invested so as to yield an interest return of 3 per cent.

The United States Treasury uses the moneys realized from the issuance of these special securities by the old-age reserve account in the same manner as it does moneys realized from the sale of other Government securities. As long as the budget is not balanced, the net result is to reduce the amounts which the Government has to borrow from banks, insurance companies and other private parties. When the budget is balanced, these moneys will be available for the reduction of the national debt held by the public….The members of the Council, regardless of differing views on other aspects of the financing of old-age insurance, are of the opinion that the present provisions regarding the investment of the moneys in the old-age reserve account do not involve any misuse of these moneys or endanger the safety of these funds.

▪▪▪

The only difference today is that Social Security can, if the trustees deem it advisable, invest in marketable securities and the interest earned is fair market, not a specified and guaranteed rate of three percent.

Notwithstanding the clear, unanimous statement made by the expert panel, consisting of representatives of business, labor, and the general public, another advisory council felt compelled, ten years later, to address the same zombie lies. Like the earlier panel, some members were among those who were instrumental in the creation of Social Security. Here is the statement of the Social Security Advisory Council of 1948:[7]

****

Report of the Advisory Council on Social Security
Appendix I-A. The Old-Age and Survivors
Insurance Trust Fund
December 31, 1948

....

[Social Security's] reserve has been invested in United States Government securities, which, in the opinion of the Council, represent the proper form of investment for these funds. We do not agree with those who criticize this form of investment on the ground that the Government spends for general purposes the money received from the sale of securities to that fund. Actually, such investment is as reasonable and proper as is the investment by life-insurance companies of their own reserve funds in Government securities. The fact that the Government uses the proceeds received from the sales of securities to pay the costs of the war and its other expenses is entirely legitimate. It no more implies mishandling of moneys received from the sale of securities to the trust fund than it does of the moneys received from the sale of United States securities to life-insurance companies, banks, or individuals.

The investment of the old-age and survivors insurance funds in Government securities does not mean that people have been or will be taxed twice for the same benefits, as has been charged. The following example illustrates this point: Suppose some year in the future the outgo under the old-age and survivors insurance system should exceed pay-roll tax receipts by $100,000,000. If there were then $5,000,000,000 of United States 2-percent bonds in the trust fund, they would produce interest amounting to $100,000,000 a year. This interest would, of course, have to be raised by taxation. But suppose there were no bonds in the trust fund. In that event, $100,000,000 to cover the deficit in the old-age and survivors insurance system would have to be raised by taxation; and, in addition, another $100,000,000 would have to be raised by taxation to pay interest on $5,000,000,000 of Government bonds owned by someone else. The bonds would be in other hands, because if the Government had not been able to borrow from the Old-Age and Survivors Insurance Trust Fund, it would have had to borrow the same amount from other sources. In other words, the ownership of the $5,000,000,000 in bonds by the old-age and survivors insurance system would prevent the $100,000,000 from having to be raised twice—quite the opposite from the "double taxation" [i.e., taxed twice for the same benefit] that has been charged.

Under present conditions the Government is operating with a budget surplus and is not borrowing. The trustees of the Old-Age and Survivors Insurance Trust Fund, therefore, when they invest the excess income in Government securities, in effect cause Government debt to be transferred from private ownership to the Old-Age and Survivors Insurance Trust Fund. The same saving of the amount of the interest for the general taxpayer will occur in this instance as in the one described above.

The members of the Advisory Council are in unanimous agreement with the statement of the Advisory Council of 1938 to the effect that the present provisions regarding the investment of the moneys in the Old-Age and Survivors Insurance Trust Fund do not involve any misuse of these moneys or endanger the safety of the funds.

▪▪▪

And nine years after that, yet another advisory council – again including some founders – sought to refute what it tactfully labeled, "some misunderstanding." With respect to those same zombie lies, the report of the 1957-59 Social Security Advisory Council, states:[8]

****

Final Report of the Advisory Council on
Social Security Financing
January 1, 1959

B. The investment of the trust funds in United States Government obligations is a proper use of the excess of income over outgo for the benefit of the contributors to the funds. The trust funds are properly kept separate from the general fund of the Treasury and have the same lender status as other investors in Federal securities.

The Council is aware that there is some misunderstanding concerning the nature of the trust funds of the program and their distinct separation from the general Treasury account. The members are in unanimous agreement with the advisory councils of 1938 and 1948 that the present provisions regarding the investment of the moneys in these trust funds do not involve any misuse of these moneys or endanger the funds in any way, nor is there any "double taxation" for social security purposes by reason of the investment of these funds in Government obligations.

Each of these trust funds is kept completely separate from all other funds in the Treasury. The income and disbursements of the Old-Age and Survivors Insurance Trust Fund and the Disability Insurance Trust Fund are not included in the administrative budget of the Government. Instead, the president reports their operations separately in his Budget Message to Congress. The debt obligations held by the trust funds are shown in Treasury reports as part of the Federal debt, and interest payments on these obligations are regularly made by the Treasury to the trust funds. The securities are sold or redeemed whenever necessary to obtain cash for disbursement by these funds.

When the trust fund receipts not needed for current disbursements are invested in Government securities, the funds are lenders and the United States Treasury is the borrower. The trustees of the funds receive and hold Federal securities as evidence of these loans. These

Government obligations are assets of the funds, and they are liabilities of the United States Government, which must pay interest on the money borrowed and must repay the principal when the securities are redeemed or mature.

The marketable securities held by the funds are identical in every way with Federal bonds bought and sold on the open market by other investors in Federal securities. The special obligations issued directly to the funds are public debt obligations backed by the full faith and credit of the United States. Interest on, and the proceeds from the sale or redemption of, securities held by each of the two trust funds are credited to and form a part of each fund. Thus the trust funds are completely separate from the general fund of the Treasury and have the same status as lenders that other investors in Federal securities have.

The confusion that there is "double taxation" for social security purposes arises because, in addition to paying social security taxes, people must also pay taxes to pay interest on, and repay the principal amount of, the obligations held by the trust funds. But the taxes that must be raised to pay interest on these obligations, or to repay the principal, are not levied for social security purposes. They are levied to meet the costs of the defense program and the other purposes for which the borrowed money was expended by the Treasury in accordance with congressional appropriations. If the trust funds did not exist, money for these purposes would have been borrowed from other sources, and in this case, too, taxes would have to be raised to pay interest and principal on the borrowings. The purchase of Government obligations by the trust funds is financially sound in relation to both the social security program and the fiscal operations of the Federal Government.

■■

The zombie lies, that all three advisory councils sought to address, remain with us today, more than a half century after those advisory councils patiently and carefully sought to set the record straight. In 2015, Florida's Sun Sentinel ran an op-ed of an Eastern Illinois University economics professor emeritus, which stated:[9]

> "Enough [Social Security] payroll taxes have been paid to cover full benefit payments until 2033. But $2.7 trillion of that money was taken by the government and spent for non-Social Security purposes. The spent money was replaced with government IOUs, called Special Issues of the Treasury."

Note that the writer flippantly uses the dismissive and derogatory label, "IOUs." As the three advisory councils carefully explained, many decades ago, what he calls IOUs are legal instruments, backed by the full faith and credit of the United States. They are purchased on behalf of Social Security contributors and beneficiaries. They are held in trust, and are accounted for in meticulous detail. They are even evidenced by written legal instruments.

Moreover, the writer emphasizes that those bonds are special issues, as if that caused them to be less valuable and secure. He, of course, fails to mention that Social Security today has the legal authority to purchase marketable securities, if the trustees who make the investment decisions deem it in the best interest of Social Security's contributors and beneficiaries.

He also fails to point out that, though the special issue bonds cannot be sold on the open market, they have an important advantage over marketable securities. Indeed, that advantage may explain why Social Security's trustees choose to purchase special issue bonds. While marketable bonds can only be redeemed for full value at their maturity dates, Social Security's special issue bonds can be redeemed at full value whenever Social Security chooses.

Most importantly, the writer fails to mention that special issue bonds, like all other Treasury bonds, are backed by the full faith and credit of the United States. They would have the same legal status and priority as marketable Treasury bonds, if the government did the unimaginable and defaulted.

As many others have done over the last more than eighty years, the writer's words suggest that legitimate, responsible, and sound arrangements represent something sinister or at least insecure. The purpose appears to be an effort to undermine confidence in Social Security.

The references to IOUs and special issue bonds are just two of a constellation of half-truths and outright false claims, designed to undermine confidence. All of the zombie claims misrepresent Social Security's prudent and responsible financing and management. And all continue to be repeated, despite efforts to set the record straight.

One More Effort to Refute the Zombie Lies and Set the Record Straight

Though some of the false claims may be, as the 1957-59 Advisory Council labeled them, misunderstandings, some are willful refusals to recognize the truth. Though they won't die, they lack merit. This lack of substance becomes clear, when one thinks carefully and thoughtfully about them. Even non-experts can see through them, once careful analysis is brought to bear.

Social Security's Assets are Held in Trust and Appropriately Invested

A common zombie claim, related to the one about worthless IOUs, is that Social Security's two trusts – the Old Age and Survivors Insurance Trust and the Disability Insurance Trust, in which Social Security reserves are kept – are not "real." To that claim, the appropriate response is that all trusts are legal entities. What does it mean for a legal entity to be "real"?

Is a trust that I set up for my children and that I fund with Treasury bonds, "real?" How about the pension trust a corporation sets up for its employees and funds with Treasury bonds? For that matter, are corporations "real?" Are those Treasury bonds "real?" And, what about the green pieces of paper that those Treasury bonds are redeemed for and that we spend in stores? Are dollar bills "real?" The piece of paper that a hundred-dollar bill is printed on is worth pennies. What makes it worth $100? Isn't that a legally accepted construct, just like trusts, corporations, and Treasury bonds? Doesn't its value come from the full faith and credit of the United States, just like all Treasury bonds, including those purchased by Social Security?

All of these are legal entities, arrangements, and understandings. Indeed, the legal entity known as a corporation goes back before the creation of the United States; it was created as part of English law. And the legal entity of a trust is even older. Trusts are thousands of years old, dating back to Roman law.

A trust is a legal arrangement where the legal ownership and the beneficial ownership are divided. The legal owner is the trustee, who has legal control over the trust. The beneficial owner is the beneficiary, in whose exclusive interest the law requires the trustee to act. Trustees and other fiduciaries have to follow certain legal rules designed to protect beneficiaries and can be held liable in court if they do not. In contrast, non-fiduciaries are not so obligated. They are free to act in their own interest.

Social Security's reserves are divided between two trusts, one for the payment of old age and survivors' benefits; the other for the payment of disability benefits. The two Social Security trusts are controlled by trustees, who are the legal owners of Social Security's revenue. American workers and their families – who have earned these benefits as part of their compensation package, just as they do retirement income provided directly from their employers – are the beneficial owners.

Trusts, like corporations, are entities recognized by the law. That legal understanding makes them real. They do not live and breathe and walk around, but they are legally recognized entities separate and apart from their living, breathing creators, trustees, and beneficiaries. In that sense, they have legal life. In 2012, then Republican presidential standard bearer, Mitt Romney, was widely mocked for exclaiming, "Corporations are people, my friend!"[10] As humorous as that sound bite was, corporations do have separate legal identities, and are treated in some ways under the law as humans are. That is true of trusts, as well. They can, for example, sue and be sued in a court of law. So can their living, breathing trustees, if those individuals fail to honor their fiduciary responsibilities.

The Social Security trusts are governed by a board of trustees, who have the same legal obligations that all trustees have. All trustees, by virtue of that position, are held to very high standards under the law. They are fiduciaries and must act, at all times, in the exclusive interest of their beneficiaries.

Whoever is then the confirmed U.S. Secretary of the Treasury is Social Security's managing trustee. The Secretary of the Treasury, along with the three other government officials who are Social Security trustees—the Secretary of Labor, the Secretary of Health and Human Services, and the Commissioner of the Social Security Administration—must wear two hats. They are in charge of their departments and they are trustees. If a conflict arises between the two roles, the trustees must resolve it in favor of the trust beneficiaries. This is not just a matter of legal theory. The Social Security trustees were sued on this very point in the fall of 1985.

At that time, President Reagan and Congress were fighting about raising the federal debt ceiling. (The debt ceiling limits federal borrowing. If the government wants to borrow beyond the specified amount, it must raise the ceiling – a politically unpopular move.)

In 1985, as Congress and the administration were arguing about the budget and the debt ceiling, the government was running out of money. The Treasury Department and the Social Security trust funds have well-established, complicated arrangements to ensure that transactions are neutral between the two entities. Secretary of the Treasury James Baker had the legal obligation, as managing trustee, to protect the Social Security trust funds.

Instead, he acted to forestall the closing of the government, at the expense of the trust funds. In September and October, he was required to transfer to the trust funds monies collected by the Internal Revenue Service. When he did not do so, the trust funds had to dip into reserves, which cost the program $10 million a day in lost interest.

When the conflict arose between his two roles, Baker was obligated under the law to act in the interest of the trust beneficiaries. When he did otherwise, several beneficiaries, several nonprofit organizations representing seniors, and several members of Congress hired a lawyer—the distinguished and illustrious Elliot Richardson. Among the many high-ranking public offices he held over his storied career, Richardson had been attorney general of the United States under President Richard Nixon. In an event instantly known as the Saturday Night Massacre, Nixon fired Richardson, during the Watergate scandal, for refusing to fire the special prosecutor.

On behalf of the plaintiffs, Richardson filed a lawsuit against the Social Security trustees in the United States District Court for the District of Columbia.[11] The civil suit, No. 85-3466, was assigned to District Court Judge Thomas F. Hogan.

The suit charged that, among other wrongdoing, "Defendant Trustees have violated and continue to violate their fiduciary obligations to the beneficiaries of the Trust Funds." The Justice Department filed a motion to dismiss the complaint. The motion to dismiss was denied by Judge Hogan. The case never went further because President Reagan and Congress resolved the debt ceiling fight the day the suit was filed, and Baker made sure that the interest due was paid to Social Security.

The claim that the Social Security trusts, with all their legal protections, are not "real" would presumably be a shock to Judge Hogan, who was appointed to the bench by President Reagan, became chief judge of the District Court in 2001, and became a senior judge in 2008. It would also be a shock to the lawyers at the Department of Justice who litigated the case, and to the late Elliot Richardson.

As that lawsuit makes clear, the trust arrangement itself provides important protection to Social Security's beneficiaries. It should be obvious that the assets contained within the trust are of very real value, as well, despite opponents disparagingly calling them "IOUs."

All of Social Security's Income and Assets are Dedicated and Must be Spent Only on Earned Benefits and Related Administrative Expenses

In addition to the claim that the Treasury bonds purchased by Social Security have no value and the trusts in which they are held are not "real," opponents darkly warn that the money underlying the assets has already been spent. The charge that the money has already been spent indicates either a misunderstanding of bonds or a desire to deceive. All those who issue bonds, whether they are corporations or government entities, do so to raise funds to be spent. Investors hope that the bond issuer uses the funds in ways that are productive and will make repayment easier. But the fact that the funds are spent, and what they are spent on, does not alter the legal obligation to repay.

Those, including Social Security, who purchase bonds are not spending their money, but investing it. The issuer of the bond spends it, but is obligated to repay all funds plus interest when due. This is similar to money placed in a savings account in a bank. Account holders are not spending their money, but saving it. The bank is using the money, but is required to return it, with interest, when the demand is made.

Opponents often add that the only way to repay the trust funds is to tax Americans, resulting in a kind of double taxation. These again are misleading zombie claims that go back to the beginning of the program. Those earlier Advisory Councils addressed that issue, as well, in the excerpts reproduced above.

The fundamental fact is that the federal government issues bonds to make up the difference between its expenditures and its tax and other revenue. If those bonds were not purchased by Social Security, they would unquestionably be purchased by others, given the ongoing worldwide demand for U.S. Treasury bonds. Similarly, when the government pays interest on its outstanding bonds or redeems outstanding bonds, that is a cost to the government which can be met from tax revenues or borrowing from others. It is immaterial who the holder of the bond is; the impact on the government is the same.

This misleading claim was well addressed in the excerpts, printed above, from the Advisory Councils of 1948 and 1959. The 1948 Advisory Council gave a concrete example, showing the fallacy in the claim. That part of the excerpt is worth repeating here:

> The investment of the old-age and survivors insurance funds in Government securities does not mean that people have been or will be taxed twice for the same benefits, as has been charged. The following example illustrates this point: Suppose some year in the future the outgo under the old-age and survivors insurance system should exceed pay-roll tax receipts by $100,000,000. If there were then $5,000,000,000 of United States 2-percent bonds in the trust fund, they would produce interest amounting to $100,000,000 a year. This interest would, of course, have to be raised by taxation.

But suppose there were no bonds in the trust fund. In that event, $100,000,000 to cover the deficit in the old-age and survivors insurance system would have to be raised by taxation; and, in addition, another $100,000,000 would have to be raised by taxation to pay interest on $5,000,000,000 of Government bonds owned by someone else. The bonds would be in other hands, because if the Government had not been able to borrow from the Old-Age and Survivors Insurance Trust Fund, it would have had to borrow the same amount from other sources. In other words, the ownership of the $5,000,000,000 in bonds by the old-age and survivors insurance system would prevent the $100,000,000 from having to be raised twice—quite the opposite from the "double taxation" that has been charged.

Increasing Social Security's Current Revenue or Reducing Its Current Costs Will Simply Increase Its Reserve and Will Not Reduce the Federal Debt

Ironically, though detractors claim that Social Security reserves are invested in worthless IOUs, some of these same detractors criticize Social Security for not being even more conservatively financed. As mentioned in the opening chapter, syndicated columnist Robert Samuelson in a column entitled, "Would Roosevelt recognize today's Social Security?" claimed that "Social Security has evolved into something he never intended and actively opposed."

Chapter one discusses the general assertion, but Samuelson was referring to a narrow question about Social Security's funding. He incorrectly claims, "Roosevelt rejected Social Security as a 'pay-as-you-go' system that channeled the taxes of today's workers to pay today's retirees."

Notwithstanding Samuelson's claim, the 1935 Act created financing that was intended to be partially pay-as-you-go (also called current-funded or contingency-funded), and partially advance-funded. The 1939 Act – it seems obvious but must be pointed out – was, like the 1935 Act, championed and signed into law by Roosevelt. The legislation intended to convert Social

Security to completely pay-as-you-go, with simply a reserve as a contingency.

Robert J. Myers was a young actuary crunching the numbers on both the 1935 and 1939 Acts. He described the financing of the 1935 Act as follows:[12]

> Self-support can be achieved by any number of different tax schedules—ranging, at one extreme, from a schedule higher in the early years than in the later ones, thus tending to produce a "fully funded reserve," to the other extreme of a schedule so slowly graded up that "pay-as-you-go" or current-cost financing would, in effect, result. The actual basis adopted initially for OASDI [i.e., Social Security] was between pay-as-you-go and fully funded—probably nearer the former—again, despite the statements of some persons that the original funding basis was "full actuarial reserves."

About the 1939 Act, Myers explains, "The 1939 Act changed the financing basis to what was generally believed to be a pay-as-you-go basis or, more properly, a contingency-fund basis."[13]

The 1939 Act was a response, in part, to the 1936 presidential campaign, where leading Republicans charged that the reserve consisted simply of IOUs. It was also a concern of some Republicans that a large Social Security reserve was unnecessary, needlessly increasing taxes in the short term. In January 1937, Senator Arthur H. Vandenberg (R-MI), a member of the Senate Finance Committee which has jurisdiction over Social Security, introduced a resolution requiring the Social Security Board to produce plans that avoided the build-up of large reserves, either by increasing benefits or reducing contributions in the short-term.

The result of the resolution was the creation of the Social Security Advisory Council of 1937-38. Its recommendations, including expanding benefits and transitioning completely to a current-funded system, were enacted as the Social Security Act Amendments of 1939, and signed into law by Roosevelt on August 11, 1939. In signing the legislation, he praised the enactment:[14]

> It will be exactly four years ago on the fourteenth day of this month that I signed the original Social Security Act. As I

indicated at that time and on various occasions since that time, we must expect a great program of social legislation, such as is represented in the Social Security Act, to be improved and strengthened in the light of additional experience and understanding. These amendments to the Act represent another tremendous step forward in providing greater security for the people of this country. This is especially true in the case of the federal old age insurance system which has now been converted into a system of old age and survivors' insurance providing life-time family security instead of only individual old age security to the workers in insured occupations.

Despite Samuelson's assertion, Roosevelt did not object to current funding, with simply a contingency reserve. What he objected to was payments from general revenue, as opposed to dedicated revenue. Whether Social Security should be financed completely through dedicated revenue or should draw on general revenue has been a matter of debate throughout its history, but has always been resolved in favor of keeping it separate and apart from the general operating fund of the federal government. As explained below, this dedicated revenue, together with Social Security's lack of borrowing authority, today keeps Social Security from adding even a penny to the federal deficit or debt.

Although Samuelson and other opponents seem to confuse the issues of advance funding and dedicated funding, they are different. Whether Social Security is current funded or advance funded is immaterial to the point about Social Security not adding a penny to the debt.

The question of whether Social Security should be advance funded, current funded, or some combination of the two, is a relatively narrow and technical question. Advance funding requires, as its name suggests, higher contributions in the early years, so that investment income can support the program in later years. Current funding, or pay-as-you-go, requires a careful matching of income and outgo, with only a contingency fund necessary to smooth out the ups and downs of income and outgo and to provide the government the time to align income and outgo when projections show the need to do so.

Current funding, advance funding, or some combination of the two all have advantages and disadvantages. The law requires private pensions to be advance funded and private insurers to maintain sizeable reserves, because the plan sponsors can go out of business. Because Social Security is sponsored by the federal government, an entity that is permanent, however, it is perfectly sound to finance its anticipated obligations from current revenue, without the need to build a large reserve.

There has to be some reserve, because in any given year, current revenues can be less than current obligations, but there will never be a time when the federal government goes out of business and must pay off future obligations immediately. This is starkly different from private life insurance companies and traditional pension plans sponsored by individual employers. Those entities can cease business; consequently, the government wisely requires those private sector arrangements to be advance funded.

Current funding may require more adjustments in Social Security's financing over time, because the working and beneficiary populations fluctuate in size over time. However, advance funding may not be the best policy for the nation's economy.

Advance funding requires higher initial contributions to build up the reserve, and lower premiums in later years, since investment income on those reserves will then be larger. However, over time, the nation has grown wealthier and standards of living have increased. That, of course, is projected to continue. Advance funding requires those less-wealthy generations to pay greater amounts for Social Security. Those earlier generations are less wealthy than future generations, as productivity and national wealth increase, so they may be the wrong ones to bear the increased cost.

Both current funding and advance funding of Social Security work and are prudent. Experts have largely come down on the side of employing predominantly current funding. The same three advisory councils that sought to dispel the idea that investment of Social Security's reserve in government obligations backed by the full faith and credit of the United States, is anything other than sound and proper, all concluded that current funding is optimal.

The 1948 Advisory Council, for example, stated, "Unlike private insurance, a social-insurance scheme backed by the taxing power of the Government does not need full reserves sufficient to cover all liabilities."[15]

Similarly, the 1957-59 Advisory Council stated:[16]

> The "full reserve" basis contemplates the accumulation during an initial period of very substantial funds which, if the pension plan were to cease operating, would be available to discharge existing liabilities. These are liabilities to the then current beneficiaries and the liabilities accrued to date for those still in active employment. In a national compulsory social insurance program it can properly be assumed that the program will continue to collect contributions and to pay benefits indefinitely into the future. The old-age, survivors, and disability insurance program therefore does not need a full reserve. It may be considered to be in actuarial balance when estimated future income from contributions and from interest on the investments of the accumulated trust funds will, over the long run, support the estimated disbursements for benefits and administrative expenses.

Ironically, though Samuelson apparently doesn't realize it, the Social Security Amendments of 1983 provided for greater advance funding of Social Security, closer to what was envisioned by the 1935 Act. Policy experts recognized that the 1990s were to be a low-cost period for Social Security. That was because the generations reaching old age in the 1990s were those born during the Great Depression and World War II, when birth rates were low, and the large post-World War II generation, the so-called Baby Boomers, would be entering their peak earning years.

Rather than reduce Social Security contributions and then raise them substantially when the baby boom generation began to retire, the 1983 Amendments allowed the contributions to remain higher than necessary for a strict current-funded system and, instead, had the excess funds used to build up an accumulated reserve, in anticipation of the retirement of the Baby Boom.

If Congress so chose, it could enact legislation to maintain this accumulated reserve, so the investment earnings could be used to offset future costs. Frustratingly, a serious analysis and discussion over whether to maintain this partial advance funding is thwarted by the zombie lies.

In addition to Social Security's very large accumulated reserve, the program is also running an annual surplus. Consequently, if Congress increased its dedicated revenue, starting right away, that increased revenue would be used to purchase additional Treasury obligations. Similarly, maintaining or even increasing Social Security's advance funding will simply maintain or increase the size of the accumulated reserve and the number and worth of the Treasury bonds in which those reserves are invested.

Yet, Social Security's detractors refuse to acknowledge that Social Security's reserves, the assets in which they are invested, or the trusts in which they are held, are real. These detractors claim that the Treasury bonds in which the reserves are invested are simply worthless IOUs. This stands in the way of a serious discussion of the best approach to fund Social Security going forward.

While the zombie lies about the reserves being filled with IOUs undercut advance funding of Social Security, other zombie lies undercut current funding of Social Security. Opponents of Social Security have sought to convince Americans that current funding is a Ponzi scheme! This, of course, is another untrue slander, as is explained in detail in chapter five.

Samuelson and other opponents of Social Security put down current funding, advance funding, the soundness of Social Security's investments, and the reality of the trust funds. One can infer that their objections are not really to the arrangements, but to the underlying program itself.

Social Security Does Not Add Even a
Penny to the Federal Debt

On top of those willful refusals to understand, Samuelson and other opponents partake in another zombie lie. They falsely claim that Social Security is adding enormously to the federal deficit and so must be cut. The truth is that Social Security does not and, by law, cannot add even a penny to the federal debt or deficit.

Social Security can only pay benefits if it has sufficient revenue to cover the costs. Its budget must be balanced, but Social Security cannot accrue the revenue needed to balance its budget through borrowing, because it has no borrowing authority. Social Security lacks the legal authority to deficit-spend, and so, cannot run a deficit. Because it cannot run a deficit, it cannot add to the federal debt or deficit.

The federal debt consists of the face value of all the outstanding Treasury bonds, which are issued in order to fund the government by filling the gap between expenditures and revenues of the general operating fund of the government. Although economists use different definitions when speaking of the nation's annual deficit, the straightforward, common understanding is that the annual deficit is simply the portion of that accumulated debt incurred in any particular year.

Neither increasing Social Security's revenue nor cutting Social Security's expenditures reduces the United States' total federal debt or annual deficits, of which the debt is comprised, by even a penny. As explained in the previous section, increasing Social Security's revenue would result in a larger reserve, which, in turn, results in the purchase of additional Treasury bonds. Though the value of the bonds held in trust for Social Security contributors and beneficiaries would increase, the overall value of the bonds issued by the government – the total federal debt – would remain the same.

The identical amount will be needed to fill the gap between general revenue expenditures and income. The bonds would be held by different creditors, but the value of the bonds issued would remain unchanged. More bonds would be held by Social Security and fewer by the public, but everything else – the total outstanding debt, the interest owed – would be the same.

The same is true if Social Security benefits were cut. Social Security would need less income to meet its reduced obligations. Consequently, that additional revenue would be invested in federal government obligations until needed, and therefore its reserve, again, would increase. Although the obligations would be issued to different investors – more to Social Security, fewer to the general public – the total outstanding federal debt and associated interest owed would, once more, remain unchanged.

This sharply differs from cuts to agricultural subsidies, defense, or other expenditures from the government's general fund. If a program paid for from general-fund revenue were cut by $100 billion and nothing else changed, the federal government's borrowing needs would go down by $100 billion. As a consequence, that year's deficit would also go down (or more realistically, given the current large deficits, it would go up less than it would have, without the cut). If the savings from that hypothetical cut were offset dollar-for-dollar by a cut in income taxes or an increase in other expenditures funded from general revenues, the federal debt and deficit would be unchanged.

In stark contrast, if Social Security benefits were cut by $100 billion, the total federal debt would remain unchanged. If the $100 billion savings from cutting Social Security benefits were offset dollar-for-dollar by a cut in income taxes or an increase in general-revenue spending, the total federal debt would increase!

For those who are used to thinking about Social Security as just another spending program, and about Social Security contributions as just another tax, the relationship between Social Security and the federal debt may be counterintuitive. To grasp that relationship, it is important to see that Social Security is a defined benefit pension plan with its own income, outgo, and reserve fund, separate from the general fund of the federal government.

The following thought experiment may help. Imagine a private pension plan whose assets are invested solely in Treasury obligations. Imagine further that the plan sponsor, Company XYZ, cuts the benefits the plan provides, but does not decrease the plan's funding in any way. In that case, the plan would have more income in relation to its expenses than it had before plan benefits were cut. The plan accordingly would use that additional income to purchase additional Treasury obligations (or to pay plan costs, if that were necessary).

The plan's increased income would have no effect on the federal deficit or debt. The federal government would have exactly the same general-fund income and outgo and, accordingly, the same borrowing needs, irrespective of the cuts to the pension plan benefits. Consequently, the Department of the Treasury would issue debt instruments totaling the exact same value, irrespective of the actions of the pension plan.

In the exact same way, if Social Security's plan sponsor, the federal government, cuts the benefits Social Security provides but does not decrease the level of contributions employers and employees are required to make under FICA, Social Security's income would increase in relation to its expenses, and Social Security, accordingly, would purchase additional Treasury obligations.

Social Security's additional income and its purchase of additional Treasury bonds would have no effect on the federal deficit or debt. Like the example of the private pension plan, the federal government would have exactly the same general-fund income and outgo and – accordingly – the same borrowing needs, irrespective of the cuts to Social Security. Consequently, the Department of the Treasury would again issue debt instruments totaling the exact same value, irrespective of the changes to Social Security.

Cutting Social Security's benefits or increasing its revenue, like cutting the benefits of a private pension plan or increasing its revenue, does not reduce by even a penny the federal deficit or the total value of debt instruments issued by Treasury. The only way to reduce the amount of federal debt Treasury issues is to reduce the expenditures of the government's general operating fund or increase its income.

Congress has codified this reality in section 13301 of the Omnibus Budget Reconciliation Act of 1990, which unambiguously states:[17]

> Notwithstanding any other provision of law, the receipts and disbursements of the Federal Old-Age and Survivors Insurance Trust Fund and the Federal Disability Insurance Trust Fund [i.e., Social Security] shall not be counted as new budget authority, outlays, receipts, or deficit or surplus for purposes of—
> (1) the budget of the United States Government as submitted by the President,
> (2) the congressional budget, or
> (3) the Balanced Budget and Emergency Deficit Control Act of 1985.

These are not mere words. Whether Social Security should be financed in part from general revenue or should be totally separate and apart from the budget of the United States was a matter over which the founders disagreed. President Roosevelt felt strongly that all of Social Security's revenue should be dedicated with no draw on the general revenue. That preference has largely prevailed. From the beginning, Social Security has been self-financing and independent of the general operating fund of the United States, with two temporary exceptions.

The first occurred during World War II, when Congress continually froze Social Security contribution rates, preventing them from rising, over the objection of the Roosevelt administration. To ensure that Social Security could continue to pay benefits notwithstanding the reduction in projected revenue caused by the frozen rates, Congress enacted legislation in 1943 that required the general fund to pay any benefits for which Social Security had insufficient revenue. Ironically, because World War II was a time of low unemployment and high workforce participation and because benefits were not increased, even though inflation was high, sufficient revenue dedicated to Social Security was received to pay all benefits and increase the holdings of the trust fund. Consequently, general revenue, in fact, never was necessary. The provision was repealed as part of the Social Security Amendments of 1950.

The second breach occurred recently. In order to stimulate the economy, President Barack Obama proposed and Congress enacted the Making Work Pay tax credit. It expired at the end of 2010, and Republicans in Congress, now in the majority in the House of Representatives, refused to go along with extending it. As an alternative – and in spite of the loud objections of Social Security advocates – it was replaced by another temporary measure, the so-called payroll-tax holiday. That reduced the level of employee premiums and made up the difference with general revenue. After two years, the temporary tax break expired.

Revealingly, those who falsely claim that Social Security is a cause of the deficit also tend to be the advocates of starving Social Security of its dedicated revenue, and replacing that revenue with deficit spending. Indeed, that proposal was reportedly under consideration by the Trump administration as part of its deliberations over its tax package. The idea could be resurrected at any time by the Republican-controlled White House and Congress, so hostile to Social Security. That would make Social Security a contributor to the debt. But, as currently structured, it is not.

The question of whether Social Security's relationship to the federal budget should be changed has been carefully considered and debated over its history. During consideration of the creation of Social Security in 1935, this issue was discussed at the Ways and Means Committee hearing on the legislation in an exchange between Representative Harold Knutson (R-MN) and Roosevelt's Secretary of the Treasury, Henry Morgenthau:[18]

> Mr. KNUTSON. Mr. Secretary, ... what is [the proposed legislation] going to cost in 1980?

> Secretary MORGENTHAU. On the contributory part of the plan [i.e., Social Security] it will cost the Government nothing. It will be self-sustaining.

> Mr. KNUTSON. What will the entire plan cost?

> Secretary MORGENTHAU. The noncontributory part [i.e., the welfare programs] of it will cost the Treasury something over $500,000,000.

> Mr. KNUTSON. That is in 1980. And that would become a fixed charge upon the Treasury annually, of $500,000,000?

> Secretary MORGENTHAU. Yes.

> Mr. KNUTSON. What about the old age part [i.e., Social Security] of it?

> Secretary MORGENTHAU. That will be zero.

> Mr. KNUTSON. You mean the old-age pension plan will take care of itself in 1980?

> Secretary MORGENTHAU. Yes, sir.

Consistent with that exchange, Social Security is self-financing today. It costs the government nothing. From the beginning, Social Security's major source of income has been premiums paid by workers and matched dollar-for-dollar by their employers. As explained at length above, excess income is invested; from the beginning, the investment income – interest on U.S. Treasury bonds purchased by Social Security – has served as an additional form of revenue.

In the future, new sources of dedicated revenue could be added. That would leave Social Security's relationship to the budget unchanged. In what would be a departure from the fundamental structure of Social Security as conceived by its founders, general revenue could be added by some future Congress. An open draw on general revenue would be a fundamental change.

For Social Security's entire history, with just the two brief exceptional periods described above, Social Security has not and, by law, could not, add to the federal debt or deficit. Consistent with that long history, that is the case today, as well.

The Understandable but Mistaken Belief That Social Security's Assets Have Been Stolen

As this chapter has detailed, the law has always required that all of the program's surpluses be invested in the safest, most conservative investment possible – interest-bearing debt instruments backed by the full faith and credit of the United States. Treasury bonds are such a safe and valuable investment precisely because they are backed by the full faith and credit of the United States.

As a sovereign nation, the United States has the power to default on any of its bonds, but it never has. It would be an outrage for the United States to honor the bonds held by foreign adversaries of the United States, such as China and Russia, but default on bonds held in trust for its own citizens.[19] It is hard to imagine that any elected officials who participated in that outcome would remain in office for long.

The commitment of the federal government to honor its debts and redeem with interest all of its obligations, including those owed to Social Security, is both a matter of law and morality. Similarly, the requirement that Social Security's revenue only be used for benefits and associated administrative costs is not only a matter of law; it represents the solemn, longstanding, fiduciary responsibility of the government, as Social Security's plan sponsor.

Historically, presidents of both parties and leaders in Congress have been extremely diligent and careful in executing their fiduciary responsibilities with respect to Social Security. Starting with the very first year after Social Security started paying monthly benefits, Congress has required Social Security's trustees to report annually, no matter the circumstances – even during times of war – on Social Security's financial status, including its accumulated surpluses which are in reserve, available whenever the monies are needed to pay scheduled benefits.

Diverting Social Security's dedicated income and assets from their intended purpose is legally and morally wrong. Not surprisingly, numerous polls indicate that the American people do not want their Social Security contributions diverted to debt reduction or governmental purposes other than Social Security. Yet, focus group data reveal that many Americans today believe that the government has already stolen their contributions or fear that it will steal Social Security's income and assets and divert them to unauthorized purposes.

The reason for this widely-held anxiety is easy to understand. The American people are constantly bombarded with irresponsible rhetoric about Social Security from some of our most influential leaders. As this chapter has already discussed, some policymakers and policy analysts casually refer to the interest-bearing United States Treasury bonds purchased by Social Security as "just IOUs." Similarly, some elected officials have warned ominously that Social Security's reserves have already been spent.

Even more reprehensibly, a chairman of the Federal Reserve argued for cutting Social Security as part of a deficit package by quoting Willie Sutton, a notorious bank robber. When asked why he robbed banks, Sutton is said to have replied, "Because that's where the money is."[20] The Fed chairman's ill-considered attempt at humor inadvertently presents a revealing picture – bank robbers and politicians, all eager to grab the money that hardworking Americans trustingly hand over every payday to what they believe is a safe institution.

All of this casual, irresponsible rhetoric is a serious disservice to the American people and explains why so many Americans believe that their contributions have been stolen.

Moreover, politicians in Washington have engaged in other behavior that suggests that they are imprudently commingling and improperly using Social Security's dedicated revenue.

Notwithstanding the clear fact that Social Security does not add even a penny to the deficit, recent Congresses have sought to cut Social Security as part of efforts to reach a bipartisan package aimed at reducing the federal deficit.[21] Moreover, these same Congresses have sought to use cuts to Social Security as supposed "pay-fors," offsetting, in some theoretical sense, totally non-related government expenditures. The opening line of a July 20, 2015 news article, for example, reported, "With 11 days left before federal funding runs out for the nation's highways, bridges and roads, lawmakers are rushing to find a way to pay for an extension. One potential fix: slash Social Security benefits...."[22]

To repeat, the only way to reduce the federal debt and the annual deficit, of which the debt is comprised, is either to increase the government's general revenue or cut programs that are paid for from general revenue. And, the only way to increase federal spending without increasing the federal debt is, also, by increasing the government's general revenue or by cutting other programs that are paid for from general revenue. Cutting Social Security does neither of these things.

The ploy of using Social Security to offset general fund spending has been undertaken by those whose expertise is the federal budget generally, not individual programs. They tend to see government revenue and expenditures as undifferentiated money-in and money-out, ignoring that Social Security premiums are dedicated exclusively to Social Security and its related administrative costs. That simplified view is distorting and fails to see that Social Security is a self-financed pension plan with its assets held in trust.

When challenged by these arguments, some opponents of Social Security have claimed that they want to address Social Security in an overall budget package "for its own sake, and not for deficit reduction."[23] But, Social Security is too complicated and too important to the American people to be addressed as part of other complicated legislation, when full attention will necessarily be diverted, and when there is no compelling or urgent reason to do so.

Including Social Security in comprehensive budget packages, as recent Congresses have sought to do, has serious costs. This is true even when the effort has been pursued by those who see themselves as supporters of Social Security. It has been a destructive exercise even though Social Security champions have been able to defeat those misguided efforts to cut Social Security. It has been destructive even when those advocating the comprehensive package implicitly acknowledge that Social Security does not and, by law, cannot add to the deficit, but seek to justify a comprehensive package, nonetheless.

The very existence of legislation designed to reduce the federal deficit that includes Social Security cuts or seeks to offset the cost of federal spending with Social Security cuts understandably erodes Americans' confidence in and support for our government. That is a serious cost, irrespective of the rationale for the inclusion.

Related to the failure to properly discuss Social Security's revenue and the misguided inclusion of Social Security in unrelated legislation, both of which have, unsurprisingly, led many Americans to believe that their money has been stolen, is another ploy by those seeking to undermine confidence in the program. In an effort to make Social Security's revenue appear less than it is, these opponents focus on what they call "non-interest income," as if the investment income is not legitimate.

The Social Security Amendments of 1983 established two Public Trustees, in an effort to boost confidence in the future of Social Security. Instead, the position most recently was filled by an individual who has been characterized as a fox in the Social Security hen house.[24] The point-person in the White House, pushing the Bush administration's privatization plan, was nominated to be a public trustee in 2009, confirmed in 2010 and served until 2015. (The positions of public trustee are vacant, as of the time this is written.) The phrases "non-interest" or "non-interest income" never appeared in a Trustees Report before 2010. In that year, those phrases appeared two times. In the 2015 report, they appeared 77 times!

Social Security's investment income is income, as it would be if it were paid to any other bondholder. The federal government pays the interest it owes on its outstanding Treasury bonds, as it should, regardless of whether the bondholder is General Motors, the Chinese government, or Social Security, whose money is held in trust for the American people.

The phrase "non-interest income" has no legal significance, but does further the goals of those seeking to undermine confidence in Social Security. Disregarding some of Social Security's revenue allows opponents to erroneously claim that Social Security is cash-negative. But as explained above, Social Security cannot deficit-spend. It is a way for opponents or others who should know better to claim that Social Security is in crisis, even though it is currently in surplus.[25]

As stated above, opponents of Social Security disingenuously argue, on the one hand, that Social Security is adding to the federal debt. On the other hand, in completely contradictory fashion, the very same people argue that Social Security is going bankrupt. It can't do both! In fact, neither is true. Social Security is neither adding to the federal debt or deficit nor going bankrupt.

Social Security cannot deficit-spend, has no borrowing authority and does not add even a penny to the deficit. Far from being in crisis, it has a steady source of revenue, has a large and growing reserve, and is projected to run a surplus in 2017 and 2018, as it did in 2016.

Social Security has three dedicated revenue streams from which to cover its costs. According to the Social Security Administration, Social Security, as of December 31, 2016, had an accumulated surplus of more than $2.8 trillion. That accumulated reserve is likely to increase, because the 2017 Trustees Report projects Social Security to have a $58.6 billion surplus in 2017 and a $44.7 billion surplus in 2018.[26]

Because there is no automatic draw on general revenues, Social Security's Board of Trustees reports every year to Congress about the long-range financial health of the program. The report comes out every year, usually in April, and projects out seventy-five years. That long valuation period and frequent reporting allows Congress more than sufficient time to act to ensure that promised benefits will always be paid on time and in full.

Whenever projecting out so many decades into the future, it is not surprising to sometimes project unintended surpluses and unintended shortfalls. But because Social Security is primarily current funded, any projected shortfall is minor. So, under the current projections, Social Security is 100 percent funded for more than a decade and a half; 93 percent funded for the next 25 years; 87 percent funded for the next fifty years; and 84 percent funded for the next three-quarters of a century.[27]

When Americans, who contribute to Social Security from every paycheck, hear the lie that Social Security is going broke, they naturally wonder if their money has been stolen. Those who understate Social Security's income and exaggerate its projected shortfall, polarize the issue and make closing the shortfall that much more complicated. The obvious inference is that they do not want to see Social Security restored to long-term actuarial balance. Rather, they want to undermine confidence as a way of cutting Social Security or, worse, ending it as we know it.

There is no question that the nation can afford Social Security, as chapter six makes clear. The cost of the projected shortfall – and, indeed, of expansions – can easily be met in a manner consistent with the founders' concept of financing Social Security. Expanding Social Security while requiring the wealthiest among us to pay their fair share is profoundly wise policy and represents the will of the people. An honest discussion would quickly produce legislation that did just that.

Because Social Security addresses the universal insecurity of the loss of wages in the event of death, disability or old age, is so soundly structured, is so responsibly financed, and is so popular, opponents are left with nothing other than their zombie lies.

A Comprehensive Effort to Correct all the Misunderstandings and Zombie Lies Surrounding Social Security's Financing

Sixty years ago, the 1957-59 Social Security Advisory Council directed its staff to draft a memorandum addressing what the Council diplomatically called misunderstandings. As the third advisory council to address the subject, its members must have seen, despite their diplomatic language, that these were zombie lies that refused to die. Nevertheless, in order to educate the public and perhaps put the false claims to rest, the memorandum is thorough and comprehensive.

Although the excellent discussion did not end the misunderstandings and false claims, it is worth reading by those who want to understand the truth. The following paper, prepared by the council's staff six decades ago, remains timely:[28]

****

Misunderstandings of Social Security Financing
(Prepared by the staff of the 1957-59
Advisory Council on Social Security Financing)

I. THE IDEA THAT THE OLD-AGE AND SURVIVORS INSURANCE TRUST FUND IS NOW $300 BILLION "IN THE RED"

Explanation

Numerous newspaper articles and editorials recently have carried the statement that the old-age and survivors insurance trust fund has a shortage of $300 billion. Similar criticisms, with different estimates of the unfunded liability of the program, have appeared during the past few years.

Clarence E. Manion, formerly dean of the law school at Notre Dame University, in a radio speech in 1954 stated that "under the 1954 amendments, the accrued liability of this huge coverage at the minimum estimate, is $250 billion"; and in a broadcast in 1956 he quoted a listener who had sent him an estimate that the trust fund was then "$280 billion in the red."

William J. Matteson of the American Institute for Economic Research, Great Barrington, Massachusetts, in a book wrote that "The fund thus far accumulated is only a small fraction of the actuarially computed reserve that would be necessary if the scheme were operating on a sound basis."

Donald F. Campbell, Jr., a consulting actuary, in a speech in 1956 stated that "$259 billion in unfunded accrued liability... should be added to the Federal debt in evaluating the overall national financial obligation in the opinion of many economists." Dillard Stokes in a book in 1956 declared that "the reserve fund, even if it were real, is pledged 10 times over." Both Mr. Campbell and Mr. Stokes referred to an estimate by the Social Security Administration that the total accrued benefit liability of the program at the end of 1954 was $280 billion of which $21 billion was funded.

Albert C. Adams, then vice-president of the National Association of Life Underwriters, in a speech in 1957 stated that "The social security trust fund has a shortage of $300 billion and it is increasing year after year." He explained that the trust fund, which at that time totaled $23 billion, had "accumulated liabilities" of $323 billion.

Answer

A compulsory social insurance program does not require a reserve fund with assets at any given time equal to the present value of future benefits payable to current beneficiaries and active members less the present value of future contributions payable by them. Private life insurance companies are legally required to have such reserves because they must be prepared to execute insurance contracts by paying off benefit liabilities or cash surrender values even if the company should cease writing any new business. A compulsory government program can be properly financed on the assumption that it will not discontinue operations in the future and that it will continue to receive contribution income. The Federal old-age and survivors insurance program is in approximate actuarial balance when evaluated in terms appropriate to such a program: over the long-range operation of this program, the scheduled contribution rates, according to actuarial estimates, will, along with interest receipts, produce roughly sufficient income to meet the benefits provided and the administrative expenses.

II. THE IDEA THAT AN EXCESS OF TRUST FUND DISBURSEMENTS OVER TRUST FUND RECEIPTS IN A GIVEN YEAR INDICATES FINANCIAL WEAKNESS IN THE PROGRAM

Explanation

The large volume of claims received from newly insured workers early in 1957 led to inquiries from the public as to whether more beneficiaries were being added to the rolls than had been expected. When data were released showing that benefit amounts were exceeding estimates, questions were raised as to the effect of the resulting larger-than-expected benefit expenditures on the financial status of the program. Statements appeared in the public press that the fund in 1957 was heading for its first deficit, with prospects that it would go deeper "into the red" during 1958 and 1959.

Articles commenting on this development in the financial position of the trust fund appeared in Barron's, Time magazine, The Wall Street Journal, Business Week, United States News and World Report, and other periodicals. Many daily news papers printed news articles, editorials, or comments by columnists on this subject. Radio and television commentators also used the item. Some of the comments combined the current analysis with repetition of long-circulated criticisms of the trust fund. Other comments used the current financial condition of the fund as a basis for warnings against any additional liberalization of the program.

Public reaction was widespread. Congressmen and the Department of Health, Education, and Welfare received many inquiries about these reports. The inquiries expressed the concern of beneficiaries and contributors about the financial condition of the trust fund and especially about the possibility that payment of future benefits might be endangered.

Answer

The financial provisions of the old-age and survivors insurance program were not designed to provide trust fund income equal to or in excess of trust fund disbursements in every year. Instead, they were designed to provide receipts exceeding disbursements in most years during the next several decades and thereafter in a rough balance between receipts and disbursements.

Total receipts of the old-age and survivors insurance trust fund exceeded total disbursements from that fund in every calendar year before 1957. In 1957, however, total expenditures exceeded receipts by about $125 million. Current estimates indicate that in calendar year 1958 and 1959 the fund's disbursements can also be expected to exceed total trust fund income.

This situation, however, will be temporary. Under the schedule provided in the Act contribution rates will increase every 5 years until 1975; as a result, the income of the trust fund is expected on the whole to rise more rapidly than disbursements. Consequently, the assets of the trust fund are expected to increase in most years for the next several decades. Disbursements of the fund nevertheless may exceed receipts in years immediately before scheduled contribution rate increases and possibly in some years of business recession.

The old-age and survivors insurance trust fund serves a two-fold function. Through its interest earnings, the fund is a source of income supplementing contribution receipts, thereby keeping down the level of contributions required to finance the program. In addition, the assets of the fund are available, when needed, to supplement current receipts in periods when disbursements temporarily rise above trust fund income. In this way, it serves as a contingency reserve. Since the fund is being accumulated partly for use in such contingencies, there is nothing alarming, or indicative of financial weakness, about temporary reductions in the size of the fund.

III. THE IDEA THAT PAYMENT OF INTEREST ON, AND THE REDEMPTION OF, SECURITIES HELD BY THE TRUST FUNDS MEANS THAT PEOPLE ARE TAXED TWICE FOR SOCIAL SECURITY

Explanation

One of the oldest and most persistent criticisms of the old-age and survivors insurance trust fund is that its investments in Federal securities involve double taxation for social security, once in the payment of social security contributions and a second time in the payment of taxes to pay interest on and to redeem the securities held by the trust find.

In 1939, Mr. John T. Flynn in an article referred to taxation for interest on the reserve fund as supplemental taxes for social security and he wrote "By the President's plan two taxes must be collected—employer-employee taxes and general taxes to pay interest." In another article in 1947 Mr. Flynn wrote: "The Government will again have to collect taxes from workers and employers in order to pay the interest on the bonds in the Old Age Reserve Fund."

Meanwhile, newspaper columnists and editorial writers had given wide circulation to the criticism of "double taxation," and comments of this type have continued up to the present time.

In a report the Senate Committee on Finance in 1943 characterized appropriations to pay interest on a reserve fund as identical with "a direct appropriation to the support of the old-age and survivors insurance system" and referred to what it characterized as "needless accumulation" of Government reserves as the result of taxation. Senator Arthur H. Vandenberg, in a speech on the floor of the Senate in 1944 repeated substantially the same view as had appeared in the report.

In 1944, Harley L. Lutz in a pamphlet characterized the taxation which furnished the money invested in bonds as "vain" and "pure illusion." In a book published in 1945 he said that the Federal Government "is merely creating a pledge that Federal taxes will be levied in future to carry and redeem these bonds."

In 1950, Lewis Mariam and Karl Schlotterbeck in their book counted the cost of interest on securities held by the trust fund as part of the total cost of the old-age and survivors insurance program.

They also stated that it is immaterial whether future citizens pay one social security tax or "a social security tax plus taxes necessary to pay interest and principal on the governmental debts held in the actuarial reserve. The only possible difference between the future taxes would be in their incidence."

Dillard Stokes in his book in 1956 counted payroll taxation as the first form of taxation for social security, general taxation to pay interest on securities held by the trust fund as a second form, and general taxation to redeem bonds held by the fund as a third form—thus developing a charge of triple taxation rather than double taxation.

Answer

Contributions are levied in the form of taxes to finance the old-age and survivors insurance and disability insurance programs, and these contributions are appropriated to the social security trust funds.

To cover expenditures for purposes duly authorized by Congress, such as armaments and highway construction, the Federal Government from time to time instead of raising additional taxes borrows money, some of it from the trust funds. When taxes are levied to repay these Federal borrowings from the trust funds and other investors, these taxes will be levied to meet the cost of the armaments, highway construction, and the other objects for which the money was borrowed. To hold otherwise would mean that taxes will never have to be levied to pay the full cost of the materials and services that the Government purchased with borrowed money.

People are taxed for social security when they pay their contributions under the program. Taxes paid to redeem the Federal securities held by the trust funds are paid for the purposes for which the money was borrowed from the trust funds, and not for social security.

Similarly, the interest the Government pays on the Federal securities held by the trust funds are payments made for purposes other than social security. Congress has recognized that it would be inequitable to contributors under the social security programs if the Treasury borrowed money from the trust funds without paying interest on these borrowings just as it would have to do if the money was borrowed from others. The taxes raised to pay this interest are levied for the purposes for which the money was borrowed and not for social security.

The Government must pay interest on all the public debt whether or not part of it is held by the trust funds. Payment of interest to the trust funds therefore does not increase the cost of servicing the debt. On the other hand, the interest received by the trust funds on their investments supplements their receipts from contributions and results eventually in lower contributions for social security than would be necessary if no interest were received by the funds. In this way, the payment of interest on securities held by the trust funds has the effect of decreasing, rather than increasing, the taxes people eventually must pay for social security.

IV. THE IDEA THAT MOST TRUST FUND ASSETS ARE FICTITIOUS BECAUSE THEY ARE IOU's ISSUED BY THE FEDERAL GOVERNMENT TO ITSELF

Explanation

Generally, the same critics who have made the criticism of double taxation also have labeled trust fund investments as IOU's issued by the Government to itself.

This criticism appears in John T. Flynn's 1939 magazine article and in Mr. Manion's radio addresses. Newspaper columnists and editorial writers have repeated it intermittently. Letters to members of Congress and the Department of Health, Education, and Welfare also refer to it.

The essential part of this criticism is the idea that securities are issued by the Government to itself. Since the old-age and survivors insurance trust fund is a Federal fund created by Federal statute, and since the promises to repay money borrowed from that fund are made by the United States Government, the obligations are described as IOU's issued by the Government to itself.

Issuance of Federal obligations to the trust fund is held to be fictitious on the ground that only investments in obligations issued by borrowers other than the Federal Government could be serviced without calling on the general taxing powers of the Federal [Government]. In this way, the criticism of double taxation is linked with the criticism that trust fund investments were IOU's issued by the Federal Government to itself.

Answer

All promises to pay, including all bonds or notes issued by the Federal Government, may be called IOU's. As evidence of debt, the Federal securities issued to the trust funds do not differ in any material respect from Federal obligations held by private investors. Obligations of the United States Government are universally recognized to be the safest possible investment. The central point to the criticism, therefore, is whether the securities held by the trust funds are obligations issued by the Government to itself.

There can be no question that the Federal old-age and survivors insurance and disability insurance trust funds and the Board of Trustees of those funds were created by and are subject to laws enacted by the Congress of the United States. To that extent, they are a part of the United States Government. These funds, however, are entities separate from and independent of the rest of the Federal Government. The income and disbursements of the funds are not included in the administrative budget of the Government. Instead, the President reports their operations separately in his Budget Message to Congress and the Board of Trustees is required to submit to Congress annually a report on the operations and status of the funds. The debt obligations held by the trust funds are shown in Treasury reports as part of the Federal debt, and interest payments on these obligations are regularly made by the Treasury to the trust funds. They are redeemed in cash by the Treasury whenever necessary for disbursements by these funds.

The old-age and survivors insurance and disability insurance trust funds are only two among several Federal trust funds that invest in obligations of the United States. All of them are entities independent of the United States Treasury which issues the Federal obligations they hold. The Treasury is as much obligated to pay interest on and redeem these securities as it is to pay interest on and redeem the Federal securities held by other investors.

V. THE IDEA THAT THE PURCHASE OF FEDERAL OBLIGATIONS BY THE TRUST FUNDS INCREASES THE NATIONAL DEBT

Explanation

An outstanding example of this view is the statement by John T. Flynn in 1947 that the Federal old-age and survivors insurance program "is a plan to add a billion or two every year to the national debt which we are supposed to reduce." From time to time newspaper writers and letters received by the Department of Health, Education, and Welfare have expressed the belief that trust fund investments cause increases in the national debt. In some comments, this idea has been linked with a belief that the availability of borrowable money due to trust fund accumulation is a temptation to Federal extravagance.

Answer

The national debt is increased only when for a given fiscal year Congress has approved expenditures that exceed tax revenues. The excess expenditures, of course, must be met by borrowing through the sale of additional Federal obligations. These obligations add to the national debt.

The purchase of Federal obligations by the trust funds does not increase the total Federal debt. If there were no trust funds, the Treasury would still borrow just as much, all of it from other investors. When the Treasury has no deficit to meet, Treasury borrowing from the trust funds can result only in the redemption of an equal amount of outstanding Federal obligations. In this way trust fund purchases of Federal obligations from the Treasury when there is no budget deficit result only in a transfer of Federal debt obligations to the trust funds from other investors; the total amount of the public debt remains unchanged.

There is no indication that the availability of trust fund money for borrowing by the Treasury ever has influenced Congress to vote expenditures not covered by general tax revenues which it would not have otherwise voted. The United States Treasury can always borrow money on the open market; the trust fund money does not increase the amount it is able to borrow. Whether borrowed on the open market or from the trust funds, money borrowed to meet a deficit increases the national debt and adds to the costs of servicing that debt.

VI. THE IDEA THAT CONTRIBUTION INCOME NOT NEEDED FOR CURRENT PROGRAM EXPENDITURES HAS BEEN WRONGLY SPENT FOR THE EXPENSES OF THE FEDERAL GOVERNMENT

Explanation

This misunderstanding is based on the fact that when the old-age and survivors insurance and disability insurance trust funds invest in Federal securities, the Treasury uses the money thus borrowed to help pay the expenses of the Federal Government. The critics usually do not mention borrowing or investment; they charge that program contributions have been wrongly used to pay the expenses of the Government. Some of these critics, chiefly newspaper writers, recognize that the borrowing has been authorized by law, but they nevertheless hold that the transactions are in effect "legalized embezzlement."

This criticism was made in the discussion of fund accumulation which preceded the 1939 amendments to the Social Security Act. In 1939, John T. Flynn in an article charged that substantial amounts of the program's contribution income would never be spent for benefits at all, "but for every sort of Government expense including, perhaps, building battleships." He described program contributions as a disguised tax levied on the lowest income groups under the pretense of old-age pension premiums. In 1947, also in an article, Mr. Flynn declared that it is dishonest to collect taxes under one guise and spend them for another purpose.

Senator Arthur H. Vandenberg, in a speech in 1942 objected to the use of contribution income for investments to finance the war, warning that "To use social security reserves for any collateral purpose other than social security benefits is to weaken the Social Security System at a vital spot."

Harley L. Lutz in 1944 charged that the old-age and survivors insurance program involves a tax levy used in part for general purposes and in part for bona fide social security payments. He wrote that "The taxes now being collected are principally devoted to general purposes and only in minor degree to genuine social security purposes"; and also that "Whether workers and employers should be required to pay so heavily toward general Federal purposes under the guise of providing for social security benefits ... is a subject which should be frankly faced."

Using a similar tone, Meriam and Schlotterbeck in 1950 pointed out that the program would provide substantial revenues for the general support of Government for a considerable number of years and commented that "Such revenues are sometimes called 'forced contributions' from special groups for the benefit of the budget as a whole." They further commented that "The taxpayers of today do not appreciate that most of the proceeds of the payroll tax ... a regressive tax, are actually being used to finance current operations."

Senator Eugene D. Millikin during the hearings of the Senate Committee on Finance on the 1950 amendments to the Social Security Act repeatedly objected to "using the contributory insurance system as a means of covering the general revenue expenditures of the country."

This charge that contribution income not needed for current program expenditures has been wrongly spent for operating expenses of the

Federal Government has had wide circulation in newspaper columns and magazines during the past 20 years. It has often been associated with a conclusion that the old-age and survivors insurance trust fund has no reality, because its moneys invested in Federal securities have been spent. The Department of Health, Education, and Welfare has received numerous letters repeating these criticisms.

Answer

Contributions paid under the old-age and survivors insurance and disability programs are earmarked for these programs. Although paid initially to the Treasury through the Internal Revenue Service, they are immediately transferred to the old-age and survivors insurance and disability insurance trust funds in accordance with the provisions of the law. The contributions are not available to the Treasury Department to be used like general revenue taxes for the operating expenses of the Federal Government.

Contribution receipts of the trust funds not needed for current disbursements under the program are invested by the Managing Trustee in Federal obligations. The trust fund money thus invested forms part of the borrowings of the Federal Treasury and, like borrowings from other investors, it is used by the Treasury to meet the general expenses of the Government. The Federal obligations purchased and held by the trust funds are part of the public debt and they are interest-bearing assets of the funds. All contribution receipts of the trust funds that are not used for the current benefit and administrative expenses of the programs thus remain invested assets of the trust funds.

VII. THE IDEA THAT EACH PERSON COVERED BY THE PROGRAM HAS AN INDIVIDUAL RESERVE ACCOUNT

Explanation

Some persons covered by the program have the idea that their contributions go into an individual account, and that any benefits paid come out of such an account. Thus they ask what happens to their money in case they and their families do not receive benefits of at least equal value to what they have paid in contributions; they expect that they should receive benefits regardless of whether they have retired; and they expect benefit amounts to vary with the amount of contributions.

Answer

Provisions guaranteeing a return of the worker's own contributions were included in the original Social Security Act of 1935 but were repealed by the amendments of 1939. Under present law benefit amounts are intended to replace, in part, the presumptive earnings loss due to the death, disability or retirement of the worker. Benefit amounts are directly related to a worker's average earnings rather than to the total earnings credited to his account or to the total contributions paid on those earnings.

VIII. THE IDEA THAT PAYMENT OF FULL-RATE BENEFITS TO INSURED PERSONS WHO HAVE CONTRIBUTED ONLY A SHORT PERIOD OF TIME IS INAPPROPRIATE

Explanation

Ever since monthly benefits first became payable in 1940, it has been possible for persons already close to retirement age when covered under the program to draw full benefits related to average earnings rather than partial benefits reflecting the small amount they had contributed. The requirements for eligibility for benefits were that the person had to have worked for roughly half the time elapsing after 1936 (the starting point for coverage) and before the year of the person's attainment of age 65. The average wage was computed over this elapsed period.

The 1950 amendments provided a "new start" for determining benefit eligibility. Under these amendments, the starting year was moved up to 1951. Workers who had been covered during half as many quarters as the number that elapsed after 1950 and before attainment of age 65 (but with a minimum of at least 6 quarters) were made eligible. Moreover, quarters of coverage earned at any time after 1936 could be counted in meeting the eligibility requirement. As a result, many people became eligible for benefits during the years 1951-54 after having contributed for only 18 months, and people are still being added to the beneficiary rolls after having contributed only a few years. In contrast, a person retiring at age 65 in June 1950 needed 6.5 years of coverage to receive any benefits and 13 years of coverage to receive full-rate benefits.

Because it was decided that full-rate or approximately full-rate benefits ought to be payable in the early years of the program to persons with only short periods of covered employment, the law provides for basing benefits on average wages rather than on total wages or contributions. The average monthly wage is defined as the total earnings after 1950 (or after attainment of age 22) and before the date of death or entitlement to old-age insurance benefits (but not counting the 5 years of lowest or no earnings) divided by the number of months elapsed during the same period. By this definition, monthly benefits for a person continuously employed for only a few years after 1950 are approximately the same as for a person with the same average monthly wage, as computed under the law, based on continuous employment (and contributions) for a much longer period.

During the years 1951-57, members of Congress and the Department of Health, Education, and Welfare have received numerous letters, principally from persons who had contributed for a number of years, protesting against the payment of full-rate benefits to people who have contributed only a short time. Persons who have criticized the old-age and survivors insurance trust fund as deficient when judged by standards applicable to individually purchased private insurance usually have objected also to this aspect of the program. Typical of this group are Mr. Manion, Mr. Matteson, and Mr. Stokes.

Answer

In the old-age and survivors insurance program, benefits are not intended to be directly and proportionately related to the amount of the worker's contributions. Instead, the benefit provisions were designed so as to relate benefits to the worker's previous earnings and to replace part of the wage loss resulting from retirement or the death of the breadwinner.

Payment of full-rate benefits to persons who have contributed only a short period of time has characterized the old-age and survivors insurance program ever since monthly benefits first became payable in 1940. If the benefits paid in the early years were no larger than the monthly amounts that could be financed by contributions paid by and on behalf of the individual beneficiary, they would be so small as to defeat the purposes of the program. Similar reasons have led private employers in their employee pension plans to grant "prior service credits" to employees near retirement age when the plan was inaugurated, so that such employees may qualify for pension amounts much more nearly adequate than they could be if they were based solely on the individual's service after the pension plan's inauguration.

In extending the coverage of the program to millions of additional workers in 1950, 1951, and 1956 Congress amended the insured status requirements and benefit provisions of the Social Security Act to afford full-rate benefits to the newly covered workers so that they would not be penalized for their late coverage. These changes were made for the same reason that similar liberal insured status requirements and benefit provisions were adopted for older workers in 1939. The new and more liberal provisions were made to apply to all workers, not just the newly covered.

In these early years of the program, a great majority of all insured workers have protection that greatly exceeds in value the contributions they have paid under the program. In no other way could the purposes of the program be accomplished. Payment of full-rate benefits to persons who have contributed only a short time, however, is a relatively temporary feature of the program. After the present transitional period, persons who have not had a substantial period of covered employment will not be able to qualify for benefits at all, and full-rate benefits will be payable only to those who have contributed regularly over most of their working lifetime.

[Sources omitted but can be found at
https://www.ssa.gov/history/reports/58advise4.html]

■■

The Best Response to the Zombie Lies

Most of the various half-truths, misunderstandings, and lies discussed in this chapter were born with Social Security itself. Many were articulated in 1936, as part of the presidential campaign. In summarizing that campaign, a Time magazine article of November 9, 1936, reporting on the just concluded election, articulated the Social Security message of the Republican Party:[29]

> Said Republicans: Wage earners, you will pay and pay in taxes...and when you are very old, you will have an I.O.U. which the U.S. Government will make good if it is still solvent.

Three days before the election, on Saturday, October 31, 1936, President Roosevelt addressed a packed crowd at Madison Square Garden, in a speech broadcast nationwide on radio. He responded to all the various charges against Social Security, including the argument that the reserves were simply IOUs and the benefits might never be paid. Eloquent and penetrating as he was, his words remain relevant today:[30]

****

Franklin D. Roosevelt
Speech at Madison Square Garden
October 31, 1936

Senator Wagner, Governor Lehman, ladies and gentlemen:

....

More than four years ago, in accepting the Democratic nomination in Chicago, I said: "Give me your help not to win votes alone, but to win in this crusade to restore America to its own people."

The banners of that crusade still fly in the van of a Nation that is on the march.

It is needless to repeat the details of the program which this Administration has been hammering out on the anvils of experience. No amount of misrepresentation or statistical contortion can conceal or blur or smear that record....

We have not come this far without a struggle and I assure you we cannot go further without a struggle.

....

We had to struggle with the old enemies of peace—business and financial monopoly, speculation, reckless banking, class antagonism, sectionalism, war profiteering.

They had begun to consider the Government of the United States as a mere appendage to their own affairs. We know now that Government by organized money is just as dangerous as Government by organized mob.

Never before in all our history have these forces been so united against one candidate as they stand today. They are unanimous in their hate for me—and I welcome their hatred.

I should like to have it said of my first Administration that in it the forces of selfishness and of lust for power met their match. I should like to have it said of my second Administration that in it these forces met their master.

The American people know from a four-year record that today there is only one entrance to the White House—by the front door. Since March 4, 1933, there has been only one pass-key to the White House. I have carried that key in my pocket. It is there tonight. So long as I am President, it will remain in my pocket.

Those who used to have pass-keys are not happy. Some of them are desperate. ...

They tell the worker his wage will be reduced by a contribution to some vague form of old-age insurance. They carefully conceal from him the fact that for every dollar of premium he pays for that insurance, the employer pays another dollar. That omission is deceit. They carefully conceal from him the fact that under the federal law, he receives another insurance policy to help him if he loses his job, and that the premium of that policy is paid 100 percent by the employer and not one cent by the worker. They do not tell him that the insurance policy that is bought for him is far more favorable to him than any policy that any private insurance company could afford to issue. That omission is deceit.

They imply to him that he pays all the cost of both forms of insurance. They carefully conceal from him the fact that for every dollar put up by him his employer puts up three dollars three for one. And that omission is deceit.

But they are guilty of more than deceit. When they imply that the reserves thus created against both these policies will be stolen by some future Congress, diverted to some wholly foreign purpose, they attack the integrity and honor of American Government itself. Those who suggest that, are already aliens to the spirit of American democracy.

Let them emigrate and try their lot under some foreign flag in which they have more confidence.

■■■

Despite the opponents' efforts to conceal the truth, Social Security today is, as it always has been, self-financing, with its own dedicated revenue streams. It does not add a penny to the federal debt and deficit.

From the beginning, continuing through today and the foreseeable future, the primary revenue for Social Security has been and remains the contributions of workers, matched dollar-for-dollar by their employers. That revenue is supplemented by investment earnings on the excess contributions, held in reserve until needed. In addition, a third source of dedicated revenue from the inclusion of a portion of Social Security benefits in taxable income for income tax purposes was added in 1983, with the strong support of three Social Security founders involved in the process: Robert M. Ball, Wilbur Cohen, and Robert J. Myers.

The founders' vision for Social Security guides the program's proponents today. Those founders, pragmatists as they were, understood that their full vision would have to be met incrementally. The structure they laid down as a cornerstone and the sound principles underlying it have guided Social Security's expansions over its more-than-eighty-year history. The next chapter explains that slow incremental growth to both the benefits and financing of Social Security. As explained in the next chapter, those principles can, and should, guide us as we further build upon that sound and sturdy structure.

CHAPTER FOUR: BUILDING ON SOCIAL SECURITY'S STRONG, STABLE, TIMELESS FOUNDATION

The founders, as chapter one illuminates, envisioned their goal as much more far-reaching than we have even come close to achieving. At the same time, they were pragmatists and understood, as chapter two details, that their vision could only be achieved incrementally. They recognized that Social Security was an enormous new enterprise, and they wanted it to succeed. They also understood that there was only so much the political world would accept in one bite.

In his message to Congress, on January 17, 1935, transmitting the proposed legislation, President Roosevelt cautioned:[1]

> It is overwhelmingly important to avoid any danger of permanently discrediting the sound and necessary policy of Federal legislation for economic security by attempting to apply it on too ambitious a scale before actual experience has provided guidance for the permanently safe direction of such efforts. The place of such a fundamental in our future civilization is too precious to be jeopardized now by extravagant action.

Reminding us of that incremental approach, President Roosevelt, when signing the Social Security Act of 1935 into law, explained, "This law…represents a cornerstone in a structure which is being built but is by no means complete."[2]

Similarly, Frances Perkins analogized Social Security to a growing child, when she spoke at the 25th anniversary celebration of the signing of the Social Security Act, at the Department of Health, Education, and Welfare, on August 15, 1960:[3]

> "I think…that as we stand here, and as we sit here and think about this precious child we want to see it grow. It has grown enormously in these years, it has improved, its administration has grown bigger and bigger as the imagination of those in charge have pointed out what could be done, but there is yet much that needs to be done and that I hope in God's good time will be done by bipartisan action as were the last amendments."

Consistent with that incremental approach, Social Security has been amended numerous times since its enactment. Just four years after its enactment, the Social Security Act Amendments of 1939 expanded Social Security's protections to include survivors' or life insurance. In addition, Social Security's retirement annuities were expanded to include joint and survivor annuities for married couples.

However, just two years after the enactment of the 1939 amendments, Japan bombed Pearl Harbor. The nation turned rapidly to war, and further expansions halted. Still, Roosevelt never lost sight of the need to expand our social security. In his 1943 State of the Union Address, at the height of the war effort, Roosevelt talked about not just what Americans were fighting against but what the nation was fighting for. He included in that vision, "assurance against the evils of all major economic hazards—assurance that will extend from the cradle to the grave. And this great Government can and must provide this assurance."[4]

In his 1945 State of the Union Address, he talked extensively about the war effort. He also talked about his vision for the post-war period. He repeated his commitment to move forward toward the achievement of greater social security:[5]

****

Franklin Delano Roosevelt
State of the Union Message to Congress
January 6, 1945

In considering the State of the Union, the war and the peace that is to follow are naturally uppermost in the minds of all of us.

This war must be waged—it is being waged—with the greatest and most persistent intensity....

...

An enduring peace cannot be achieved without a strong America-strong in the social and economic sense as well as in the military sense.

In the State of the Union message last year I set forth what I considered to be an American economic bill of rights under which a new basis of security and prosperity can be established for all—regardless of station, race, or creed.

....

An expanded social security program, and adequate health and education programs, must play essential roles in a program designed to support individual productivity and mass purchasing power. I shall communicate further with the Congress on these subjects at a later date.

■■

That later date never came. Three months and six days later, Roosevelt died. His further communication with Congress was not to be. But his vision and that of the other founders remained a guiding light.

Consistent with the founders' intent for steady, incremental expansion, Social Security was increased once World War II was over and Congress was once again in Democratic control. Democrats controlled Congress during World War II, but were focused on the war effort and did not expand Social Security. Democrats lost control in the 1946 election. Roosevelt's vice president and successor, Harry S. Truman, ran against what he labeled the "Do-Nothing-Congress" and was elected in a surprise victory. In that same election, Congress was returned to Democratic control.

Throughout his seven and a half years as president, Truman pushed hard for expansions of Social Security, particularly the one piece jettisoned in 1935 – universal, national health insurance. Though he was unable to enact national health insurance, he did succeed in securing the enactment of the Social Security Act Amendments of 1950. Those built on Social Security's promising incremental start that had stalled as a result of World War II and Republican control of Congress thereafter.

The 1950 legislation increased benefit levels and expanded coverage. Social Security was further expanded in 1952, and then approximately every other year after that, during the presidency of Dwight Eisenhower and beyond. In 1956, long-term disability insurance was added. In 1965, Medicare, as a step toward universal national health insurance, was added. Along with additional areas of protection, coverage was expanded and benefit levels were increased to keep pace with inflation and growing standards of living.

But much work remains. Short-term disability insurance, including paid sick leave and parental leave, has not been added yet, despite the sweeping vision of the original architects. Nor has Medicare been expanded to include everyone. And benefit levels remain modest.

It is common to hear today that Social Security has changed in ways that the founders never intended, indeed in ways they wouldn't even recognize, ways that go far beyond their goals. And that proposals to expand Social Security are inconsistent with what they intended.

None of these assertions are grounded in fact. The expansions of Social Security, enacted over the last eight decades, though incremental in nature, are completely consistent with the founders' vision. They fit perfectly on the basic structure laid out by the founders and described in chapters two and three.

In describing the incremental growth of Social Security, this chapter seeks to set the record straight about much of today's conventional "wisdom" that is just plain wrong.

The Envisioned Size and Role of Social Security's Benefits

Take today's misunderstanding about the intended size and role of Social Security. The metaphor of a three-legged stool for the nation's patchwork of retirement income programs is used routinely today. The three legs are generally today described as Social Security, employer-sponsored pensions, and savings. Along with the reference to the metaphor is the comment, often expressed, that the architects "never intended" Social Security to be a worker's only source of retirement income.

Even supporters and supposedly objective reporters assert that Social Security was intended to be part of a three-legged stool, supplemented by employer-sponsored pensions and savings. A Money columnist and reporter for USA Today, for example, has written, without any evidence, "Social Security was never intended to be a pension you could live on. Instead, it was designed to be a supplement to retirees' income."[6]

In fact, the history belies this widespread belief. The founders designed Social Security to require employers to match, dollar-for-dollar, their employees' Social Security premiums. There is no evidence whatsoever that the founders expected employers to do more. There is no evidence that Roosevelt and his colleagues intentionally designed Social Security simply to be part of what is needed, with the expectation that individual employers would make up the difference through their own individual plans. Not only does the legislative history of the Social Security Act of 1935 offer no evidence for that widespread belief, there is substantial legislative history that indicates the exact opposite was true.

At the time Social Security was enacted, private pensions were rare and unreliable. They were voluntary arrangements, set up to satisfy employer goals. Like today, employers were free to terminate them at will. The arrangements were unregulated and often were unfunded.

They generally contained broad disclaimers regarding the employer's legal obligations to pay the promised benefits. By the early 1920s, a number of courts had upheld the validity of these disclaimers. Many court decisions permitted employers to arbitrarily retract the pension promise, finding that the pension was merely a gift and therefore the promise could be broken without penalty. In addition, these employer plans generally imposed onerous requirements and restrictions on receipt of benefits, such as working continuously for the same employer for at least twenty years and not leaving before retirement.

For all these reasons, activists in the American old-age security movement were hostile to employer-sponsored pensions, viewing them simply as employer devices to control workers and believing them to be inherently insecure. The Great Depression compounded that insecurity. Between 1929 and 1932, almost 10 percent of all existing pension plans were discontinued, closed to new employees, or suspended. Those that remained were in shaky financial shape.

The Committee on Economic Security shared the activists' skeptical view of private pensions. The shortcomings of private pensions were articulated at length in a CES report, which was released in 1937:[7]

****

Committee on Economic Security
Social Security In America
(Published by the Social Security Board, 1937)
(Drawn from unpublished staff reports)

Part II

OLD-AGE SECURITY

Chapter VIII

PROVISIONS FOR THE AGED IN THE UNITED STATES
....
The half century of experience with voluntary pension plans has shown that they have been inefficient and inadequate as sound social insurance measures. The proportion of all employees in the field affected has been small, never rising above 15 percent; nor are there

very good grounds for supposing that the field is capable of any material expansion....

Even within the field which these voluntary pension systems embrace, the terms of the plans are restricted so that relatively few employees qualify for pensions.....
....
Moreover, these voluntary plans contain many elements of discrimination....And, as has already been pointed out, there are many elements of insecurity, inadequate financing, and lack of sound legal basis in pension systems even at the present time.

Apart from these inadequacies in the plans themselves, industrial retirement systems have entailed certain unfortunate social consequences. A concomitant of these plans is a hiring-age limit which forbids the employment of persons over 45 to 55 years old. ...Moreover, the provisions of pension plans which attempt to tie employees to a particular firm are undesirable even though their actual effectiveness is open to question. Insofar as they have been effective in this direction, however, they are not desirable.

Generally speaking, industrial pension systems viewed as a managerial device to limit superannuation among the personnel, clear channels of promotion, and add to the relative attractiveness of the employment of a particular firm, and, in general, improve personnel efficiency can be helpful and successful, although for various reasons they have frequently not had such results. Viewed as a means of providing security to industrial workers in old age, because of their limited application and restrictive provisions requiring long and continuous service for a single employer, they are wholly inadequate. Nor do they give promise of substantially adequate protection in the future. Social insurance with a far broader coverage and without these restrictions is essential to old-age security...

While the creators of Social Security recognized that employers might, for their own reasons, continue to provide some workers with private pensions, these arrangements were not seen as part of a widespread, serious solution to old age insecurity.

The attitude of Social Security's architects toward employer-sponsored pensions, which ranged from indifference to outright hostility, is apparent in the legislative history of a major amendment, one that came close to defeating Social Security. The amendment would have made no sense, if the system described by the metaphorical three-legged stool was indeed the system envisioned by the founders.

The amendment would have allowed employers to opt out of Social Security if they provided equivalent private pensions to their employees. Not larger benefits, but simply equivalent benefits. It was developed by Walter Forster, a partner in the well-known insurance brokerage firm, Towers, Perrin, Forster and Crosby, and championed by Senator Bennett Champ Clark (D-MO), a member of the Senate Finance Committee.

This was not some minor amendment. It came very close to being enacted into law, despite the strong opposition of the Roosevelt administration. The Clark amendment was defeated on a tie vote in committee, with several members absent and not voting – members who later voted for the amendment when it came to the Senate Floor. Debate over the Clark amendment on the Senate Floor lasted two days. Lobbying on both sides was fierce. In this Democratically-controlled Senate, the Clark amendment passed by a vote of 51 to 35.

The day after the Senate passed the Social Security Act, both chambers appointed conferees to reconcile the House and Senate versions. After a month of wrangling over differences, the conference committee had resolved every disagreement but one, the Clark amendment.

In mid-July, the conferees, unable to reach agreement on this one remaining point, requested instructions from their respective bodies. On July 17, both the Senate and the House instructed their conferees to hold firm. The House of Representatives stated emphatically that it would never pass a bill with the Clark amendment; the Senate made clear it would not enact the bill without it.

Time was running out on Social Security, at least for this session. Congress was within weeks of adjournment, and the conferees were deadlocked, apparently irreconcilably. The House conferees kept raising problems with the drafting of the Clark amendment. They were pointing out problem after problem, different ways the language could permit inadequate or sham retirement plans to qualify for exemption, and the Senate conferees were scrambling to come up with answers. Finally, the conferees assigned three staffers the job of redrafting the Clark amendment to make it work.

The three worked around the clock, as hard as they could. As they became more and more immersed in the details, they became more and more bogged down. After two weeks of excruciatingly long and frustrating hours of work, the three reported back that it would take many months more of intense effort—well beyond the end of the congressional session—to work out all the difficulties.

At that point, a compromise was reached. The Senate conferees agreed to report the bill without the Clark amendment in exchange for the appointment of a special joint committee to develop a more workable proposal that would meet the concerns of both sides. The understanding was that, if a workable proposal could be drafted, it would be taken up in the next session.

With that agreement in place, the conference report was agreed to and the Social Security Act of 1935 passed both chambers and was sent to the President. Congress adjourned shortly thereafter.

In early 1936, the Senate Finance Committee appointed a subcommittee to revise and report out a workable Clark amendment. In addition, the Finance Committee met a few times with the Ways and Means Committee, but the issue went no further.

Thomas H. Eliot had been Counsel for the Committee on Economic Security, the 1934 interagency task force that developed the Social Security legislation, and then became General Counsel for the Social Security Board (predecessor of the Social Security Administration). He was one of the three individuals tasked, during the conference, with developing a workable proposal. In a first-hand account of the enactment of Social Security, in a 1961 speech, here is what he said about the Clark amendment:[8]

****

Thomas H. Eliot
Address Before a General Staff Meeting at Social Security
Administration Headquarters, Baltimore Maryland
February 3, 1961

THE LEGAL BACKGROUND OF THE
SOCIAL SECURITY ACT

....

CLARK AMENDMENT ADDED IN SENATE

The [Social Security] bill then went to the Senate. Again there was very little opposition to it, except on one point. This is the one time when Administration really had to fight to round up votes. And it lost that fight at first....[A] company of about four men...had devised various kinds of retirement pension plans and made their living by going around selling these to employers and installing the plans. They were expert advisors as to how to have a private insurance plan. This group was headed by a great friend of my father's, a big, tall fellow named Forster from Philadelphia, and he was a wonderful lobbyist. His intent was to exempt from the old-age provisions any employer and his employees having a reputable retirement plan in operation.

This threw a panic into the insurance-minded people who had helped to devise the original old-age insurance program in the bill. This, they pointed out, would destroy its actuarial soundness. It would exempt many of the so-called best risks from the plan and would throw all their calculations out of kilter. Another thing that did worry a good many people was the possibility that companies could get out of the old-age insurance requirements and, at the same time, have a "phony" retirement plan. Too often during those weeks we were brought into contact with people who gave us the evidence that they, as employees, had been covered by a voluntary retirement plan which promised them a retirement pension when they reached 65 in the companies which employed them and who had been fired a week before their 65th birthday so that the company didn't have to pay them any benefit after all. How were you going to prevent this, even if you wanted to do what Mr. Forster and Senator Bennett Clark of Missouri wanted to do? How were you going to prevent the fly-by-night plan from destroying the old-age insurance system? How would you avoid exempting large numbers of employees who weren't really making adequate provision for their employees?

That was the question. And the big battle in the Senate was over the so-called Clark Amendment to exempt private pension plans.

The Clark Amendment did not adequately safeguard the interests of the employees or of the Government. It did not close the door to the "phony" plans. It did, as it was intended to do, permit the reputable plan to work outside of the old-age insurance system and to exempt the people that were covered by the reputable plan; but it also permitted disreputable plans to exist. It was a very hard thing, purely from a technical standpoint, to draft something to close all the loopholes and to distinguish between the valid and "phony" plans. It was a battle! The President got indirectly involved. Three of us, the President's legislative liaison man, Charlie West, a former congressman; Tom Corcoran, whom I mentioned earlier, a man working on legislation; and myself, each were assigned four senators. Forster was lobbying like fury. He told my father later that he spent $50,000 in entertaining members of Congress. He wasn't fighting. He was educating them. He had materials—perfectly legitimate stuff—to explain how the various plans would be hurt if the old-age insurance system didn't exempt them. This was an entirely legitimate operation and I greatly respected him and his ability, but we certainly fought on the other side. Tom took four senators, I took four senators, and Charlie West from the White House took four senators. The outcome was, I think, the measure of our skill as lobbyists. Charlie West got nobody. All of his senators voted wrong. They all voted for the Clark Amendment. I got two and lost two. Corcoran got all his four. But the Senate, in spite of all our efforts, adopted the Clark Amendment. It had a very great appeal. Why do you want to destroy these good pension plans? We lost in a close vote. The bill then went to conference.

CONFERENCE COMMITTEE ACTION

There were a good many differences, and these were battled over for a month. Eventually all differences were settled except whether or not the Clark Amendment should be included in the bill. Here the President did bring pressure on the House leadership which was much more amenable to his leadership and influence than was the Senate. The House was solidly against the Clark Amendment and indicated that it would never vote for the bill if the Clark Amendment was in it. The Senate was equally obdurate in insisting that the Clark Amendment stay in the bill. Eventually Harrison's assistant, Leonard Calhoun, a counsel from St. Louis brought in by Senator Clark, a very able fellow named Bill Woodward, and I were designated by the conference committee to see if we could redraft the Clark Amendment to close all the conceivable loopholes so that only the really reputable private pension plan could be exempted from the national scheme. We spent 2 weeks of very hard work. We could not close the loopholes. This was going to be an exceedingly difficult job. We had to learn absolutely everything about the possibilities in this old-age pension retirement plan system kind of thing, and we just couldn't do it in the short time that had been given us. We finally signed a report to that effect and agreed to continue to meet if the Senate wanted us to and to have a new version of the Clark Amendment ready sometime the following winter or spring. With that understanding, the Senate dropped its insistence on the Clark Amendment. The conferees agreed, and on August 14 the bill was passed and signed by the President.

CLARK AMENDMENT DROPPED

Now an interesting little-addition to that issue is what happened the next winter. I was by then General Counsel and Leonard Calhoun was one of my assistants. He talked to me about this. I called up Senator King, who was Acting Chairman of the Finance Committee, and said, "Look, you were one of the people who was most active for the Clark Amendment, and you remember that Leonard and I and Bill Woodward pledged ourselves to do our best to write a new Clark Amendment. When do you want it? It's getting on into March now, and Congress isn't going to sit forever. When do you want the amendment? We haven't heard from you." He laughed and he said, "Oh! Mr. Forster was in the other day. You can forget the amendment. Mr. Forster said he'd made a terrible mistake. He thought that the passage of the old-age insurance bill would ruin his business of selling private pension plans. Instead the passage of the Social Security Act has got everybody thinking about pension plans. He doesn't want any Clark Amendment. You can forget it forever." So that's why there isn't an exemption for private pension plans in the present social security law.

· ·

The Clark amendment would have made no sense, if Social Security was intended simply to be part of a three-legged stool, along with private pensions. Indeed, during the long debate over the Clark amendment, the administration and its allies offered numerous arguments in opposition but never that Social Security was simply supposed to be a foundation on which private pensions would build.

Patchwork Retirement Income System is an Historical Accident

Today's patchwork retirement income system, described metaphorically with the image of a three-legged stool, is in many ways an historical accident – certainly not a carefully considered, rational policy response to the quest for secure, adequate, universal retirement income for the nation's workers.

Other than the Clark amendment, private-sector employer-sponsored pension plans were not a focus of discussion in the debate over Social Security. Nor were they in 1939, just four years after the enactment of Social Security, when Congress expanded Social Security to add life insurance, convert the retirement life annuities into joint and survivor annuities, and substantially increase the benefits of those then close to retirement age. After the enactment of Social Security and its expansion in 1939, though, several events spurred the growth of private pensions.

Shortly after this propitious start of incremental Social Security growth, the United States entered World War II. During the war, no further expansions of Social Security were enacted. Moreover, because Congress failed to raise Social Security benefit levels even to keep pace with inflation, Social Security benefits eroded in value substantially during this period. Not only was about half the workforce not covered by Social Security – another item subjected to revisionist history, as discussed below – the benefits became less and less adequate for those who were covered.

At the same time, several events conspired to boost the numbers of employees covered under private-sector, employer-sponsored private pensions. One was the desire to escape income taxes.

Roosevelt was the first president to make serious use of the income tax in peacetime. The Revenue Act of 1935 – colloquially called the Soak-the-Rich Tax – taxed the wealthy at high rates, including a rate of 75 percent on incomes over $5 million. Even with the Revenue Act of 1935, only five percent of Americans were required to pay income tax, but that five percent was not happy. They didn't like the tax, and they didn't like the New Deal programs the tax was financing.

Some of the wealthiest businessmen in America, according to a Time magazine retrospective on the twentieth century, spent the Roosevelt years "in their clubs denouncing 'that man in the White House,' 'that traitor to his class.'"[9] They also spent time looking for ways to avoid the "Soak-the-Rich" Tax.

Although Congress enacted a federal income tax in 1913, after the ratification of the Sixteenth Amendment, only the very wealthiest were subject to it, and, even then, the effective rates were modest. It was in that context that the tax treatment of private pension plans had developed. The treatment developed incrementally as issues arose, in accordance with general tax principles, and was set by the 1920s.

Despite the effort to simply be fair, the treatment was identical to the so-called preferential tax treatment today enjoyed only by those plans that qualify by complying with extensive statutory and regulatory requirements under the Internal Revenue Code. The tax treatment is considered preferential because it is more favorable than that accorded current cash compensation. It is important to understand that it is extremely difficult, and perhaps impossible, to devise a fair and administratively feasible method of taxing these arrangements in a neutral manner. The tax treatment can provide tax savings or a penalty.

The early decisions to err on the side of favorable tax treatment were of little consequence when the decisions were made, because so few plans existed and because so few taxpayers were subject to federal income tax. However, with the enactment of the "Soak-the-Rich" Tax in 1935, the incentive to discover ways to avoid taxation was created.

Starting around 1937, enterprising insurance agents recognized the favorable tax treatment and began to market pension plans aggressively. The National Underwriter Company, for example, published in its weekly newsletter dated April 23, 1937, a piece entitled "Pension Trusts are Termed Richest Field Yet Untapped."[10]

Plans that benefited only the owners, designed to escape income taxes, started coming to life. The Roosevelt administration noticed. The pension scheme was just one of a variety of tax-avoidance schemes that the government identified. Another was the incorporation of yachts and country estates in order to take advantage of provisions allowing for depreciation and deduction of expenses meant to be for legitimate businesses.

To stop these and other tax-avoidance schemes, Roosevelt called on Congress to act against what he described as "efforts at avoidance and evasion of tax liability so widespread and so amazing both in their boldness and their ingenuity, that further action without delay seems imperative."[11] Although some of the schemes were addressed in 1937, it took Congress until 1942 to prohibit the discrimination of pension plans in favor of officers, shareholders, supervisors and the highly paid. That enactment meant that employers who wanted to avoid taxes by establishing pension plans now had to cover more of their employees.

In addition to the change in the tax law, requiring employers to provide pensions for more than just those at the top in order to obtain the favorable tax treatment, another event in 1942 caused the growth of private pensions. The cost of living, which had gone up 15 percent since 1939, was projected to increase at least 23 percent more in 1942 alone. In response to the raging inflation, the federal government imposed controls on prices and wages.

But, deferred wages were exempt from the controls. Private pensions became a convenient vehicle to escape the government controls and compete for labor at a time when it was very scarce, made tight by the demands of the war. The combination of wage controls, high corporate tax rates, high individual income taxes, the excess profits tax, and the tight labor market propelled employers to create and expand private pension plans. In 1940, employer contributions to private pension plans were $180 million. By 1945, the money contributed annually had risen to $830 million.

In 1946, the first election following the end of World War II, the Republican Party gained control of Congress. Labeled the "Do Nothing Congress" by President Truman, the Republican-controlled Congress failed to raise Social Security benefit levels.

In that same year, 1946, the United Steelworkers of America went out on strike against Inland Steel. A key demand was for pensions. Partly in response, the National Labor Relations Board in 1948 ruled that it had jurisdiction over labor disputes regarding pensions, under the National Labor Relations Act's reference to "conditions of employment."

At the time the three-legged stool metaphor was coined, the Social Security system covered only about half the workforce and benefits continued to erode in value. Private pensions had become an attractive mechanism to avoid taxes. Workers had become used to receiving private pensions as substitutes for current compensation, and unions aggressively bargained for them.

These were the conditions under which the three-legged stool metaphor was born. In 1949, an executive with the Metropolitan Life Insurance Company used the three-legged stool metaphor in a speech, and it caught on. The executive, of course, had a professional stake in selling private sector annuities that supplemented Social Security.

As a simple description of circumstances at that time, the metaphor was accurate. Social Security benefits had not been increased for a decade, and there was no guarantee that Congress would act in the near future. The minimal Social Security benefits would have to be supplemented to have any hope of beneficiaries receiving adequate retirement income.

But it is unquestionably revisionist history to say that the metaphor reflects the intent of the founders that Social Security should provide benefits that are minimal and require supplementation. Indeed, a minority report, signed onto by all the

Republicans on the House of Representatives' Ways and Means Committee, opposed what would become the Social Security Act Amendments of 1950, a major expansion of Social Security. In expressing their opposition, the Republicans expressed their belief that Social Security benefit levels should be kept low, in need of supplementation, to provide workers with adequate retirement income. The clear inference is that the majority disagreed:[12]

> **In our opinion**, the purpose of compulsory social insurance is to provide a basic floor of economic protection for the individual and his family and in so doing to encourage and stimulate voluntary savings through personal initiative and ambition. It should not invade the field historically belonging to the individual. [Emphasis added.]

It is instructive to recognize that the laws and policies regarding Social Security and private retirement arrangements have developed compartmentalized from each other. Congress has traditionally considered Social Security and private pension legislation in separate legislative vehicles, generally in different years, and usually without reference to the impact of the changes on other parts of the retirement income system. Congressional and administrative jurisdiction is divided: Different congressional subcommittees have jurisdiction over private pensions and Social Security, and four different agencies of the federal government have administrative responsibilities for major parts of the retirement income system.[13]

The idea that Social Security provides merely a foundation is empirically true today, as it was in 1949, when the three-legged stool metaphor was coined. Social Security's benefits then and now are inadequate. The idea that the intent of the founders was to provide benefits that are inadequate without supplementation, though, is not supported by history. In fact, the exact opposite may be the better reading of that history.

Founders Proceeded Carefully to Ensure Success

While Social Security's benefits have never been adequate, the size of the benefits is easily explained by Roosevelt's commitment to proceeding cautiously and incrementally. As he said, enactment and a solid start was "too precious to be jeopardized now by extravagant action."[14]

Another part of the legislative history reinforces this inference. The administration's proposal included a provision that would have authorized the government to sell annuities. Edwin Witte, executive director of the Committee on Economic Security, the interagency task force that developed the legislation, explained during congressional hearings, "The primary purpose of the plan is to offer persons not included within the compulsory system a systematic and safe method of providing for their old age."[15]

The provision was dropped in Committee. There is no indication that the Roosevelt administration felt strongly about the provision or made efforts to convince the majority Democratic Congress to keep it. Indeed, the plan, all along, was to eventually include everyone under Social Security. That ultimate goal made the need for voluntary annuities for those who remained uncovered of less concern. Presumably, if the system being developed were understood as part of a three-legged stool, the administration would have fought harder for this additional source of economically-priced retirement income protection.

As a related matter, some opponents of Social Security claim that today's modest benefits are much more lavish than the original legislation called for or than the founders intended. This too is incorrect. The late Robert J. Myers, a lifelong Republican, remains the longest serving chief actuary of Social Security in the history of the program. In 1934, he was a young actuary on the staff of the Roosevelt task force that developed the Social Security Act. More recently, in 1983, he was executive director of the bipartisan commission that was chaired by Alan Greenspan and developed the recommendations that were largely enacted as the Social Security Amendments of 1983. He remained involved in Social Security matters until his death in 2010.

Myers had both the knowledge and the expertise to know the truth. In his landmark, exhaustive treatise, Myers explains:[16]

> At times, people assert that the [Social Security] benefit level has been overexpanded over the years. They tend to believe this because they consider only the dollar figures involved....What is significant, for proper analysis, is the

relative levels, because both the value of the dollar and general wage levels have changed so drastically over the years.

Properly analyzed, Myers's conclusion is likely to shock most people:

The level of [Social Security benefits payable to retired workers, once fully phased in] under the original 1935 law is actually significantly higher than under present law.

It is instructive to note that, as a result of the Social Security Amendments of 1983, benefit levels have been cut, and continue to be cut, as the changes continue to phase in.[17]

In 1939, benefits for those near retirement were increased. Ultimate benefits were lowered in order that the overall cost remained fixed, but, not surprisingly, the focus of debate and discussion was on increasing the benefits for those close to retirement, as well as adding family benefits.

Roosevelt was a visionary, committed to as much economic security as possible, yet he was also a pragmatist, aware of the risks of "extravagant action." That, together with the ongoing Great Depression and the efforts to restore the economy to health, may explain why the architects did not propose higher benefits at the start, revisionist history about a supposed "three-legged stool," notwithstanding.

Incremental Approach to Universality

The goal of ensuring success by proceeding carefully and incrementally also explains the original limitation in coverage, revisionist history notwithstanding. Social Security, as enacted, was limited to wage and salaried workers employed in industry and commerce.

That meant that 56.1 percent, a bit more than half of the workforce, was covered initially. Excluded from coverage were, among many other groups, domestic and agricultural workers, who were disproportionately African American. It is widely claimed today that the initial limited coverage of Social Security was done for racist reasons.

Obviously, the nation was much more overtly racist in the 1930s than today, but there is no evidence that racism had any effect on Social Security's coverage or any other aspect of the program. Indeed, there is extensive and powerful evidence that there was no racial bias.

Roosevelt and the other architects make clear in many statements, speeches, and memoranda that they intended that Social Security be universal, covering every worker in the country on a mandatory basis. This was and is important to the functioning of the program, because Social Security is based on the insurance principle of risk that is widely pooled.

At the same time, as pragmatists, the founders wanted to make sure that the vast new undertaking would be successful. This was, after all, 1935 – a time before smartphones, computers, copiers, and so many other devices that we today take for granted. Moreover, the United States had never before in its history taken on a job that would reach so many workers. There was understandable concern about the capacity of the government to undertake such a technically complicated, administratively difficult, and far-reaching job.

The decision to exclude those categories of workers, along with a number of other categories, originated within the Roosevelt administration. In the context of the times, the Roosevelt administration was extremely progressive on racial issues, and is widely recognized for its efforts to advance the cause of racial equality and justice. As just one example, the administration issued an executive order banning racial discrimination in federal hiring – an action that has been described as the most important affirmative action in the cause of civil rights taken by a president after Reconstruction, prior to the enactment of the Civil Rights Act of 1964.

The executive director of the Committee on Economic Security, Edwin Witte, who many have called the father of the Social Security Act, has described how the task force wrestled with the issue of coverage:[18]

****

Edwin Witte
The Development of the Social Security Act
(Madison, WI: University of Wisconsin Press, 1962)

The staff of the Committee on Economic Security recommended that the old age insurance taxes and benefits be limited to industrial workers, excluding persons engaged in agriculture and domestic service. The Committee on Economic Security struck out this limitation and recommended that the old age insurance system be made applicable to all employed persons. This change was made largely at the insistence of Mr. Hopkins, but was favored also by Secretary Perkins.

Subordinate officials in the Treasury, particularly those in charge of internal revenue collections, objected to such inclusive coverage on the score that it would prove administratively impossible to collect payroll taxes from agricultural workers and domestic servants. They persuaded Secretary Morgenthau that the bill must be amended to exclude these groups of workers, to make it administratively feasible. Secretary Morgenthau presented this view in his testimony before the Ways and Means Committee. … In the executive sessions of the Ways and Means Committee, the recommendations of Secretary Morgenthau were adopted, practically without dissent.

■■

As Witte reports, the limitation on coverage was raised by Secretary Morgenthau out of concern about administrability of the large new undertaking. The following is the transcript of that testimony:[19]

****

Hearings on the Economic Security Act
Before the House Ways and Means Committee
February 5, 1935

Secretary MORGENTHAU. Before taking up the next paragraph, which is entitled "Administrative Simplification", I would like to say that from here on, I am presenting the Treasury's own attitude toward the collection of this tax; that is, this is the attitude of the Bureau of Internal Revenue on whom the burden of collecting these taxes will fall. As I say, this is purely the Treasury's statement. Up to this point, those of us who have worked on this bill are in complete accord. But I wish to point out that from here on the matter discussed is one which has been brought to my attention by the Bureau of Internal Revenue. I feel it is my duty to point that out to the committee, and I want to emphasize once again that this is purely the Treasury's attitude.

....

Mr. COOPER. By that, Mr. Secretary, we are to understand that the Economic Security Committee is in agreement and submits jointly all of the statement which you have read up to this point?

Secretary MORGENTHAU. Up to this point, yes.

....

Mr. TREADWAY. From the point where you are now about to read, your Department is not in agreement with the bill as submitted to us? Is that what you mean, Mr. Secretary?

Secretary MORGENTHAU. I would not put it that way. I simply feel that this is a matter the responsibility for the carrying out of which will fall on the Bureau of Internal Revenue. They raised the point as to whether they can enforce this, and I, as Secretary of the Treasury, feel that I should bring it to the attention of this committee.

Mr. TREADWAY. I assume that you concur with the Bureau of Internal Revenue on this point?

Secretary MORGENTHAU. Oh, yes.

....

Secretary MORGENTHAU. I want to make it clear that Miss Perkins and I are in complete accord, but this particular matter is purely one of administration.

The CHAIRMAN. Please proceed.

Secretary MORGENTHAU.

ADMINISTRATIVE SIMPLIFICATION

This committee is well acquainted with the Treasury's attitude on law enforcement. If there is a law on the statute books to be enforced by the Treasury, we insist on enforcing it to the utmost of our powers. But in one respect the bill in its present form imposes a burden upon the Treasury that it cannot guarantee adequately to meet. The national contributory old-age annuity system, as now proposed, includes every employee in the United States, other than those of governmental agencies or railways, who earns less than $251 a month. This means that every transient or casual laborer is included, that every domestic servant is covered, and that the large and shifting class of agricultural workers is covered. Now, even without the inclusion of these three classes of workers, the task of the Treasury in administering the contributory tax collections would be extremely formidable. If these three classes of workers are to be included, however, the task may well prove insuperable—certainly, at the outset. I want to point out here that personally I hope these three classes can be included. I am simply pointing out the administrative difficulty of collecting the tax from those classes.

Mr. REED. Mr. Secretary your views with regard to the difficulty of collecting this tax coincide with the experience of Great Britain insofar as the domestic-service class is concerned over there.

Secretary MORGENTHAU. I am sorry, Mr. Congressman, that I am not familiar with the experiences of Great Britain. I am simply pointing out what I feel is a difficulty. Perhaps we can work out some way of overcoming that difficulty.

Mr. REED. The British Government had that difficulty, exactly along the lines you mention, and those people were eliminated from the provisions of their security act.

…

The CHAIRMAN. In other words, you are presenting a very serious difficulty which you have thus far not been able to find a way of overcoming?

Secretary MORGENTHAU. Up to now. But I am asking the Bureau of Internal Revenue to try their best to find some way whereby this tax can be collected. As soon as they find a way, I shall ask them to bring it to this committee's attention. Under the income-tax law, the Bureau of Internal Revenue last year handled something less than 5 million returns; with the present nearly universal coverage of the bill's provisions with respect to contributory old-age annuities, we estimate that some 20 million returns would be received. In addition, there would be required the sale of stamps to be used in connection with hundreds of thousands of odd payments for casual work, often for only a few hours' duration. **We recognize, without question, the need of these classes of workers for the same protection that is offered other employed workers under the bill.** But we should like to ask the committee to consider the question whether it is wise to jeopardize the entire contributory system, as well as, possibly, to impair tax-collecting efforts in other fields, by the inclusion under the system of the necessity for far-flung, minutely detailed, and very expensive enforcement efforts. In view of the great importance of our objective, we should greatly regret the imposition of administrative burdens in the bill that would threaten the continued operation of the entire system. **After the system has been in operation for some years, more inclusive coverage may prove to be entirely practicable; but we should like to see the system launched in such fashion that its administrative as well as its financial provisions contribute directly to the assurance of its success.** [Emphasis added.]

….

Mr. KNUTSON. Mr. Secretary, you are making some recommendations of changes in the bill that we have before us?

Secretary MORGENTHAU. Yes, sir.

Mr. KNUTSON. It was my understanding that the bill we have before us, H. R. 4120, was the product of the Economic Security Committee appointed by the President.

Secretary MORGENTHAU. That is right.

Mr. KNUTSON. When were these changes agreed upon, Mr. Secretary?

Secretary MORGENTHAU. Mr. Knutson, the fact that the changes have been made as late as this is purely my own fault. Unfortunately, I had so many administrative duties to perform. I worked for 3 months on the $4,800,000,000 bill that was recently before the Congress. I took part in the preparation of the Budget. So it is my fault that I did not get to this earlier. I simply felt that I had better be late and be right.

Mr. KNUTSON. We have put in 2 weeks of hearings on H. R. 4120. I am just wondering whether the changes that you have proposed this morning would necessitate continued hearings, perhaps for as long a time as we have been in session on this bill.

Secretary MORGENTHAU. Of course, that is up to the committee, as to whether they want to have further hearings on the bill.

Mr. VINSON. May I suggest to the gentleman from Minnesota that several of these suggestions that have been made this morning were mentioned during the course of the hearings. For instance, the exclusion of the agricultural workers, domestics, and the casual workers from the compulsory contributory plan was discussed freely, as I recall it. Dr. Witte made the statement that the exclusion of those from the contributory system could be had without any added burden to the fund or to the system.

Mr. KNUTSON. That is true.

The CHAIRMAN. If Mr. Knutson will yield.

Mr. KNUTSON. Of course.

The CHAIRMAN. The Chair would like to suggest that unless someone should request to be heard in opposition to the proposed changes, further hearings will not be necessary on those proposed changes. Should any one request that they be heard in opposition to those changes that might change the situation.

....

Mr. MCCORMACK. Mr. Secretary, referring to the casuals, and the domestics, and I assume those engaged in agricultural pursuits, they are the ones you have in mind in connection with your expression of doubt conveyed to the committee of the feasibility of practical administration of the provisions of the bill as applied to them, is that right?

Secretary MORGENTHAU. Yes, sir.

Mr. MCCORMACK. How many are involved in number?

Secretary MORGENTHAU. I am told an approximate estimate would be about 7,000,000, all told.

Mr. MCCORMACK. And the bill in its present form embraces about how many?

Secretary MORGENTHAU. Mr. Haas says about 20,000,000.

Mr. MCCORMACK. Twenty million?

Secretary MORGENTHAU. The bill would affect about 20,000,000.

Mr. MCCORMACK. That is, under the unemployment features?

Secretary MORGENTHAU. That is the old-age provision.

Mr. MCCORMACK. Is there any estimate as to how many of those 20,000,000 will be affected by the old-age provisions?

Secretary MORGENTHAU. Now you are getting a little beyond my depth, Mr. McCormack. If you do not mind, I will ask Mr. Altmeyer to answer those questions.

Mr. ALTMEYER. There are about 7,000,000 who are over 65 at the present time. As the years go by, that number will increase. In about 30 or 40 years you will find it will run up to about fifteen or twenty million. Those figures are contained in the supplement of the committee report, which I shall be glad to file with the committee.

Mr. MCCORMACK. That is based on the tables of mortality?

Mr. ALTMEYER. Yes, sir.

Mr. MCCORMACK. Why should they be excluded from the benefits of old-age assistance?

Secretary MORGENTHAU. Who, Mr. McCormack?

Mr. VINSON. May I suggest to the gentleman from Massachusetts that they are not excluded.

Mr. MCCORMACK. Is it proposed by you that they should be?

Mr. VINSON. They are merely relieved from the compulsory contributory features not excluded from old-age pensions.

Secretary MORGENTHAU. I tried to make clear, and I am glad to have the opportunity again, that I do not suggest that anybody be excluded. I simply point out that the Bureau of Internal Revenue feels that a plan has not yet been devised which will make it practical to collect this tax. We just came out of one of the most difficult eras of selling liquor, have been struggling with that for about 13 months. We are beginning to see daylight now, and getting the public to realize that it is a question of buying tax-paid or non-tax-paid liquor. The American public got itself into a frame of mind where they just did not think they had to obey the Federal laws. What I am afraid of is that if we make it so difficult to collect this tax that we may again build up a large population or group who will get themselves into that same sort of frame of mind. I feel that it is up to us to find a way to collect, that tax, and the Internal Revenue Bureau should do that. But we have not been smart enough yet to do it. I want to make it very clear that we are not recommending that any group should be excluded.

Mr. VINSON. May I suggest that the testimony before the committee, Mr. Secretary, has shown that the moneys that would be paid in by this group in taxes, under the contributory plan, would buy very small annuities. You would take the benefits that would accrue, and, of course, there is no suggestion here that this group would be excluded from the noncontributory features, or what we generally call the old-age pension plan.

Mr. MCCORMACK. I recognize the force of the argument that there are administrative difficulties, but that is taking an attitude of defeatism, it seems to me. If we do not get them in the bill, then you are going to have a lot of difficulty in the future getting them into the bill. If we are going to do anything, we might as well embrace them now, and if necessary suspend payments from them for a year or two until you have devised a method of obtaining those payments in a practical way. That would be my thought on the matter.

Secretary MORGENTHAU. I would say that that would be ideal.

The CHAIRMAN. If there are no further questions, we thank you for your appearance and the testimony you have given the committee, Mr. Secretary.

• •

Secretary Perkins, who was testifying with Secretary Morgenthau, was taken by surprise and felt shocked and dismayed. Here is how she, in her memoir, *The Roosevelt I Knew*, described what happened:[20]

****

Frances Perkins
The Roosevelt I Knew
(NY: Viking Press, 1946)

Once the social security bill was introduced in the Congress it was our duty to see that the congressional committee hearings were prepared with sufficiently clear and varied testimony. The members of Congress must have a true opportunity to study the bill and to support it intelligently. It is interesting to note that the public educational work in the year and a half preceding the introduction of this bill had been sufficient to insure wide backing from the constituents of the congressmen.

At the first hearing before the House Ways and Means Committee we were startled to have Secretary Morgenthau make an appearance with a carefully prepared formal memorandum in which he apologized to his fellow members of the Committee on Economic Security. He said that the Treasury had decided, and he had concurred, that it would be unwise to give universal coverage under this act. He argued that it would be a difficult problem to collect payments from scattered farm and domestic workers, often one to a household or farm, and from the large numbers of employees working in establishments with only a few employees. He begged to recommend that farm laborers, domestic servants, and establishments employing less than ten people be omitted from the coverage of the act.

This was a blow. The matter had been discussed in the Committee on Economic Security, and universal coverage had been agreed upon almost from the outset. One could concede that it would be difficult for the Treasury to collect these taxes. But the whole administration of the act was going to be difficult.

The Ways and Means Committee members, impressed by the size of the project and the amount of money involved, nodded their heads to Secretary Morgenthau's proposal of limitation. There was nothing for me to do but accept, temporarily at least, though I continued to recommend universal coverage as the best and safest way for the United States.

■■

The exclusions were supported by a number of witnesses in hearings before both the House Ways and Means Committee and the Senate Finance Committee. Notably, Abe Epstein, the progressive founder of the American Association for Old Age Security (changed to the American Association for Social Security in 1933), who had dedicated his professional life to improving old age security, testified against including agricultural and domestic workers, initially. In testimony before the House Ways and Means Committee, he argued:[21]

****

Hearings on the Economic Security Act
Before the House Ways and Means Committee

Statement of Abraham Epstein, Executive Secretary
American Association For Social Security, New York City

…I have spent about 20 years in this movement for social security. I have been probably the most active person in promoting legislation of this kind and have done, probably, most of the writing on the subject in this country. So that I feel that I come to you with at least considerable experience and considerable knowledge of the whole subject.

….

First of all, I should like to begin my statement, gentlemen, by saying that the entire program as presented by the President is the most outstanding and courageous program that has ever been attempted in the history of the world—not only in this country.

No man, not even Bismarck or Lloyd George, ever dared to present as comprehensive, as thorough-going, as vital a program in its all-embracing aspects as is included in the President's message. It is the most courageous, the most daring proposal that has ever been made, and all of us, of course, are greatly indebted and feel that this has been the greatest contribution in this line in American history.

I do want to caution you, however, that even if the entire program that is presented here is adopted this year, this country will still be from 25 to 30 years behind European countries in the adoption of social-security legislation. In other words, daring as the program is from a political point of view, courageous as it is from a social point of view, in actual practice, even if we adopted it entirely, we will still be almost a generation behind other progressive nations. That is to say, this program is not a revolutionary program. It is not a program that has not been tried or experimented with. It is a program that we know pretty much everything about. We know of its benefits, we know its workings, and there is sufficient evidence to warrant our going ahead.

Now I come down to the bill, and I should like to analyze at least the outstanding provisions in the bill and state some of our own reactions to it.

....

...There is one thing I want to call your attention to, and that is this; and it is a very important thing: It is that the present provision in the act concerning contributory pensions takes in everybody in this country; small employers, farmers, and everybody else.

This may sound strange, coming from me; that is, it may sound strange that I should be trying to restrict the pension system in this country. Yet I think it is logical that it should come from me, because I am interested, gentlemen, in seeing that we have a decent system of old-age security in this country. I am interested, perhaps, more than anyone else. I do not want to have Congress do something that will come back and plague us a year from now and may antagonize the country 2 years from now so that another Congress will come in and repudiate the whole business.

I would rather start mildly and softly, but soundly. Give us, first, this pension of $15 a month. Do not rush us to $25, and when that money is wasted, have another Congress come along and rip the whole system out. Start modestly. You will have time enough to make increases a year from now.

Do not try to collect now from the farmers. Do not try to collect from the domestic servants. You cannot collect money from farmers. You cannot collect money from domestic servants. If you try to do that, you are going to have to spend more money in administering the act than you will ever collect. And when that leaks out they will come to me and say, "You are a hell of an advocate of social insurance. Look what you did; you made a mess of it." I am standing here before you, and I appeal to you, do not, for God's sake, ruin this legislation by overdoing it at first, and undertaking things that you cannot possibly do.

You cannot make collections from farmers at this time. You cannot collect contributions from domestic servants. You cannot collect contributions from push-cart peddlers and small-store proprietors. It will cost you twice as much to collect as the amount of money that you will collect.

So, for God's sake, start mildly, start modestly. Let me tell you that no other country on earth—not only the big countries like ours, but other countries that are not spread out as ours are—no other country dared to try to include the agricultural workers and the domestic servants at first. And if that is so, why should you, with such an immense country like ours, with such a problem of administration to tackle, why should we undertake all these things and then fail in the administration of them so that it will all come back to us to plague us for the next generation.

I do not want to see that done. Include those employers from whom you can collect. You can collect from an employer of three or more people. That will not cost so much. But you cannot collect from farmers, you cannot collect from domestic servants. You cannot possibly do it.

Frankly, I do not want the farmers to come in here and fight us. We will have enough of a fight with the manufacturers' association. Why take on the farmers at the same time?

We have had enough of a fight for the last 20 years. Good Lord, I know what that fight means. Why give us all of this extra trouble by including the farmers in addition? After this has been tried, after it has been experimented with, and the farmers see what great benefit it is to everybody, the farmers then may want to come in. We will see. When they do, we will say "Amen", and we will welcome them with open arms and say, "Yes; please come in. We will be happy to have you."

But do not let us undertake too much now. Do not let us undertake a fight that will defeat us. Do not try to take a bite that will choke us in trying to swallow it. We just cannot do it.
….
…Do not overload yourselves. Do not try to tax the people too much by making this a 3-percent tax on old-age and another tax on unemployment insurance. We will also want health insurance. If you do that, you are going to arouse the American people, on account of the tremendous amount of the tax.

For God's sake do not let us do these things too suddenly. We can kill ourselves by a sudden jolt. Let us do these things gradually. One percent for the next 5 years will be sufficient and will provide us sufficient money for our purposes. We may begin to run into a deficit in 1960 or 1965 or 1970, and we will make up the deficit. But let us not run headlong into a stone wall and crack our heads. Let us go slowly and keep before us the purpose of laying a solid foundation on which we can build in the future. We must not run like an insane person into a stone wall and crack our heads.

■■■

In case there is doubt that Epstein was simply indifferent to the needs of agricultural and domestic workers or, worse, racist himself, he said in testimony before the Senate Finance Committee:[22]

I want to say again when I say that the farmer should not be included or the domestic servant should not be, I hope I will not be understood to mean that I do not believe that the farmer does not need this or the domestic servant. They need to have it as much and even more so than the industrial workers, but there is the problem of administration. You are not going to collect it. We have no administrative machinery. The administrative machinery on a program like this is a terrifically difficult thing. I do not want to see this country saddled with an administrative problem which will become a fizzle and therefore react ultimately against the whole plan.

The House Ways and Means Committee followed the Morgenthau recommendation limiting coverage, and the provision remained unchanged all the way to final passage. In addition to excluding agricultural and domestic workers, other categories of workers were excluded, many predominantly white, including self-employed doctors and lawyers, as well as employees of state, local and federal governments and of nonprofit employers.

Part of the historical confusion about this arises because the jointly-administered federal-state means-tested welfare programs enacted as part of the Social Security Act of 1935 were unquestionably tainted by deep racism. On that, the historical record is clear.

Arthur Altmeyer was the first Social Security Commissioner and was more influential than anyone else during the first twenty years of the development of Social Security. In 1934, he was Assistant Secretary of Labor. On behalf of Secretary of Labor Frances Perkins, the Chair of the Committee on Economic Security, Altmeyer served as liaison to the Committee's Executive Director, Edwin Witte, and his staff.

In Altmeyer's landmark book, *The Formative Years of Social Security*, he gives a first-hand, inside account of the enactment and implementation of Social Security. Title I of the Social Security Act established the joint federal-state means-tested old age assistance program. (That program is the predecessor of today's means-tested SSI program.) What we today think of as Social Security was contained in Title II.

In his insider account, Altmeyer highlights the concerns Southern senators had with Title I, the means-tested, joint federal-state piece of the legislation. Altmeyer reports:[23]

> Most of the questioning had to do with old age security, particularly old age assistance. Senator Byrd of Virginia focused his questioning on the requirement to be met by states, in order to receive federal grants for old age assistance, that a state plan must furnish assistance at least great enough to provide, when added to the income of the aged recipient, "a reasonable subsistence compatible with decency and health."
>
> Dr. Witte pointed out that this provision was taken from the Massachusetts and New York laws and constituted a flexible standard related to varying circumstances throughout the country. However, Senator Byrd forced Dr. Witte to admit that in the final analysis this requirement meant that a federal official had the right to determine what constituted reasonable subsistence compatible with decency and health. The result was that the committee eliminated this clause from the bill.

In Witte's own insider account, *The Development of the Social Security Act*, the executive director is even more explicit about the racist nature of the changes to Title I, Grants to States for Old-Age Assistance, the means-tested state-federal welfare program:[24]

> Title I of the original bill was very bitterly attacked, particularly by Senator Byrd, on the score that it vested in a federal department the power to dictate to the states to whom pensions [i.e. old age assistance] should be paid and how much. In this position, Senator Byrd was supported by nearly all of the southern members of both committees, it being very evident that at least some southern senators feared that this measure might serve as an entering wedge for federal interference with the handling of the Negro question in the South. The southern members did not want to give authority to anyone in Washington to deny aid to any state because it

discriminated against Negroes in the administration of old age assistance.

There is no question that racist politicians were extremely concerned about the federal-state means-tested programs, as they continued to be after enactment. State administration included racist, discriminatory, demeaning implementation, particularly of the Social Security Act's Aid to Dependent Children. But that has never been the case with respect to the federal-sponsored contributory Social Security insurance.

Altmeyer and Witte were very clear about the racist concerns surrounding Title I, and the political compromise it necessitated. As Witte explained:[25]

> It was my position in the prolonged questioning which I underwent from Senator Byrd that there was no intention of federal dictation. The fact is that it had never occurred to any person connected with the Committee on Economic Security that the Negro question would come up in this connection. After the first days of the committee hearings, however it was apparent that the bill would not be passed as it stood and that it would be necessary to tone down all clauses relating to supervisory control by the federal government.

Witte then proceeded to discuss four specific changes in the legislation as the result of the racist concerns of the southern senators. It does not make sense that he or Altmeyer, in their candid accounts, would be so explicit about the racist motivations behind these changes but hide some racist motivation behind limiting the original coverage of Title II (what we now call Social Security) if racism indeed played a role in the exclusion.

As further evidence that the initial exclusion of agricultural and domestic workers was motivated solely by administrative concerns, not racist ones, it is instructive to read both the House Ways and Means Committee and the Senate Finance Committee testimony of Charles H. Houston, the former Dean of the Howard University Law School and special counsel to the NAACP, on whose behalf he testified. He was more constrained by time before the House, but the thrust of his testimony was the same before both bodies. Not surprisingly, he expressed serious concern in his Senate committee testimony about state administration of Title I, the means-tested old age assistance program:[26]

> [T]he old-age-assistance program does not become operative in any State until the State has first accepted the act and established a State old-age authority and a State old-age plan satisfactory to the Federal administrator. When we look at the States which now have old-age pension laws according to the supplemental report of the President's committee, we note that there is not a single Southern State with such a program. And as practical statesmen you know the difficulties there will be in getting any age-assistance plan through the legislature of any Southern State if Negroes are to benefit from it in any large measure. If the Southern States do pass old-age-assistance laws under such circumstances, it will be more than they have done for Negro education or Negro public health or any of the other public services which benefit the Negro masses.

> Therefore the national association favors a strictly Federal old-age-assistance program either with direct benefits or with Federal grants in aid to the States, and such guaranties against discrimination which will insure that every American citizen shall receive his fair and equal share of the benefits according to his individual need.

He also objected to Title II, the program we today call Social Security. His comments before both the House and Senate reflected the legislation, as introduced, so with domestic, farm, and casual workers included. (Both chambers held hearings basically simultaneously. The House Ways and Means Committee held hearings from January 21, 1935 through February 12, 1935. The Senate Finance Committee hearings ran from January 22, 1935 through February 20, 1935.)

Speaking about the inclusion of these groups, Houston testified that the administrative problems and the structure of Social Security were such that those groups would not, in practice, benefit. Before the House Ways and Means Committee, he explained:[27]

Our understanding is that the old-age assistance is a provision for supplementing income up to a reasonable, decent level. On the other hand, old-age annuity is a substitute for income, because the bill provides that a person who is employed by another is ineligible for old-age annuity.

…

The point that I am making is that in order to qualify for the old-age annuity there is a provision that taxes must be paid on behalf of this person prior to the day when he reaches 60 years.

Now, for the benefit of Negroes, I want to inquire who would be benefited or excluded by that provision?

First, and very serious, Negro share croppers and cash tenants would be excluded. I take it that I do not need to argue to this committee the fact that of the Negro population and of the population of the country generally, your Negro share cropper and your Negro cash farm tenant are just about at the bottom of the economic scale. He is not employed. There is no relation necessarily of master and servant by which he gets wages on which a tax could be levied. Therefore this population is excluded from the entire benefits of the old-age annuity, and that represents approximately, according to the 1930 census, 490,000 Negroes.

Next: Domestic servants are in substance excluded from the act and the benefit of the old-age annuity, because the system of employing domestic servants is so loose that the chances are, from the standpoint of the administration of the act as an excise contributory tax, it would be impossible to make a regulation which would go down far enough to pick up all the miscellaneous wages of your domestic servants who, as you may know, are sometimes employed on the basis of day labor, sometimes employed on the basis of hour labor, and less frequently employed either by the week or by the month.

In addition to that, from the standpoint of present persons unemployed, likewise this old-age annuity does not provide for these and I take it again I do not need to argue to the committee that Negroes have suffered from unemployment more than any other class of the community.

Houston made the same points before the Senate Finance Committee, but had more time to speak. Before that body, he addressed the administrative costs, as well as the likely outcome that many African Americans might pay into Social Security but never receive benefits:[28]

> As to…the old-age annuity plan, this plan differs from the old-age assistance in being a substitute for earnings as distinguished from old-age assistance which is a supplement to earnings.
>
> ….
>
> … Every employee is subject to the tax without any exemptions whatsoever, just so long as he is under 60 years of age on 1937, but he can only qualify for the annuity if he has had the tax paid for him at least 200 different weeks in not less than a period before he attains the age of 65 years. Whom does this provision eliminate? It eliminates all casual workers because in substance it provides a worker must be employed an average of 40 weeks out of the year for 5 years. It eliminates all domestic and agricultural workers because it is almost impossible to standardize their wages sufficient for the tax to be collectible as they work by the hour, by the day, or by the week. And I call your attention to the fact that no person is eligible for old-age annuity unless a tax has been paid on his behalf.
>
> Further, it eliminates the share cropper and the tenant farmer, because from the nature of their relationship to the landlord they do not draw wages….
>
> ….
>
> … No argument is necessary to demonstrate that the overhead of administering and really enforcing pay-roll tax on casual, domestic, and agricultural workers would

practically consume the tax itself. But from the standpoint of annuity benefits what is the situation?

Since the "average monthly wage" is at the basis of computing the annuity, and the "average monthly wage" includes part-time as well as full-time wages it is safe to say that the average monthly wage would be less than $30 per month. Those workers ordinarily would qualify only for the smallest annuity, 15 percent, which would amount $4.50 per month, or $54 per year. It is perfectly obvious that this can be no substitute for a working wage.

....

Now, as to the casual worker—under this bill, where you have no exemptions whatsoever for any employees, the casual worker who loses out with 199 weeks in a 5-year period has contributed his share of the tax for the benefit of the annuity of those who have 200 weeks out of a 5-year period; in other words? you are penalizing your casual worker in order to pay the annuity for the steady worker.

Consequently, Houston urged that, rather than Social Security and a state-federal welfare program, there be substituted a federal program of means-tested assistance for all workers.

Looking back over the last eighty years, Social Security has been particularly important to African Americans, as highlighted in chapter five. At the moment of its birth, though, it was far from clear that it would be. It is revisionist history and a boot-strap argument to attribute knowledge of how important Social Security would be to that segment of the population today and then assert that they were undoubtedly excluded for racist reasons.

Perhaps the most comprehensive, exhaustive refutation of the erroneous accusation that Social Security was born in racism is the following article, written by Larry DeWitt, who served as Historian at the Social Security Administration from February 1995 until his retirement in June 2012:[29]

****

Larry DeWitt
Social Security Bulletin, Vol. 70, No. 4 (2010)

THE DECISION TO EXCLUDE AGRICULTURAL AND DOMESTIC WORKERS FROM THE 1935 SOCIAL SECURITY ACT

The Social Security Act of 1935 excluded from coverage about half the workers in the American economy. Among the excluded groups were agricultural and domestic workers—a large percentage of whom were African Americans. This has led some scholars to conclude that policymakers in 1935 deliberately excluded African Americans from the Social Security system because of prevailing racial biases during that period. This article examines both the logic of this thesis and the available empirical evidence on the origins of the coverage exclusions. The author concludes that the racial-bias thesis is both conceptually flawed and unsupported by the existing empirical evidence. The exclusion of agricultural and domestic workers from the early program was due to considerations of administrative feasibility involving tax-collection procedures. The author finds no evidence of any other policy motive involving racial bias.

....

Introduction

In recent years, some scholars have argued that the U.S. Social Security program—like some other social institutions—is biased against women and African Americans. One major contention along these lines involves the original coverage exclusions of the Social Security Act of 1935.

The 1935 act limited its provisions to workers in commerce and industry (this is what is known as the program's "coverage"). This meant that the new social insurance program applied to about half the jobs in the economy. Among those left out were farm and domestic workers. Contemporary scholars have looked at this provision of the 1935 act, realized that a disproportionate number of African Americans were in these two occupational groups, and concluded that the disproportionate impact is evidence of a racial bias as the motive for this coverage exclusion.

An important key to the argument is the additional assumption that Southern Democrats in Congress were the agents who engineered this restrictive coverage policy. Thus, the full argument is that Southern Democrats in Congress—motivated by racial animus—moved to block African Americans from participation in the new Social Security program and that this was the reason for the provision excluding farm and domestic labor (Gordon 1994; Brown 1999; Lieberman 1995; Williams 2003; Poole 2006).

The Race Explanation

The description of Social Security's restrictive coverage policy has become so epigrammatic that it has passed over from historical narrative to background historical fact; it has been assumed and repeated as a basic datum about the program's origin.

For example, one recent labor-history text summed up the issue of Social Security and race this way:

> The Social Security Act was also racially coded—in part because of the power of Southern Democrats in the New Deal coalition. Southern politicians, reported one architect of the new law, were determined to block any 'entering wedge' for federal interference with the handling of the Negro question. Southern employers worried that federal benefits would discourage black workers from taking low-paying jobs in their fields, factories, and kitchens. Thus neither agricultural laborers nor domestic servants—a pool of workers that included at least 60 percent of the nation's black population—were covered by old-age insurance. (Lichtenstein and others 2000, 429)

One of the strongest early statements of the thesis was given by Robert C. Lieberman (1995, 514–515), who asserted, "The Old Age Insurance provisions of the Social Security Act were founded on racial exclusion. In order to make a national program of old-age benefits palatable to powerful Southern congressional barons, the Roosevelt administration acceded to a Southern amendment excluding agricultural and domestic employees from OAI coverage."

Linda Gordon (1994, 514–515) in her influential study of the welfare state, merged a discussion of the public assistance titles of the 1935 Social Security Act with the contributory social insurance title and offered a misleading critique of both: "Social Security excluded the most needy groups from all its programs, even the inferior ones. These exclusions were deliberate and mainly racially motivated, as Congress was then controlled by wealthy southern Democrats who were determined to block the possibility of a welfare system allowing blacks freedom to reject extremely low-wage and exploitive jobs as agricultural laborers and domestic servants."

Alston and Ferrie (1999, chapter 3), in their book *Southern Paternalism and the American Welfare State*, offered a variation on this account. They argued that class—in the form of racially based landlord/tenant paternalism—played a stronger role than simple race prejudice or other factors, such as federalism, in shaping the programs under the Social Security Act in general and relative to the coverage exclusions in particular.

Probably the best detailed look at the exclusion issue in the academic literature is provided by Lieberman (1998)—*Shifting the Color Line*. Lieberman did not suggest that any members of Congress were the direct agents of the coverage exclusions, although he did imply that the coverage exclusions were some-how engineered by Southern members of Congress. Here, for example, is one way he described the exclusions: "the CES's [Committee on Economic Security] decision that all workers should be covered came under immediate and persistent question at the hearings … In the end, an important step behind congressional acceptance of a national program of old-age insurance was the racial manipulation of the program's target population so that a national program was sure to be a segregated one" (39). At another point he summarized the history this way: "In order to pass national old-age and unemployment insurance plans, the Roosevelt administration had to compromise inclusiveness and accept the exclusion of agricultural and domestic employees from the program, with notably imbalanced racial consequences" (25).

As we will see, these kinds of generalizations overlook the degree to which members of the Roosevelt administration were the principal advocates of the coverage exclusions—the administration did not have to "accept" the exclusions; *it was the source of the idea.*

This thesis has worked its way, unquestioned, into general-interest and survey-history texts. Matters have reached such a state that if a survey-history text makes three or four general observations about Social Security, one of them will often be that African Americans were excluded from participation via the coverage exclusions owing to racist motivations on the part of Southern members of Congress. This thesis thus becomes one of the few "facts" that beginning students of history learn about the Social Security program.

Typical of the treatment the subject receives in some general history books is Gordon and Paterson's *Major Problems in American History 1920–1945.* The authors introduced their selections on Social Security with this summing up:

> Before and after 1935, the New Deal was always dependent upon the votes of conservative Southern Democrats ... but Southerners saw the labor and welfare legislation of 1935 as a clear threat to Southern race relations and economic competitiveness. In many respects, Southern legislators were able to shape federal law (winning both the exemption of agricultural and domestic workers from Social Security and local control over its administration, for example). (1999, 304)

Gordon and Paterson (1999, 304–305) then provided as their underlying source document an excerpt from Edwin Witte's (1962) memoir of the development of the Social Security Act.[1] In this document, according to the authors, "one of the drafters of the Social Security Act explains how both political and administrative considerations led to the exemption of agricultural and domestic workers."

Gareth Davies and Martha Derthick (1997, 217–235) examined some key aspects of the racial-bias thesis and put the decisions made in the 1935 Social Security Act in comparative international perspective; they gave an overview of how the coverage exclusions came about, as well as a differing explanation of how and where racial concerns were in play in the Congress (in the welfare provisions of the 1935 act). The authors argued that race was relevant in shaping the welfare provisions; but they also argued that nonracial factors—such as federalism and state-specific economic considerations—were more significant determinants.

Perhaps the most pertinent contribution of Davies and Derthick was to make clear the distinction between the contributory Social Security program and the various public assistance provisions and to point out that Southern Democrats in the Congress were not the source of the Title II coverage exclusions. Unfortunately, many scholars are still confused about the distinction between the public assistance programs and the contributory social insurance program under the 1935 act.[2]

Understanding the Social Security Act

The Social Security Act of 1935 was an omnibus bill, containing 11 titles authorizing 7 distinct programs, only 1 of which (Title II) was the program we commonly think of as Social Security.[3] These various programs had unique features that make presumed equivalences among them sources of serious error.

The Title II program was a new form of federal social provision in which workers and their employers paid taxes into an insurance fund that would pay the workers retirement benefits in the future, typically after many years of paying into the system (when the worker had attained age 65). Title I was the more familiar state-based welfare program that paid immediate benefits to the needy elderly, using some federal money and some federal policy oversight. Title III was likewise a new program of unemployment benefits administered as state programs, but funded by federal dollars (and governed by federal mandates).

Because Title II was the only exclusively federal program in the 1935 act, all of its policies were federal with no state administration or policy involvement. The Title I and Title III programs, by contrast, were state-administered and partially federally financed, so there was both state and federal policymaking involved, and conflicts over federalism and related issues arose in those programs. For example, initially the Roosevelt administration proposed a federal standard that the welfare payments under Title I should be sufficient to provide "a reasonable subsistence compatible with decency and health." Some Southern legislators found this language potentially threatening to economic and social arrangements in their region. Much of this concern may well have been racially motivated, but this issue had nothing to do with the Title II program, in which such policy constructions had no role.

It is important to make these distinctions because, as it turns out, many of the claims of racial bias in the coverage decisions involve confusion regarding these programs—or if not outright confusion, oblique arguments that political factors known to have influenced one of the other programs could somehow be presumed to have also been active in shaping the Title II program.

For example, in the quotation from the labor-history textbook cited earlier, Lichtenstein and others (2000) were clearly confusing the Title II coverage issue with features of the Title I old-age welfare benefits when they argued that "Southern employers worried that federal benefits would discourage black workers from taking low-paying jobs in their fields, factories, and kitchens. Thus, neither agricultural laborers nor domestic servants—a pool of workers that included at least 60 percent of the nation's black population—were covered by old-age insurance." The worry here was that immediate welfare benefits (under Title I) might be a disincentive to work. But coverage for a potential retirement benefit expected years or decades down the road (Title II) could hardly be a disincentive to present labor—indeed, present labor *is required* in order to build the credits necessary to qualify for a contributory retirement benefit in the future.[4]

Probably the most explicit example of the confusion appears in the Gordon and Paterson quotation previously cited. After making their argument about the central connection between the coverage exclusions and the "Southern concession," the authors provided the source document underlying their analysis. It is an excerpt from the contemporaneous memoir of Edwin Witte (1962), who was the executive director of the cabinet-level Committee on Economic Security (CES) that President Roosevelt appointed to design his legislative proposals. Here are Witte's observations, as reprinted in Gordon and Paterson (1999):

> In the Congressional hearings and in the executive sessions of the Committee on Ways and Means, as well as in the House debate, the major interest was in the old age assistance.... Title I of the original bill was very bitterly attacked, ... it being very evident that at least some Southern senators feared that this measure might serve as an entering wedge for federal interference with the handling of the Negro question in the South. The Southern members did not want to give authority to anyone in Washington to deny aid to any state because it discriminated against Negroes in the administration of old age assistance.[5] (312–313)

The thing to notice about this passage is that it has absolutely nothing to do with the contributory social insurance program under Title II of the 1935 act nor with the decision to exclude agricultural and domestic workers from the program. It is a passage describing congressional interest in the old-age assistance provisions under Title I of the act. Senator Harry Byrd (D-VA) and others objected to features of Title I for the reasons Witte states.

The fact that many authors have mistaken the evidence in Witte as showing something it manifestly does not is especially surprising because Witte discussed the Title II coverage exclusions in his book, in the section "Exemption of Agriculture and Domestic Service." Here is Witte's (1962) explanation of how the coverage decision came about:

> The staff of the Committee on Economic Security recommended that the old age insurance taxes and benefits be limited to industrial workers, excluding persons engaged in agriculture and domestic service. The Committee on Economic Security struck out this limitation and recommended that the old age insurance system be made applicable to all employed persons. This change was made largely at the insistence of Mr. Hopkins, but was favored also by Secretary Perkins.
>
> Subordinate officials in the Treasury, particularly those in charge of internal revenue collections, objected to such inclusive coverage on the score that it would prove administratively impossible to collect payroll taxes from agricultural workers and domestic servants. They persuaded Secretary Morgenthau that the bill must be amended to exclude these groups of workers, to make it administratively feasible. Secretary Morgenthau presented this view in his testimony before the Ways and Means Committee...In the executive sessions of the Ways and Means Committee, the recommendations of Secretary Morgenthau were adopted, practically without dissent. (152–154)

So the historical evidence of record tells a very different story than that associated with a racial motivation behind the Title II coverage exclusions. Before we look at the historical evidence in careful detail, we need to examine the logic underlying the race explanation.

Examining the Race Explanation

First, note that the coverage decision made in 1935 was *not* to exclude farm and domestic workers, which, had that been the factual circumstance, might have lent more credence to a charge of racial bias. Rather, the decision was to include only those workers regularly employed in commerce and industry. Thus, the coverage decision also excluded the following.

- Self-employed individuals (including farm proprietors)
- Persons working in the nonprofit sector
- Professionals such as self-employed doctors, lawyers, and ministers
- Seamen in the merchant marine
- Employees of charitable or educational foundations
- Employees of the American Society for the Prevention of Cruelty to Animals
- Persons aged 65 or older
- Casual laborers
- Members of Congress
- Employees of federal, state, and local governments—everyone from the president of the United States to post office clerks

Indeed, of the 20.1 million gainfully employed workers that the president's Committee on Economic Security estimated were excluded from participation in the Social Security system, at least 15 million were white.[6]

Moreover, African Americans, to the extent that they were members of these other professions, would be excluded from coverage because of their membership. For example, in 1935 African Americans made up about 4 percent of the federal government's workforce in six of the largest agencies and comprised more than 20 percent of the workers in such agencies as the Government Printing Office. All of these workers were excluded from Social Security coverage because of their employment, not because of their race (Rung 2002, 73–74). Other African Americans were likewise excluded for reasons having nothing to do with race. The professional employees of the National Association for the Advancement of Colored People (NAACP), for example, were also excluded from coverage on the grounds that they were employed by a nonprofit institution. Indeed, most of the members of President Roosevelt's informal "black cabinet" were blocked from participating in the Social Security system because they worked in either the federal government or in nonprofit organizations.[7] The point here is that some African Americans were excluded from the program for *occupational reasons* rather than their race. This lends credence to the idea that the other large group of excluded African Americans (those in agricultural and domestic work) might also have been excluded from coverage because of their occupation features rather than racial bias.

It is true that from the 1930 Census (the closest available data point and the main information base available to Social Security policymakers in 1935), we can observe that about 65 percent of gainfully employed African Americans worked in the agricultural or domestic sectors of the economy. This statistic, stated alone, does create an impression that African Americans might have been the target of the coverage exclusions. But there are a couple of other statistics here that are worth noting. See Table 1, for a more comprehensive view of coverage exclusions.

Table 1.
Noncoverage of agricultural and domestic workers, by occupational categories and race

Occupational category	White	Negro [sic]	Other [a]	Total, all races
Agriculture	8,192,181	1,987,839	291,978	10,471,998
Domestic and personal service	3,268,725	1,576,205	197,521	5,042,451
Total workers excluded from coverage	11,460,906	3,564,044	489,499	15,514,449
Percentage of excluded workers	74	23	3	100
Total workers in all occupations	42,584,497	5,503,535	741,888	48,829,920
Excluded workforce as a percentage of total workers	27	65	66	. . .
SOURCE: Census Bureau (1933, Table 12, p. 24).				
NOTE: . . . = not applicable.				
a. Other category includes Mexicans, Indians, Japanese, Filipinos, Hindus, Koreans, Hawaiians, and so forth.				

Although 65 percent of the African American workforce was excluded by this provision, it was also the case that 27 percent of the white workforce was likewise excluded from coverage. Moreover, African Americans were not the most heavily impacted group: 66 percent of "other" races were excluded as well. Of those individuals excluded under the provision, 74 percent were white, and only 23 percent were African American. This hardly constitutes a compelling initial case for the assumption that the provision targeted African Americans.[8]

Moreover, the coverage exclusions had less impact than the gross 1930 Census numbers suggest because the Bureau of Internal Revenue—subsequent to the passage of the law—had to develop regulations to put the generalities of the law into practical language. They had to define, for example, what type of work was and was not considered "agricultural." Ultimately the regulations excluded from agricultural work (and hence *included* for participation in Social Security) jobs in industries such as cotton and rice gins; milk bottling, delivery, and sales; growing, harvesting, processing, and packing gum naval stores; chicken hatcheries; raising animals for fur; and several other agricultural-type occupations. The bureau also defined any job that was not in fact agricultural in nature (such as a mechanic, bookkeeper, carpenter, and so forth) as nonagricultural, even if it was performed entirely on a farm (Schurz, Wyatt, and Wandel 1937, 91–97).[9]

Also, occupational categories are not necessarily life assignments; workers in noncovered occupations could earn coverage by working part time in covered jobs, even if their primary occupation was excluded. The Social Security Board (1945, 14) estimated that around 22 percent of agricultural workers had earned some coverage by the end of 1940; about 25 percent of white domestic workers and 13 percent of black domestic workers had some covered earnings during the first few years of the program.[10]

Finally, if Southerners engineered the coverage exclusion of agricultural and domestic workers out of economic self-interest, we have to question whether or not the coverage exclusions would have been a rational way to proceed. If Social Security coverage was considered to be a positive, the exclusions might have acted as an incentive for workers to leave their agricultural and domestic jobs and seek employment in factory work or in other covered industries. On the other hand—to the extent that future Social Security benefits would be seen as an economic incentive—covering agricultural and domestic workers under Social Security would have served as an incentive to keep them in those jobs. So if racist Southerners were acting out of their economic self-interest here, it would seem more likely that they would have urged coverage of their agricultural and domestic workers, not their exclusion.

The Historical Context of the Coverage Decisions

In order to appreciate the legislative history of the coverage exclusions, the historical context in which the coverage decisions were made should be clarified.

One of the pitfalls here is a tendency to generalize about the South and Southern politicians in ways that are historically inaccurate. Not only was the South not a monolith culturally or politically in the 1930s, neither was the "Southern block" in the U.S. Congress of a single mind or interest. The plantation economy of the Piedmont did not necessarily always have the same economic agendas as the Southern towns whose economies centered around the textile mills. Nor certainly did the planter economy of the Mississippi Delta always have the same political interests as a border state like Delaware.[11] Indeed, work by Howard Reiter (2001, 107–130) has up-ended old assumptions about conservative Southern Democrats. Reiter showed that before the late 1930s in the House and the mid-1940s in the Senate, Southern Democrats were actually more liberal than their Northern counterparts. In his study of congressional reform, Julian Zelizer (2004, 22–29 and chapter 2) supported this same insight, observing that outside of the issues of civil rights and unionization, Southern Democrats were generally supporters of New Deal liberal reforms through 1937.

The size and influence of the Southern block has also been exaggerated. On the Senate Finance Committee, 6 of the 21 members were from Southern states; on the House Ways and Means

Committee, only 4 of the 18 members were from the South. The proportions can be inflated here by only considering the Democrats (as Lieberman (1998) did at one point), or by adding in border state members (as Alston and Ferrie (1999) did). But members cannot be aggregated by state without looking at the details behind the generalization. It matters who the specific members were.

For example, Rep. David Lewis of Maryland (the cosponsor of the bill in the House)[12] would be classified as being from a border state; but he was a liberal former coal miner and union official from western Maryland, in a part of the state that had much more in common with Pennsylvania than with Mississippi. And even Mississippi cannot always be assumed to act like Mississippi. Senate Finance Committee Chairman Senator Pat Harrison's (D-MS) biographer, for example, explicitly rejected the idea that Harrison shared the racial concerns of some Southerners over the bill (Swain 1978, 83).

We should also remember what the voting was on the coverage provision. As Witte (1962) reported, excluding coverage of agricultural and domestic workers was adopted in the House Ways and Means Committee "practically without dissent" and was implicitly adopted unanimously in the Senate Finance Committee (since the Finance Committee never raised the topic). Thus, essentially all the members of both committees—of both parties and all regions of the country—voted in favor of the exclusion, not just Southerners. This suggests the presence of some other motive than Southern racism.

Many scholars also misunderstand the circumstances and attitudes of the historical actors of the 1930s when faced with the novel expansion of the social welfare system represented by contributory social insurance. In fact, many workers and their employers in 1930s America *did not want to be covered* under the Social Security system and would have been relieved to have been in the cohort of the excluded.

Remember that in the 1930s, the Title II program was an unprecedented new form of social provision, in which workers were asked to buy social insurance from the federal government—with employers paying half the cost. Money would be taken out of a worker's paycheck every payday and sent to the federal government, with the promise that some years hence, the government would pay the worker a retirement pension. In other words, the mechanism of the Social Security program involves a form of what economists call "deferred consumption," or what can be described more simply as delayed gratification.

Many workers in Depression-era America were reluctant to take an immediate cut in take-home pay for the promise of a benefit in the distant future. Recall also that the original law of 1935 contemplated payroll-tax withholding beginning in January 1937, but the first monthly retirement benefits were to be paid in 1942. So 1935-era workers not only had to take on faith the idea that they would get a future benefit from the government when they retired, but it was also going to be several years before they could see examples of other people going before them for whom the government had kept its promise.

Indeed, almost all of the disputes, protests, lawsuits, and so forth, involving the program in the early years were efforts by individuals who were in the covered population to *get out* of that population for the reason that they did not want to pay the taxes involved in the new system. Indeed, the three lawsuits that led in 1937 to the U.S. Supreme Court rulings on the constitutionality of the Social Security Act were all lawsuits filed by covered employers seeking to avoid coverage by having the law declared unconstitutional.[13]

During the legislative process, some interest groups lobbied to have their professions *added* to the list of *excluded groups*. Witte (1962, 154–157) detailed, for example, how lobbying by religious organizations led to the exemptions for charitable, educational, and religious institutions. The single most contentious policy debate regarding the Old-Age Insurance program concerned a provision introduced in the Senate excluding from coverage any company with its own private pension plan. This provision, known as the Clark Amendment, was being pushed by insurance interests and, as Witte reported, "a vast amount of lobbying was carried on in connection with this amendment" (105–108). The lobbying and the dispute was so intense that the entire bill was held up in conference for nearly 2 months, while the administration sought some compromise to permit passage of the bill.[14]

There is also some evidence that farm proprietors did not want to be covered under the 1935 law. Witte's (1962) eyewitness report conveyed that proprietors wanted to be excluded to avoid paying the relevant taxes. Also, the American Farm Bureau—the largest lobbying group representing farmers—continuously opposed the coverage of farmers, not only under the 1935 law, but all the way through 1954 when self-employed farmers were finally covered (Altmeyer 1966, 241 and 248). Arthur Altmeyer (the top program administrator during this period) also indicated that farmers wanted to be excluded for similar reasons. He told an interviewer "we were smart enough politically to know there was no chance of covering the farmers to begin with. They had been excluded traditionally from all forms of regulatory legislation, labor legislation, particularly workmen's compensation even to this day. No, they're the last stronghold of individualism, reactionism, independence—whatever you want to call it. I thought when we got them under in 1950 we'd really crossed the mountain."[15] This point was further illustrated by a story that Altmeyer recounted. During consideration of the 1939 amendments, Altmeyer had been urging extending coverage to agricultural workers. He repeatedly lobbied Ways and Means Committee Chairman Robert Doughton (D-SC) on the issue. At one point Doughton turned to Altmeyer in exasperation and said, "Doctor, when the first farmer with manure on his shoes comes to me and asks to be covered, I will be willing to consider it" (Altmeyer 1966, 103).

In other words, the available evidence suggests that Southern agricultural producers wanted their employees excluded from coverage because they did not want to be taxed to support the Social Security system. Indeed, the evidence suggests that they did not want to pay the requisite taxes for any of their workers—white or black—or for themselves, for that matter.

Unfortunately, there is no direct evidence on the attitudes of farm workers regarding their exclusion from coverage. All that can be said with certainty is that coverage under Social Security was not universally perceived as a boon by the workers and employers of the 1930s.

Once the law was passed, one of the major administrative struggles undertaken by the Social Security Board in the early years of the system was the effort to get covered workers and employers to participate—that is, to accept the fact that they were covered. Until the mid-1940s—when benefits were finally flowing in noticeable volume—many workers and employers in all occupational categories tried to avoid coverage. Indeed, the Social Security Board had full-time positions in its field offices called field representatives, and one of their main functions was to go out into the community and find noncompliant workers and employers and convince them that they had to accept the fact that they were covered by the law.

We can gain some insight into the attitudes of domestic workers and their employers by observing what occurred after 1950, when domestic work was brought into coverage.[16] There is quite a bit of evidence of resistance from employees and employers alike. One St. Louis housewife told the *Wall St. Journal*, "I haven't paid the tax so far, and I'm not going to pay it until someone yells."[17] A Pittsburgh woman told the *Journal*, "I've never given it any thought, and I don't suppose my cleaning girl has either; she's never mentioned it."[18] According to the *Journal's* investigation of the issue, "Many domestic servants queried about the new Social Security provisions said they definitely would object to the withholding from their pay. Some simply don't want to lose the 2% in cash wages."[19]

One group of domestic-employing housewives in Marshall, Texas formed a rump resistance to coverage, initiating a lobbying campaign and a federal lawsuit against coverage of their employees—a lawsuit they pursued all the way to the U.S. Supreme Court, but lost in January 1954.[20] Ironically, the housewives' rebellion became a political cause championed by the leading newspaper of the area—the *Houston Post*—whose publisher, Oveta Culp Hobby, would become Eisenhower's secretary of Health,

Education, and Welfare in 1953 and would thus be the federal official charged with responsibility for administering the Social Security Act.

Over the years, domestic workers often tried to avoid coverage, usually by persuading their employers to pay them "under the table" so that there was no record of their earnings. This would mean, of course, that they would not be eligible for benefits in the future.

We saw evidence of this attitude on the part of these lower-paid workers when the issue of coverage for domestic workers broke into public attention in 1993 with the failed nomination of Zoe Baird to be U.S. attorney general. Baird had been paying her domestic help "under the table" for years, at the request of her employee. At the time the Zoe Baird case broke into public view, officials of the Internal Revenue Service estimated that only about 500,000 of the "several million" who employed domestic workers were in fact complying with the coverage requirements of the 1950 law.[21] What these incidents all reveal is that even now, domestic workers resist being covered by Social Security, and it suggests that they would not in fact have agreed in 1935 that the decision to exclude them was adverse.

Contemporary scholars tend to look back on 1935 from their present vantage points, and they see something of value (Social Security coverage) being withheld from African Americans. But this distorts the historical context in which the coverage decisions were actually made. There is good reason to believe that many agricultural and domestic workers in 1935 may not have agreed that something of value was being denied them.

Also, the race critique misrepresents the factual history of the exclusions, how they developed, and what the evidence of record says about the decision to exclude farm and domestic laborers from coverage.

The Legislative History of Coverage Exclusions

The Roosevelt administration's Social Security proposals were developed by an executive branch ad hoc Committee on Economic Security, headed by Secretary of Labor Frances Perkins, which was comprised of five cabinet-level administration officials.[22] The CES was supported by a four-part organization: At the top was the executive director (Professor Edwin Witte of the University of Wisconsin); under Witte was a technical board (headed by Arthur J. Altmeyer), which contained several dozen volunteer staffers on loan from federal agencies; and finally, within the CES, there was a cadre of subject-matter experts who were recruited from academia and related entities. From outside the CES, there was also an advisory council composed of representatives from business, academia, and interest groups. All of these individuals and groups had input in the CES's decisions.

The subject-matter experts within the CES were divided into "working groups" by topical area. The group developing the Social Security proposals (who made the initial program-design decisions) was known as the Old-Age Security Staff and was composed of three experts: Barbara Nachtrieb Armstrong, associate professor of law, University of California; J. Douglas Brown, director of the Industrial Relations Section, Princeton University; and Murray W. Latimer, chairman of the Railroad Retirement Board. Working for these three experts were numerous researchers and assistants who prepared literally dozens of background papers for the staff's consideration.

Thus, any decision on Social Security policy, such as coverage recommendations, went through the following six-step decision process.

1. Staff recommendations were made initially by the Old-Age Security Staff.
2. The advisory council offered its recommendations to the technical board.

3. The Old-Age Security Staff and the advisory council recommendations were subject to a review by Altmeyer and the executive staff of the technical board.
4. The recommendations were then subject to a review by Witte.
5. The CES itself then made the final decision as to its recommendations.
6. President Roosevelt reviewed the CES recommendations and made the final policy decisions that would be in the administration's legislative package.

The Old-Age Security Staff recommended four broad exclusions from coverage: white-collar workers earning more than $50 per week, government employees, railroad workers, and agricultural and domestic workers. The rationale given by Armstrong, Brown, and Latimer for excluding farm and domestic workers were reasons of administrative efficiency.[23] The matter was described in the Social Security Board's (1937) book, *Social Security in America* (which was a summary report of the CES work):

> Administrative difficulties suggested further limitations of coverage to eliminate, at least in the early years of a system, certain types of employments in which it would be difficult to enforce the collection of contributions. In the case of farm labor and domestic servants in private homes, a large number of individual workers are employed in small establishments scattered over a wide area, frequently at some distance from any city or town. The close relationship which exists between employer and employee, the frequent absence of accounting records, and the usual provision of a part of compensation in the form of maintenance would greatly handicap effective enforcement. While the need of these groups for protection in old age was very apparent, it seemed expedient to postpone their inclusion until after administrative experience could develop in less difficult areas of operation. (208)

The recommendation of the advisory council was a slight variation on that of the CES staff. The council suggested four exclusions: white-collar workers earning more than $100 per week, government employees, railroad employees, and agricultural workers. The council's rationale for excluding agricultural workers was the same as that of the CES staff—administrative difficulties.

Altmeyer and Witte supported the recommendations of the CES staff, including the exclusion of agricultural and domestic workers. This was the proposal submitted to the CES. At the CES, both Frances Perkins and Harry Hopkins objected to the exclusion of farm and domestic workers, arguing that the program should be as nearly universal as possible. As a consequence, the final report from the CES to President Roosevelt dropped the exclusion of agricultural and domestic workers and moved toward a higher dollar amount for white-collar workers, as advocated by the advisory council. In the end, the CES's final report contained three recommendations for exclusions: white-collar workers earning more than $250 per month, government employees, and railroad workers.[24]

Alston and Ferrie (1999, 62–66) have added some confusion to accounts of the initial decision making by the CES by reading too much importance into some of the background papers produced by the research staff, who generally wrote more favorably of the possibility of including agricultural workers (although not domestic workers). The authors incorrectly reported that the CES staff recommended universal coverage. In fact, the Old-Age Security Staff, the advisory council, Altmeyer and the technical board, and Witte all made the contrary recommendation.

Alston and Ferrie (1999, 66) also incorrectly stated that the draft administration bill included "a special scheme to cover 'farm owners and tenants, self-employed persons, and other people of small incomes.'" They then argued that when this "special scheme" was dropped during congressional consideration of the bill, this was evidence of a congressional influence on the coverage exclusion of agricultural workers. As Alston and Ferrie put it: "The special Old-Age Insurance program for tenants, croppers, and farm owners was similarly deleted without much ceremony by the committees" (68).

The special scheme referred to was in fact a proposal for a supplemental system of voluntary annuities to be sold in the marketplace by the Treasury Department, as an adjunct to the compulsory old-age insurance pensions. It had two aims, according to Witte's testimony and the CES's final report: (1) to supplement the pensions of those covered by the compulsory system, and (2) to permit those not covered to purchase marketplace annuities to provide for their own retirement security. This was not a proposal to create a "special" coverage rule for agricultural workers. Essentially anyone in America would have been able to purchase the market-based annuities—rich, poor, and middling alike—regardless of their occupations and regardless of whether or not they already were covered under the program.

The quotation Alston and Ferrie (1999) provided—referring to "farm owners and tenants, self-employed persons, and other people of small incomes"—was in fact a comment made by Edwin Witte during his testimony as part of a suggestion that Congress study the possibility of providing subsidies to low-income individuals to help them purchase these voluntary annuities (Economic Security Act 1935a, 46–47).[25] It was not itself a "program" of any kind, and it had nothing to do with providing Social Security coverage to anyone. As it happened, the recommendation was rendered moot since Congress refused to adopt the voluntary annuity scheme. It was not, however, "deleted without much ceremony by the committees." Actually, it was dropped in the House by a unanimous vote within the Ways and Means Committee (as part of a larger political maneuver involving other provisions of the bill), approved by a 7 to 5 vote in the Finance Committee, and finally disposed of in the Senate by a motion proffered on the Senate floor by Senator Augustine Lonergan of Connecticut, on behalf of his state's insurance interests—anxious to keep the federal government out of the annuity business.[26]

After the CES's final report went to the president, he reviewed it with some care, even forcing the CES to rewrite the financing provisions to make the program more clearly self-supporting (Witte 1962, 74).[27] But he accepted the recommendations on coverage. Therefore, the report from the president to the Congress on January 17, 1935, and the associated draft administration bill included coverage for farm and domestic workers and contained only the three other exclusions recommended by the CES.[28] This was in keeping with the final recommendation of the CES, as signed-off on unanimously by all five members, including Secretary of the Treasury Henry Morgenthau, Jr.

Because the president had at the last minute pulled the actuarial tables from the CES document, the proposal went to Congress without benefit of the supporting financials, and Secretary Morgenthau had to appear during the House hearings on the bill to present the revised financing scheme. He did so during testimony on February 5, 1935. At the hearing, Morgenthau presented a set of revised financial estimates and asked the Ways and Means Committee to substitute these actuarial tables for the missing data in the original report. However, he also took the opportunity to do something quite unexpected. During his testimony he complained to the Ways and Means Committee that the idea of virtually universal coverage of all workers in the country would impose an intolerable administrative burden on the Treasury Department (which would have responsibility to collect the taxes at a time well before automatic payroll deductions or computers). He thus suggested to the committee and to a startled Frances Perkins, who was present at the hearing, that coverage be dropped for certain groups of workers who would present tax-collection problems for the Treasury. He specifically recommended dropping "casual laborers," "domestic servants," and "agricultural workers." As Frances Perkins (1946) recalled the event:

> He argued that it would be a difficult problem to collect payments from scattered farm and domestic workers, often one to a household or farm, and from the large numbers of employees working in establishments with only a few employees. He begged to recommend that farm laborers, domestic servants, and establishments employing less than ten people be omitted from the coverage of the act. ... The Ways and Means Committee members, impressed by the size of the project and the amount of money involved, nodded their heads to Secretary Morgenthau's proposal of limitation. There was nothing for me to do but accept. (297–298)

Morgenthau's testimony was quite specific as to his motives and will be considered in some detail here.[29] Morgenthau began by interrupting his own testimony to alert the committee that he was about to make a "personal" statement, representing the views only of the Treasury Department and not the president or the CES. He told the committee that the Bureau of Internal Revenue (which reported to him) had presented him with a report indicating that they had serious concerns about the coverage provisions and he felt duty-bound to support them. Morgenthau told the committee: "I simply feel that this is a matter [of] the responsibility ... which will fall on the Bureau of Internal Revenue. They raised the point as to whether they can enforce this." Congressman Treadway (R-MA) interrupted Morgenthau at this point to clarify Morgenthau's own views as distinct from those of the Bureau of Internal Revenue. He asked Morgenthau, "I assume that you concur with the Bureau of Internal Revenue on this point?" "Oh yes," Morgenthau replied. To make sure, Treadway asked again, "You approve what they are recommending for you to submit to the committee?" "Yes," Morgenthau insisted, "Otherwise I would not read it."[30] Morgenthau then turned to his specific arguments for restrictions on coverage:

> [T]he bill in its present form imposes a burden upon the Treasury that it cannot guarantee adequately to meet. The national contributory old-age annuity system, as now proposed, ... means that every transient or casual laborer is included, that every domestic servant is covered, and that the large and shifting class of agricultural workers is covered. Now, even without the inclusion of these three classes of workers, the task of the Treasury in administering the contributory tax collections would be extremely formidable. If these three classes of workers are to be included, however, the task may prove insuperable—certainly, at the outset.[31]

At the very end of Morgenthau's testimony he made another argument for delaying coverage—an argument that turned out to be prescient. He worried, he told the committee, that difficulties in enforcement would create incentives for these groups to become scofflaws, evading their taxes and thereby undermining the

Treasury's mission. This is precisely what happened in the case of domestic workers.

Alston and Ferrie (1999, 67–69) depicted Morgenthau as only lukewarmly interested in the exclusion of agricultural and domestic workers and as being stampeded to this view by Vinson and other Southerners on the Ways and Means Committee. The authors made a particular point of claiming that "Morgenthau found several other options equally satisfying, including bringing agricultural workers under the bill immediately and dealing later with the peculiar problems their inclusion might pose."

From the extensive quotations offered here, it should be clear that the Alston and Ferrie interpretation is inconsistent with the record. And the specific claim that Morgenthau abandoned the coverage exclusion position in favor of some more "ideal" option is based on a single passing remark, which comes literally as the last sentence in Morgenthau's 15 pages of testimony and as part of a jumbled discussion among Morgenthau, John McCormack (D-MA), Arthur Altmeyer, and Fred Vinson (D-KY).[32] What Morgenthau responded favorably to was a fleeting suggestion that these categories of workers could somehow be covered "in principle" immediately, but not in practice until sometime later when the administrative problems had been solved. It is beyond reasonable doubt that Morgenthau strongly recommended excluding agricultural and domestic workers in the initial years of the Social Security system, on grounds of the administrative difficulties that he believed their inclusion would present the Bureau of Internal Revenue in its tax-collection process under the law.

No Southern member of the Ways and Means Committee spoke out either in favor of or against Morgenthau's proposal during his hearing testimony. In fact, the only member who took a position on either side of the issue was John McCormack (D-MA), who worried and went on to explain, "if we do not get them in the bill, then you are going to have a lot of difficulty in the future getting them into the bill."[33]

Apart from Morgenthau's surprise testimony, the topic of the exclusions was raised on only a handful of other occasions during the hearings. It was first broached by Edwin Witte in a dialog with Fred Vinson. Witte raised the issue of coverage of domestic workers in the context of the administrative difficulties in general and how taxes might be collected. He mentioned the stamp-book system in use in Britain and used domestic workers as an example of a group for whom tax collection was difficult. An exchange followed in which Vinson asked Witte if the issue about potential administrative difficulties applied to agricultural and casual laborers, as well as domestic workers. Witte conceded that it did. The context in which they discussed all three categories, however, mostly involved program costs. Vinson was apparently worried about loss of revenues from excluding these groups, although Witte apparently misunderstood his point, and they talked past each other for most of their dialog. Vinson clearly initiated the topic of excluding these categories of workers, and his colloquy with Witte did occur prior to Morgenthau's appearance before the committee. This was the sole instance in the hearings in which any member of either committee (Southerner or otherwise) discussed the topic. Vinson specifically asked Witte to give the committee assurances that excluding these groups would not have any adverse financial impact. Witte assured him that the financial impact would be minimal, and that was that (Economic Security Act 1935a, 112–113).

In Witte's Senate testimony, he and Finance Committee Chairman Harrison had a brief dialog concerning the exclusion of agricultural workers. Harrison broached the topic, whose comments on the exclusion of agricultural workers consisted of a one-sentence question to Witte asking whether the CES had given any thought to excluding agricultural workers; he then asked Witte a few follow-up questions as to who had represented the agricultural perspective within the CES structure (Economic Security Act 1935b, 219–220). In his testimony before both the House and Senate, Marion Folsom, representing the Advisory Council on Social Security, briefly mentioned its support for the recommendation to exclude agricultural workers (and now domestic workers too) on grounds of administrative difficulty. Folsom's testimony in both committees occurred after Morgenthau's, so the Morgenthau proposals were already on the table, and Folsom stated that the advisory council supported them. In the House, no member of the committee made any comments on Folsom's testimony on the issue.

In the Senate Finance Committee, Folsom also testified on the issue. After a long discussion about the financing of the contributory system and especially about the prospects for a large trust fund reserve—which was in fact the main topic of interest among all parties throughout the hearings when it came to the Social Security program—Folsom volunteered, "I agree that agricultural workers and domestic service should come out. Our advisory council recommended that it [sic] be excluded also. The Cabinet committee plan included them, but we think they should be excluded. Eventually they might be brought in, but right now we would cut them out" (Economic Security Act 1935b, 576–577). Chairman Harrison and Folsom then had a brief dialog on the issue.

> Harrison: "Do I understand you to say that the tax should not be imposed on the employer in agriculture?"
>
> Folsom: "They would not be eligible at all."
>
> Harrison: "How about the fellow when he got to be 65 years of age, who had been engaged in agriculture? Would he have to depend on the pension?"
>
> Folsom: "On the old-age assistance."[34]

Harrison's apparent interest here was in worrying about the loss of benefits to agricultural proprietors and workers if they were not covered by the program—not in keeping African Americans, or anyone else, *out* of the program.

In his testimony before the two committees, J. Douglas Brown repeated the CES Old-Age Security Staff recommendation that agricultural and domestic workers be excluded on grounds of administrative difficulty, and no members engaged him in comment on the point.

U.S. Chamber of Commerce President Henry Harriman, in his testimony before the Senate Finance Committee, also advocated the exclusion of "agricultural workers, domestic servants, and casuals" on grounds of administrative difficulty. Harriman told the committee, "I should think that it would be, as a practical matter, practically impossible to collect the tax on, for instance, the casual worker—the man who comes and works in your garden for a day or two, or he shovels snow. I think the burden of setting up an organization to collect such taxes would be substantially impossible; and I believe that, certainly at the start, it would be very much better to remove those three classes."[35]

The exclusion of farm and domestic labor because of the administrative difficulties involved in tax collection was supported by political activist Abraham Epstein, who generally criticized the Social Security program from the political left, complaining it was not generous and comprehensive enough. Epstein testified before both the House and the Senate committees and made the most sustained argument of anyone in support of excluding farm, domestic, and casual workers on the grounds of administrative difficulty. Epstein was worried that if the new program foundered over administrative glitches, support would be undermined for the liberalizations he wanted to see down the road.[36] During Epstein's House testimony, Rep. Frank Buck (D-CA) asked if he also advocated excluding agricultural workers, at which point Epstein replied that he did. Fred Vinson asked if he was also advocating excluding casual laborers, and Epstein replied that he was. During Epstein's long Senate testimony, no member commented on his recommendations for excluding agricultural and domestic workers.

The only witness in the hearings to speak out against the exclusion provision was NAACP official Charles Houston. Houston pointed out the adverse impact of the provision upon African Americans, as part of an overall critique designed to persuade the Congress to *drop the whole Social Security program entirely*. He wanted a single, universal, federal welfare benefit in lieu of a contributory social insurance system. Houston conceded Morgenthau's point about administrative difficulty, telling the Finance Committee, "No argument is necessary to demonstrate that the overhead of administering and really enforcing a pay roll tax on casual, domestic and agricultural workers would practically consume the tax itself."[37] So Houston was not advocating coverage for domestic and farm workers, but rather rendering the whole issue moot by rejecting the Social Security system *entirely.*

Lieberman (1998, 43) made much of Ways and Means Chairman Robert Doughton's (D-NC) supposed disengagement and lack of comment during the hearings on the bill. He depicted Doughton as sitting silently through much of the witness testimony. Lieberman then suggested that Doughton, and Harrison in the Senate, only displayed an active interest in the specifics of the hearings when topics like the coverage exclusions were raised—suggesting, for Lieberman, a more active involvement on the part of the two chairmen in shaping the issue.

Lieberman's characterization of the two chairmen is problematic. For example, during the House hearings, we can find Doughton carrying on colloquies with witnesses on a variety of subjects, including the qualifications of members of the advisory council; under what conditions dependent parents might be eligible for aid under state welfare programs if their adult children fail to support them; the Townsend Plan; cost estimates for the old-age pensions; the staffing, compensation, and organizational placement of the Public Health Service; the tax rates under Unemployment Insurance; and other topics, as well as defending against Republican criticisms of administration testimony.

In the case of Harrison, Lieberman (1998, 43) cited Witte's Senate testimony as an example of the disengagement he perceived in the hearing testimony. Because this kind of impressionistic argument is subjective, it might be illuminating to perform a simple empirical test. If we count the number of instances of comment by Chairman Harrison during Witte's testimony, we will discover that he commented 180 separate times, of which precisely 12 involved the topic of the exclusion of agricultural workers.[38] This is hardly indicative of an obsessive focus on the exclusion of agricultural workers.

Although I think Lieberman's characterization of the involvement of both chairmen is debatable, his observations overlook the specifics of Doughton as an individual. For one thing, Doughton was already 72 years old by the time of the Social Security hearings, and he was hard of hearing, which may explain some of his "disengagement" during the testimony. Arthur Altmeyer (1966, 100) observed one of his experiences with the testimony before Doughton's committee: "There was no microphone, and the acoustics of the room were such as to make even a shout almost inaudible. Moreover, Robert L. Doughton, the Chairman, was very deaf and disdained the use of a hearing aid. I can never forget how the elderly Chairman would say, 'Speak up, young man, speak up,' although I was shouting at the top of my voice at the time." Morgenthau privately made a similar observation, telling his staff on one occasion that when they presented an excess-profits tax proposal to Doughton, "we will have to shout it four times" (Swain 1978, 228). Also, according to Altmeyer (1966, 30), Doughton was reticent to speak up on subjects on which he was uncertain and would typically let other members take the lead in the questioning during hearings; the administration's economic security bill was very much in this category.

During the House floor debate, Fred Vinson, David Lewis, John McCormack, and Jere Cooper (D-TN) voiced the administrative-difficulty argument in support of the exclusions. When a Republican member challenged McCormack over the idea of excluding domestic workers, Vinson voluntarily responded, "The tax levy in title VIII is upon wages. Taking as a basis the total wage of the domestic servants ... you would not have money in the account sufficient to purchase a substantial annuity. You would have a nuisance feature, such as a person being paid [a] $1 wage and taking out 1 penny and having at the end of the road a small sum that would purchase a very small annuity. The same thing applies to agriculture, and the same thing applies to other occupations."[39] This reinforces the reading of the hearing testimony, which suggests that even Vinson was primarily interested in financing issues, not the racial makeup of the excluded groups.

Daniel Reed (R-NY) voiced the only opposition to the coverage exclusions. Reed was an opponent of the entire 1935 act, and he voted against it as unconstitutional and as "an invasion by the Federal Government." In an effort to have the whole Federal Old-Age Benefits program dropped, he made this argument: "You propose to whip and lash the wage earner into paying this tax, but you are not treating everybody alike. Millions who labor will be exempted from benefits. [Referring to the exclusion of domestic and farm labor] ... why talk about the difficulty of administering the act as a justification to exclude them? You found no difficulty in providing for administration of title I of the act ... but when it comes to certain classes you discriminate. This title ought to be removed from the bill."[40] In other words, it was not fair that the bill failed to whip and lash farm and domestic workers like everyone else, so the whole Social Security program should be dropped on grounds of equity.

In responding to Reed, McCormack explained the rationale for the differential treatment between the Title I and Title II laws:

> Title I is a noncontributory law. Title II is a contributory law. Title I, being noncontributory, every person in need ... without regard to their previous employment, should receive the amount set out, provided and intended by this bill.
>
> When we come to the contributory provision, there is an entirely different situation. The administrative cost enters into the picture. Furthermore, whether or not farm laborers and domestic servants receive a salary so that when they reach the retirement age they will receive an earned annuity about $10 a month [the minimum in the law] is also a matter of consideration. We have also excluded those employed in educational and religious activities and in all kinds of charitable activities. The committee has tried to draft a contributory annuity provision which not only [meets] the purposes desired but [does] so in a manner that can be administered without any great difficulty.[41]

No mention of excluding agricultural and domestic workers occurred during the Senate debate.

So the only real attention given to the issue of the exclusions by any member of Congress, North or South, was from Fred Vinson, the first to mention the administrative difficulties associated with agricultural and casual labor; and Senator Pat Harrison, who fleetingly raised the matter of agricultural workers with Edwin Witte.

Also to clarify what the policy decision really was here— Morgenthau, Epstein, Brown, Folsom, and Harriman were not, as their testimony made clear, urging the *exclusion* of agricultural and domestic workers from the system, but only a *delay in their inclusion*. Indeed, as events transpired, almost all agricultural and domestic workers would be included by 1950 and the remainder by 1954. The real aim of the proponents of the exclusion was not to exclude agricultural and domestic workers, but to include them later. The difference matters. We cannot impute racism to the Social Security program on the assumption that this provision was designed to exclude from coverage African Americans if in fact exclusion was not the purpose. If delay in covering workers in these occupational categories was the purpose, this lends credence to the view that the provision was motivated by administrative practicality and not racism.

Administrative Difficulties Reconsidered

Some scholars have argued that there were no genuine administrative difficulties involved in extending coverage to agricultural and domestic workers in 1935, and thus their exclusion from the 1935 act could not have been on this basis.

Finegold (1988, 209), for example, said of the administrative-difficulties argument, "Opponents of extending contributory social insurance stressed its administrative difficulties, but their arguments should not be taken at face value: they showed little interest in exploring ways to address the practical problems, as had already been done in other countries, and would eventually be done rather easily in the United States."

Lieberman (1998 41–42, 96–98) made much of the idea of a stamp-book system for recording earnings. He noted that Witte mentioned it (albeit in an ambiguous way); that J. Douglas Brown testified at length in favor of it; that there was precedent for it in some European systems (the system in use in Great Britain being specifically touted); and that during consideration of the 1939 amendments, the Social Security Board produced briefing papers suggesting it could be used to overcome the administrative difficulties involved here.[42] Many other scholars mentioned the stamp-book system, counter-example to undermine the administrative-difficulties argument.[43]

Lieberman reported that the stamp-book idea was dropped by the Ways and Means Committee, suggesting again the influence of Southern congressmen.[44] Actually, the stamp-book idea was not dropped by Ways and Means; it remained in the final enacted version of the law, under section 807, as an option left open to the program's administrators. It was the Treasury Department that dropped the idea of a stamp-book system—in 1936, in a letter to the Social Security Board[45]—because that agency was still convinced it was not a practical method of addressing their administrative problems, and it was the judgment of the Treasury Department that was the driver behind the whole sequence of legislative policymaking.

Contrary to Finegold's assumption, the matter of administrative options (and especially the stamp-book scheme) was explored in detail both by the CES and the Social Security Board. And contrary to Lieberman's report, the Social Security Board's internal studies around the time of the 1939 amendments often concluded that the stamp-book scheme was unworkable—despite the board's stated policy objective of extending coverage. One summary study of the issue listed five advantages of the stamp-book system, along with twice as many disadvantages.[46]

But of course a study from 1939 speaks only indirectly to policy decisions made in 1935. The pertinent study on this question was the one prepared by the CES researchers in 1934. Their main report on the issue, *The Case for Payroll Recording as Against the Stamp*

System, was presented to the technical board on October 16, 1934, by CES staffer Merrill G. Murray.[47] Not only did Murray tell the technical board that the stamp-book scheme had insurmountable problems—such as being too complicated; incapable of dealing adequately with part-time employment; less capable of yielding useful program statistics; more difficult to coordinate with other social insurance measures; and more prone to fraud—he also attached a special addendum in which he detailed the fraud and other well-known abuses that afflicted the British stamp-book system. This report by Murray and the internal study by the Treasury staff constituted the available information the CES had and used in making their decisions about the stamp-book system during the 1934–1935 period, no matter what the Social Security Board may have believed in 1939.[48]

Because the idea of a stamp-book system is used so widely to discredit the administrative-difficulties thesis of the coverage exclusions, it might be useful to explore in a little more detail just why the staffs of the Treasury Department and the CES considered it unworkable. Consider just two of the many problems with the stamp-book scheme.

First, under the U.S. system adopted in 1935, employers made their tax payments quarterly, based on the actual wages paid during the preceding quarter. Under a stamp-book system, employers would be required to prepay their taxes by purchasing stamps equal in value to their expected tax burden in the ensuing pay period. Also, under a stamp-book system, purchase of the stamps by the employer is the method of tax payment; this is how the tax-collection problems for Treasury are overcome. Prepayment of taxes is required, and the employer must paste stamps in the workers' stamp books whenever earnings are paid; this is how earnings are certified so that the worker may eventually qualify for a benefit. Employers have to purchase stamps at the beginning of each pay period—weekly, biweekly, monthly, or whatever the pay periods may be for their employees—sufficient to cover the upcoming payroll. Thus, the administrative burdens of tax collection and earnings certification are shifted from the Treasury Department to the nation's employers.

This is something many employers would most likely find highly objectionable.

Second, under the U.S. system, the government goes to the effort and expense to maintain the earnings histories of every covered worker for the duration of their working lives. Then when they retire and file a claim, the workers have no burden to establish their earnings history; they only need to prove that they are of retirement age. Under a stamp-book system, the entire burden shifts either to the worker or the employer, who must maintain and preserve the stamp books until they can be turned over to the Social Security Board. If the stamp books are lost, damaged, or destroyed, the worker has no certified record of earnings to use in establishing entitlement to a benefit. Shifting the burden of proof in this way would almost certainly have created enormous administrative difficulties, not for the government, but for millions of workers and employers. For these and other reasons, the stamp-book scheme was one never likely to be enacted into law.

It should be noted that the administrative challenges were in fact still formidable nearly 20 years later when all agricultural and domestic workers were finally covered by amendments enacted in 1950 and 1954. The top administrator at the time, Robert M. Ball, described extending coverage to agricultural workers as "one of the toughest things that Social Security ever undertook," and he has given a fairly detailed account of some of the administrative difficulties the government faced when coverage became available.[49] Also, it is interesting to note that during the 1950s, the Social Security Administration had to more than double its staff—from 12,000 to 25,000—in order to cope with the challenges of the expansions in coverage.[50]

Conclusions

It was the surprise testimony of Henry Morgenthau, Jr., rather than any initiative by any member of Congress, that was the source of the decision to exclude farm and domestic workers from coverage. It was not presumptively racist Southern politicians who moved to delete coverage for these workers, but northeastern patrician Henry

Morgenthau, Jr., who was trying to avoid an onerous task for the Treasury.[51] Congress was only too happy to oblige Secretary Morgenthau by excluding several million workers and their employers from the burden of paying those taxes.

It is more in keeping with the evidence of record to conclude that the members of Congress (of both parties and all regions) supported these exclusions because they saw an opportunity to lessen the political risks to themselves by not imposing new taxes on their constituents.

It is not as if observers of these events were oblivious to the issue of race as it influenced particular provisions of law. As we saw, Witte recounted how race was a factor in the development of Title I of the 1935 act. Another contemporary observer, Paul Douglas (1936, 100–102), also pointed an accusing finger at Southern Democrats in Congress when it came to the Title I program.[52] Yet neither Witte nor Douglas reported any such influence on the Title II program coverage issue. Nor did other eyewitnesses—such as Arthur Altmeyer, Frances Perkins, or Thomas Eliot—mention any such influence in their memoirs (Eliot 1992).[53]

The actual historical sequence of coverage exclusion follows.

- The Old-Age Security Staff, the Advisory Council on Social Security, Arthur Altmeyer and the technical board, and Edwin Witte all recommended excluding agricultural and/or domestic workers on the grounds of administrative simplicity.
- The CES overruled them and included such workers.
- President Roosevelt supported agricultural and domestic worker coverage.
- Little notice or mention of the issue appeared in the Congress before Henry Morgenthau, Jr., urged the House Ways and Means Committee to adopt the exclusion.
- Little notice or mention of the issue occurred in the Congress after Morgenthau's testimony.

- The exclusion was adopted without any reported debate by Ways and Means, acceded to in the Senate Finance Committee, and adopted in both chambers without real debate and only passing mention.
- At no point did Southern Democrats create the exclusion or push it through Congress.

The overwhelming bulk of the evidence here suggests that it was bureaucratic actors who were the effective parties in shaping and moving this policy. This was preeminently a policy promulgated by the bureaucracy to satisfy its own administrative needs.

The allegations of racial bias in the founding of the Social Security program, based on the coverage exclusions, do not hold up under detailed scrutiny.

[Endnotes and references omitted but can be found at https://www.ssa.gov/policy/docs/ssb/v70n4/v70n4p49.html**]**

■■

It is revealing that in 1950, coverage of Social Security was expanded to include domestic and farm workers. Altogether, the 1950 amendments extended coverage to approximately 10 million additional people from categories excluded in 1935. In addition to domestic and farm workers, they included non-farm self-employed other than doctors, lawyers, engineers, and members of certain other professional groups; federal employees not covered under the Civil Service Retirement System, workers in Puerto Rico and the Virgin Islands, and others. In addition to the automatic, mandatory coverage extended to these groups, state and local governments and non-profits were given the ability to choose to opt into Social Security.

If the exclusion of domestic and farm workers was racially motivated in 1935, it is hard to explain why those forces would not have been equally at play in 1950. It is hard to argue that 1950 was substantially less racist than 1935. Just two years before, in 1948, Southern delegates to the Democratic Convention walked out over civil rights and formed their own breakaway Dixiecrat Party. A much better, more accurate explanation is that the architects decided to work toward universality on an incremental basis in order to allow the best chance of a successful launch.

Incremental Approach to Types of Risks Covered

In addition to adopting an incremental approach to coverage and, arguably, benefit levels, the founders embraced an incremental approach to types of risks covered. Though the Roosevelt administration contemplated proposing universal health care as well as long-term and short-term disability, those expansions did not occur in 1935.

Disability Insurance

As the 1935 legislation was being developed, disability was certainly understood as an economic risk for which social insurance could provide protection. The papers of the Committee on Economic Security, the interagency task force that developed the legislation, includes "Memorandum Concerning The Interests of the Physically Handicapped As Affected By Social Insurance Proposals, Particularly Old-Age Pensions with an Invalidity Corollary, and Unemployment Insurance," written by Oscar M. Sullivan, who was Secretary-Treasurer of the National Council for the Physically Handicapped. The memorandum states:[30]

> An old-age pension system is theoretically incomplete unless it provides for invalidity pensions as well. While so large a coverage may not be feasible at the present time the desirability of it in a complete scheme of social insurance should, we feel, be pointed out in the report, on the subject. Such a system should probably at the beginning allow pensions only for total and permanent disability.

Insurance for total and permanent disability, indeed, was added in 1956, though just for workers aged 50 to 64 and for adult children of retired or deceased workers, if the disability occurred before the child reached age 18. In 1958, disability insurance benefits were extended to the families of workers with serious and permanent disabilities. And in 1960, long-term disability insurance was extended to workers of all ages and their families. As discussed below, partial disability protection and short-term disability insurance, covering risks such as sickness and the birth or adoption of a child, have not yet been added.

Universal National Health Insurance

Another protection considered but not included in 1935 was health insurance. Roosevelt reluctantly decided against proposing universal health care as part of Social Security. Edwin Witte discussed the decision in remarks entitled, "Reflections on the Beginnings of Social Security," delivered at an event celebrating the twentieth anniversary of the enactment of the Social Security Act, at the Department of Health, Education and Welfare, on August 15, 1955. As he described it:[31]

> Health insurance was ... intensely studied by the health insurance staff of the Committee [on Economic Security] and received a good deal of attention at top Committee levels and at the White House. Originally, it was expected that the Committee would ... deal with this subject in its recommendations...[Instead] the Report merely stated that the Committee on Economic Security would make a later report on the subject, and the Administration bill merely provided for Federal aid for public health services, with a provision that the Social Security Board should study the need for and possibility of improving the social security protection of Americans, including, among others, health insurance. This innocent reference to health insurance led to the first special Meeting of the House of Delegates of the American Medical Association, in the false belief that the Administration was secretly trying to foist compulsory health insurance on the country. Immediately, the members of the Ways and Means Committee, then considering the social security bill in executive sessions, were deluged with telegrams from all parts of the country protesting against this "nefarious plot." The upshot was that the...President

deemed it inadvisable to proceed along that line and the report was never even published. ...

Arthur Altmeyer offered another first-hand account of the efforts to enact universal health care, by the administrations of Presidents Roosevelt and Truman, for whom he served:[32]

****

Arthur J. Altmeyer
Address Presented at the 10th Anniversary Award Banquet,
NASW, Honoring Wilbur J. Cohen, Under Secretary, HEW
Washington-Hilton Hotel
December 9, 1965

SOCIAL SECURITY—YESTERDAY AND TOMORROW

. . . .

Of course, the great omission in the 1935 Social Security Act was health insurance. The Committee on Economic Security stated in its report that its staff had prepared a tentative plan which was being studied by several professional advisory groups which had requested an extension of time. The Committee further stated that, therefore, it could not present a specific plan. But the Committee did list what it called "broad principles and general observations which appear to be fundamental to the design of a sound plan of health insurance."

In 1938, after a conference with the President, it was decided to call a National Health Conference. The public support for a national health program which included health insurance was amazing. The President was so enthusiastic that his first inclination was to make the health program an issue in the 1938 campaign. He then said he thought it would be better to make it an issue in the 1940 Presidential campaign. World War II then intervened.

. . . .

The Social Security Board ... did recommend to the President in 1941, just before Pearl Harbor, that a comprehensive social insurance system be established, including not only old-age and survivors' insurance, but also temporary and permanent disability benefits, unemployment insurance and cash hospitalization benefits. The Board also recommended federal grants for public assistance to all needy persons. It is interesting to note that, although President Roosevelt said at his first press conference following Pearl Harbor that "old Dr. New Deal" had to be replaced by "Dr. Win-the-war", he included in his January 1942 Budget Message all of the recommendations the Board had made except federal aid for all needy persons.

....

In his last Message on the State of the Union in January 1945, he again urged an expanded social security program and health and education programs, saying, "I shall communicate further with the Congress on these matters at a later date." But he died three months later.

President Truman, in a message on September 6, 1945, signalling the beginning of the Fair Deal, said he favored "extending, expanding and improving our entire social security program." A few months later he sent a message to Congress outlining a broad national health program, including a federal health insurance system. Bills were introduced by Senators Wagner and Murray and Congressman Dingell to give effect to the President's program but no hearings were held until 1946.

In 1946, 1947 and 1948 the President repeated his recommendations regarding improvements in the Social Security Act. In May 1948 he sent a special message on social security. But his recommendation regarding health insurance attracted the most attention.

Republican leaders introduced rival health bills. The major difference between the Republican bills and the Administration bill was that the Republican bill provided only for grants-in-aid to the States to assist them in furnishing medical care for needy persons instead of a national health insurance system covering the cost of medical care without applying a means test.

Extended hearings were held throughout 1946, 1947 and 1948. Some health legislation resulted, notably the 1946 Hospital Survey and

Construction Act and the expansion of the National Institutes of Health. But no legislative action was taken on health insurance.

....

The great gap in our present Social Security Act is its failure to include two forms of social insurance which are found in the social security systems of practically all other industrialized countries: insurance to cover wage loss resulting from temporary disability and insurance to cover the cost of medical care for all workers. I believe both of these forms of social insurance should be included under the Federal Old-Age Survivors' and Disability Insurance System.

■■

Having suffered so many defeats over national health insurance, including when Democrats controlled Congress, as well as the White House, supporters began to contemplate an incremental approach. One key player was Wilbur J. Cohen. He had graduated from the University of Wisconsin in 1934. While there, he had become close to two professors, Ed Witte and Arthur Altmeyer, both of whom were now working in Washington. Witte hired Cohen in 1934 to be his personal assistant in his role as executive director to the task force developing the Social Security legislation.

Once Social Security was enacted, Cohen went to work as the assistant to Altmeyer who was picked to run the new program as part of the three-person Social Security Board. Cohen spent the rest of his life involved in Social Security policymaking. From 1960 to 1961, he was Chairman of President John F. Kennedy's Task Force on Health and Social Security. Between 1961 and 1968, he worked at the Department of Health, Education, and Welfare ("HEW"), the agency that had jurisdiction over Social Security and health programs. Cohen served in increasingly powerful positions until he ultimately rose to the top, cabinet-level position of Secretary of Health, Education, and Welfare.

After the ongoing failure of enacting universal health insurance, he and his colleagues decided to shift tactics. In "Reflections on the enactment of Medicare and Medicaid," an essay published just a few years before his death, Cohen explained his thinking:[33]

Although I had been a strong advocate of a comprehensive and universal nationwide health insurance plan since 1940, I was conscious of the monumental administrative and management problems involved in such a large undertaking.... The primary source of my early and long association with Medicare is that I suggested it to Oscar Ewing [a close confidant of President Truman and, at that time, the head of the Federal Security Agency, which had jurisdiction over Social Security] in 1950 as a fall-back position after the defeat of the Truman national health insurance proposal and the Wagner-Murray-Dingell bill to carry it out.

Cohen was key to the enactment of Medicare. Another key player and close associate was Robert M. Ball. As Commissioner of Social Security when Medicare was enacted, Ball was instrumental not only in the drafting of Medicare but its implementation, as well. Like Cohen, he has written what he and the others had in mind, in their decision to stop their push for universal health insurance and instead push for the more limited Medicare. In "Perspectives On Medicare: What Medicare's Architects Had In Mind," Ball explains:[34]

What were we hoping to accomplish when we proposed a national hospital insurance plan for the elderly? No other country, as far as I know, had ever considered such an approach. Certainly the elderly were the most expensive and difficult group to cover, and, for the money spent, they clearly would yield the least return of any age group...

A first step toward universal coverage. For persons who are trying to understand what we were up to, the first broad point to keep in mind is that all of us who developed Medicare and fought for it...had been advocates of universal national health insurance. We all saw insurance for the elderly as a fallback position, which we advocated solely because it seemed to have the best chance politically. Although the public record contains some explicit denials, we expected Medicare to be a first step toward universal national health insurance, perhaps with "Kiddicare" as another step.

Consistent with the approach of gradually expanding Medicare until it was universal, Medicare was expanded to cover people with disabilities in 1972. Further expansion of what experts today refer to as traditional Medicare stopped at that point. As described in chapter five, some ideologues have never supported government-sponsored insurance. Though they have been unsuccessful in converting Social Security into welfare or privatizing Social Security, they have been successful in adding private features into Medicare, in the form of Medicare Advantage plans and prescription drug coverage.

At the time of this writing, momentum is building for Medicare for All, which fits solidly within the visionary goals of President Roosevelt and the other Social Security founders. Achieving Medicare for All, as well as other parts of the founders' vision, is discussed in chapter six.

Financing of Social Security

From its start, the primary source of Social Security's revenue came from the premiums of covered workers, matched dollar-for-dollar by their employers. That continues to be the case today. A small part of Social Security's revenue, from the beginning, has come from interest on the investments made with surplus contributions, not yet needed for the payment of benefits.

In 1983, a new source of revenue was added. For the first time, a portion of benefits paid were counted as income for purposes of calculating income tax liability. Normally, that extra tax revenue would go into the general fund of the federal government, to be used for a range of goods and services provided by the government. Instead, this particular revenue was not paid to the general fund but rather was dedicated to Social Security just as the employer and employee federal insurance contributions are.

Because these payments are dedicated and there is no open-ended draw on general revenue, Social Security's self-financing is maintained. As President Roosevelt explained in his message to Congress transmitting the legislation in 1935:[35]

[T]he system adopted, except for the money necessary to initiate it, should be self-sustaining in the sense that funds for the payment of insurance benefits should not come from the proceeds of general taxation.

This is a point not understood well, even by some experts. As long as the funds are specifically dedicated to Social Security, and Social Security's revenue is limited to its dedicated revenue, with no open-ended draw on the government's general fund, Social Security's basic structure is maintained. Its revenue does "not come from the proceeds of general taxation."

Understanding this, President Ronald Reagan, who was president at the time this additional source of revenue was created, made that simple point perfectly clear in 1984. As Secretary Morgenthau said at the hearing in 1935, President Reagan, a half century later, repeated, "Social Security has nothing to do with the deficit."[36]

A founder of Social Security, the late Robert M. Ball, identified Social Security's self-financing as one of the fundamental principles of Social Security. His essay "The Nine Guiding Principles of Social Security" is reproduced in chapter two. As the proponent of the additional funding source, enacted in 1983, he understood as well as anyone that it did not violate the guiding principle he articulated.

Self-financing is violated if there is an open-ended draw on general revenue, such as the payment of one-third of the cost, as has been proposed over the years, or a guarantee that any shortfall would be made up by general revenue, as was the law during World War II. Those kinds of provisions would violate the self-financing principle. But dedicated revenues, no matter the source, do not. They are not an open-ended draw on the general fund.

The new dedicated source of revenue could be an entirely new source of revenue, such as a wealth tax or a financial transactions tax. However, it would not violate Social Security's basic structure if that new source of dedicated revenue is one like the estate tax, which would have already existed but whose revenue would no longer go into the general fund, but after the transformation, would be dedicated to Social Security.

The key is that the revenue is dedicated, so that it can only be used for the one limited, dedicated purpose. As just mentioned, the late Robert M. Ball was a founder who identified Social Security's self-financing as one of the fundamental principles of Social Security. It was his idea and he was the reason that the 1983 amendments dedicated to Social Security a new source of revenue – proceeds from the imposition of the federal income tax on Social Security benefits.

It is instructive to know that, in response to the current projected shortfall, Ball proposed that the federal estate tax, whose proceeds currently go to the general fund, be converted into a dedicated Social Security tax. Ball understood better than anyone what would and would not violate the guiding principle of self-financing he himself articulated. He knew that dedicating the estate tax – or the proceeds of any other tax – would not violate the self-financing principle to which Ball wholeheartedly subscribed.

Given the extreme income and wealth inequality now plaguing our nation and the aging of our population, new sources can be added in the future as they were in 1983. That is consistent with the incremental growth of the program, building on the basic structure laid down in 1935.

Additional Expansions of Social Security to Turn the Founders' Vision into Reality

Roosevelt and other founders envisioned Social Security as cradle to grave protection from all economic insecurities to which working families are exposed. Wages can be lost as the result of unemployment. Unemployment insurance, enacted in 1935, insures against lost wages as a result, but the program should be expanded and updated.

Wages can also be lost as the result of old age, disability, or death. The provision of joint and survivor benefits and life insurance were added in 1935 and 1939, and disability insurance was added in 1956. The benefit amounts, which are all generated from the same formula, were increased historically every few years until the Social Security Amendments of 1972, when benefit amounts were indexed, essentially frozen at their then-replacement rates. Since then,

Congress enacted cuts, which are still being phased in, so those benefits will replace even lower percentages of wages in the future. As the following chart shows, those benefits, even before the cuts are fully phased in, are extremely low compared to other industrialized countries. (The bars designating U.S. benefits are highlighted with arrows):[37]

Social Security Replacement Rates in OECD Countries by Earnings Level

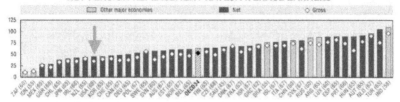

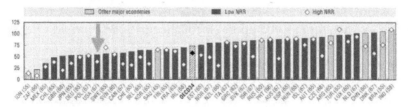

Note: The three-letter codes for the countries in the chart are available at https://unstats.un.org/unsd/tradekb/knowledgebase/country-code. The number in parentheses after the country code is that nation's legislated retirement age.
Source: OECD (2015), *Pensions at a Glance 2015: OECD and G20 indicators*, p. 145, OECD Publishing, Paris.
https://www.keepeek.com//Digital-Asset-Management/oecd/social-issues-migration-health/pensions-at-a-glance-2015_pension_glance-2015-en#page147

In addition to more adequate benefit levels, other protections have not yet been enacted. Wages are lost as the result of sickness of the worker or another family member for whom the worker provides care. Expenses increase and wages are also lost as the result of the birth or adoption of a child. The United States stands out among industrialized countries in providing no nationwide paid family leave or sick leave. Yet the founders talked about short-term disability insurance, which could cover both those risks.

If Social Security is seen not simply as the insurance program that today provides wage replacement in the event of death, disability or old age, but rather also social security produced by healthy, enriched childhoods; education; affordable, safe housing; clean air and water; safe food; and guaranteed employment at good paying jobs where the work environment is safe, there is much work to do. Expansions could include affordable, safe daycare; a significant increase in the minimum wage; guaranteed public employment if no private sector jobs exist; as well as stronger occupational health and safety rules and enforcement, along with stronger protection of the environment.

Expanding Social Security is profoundly wise policy, consistent with the vision of its founders. There is no question we can afford the vision of the founders. We are much wealthier, as a nation, than we were during the Great Depression when the founders articulated their vision. Indeed, we are wealthier than other industrialized countries that provide a social security that is closer to the vision of the founders. In fact, we are the wealthiest nation in the history of the world! Moreover, numerous polls show that the American people overwhelmingly support Social Security and would like to see it expanded.

Standing in the way, though, is a small but determined group that has waged a campaign against our Social Security system, since before its enactment. Some of the arguments used in this campaign have been addressed already. The next chapter examines the campaign more thoroughly and in more detail. It traces the continuous chain of opposition from the beginning. It addresses the zombie lies as well as the more recent tactics used to undermine our Social Security system.

It is imperative that all of us who would like to see our economic security increased through Social Security understand clearly who is standing in the way and what tactics they employ in an effort to win their way. Chapter five seeks to pull the curtain back and expose the truth.

CHAPTER FIVE: IN THE IMMORTAL WORDS OF YOGI BERRA, THIS IS DÉJÀ VU ALL OVER AGAIN

The last chapter ended with a call to expand Social Security, consistent with the founders' vision. Whether to increase or decrease Social Security's modest benefits, whether to add new protections or take current protections away, and whether to retain or change Social Security's fundamental structure are questions of values and collective choice.

An overwhelming majority of Americans have always supported Social Security, valuing the basic economic security it provides by pooling risk. They understand that there are some undertakings that government does better than the private sector. Security, both physical and economic, is one of them. To promote economic security in this country and indeed around the world, government-sponsored insurance has proven to be extremely effective. Indeed, more than 170 countries have enacted their own social security.

Americans appreciate that our Social Security system's benefits are earned and that work is a condition of their receipt. Indeed, the values that underlie Social Security are basic American values: reward for work; individual responsibility; shared participation, risk, and benefit; responsible, prudent financing; and protection of our families.

Those of us who want to see Social Security remain strong and see its modest but vital benefits expanded can triumph as long as we are engaged and informed. To win, we must be vigilant, hyper-sensitive to the goals and tactics of those who would like to see our Social Security system dismantled brick by brick.

Though opponents' tactics have changed somewhat over time, their goal has been constant. This chapter will analyze in detail both the goals and tactics of opponents throughout Social Security's history, so supporters of Social Security are well-informed and armed.

The "Tiny Splinter Group" with Oversized Influence

A small minority has always believed that all but the neediest individuals should be completely on their own and has long fought a campaign against Social Security. People holding those views want, as lobbyist Grover Norquist vividly remarked, "to shrink government to the size where we can drown it in the bathtub."

Those who oppose Social Security have always been a tiny fraction of Americans, but have had oversized influence because they are generally of great wealth. President Eisenhower astutely explained, in a November 8, 1954 letter he wrote to his brother, just who those opponents of Social Security are and what he thought of them:[1]

> Should any political party attempt to abolish social security [and] unemployment insurance...you would not hear of that party again in our political history. There is a tiny splinter group, of course, that believes you can do these things. Among them are H. L. Hunt (you possibly know his background), a few other Texas oil millionaires, and an occasional politician or business man from other areas. Their number is negligible and they are stupid.

Some members of that "tiny splinter group" are libertarians, who want to be free of all constraint. Others are wealthy individuals who don't believe they need to pool their risk, because they are wealthy enough to self-insure, and don't want the cost associated with a collective program of insurance. Still others are unenlightened business people who define their self-interest narrowly, with no regard for the common good, and want to increase their profits and wealth by reducing the cost of mandatory contributions to the government.

And others are people who make their living from Wall Street, and recognize that if people were not receiving Social Security, they would purchase more stocks, bonds, annuities, and other financial instruments in the private market in an effort to protect their economic security. What unites all of these opponents is the desire to undo universal government-sponsored insurance in the form of Social Security and Medicare.

People who share those views sought to defeat Social Security when it was first proposed and, when that proved unsuccessful, to change its basic structure and function, as described below. The history of Social Security shows a continuous chain of opposition, but with different actors over time, of course. Interestingly, in some cases, the most prominent opponents over time have been related. The progeny of some of the wealthy opponents in the 1930s are fighting Social Security today.

The grandfather of President George W. Bush, who sought to radically transform Social Security in 2005, was a man named Prescott Bush, who was a contemporary of President Roosevelt. He once remarked of Roosevelt: "The only man I truly hated lies buried in Hyde Park."[2] Similarly, the father of the highly ideological Koch brothers, Charles and David Koch, who have financed efforts aimed at dismantling Social Security, was a Texas newspaper publisher who used that position to rail against Social Security and other New Deal programs.

Opponents and supporters have not fallen neatly into political party affiliation. Among the electorate, Republicans, Democrats, and Independents alike have always supported Social Security, because they have understood how important it is to their economic security and to the nation.

In addition, once Social Security was established, some Republican leaders like President Eisenhower have supported the program, at least in limited, foundational size. In recent years, though, the Republican Party has endorsed proposals to dismantle Social Security, despite the claim made by virtually all Republican politicians that they support it.

Moreover, as the mistaken view of Social Security as a drain on the federal budget and economy gained traction in the last few decades, some Democratic leaders have, perhaps unwittingly, pushed for changes that would undermine and weaken Social Security's protection, as well. Nevertheless, though not all Democrats have supported Social Security, nor all Republicans opposed it, support for Social Security over its history has largely come from Democrats; opposition from Republicans.

The Invaluable Role of the American People

When Congress first debated Social Security in 1935, Republicans offered no alternative, other than support for means-tested benefits already in the Roosevelt package. However, there was an enormous grassroots demand for old age annuities and so, despite some close votes and amendments that would have derailed Social Security, it was enacted and signed into law on August 14, 1935.

The grassroots energy at the time in favor of financial support for the old is hard to overstate. It started in the unlikeliest of ways. In 1933, Francis E. Townsend, a doctor from Long Beach, California, found himself at age 66 unemployed with no savings. He knew he wasn't alone in his plight. One day, he happened to look out his window and see an old woman digging through a garbage can, looking for something to eat. The sight upset him. It also motivated him. Dr. Townsend wrote a letter to the editor of the *Long Beach Press-Telegram*, his local newspaper, detailing the incident he had witnessed and proposing a solution.

His idea, published on September 30, 1933, was that the federal government should provide every person aged 60 or older a payment of $200 a month, a princely sum in the 1930s. The only requirement, in addition to being retired and not a criminal, was that the recipient had to spend every penny within 30 days of receipt.

Townsend's idea spread around the country at a rate astonishing to believe in that pre-Internet world. A year after Townsend wrote his letter to the newspaper, *Time* magazine reported in its October 15, 1934, issue: "There were Townsend Clubs in every State except Delaware....Between 2,000,000 and 5,000,000 people had put their names to petitions begging their Congressmen to vote the Plan into effect at once."[3] In some congressional districts, a candidate's position on the Townsend plan determined the outcome of the election.

The Townsend movement is simply the first example in Social Security's long history where the American people stepped up to advocate for and protect the economic security our Social Security system provides. In every battle to protect and expand Social Security, the American people have been united in support.

Recognizing, even as far back as the start of the program, that the demand for the economic security that old age pensions brought was powerful and unstoppable, the Republican Party chose in the 1936 election not simply to oppose Social Security but to offer an alternative. The alternative, included in the 1936 Republican Platform, is the same one offered by opponents today, as explained toward the end of the chapter. But the real goal, from the beginning, has been to end Social Security as we know it. So far, though, the American people have never let it happen.

The Eight-Decade Effort to End Social Security

From the moment that Social Security was first debated in Congress, opponents sought to defeat it. At the start, opponents spoke clearly and straightforwardly about their ideological opposition to Social Security. While some opposed it, because they didn't think it went far enough, most opposed it because they thought it gave the government too much power.

In the debate on the House floor, Representative Thomas A. Jenkins (R-OH) argued that Social Security is "compulsion of the rankest kind."[4] Representative Daniel Reed (R-NY), who in 1952 would become chairman of the Ways and Means Committee, charged, "The lash of the dictator will be felt and 25 million free American citizens will for the first time submit themselves to a fingerprint test."[5] Representative James W. Wadsworth (R-NY) accused, "This bill opens the door and invites the entrance into the political field of a power so vast, so powerful as to threaten the integrity of our institutions and to pull the pillars of the temple down upon the heads of our descendants."[6]

In hearings before the Senate Finance Committee, which included some of the most conservative members in that body, Senator Thomas P. Gore (D-OK), who believed that the proposal unwisely sought to substitute Social Security for what he perceived as the laudable individual struggle for existence, asked Frances Perkins, "Isn't this Socialism?" When she strongly reacted, "Oh, no," he smiled gently, leaned forward in his chair, and, as if Perkins were a child who was not being totally candid, rhetorically asked, "Isn't this a teeny-weeny bit of Socialism?"[7]

The same ideological attacks continued during the election of 1936. The Hearst-run Washington Herald, for example, ran a May 28 editorial which argued that Social Security would "reduce millions of Americans to the condition of 'STATE PARASITES.'"[8] (Capitalization in original.) Republican presidential standard bearer Alf Landon similarly charged that Social Security would undermine freedom, and promised that "the Republican party will have nothing to do with any plan that involves prying into the personal records of 26 million people."[9]

Other opponents of Social Security echoed these sentiments. Industrialist Henry Ford issued a statement denouncing Social Security:[10]

> Under some social security systems abroad a man cannot quit his job, or apply for another, or leave town and go to another even to get a better job because that would break the "economic plan." Such a restriction of liberty will be almost a necessity in this country too if the present Social Security Act works to its natural conclusion.

Despite Roosevelt's landslide victory, a small, well-financed group continued to oppose Social Security. But with continued Democratic control of Congress and the White House, and the nation's entrance into World War II, Social Security receded as an issue. When Republicans regained control of Congress in 1946, opposition to Social Security re-surfaced. In 1947 and 1948, the 80th Congress included in several bills technical provisions which had the impact of denying Social Security coverage to over a half million workers. President Truman vetoed every bill. In one of his veto statements, he explained:[11]

> In withholding my approval from H.R. 3997 last August, I expressed my concern that such a bill would open our social

security structure to piecemeal attack and to slow undermining. That concern was well founded. The House of Representatives has recently passed a joint resolution which would destroy the social security coverage of several hundred thousand additional employees....The present bill must be appraised...as but one step in a larger process of the erosion of our social security structure.

The security and welfare of our nation demand an [expansion] of social security to cover the groups which are now excluded from the program. Any step in the opposite direction can only serve to undermine the program and destroy the confidence of our people in the permanence of its protection against the hazards of old age, premature death, and unemployment."

Two months later, he vetoed another bill restricting coverage and again highlighted the bigger picture behind these seemingly technical bills:[12]

If our social security program is to endure, it must be protected against these piecemeal attacks. Coverage must be permanently expanded and no employer or special group of employers should be permitted to reverse that trend by efforts to avoid a tax burden which millions of other employers have carried without serious inconvenience or complaint.

In 1949, with Congress back in Democratic control, the Ways and Means Committee of the House of Representatives reported out, on a party-line vote, what became the Social Security Act Amendments of 1950, a major expansion of Social Security. A minority report signed onto by all the Republicans on the Committee expressed the ideological disagreement to universal government insurance that provided more than a floor on which to build:[13]

Our opposition to certain features of the bill is based, in addition to the cost factor, on our strong conviction that they are inconsonant with the fundamental purpose of compulsory social insurance.

In our opinion, the purpose of compulsory social insurance is to provide a basic floor of economic protection for the individual and his family and in so doing to encourage and stimulate voluntary savings through personal initiative and ambition. It should not invade the field historically belonging to the individual.

We believe that such a form of compulsory social insurance which unnecessarily takes from the individual funds which he would invest or otherwise use for building his own security is incompatible with our free-enterprise system. Accordingly, we do not conceive it to be a proper function or responsibility of the Federal Government either to compensate individuals for all types of losses in earning capacity or to provide a scale of benefits which pay substantially higher amounts to those with higher income.

In a separate minority view, Representative Carl T. Curtis (R-NE) called Social Security, "unmoral."[14]

Other opponents at the time were equally outspoken about their opposition. Senator Barry Goldwater (R-AZ), who would become the Republican presidential nominee in 1964, failed to distinguish Social Security from welfare which, he claimed, gives the federal government "unlimited political and economic power...as absolute...as any oriental despot," and transforms those who receive the benefits "into a dependent animal creature."[15]

Advising Goldwater was Milton Friedman, who in 1962 published *Capitalism and Freedom*, in which he asserted, "The 'social security' program...involves a large-scale invasion into the personal lives of a large fraction of the nation without, so far as I can see, any justification that is at all persuasive."[16]

Nevertheless, the opponents, accurately described as "a tiny splinter group" by Eisenhower, became increasingly marginalized. In 1955, Social Security celebrated its twentieth birthday. The Republican president strongly supported Social Security and the program, now firmly established, was well known to the American people. By that time, around 68 million workers were contributing to Social Security, and over 7 million beneficiaries were receiving benefits. Consequently, the ideological arguments about Social Security as a symbol of the government having too much power lost their potency.

Though the battles were hard fought, the program continued to expand, with the addition of Disability Insurance in 1956 and Medicare in 1965. And in 1972, President Richard Nixon signed into law legislation that increased Social Security's benefits and then provided that they would be automatically indexed annually. In signing the legislation into law, Nixon emphasized the importance of the indexing provision, stating:[17]

> One important feature of this legislation which I greet with special favor is the automatic increase provision which will allow social security benefits to keep pace with the cost of living. This provision is one which I have long urged, and I am pleased that the Congress has at last fulfilled a request which I have been making since the first months of my Administration. This action constitutes a major break-through for older Americans, for it says at last that inflation-proof social security benefits are theirs as a matter of right, and not as something which must be temporarily won over and over again from each succeeding Congress.

But then, eight years later, Ronald Reagan, an outspoken opponent of Social Security, became president. Four years prior to his successful run, Reagan had challenged President Gerald Ford for the nomination. In the Florida primary, Ford made an issue of Reagan's hostile views toward Social Security. Ford won the primary and eventually the nomination.

Apparently, that experience taught Reagan an important lesson about the power of the Social Security issue. During the second debate of the presidential campaign, Democratic President Jimmy Carter accused Republican nominee Ronald Reagan of advocating a voluntary Social Security system. Reagan implicitly disavowed his earlier view and said, "I, too, am pledged to a Social Security program that will reassure these senior citizens of ours that they are going to continue to get their money."[18]

Nevertheless, opponents of Social Security held out hope. At first, Reagan did not disappoint. He named Representative David Stockman (R-MI) to be the director of the Office of Management and Budget (OMB). Stockman saw Social Security, which he called "closet socialism," as simply one more part of the overblown welfare state. As part of the transition, Stockman prepared a memorandum entitled "Avoiding a GOP Economic Dunkirk." He recommended that in Reagan's first 100 days in office, the president propose an economic package consisting of both tax reductions and substantial cuts to Social Security and other programs in the federal budget, which he claimed had "become an automatic 'coast-to-coast soup line.'"[19]

On Stockman's recommendation, the administration proposed $2.5 billion of Social Security cuts as part of its omnibus budget bill, which was enacted into law. However, two years later, Reagan championed and signed into law the Social Security Amendments of 1983, which restored Social Security to long-range balance while maintaining its fundamental structure, present from the beginning, described in chapters two and three.

How, in just two years, Reagan went from pushing cuts to Social Security as part of a budget bill to championing a package that maintained Social Security's structure and restored it to long-range actuarial balance is a long story that I and other participants in the process have written about elsewhere. The important point is that Reagan's signature on the 1983 amendments to the Social Security Act was undoubtedly disappointing to opponents of the program.

Reagan's embrace of traditional Social Security dashed the hopes and plans of activists determined to finally radically transform Social Security, that symbol of big government that works for the people. Adding insult to the injury of Social Security opponents, Reagan proclaimed at the signing ceremony:[20]

This bill demonstrates for all time our nation's ironclad commitment to social security. It assures the elderly that America will always keep the promises made in troubled times a half a century ago. It assures those who are still working that they, too, have a pact with the future. From this day forward, they have our pledge that they will get their fair share of benefits when they retire.

The whole episode had to be disheartening to those who wanted to dismantle Social Security. The president had been an outspoken critic of the program, which was projecting shortfalls that required action. Those opponents must have thought that they had finally been tantalizingly close to their goal, only to have those hopes dashed. In addition to the experience being discouraging, it appears also to have been a wake-up call.

The program was now nearly a half century old and a president who previously had favored dismantling Social Security, as they did, had signed into law amendments that seemed to ensure that Social Security was here to stay. Opponents presumably finally acknowledged to themselves that their ideological concerns were not shared by the overwhelming majority of the nation.

They appear to have decided that to be successful in their goal of ending Social Security, they had to change their tactics. It must have become abundantly clear that, given the powerful support that Social Security generates, they needed to undermine public confidence in the future of the program, rather than straightforwardly object to Social Security on ideological grounds.

Within months of the signing ceremony, the libertarian Cato Institute dedicated its fall journal to Social Security. The journal published a set of conference papers critiquing the just-enacted amendments and discussing how to achieve radical reform. One particularly illuminating article addressed the question of tactics directly. Entitled "Achieving Social Security Reform: A 'Leninist Strategy,'" the article laid out, in true Leninist fashion, the elements necessary to achieve "a radical reform of Social Security."[21]

The authors explained that their Leninist strategy was to wage "guerrilla warfare against both the current Social Security system and the coalition that supports it." Their proposed guerilla war included a number of attacks. One was to undermine confidence in Social Security, in particular convincing younger Americans that their retirement would be more secure and adequate with individual savings, rather than with Social Security, because, the Leninist strategists would claim, Social Security was supposedly unsustainable. Another was to assure those at or near retirement that their benefits would remain untouched or, even better, would be higher under the proposed reform.

Part of the strategy was to make private retirement savings accounts more widespread and attractive, and to activate Wall Street, which had profits to be made, into the fight on the side of those who wanted to dismantle Social Security. In that way, the authors sought to create, in the authors' words, "an alternative" to Social Security, one "with which the public is familiar and comfortable, and one that has the backing of a powerful political force." As explained below, this was not a new alternative, just an old one with some new trappings.

As the title of their article suggests, the authors considered themselves revolutionaries, seeking to overthrow Social Security, just as Lenin had plotted against capitalism. The article concluded by cautioning fellow revolutionaries to "be prepared for a long campaign," adding, that "as Lenin well knew, to be a successful revolutionary, one must...be patient and consistently plan." That campaign continues to this day.

Hiding Motives and Intensifying Efforts to Undermine Confidence and Support

Reagan's statement at the signing ceremony seems to have crystallized for Social Security's opponents that they would have to hide their true opposition to Social Security, if they were ever to achieve the goal of ending Social Security as we know it. By the 1980s, outright public criticism of the concept of Social Security largely disappeared. Today, few politicians explicitly attack Social Security on ideological grounds. No politicians today argue that Social Security is an inappropriate role of government, or, more bluntly, that it is socialism. Very occasionally, an opponent will say that the Supreme Court got it wrong, and Social Security is unconstitutional, as Donald Trump's OMB Director, Mick Mulvaney, has claimed. But even that level of frontal attack is rare.

Rather, today's opponents are much more duplicitous. Indeed, today it is hard to tell opponents from supporters. They talk about "saving," "fixing," and "strengthening" Social Security, and they even praise it. Often, though, the praise comes with veiled or not-so-veiled undermining comments. President Bush, for example, in presenting his plan to radically transform Social Security, said:[22]

> Social Security was a great moral success of the 20th century, and we must honor its great purposes in this new century. The system, however, on its current path, is headed toward bankruptcy. And so, we must join together to strengthen and save Social Security.

The Leninist strategists must have realized that not only would they have to hide their own ideological opposition, they would have to willfully refuse to see that Social Security is insurance. They certainly could never publicly acknowledge that fact.

Prior to the change in, and intensification of, tactics, opponents would occasionally mischaracterize Social Security as forced savings, as Landon did, but generally would refer to it as the insurance that it is. Starting in the 1950s, opponents like Goldwater and Reagan began to mischaracterize it as welfare. Nevertheless, the battle was clearly over ideology. That was true for the battles in the 1930s, 1940s, 1950s, and 1960s. Opponents of Social Security made no effort to hide their opposition to Social Security on ideological grounds.

Today, opponents sometimes imply that Social Security is forced savings, proposing as President Bush did that workers be able to divert a portion of their Social Security insurance premiums into private savings accounts. However, the argument today is never waged in terms of whether insurance or savings are what is needed. More often, today's opponents imply that Social Security is welfare, and sometimes push to means-test the benefits. The issue is never joined in terms of an open and honest debate about whether universal wage insurance, forced savings, or welfare is the best solution to ensure economic security when wages are lost.

Before the change in tactics, the debate over Social Security was largely a straightforward one, where people on both sides were open about their values and ideology. That is a crucial element at the heart of our democracy. It depends at base on agreeing to the facts of a situation. It depends on accurate information. And it depends on politicians who are willing to state their views openly and honestly, and willing to take political accountability at the polls for those views.

But that is not the case today. Opponents' policy prescriptions, when closely examined – as is done towards the end of this chapter – have remained largely unchanged since 1936. What has changed is the honesty of the debate.

Along with the cessation of clear opposition on ideological grounds has come an intensification of certain tactics and the creation of new tactics. Instead of being clear about their values, opponents seek to subtly subvert support for, and undermine confidence in, Social Security. Rather than a straightforward debate over the kind of nation we want, the debate is fear-based, in an effort to achieve ends that an honest debate did not and will not yield. Today's opponents raise doubts about the future receipt of benefits and use language which subtly but inexorably mischaracterizes what Social Security is and is not.

Raising Doubts About the Receipt of Benefits

As chapter three explains in detail, Social Security's opponents have warned sinisterly, from the beginning, that the program will not pay benefits at some future time. Republican presidential nominee Alf Landon claimed that Social Security was "a fraud on the workingman." He and other opponents claimed that the funds would be insecure, backed simply by IOUs, the money having already been spent. Therefore, beneficiaries were supposedly at the mercy of some future Congress to provide the benefits. A future Congress that could change its mind.[23]

Fear-Mongering Threat That Congress Can and Will Arbitrarily Stop Paying Earned Benefits

Days before the 1936 election, the Republican National Committee mailed, to employers across the country, millions of pamphlets, posters, and pay envelope inserts, all attacking Social Security. On the Friday before the election, workers all over the country opened their pay envelopes and found inserted what looked like an official government notice. It was captioned "Notice— Deductions from Pay Start Jan. 1," and at the bottom of the insert were the words, in big, black letters, "Social Security Board, Washington, D.C." Included with a worker's pay, the notices stated:[24]

> Effective January, 1937, we are compelled by a Roosevelt "New Deal" law to make a 1 per cent deduction from your wages and turn it over to the government. Finally, this may go as high as 4 per cent. You might get this money back...but only if Congress decides to make the appropriation for this purpose. There is NO guarantee. Decide before November 3—election day—whether or not you wish to take these chances.

Reading the notice, a worker was left with the clear impression that Social Security was merely a gimmick to raise taxes, not a contributory retirement program. Reports started coming into both the Democratic and Republican headquarters about workers tearing Roosevelt campaign buttons from their shirts and throwing them on the ground, stripping Roosevelt bumper stickers off cars, and ripping Roosevelt posters off walls. Republicans got an excited call from a campaign headquarters in Ohio: "The labor vote has stayed unimpressed and adamant until now that the Social Security issue is brought home to them. This state is all agog over payroll reduction." Local Democratic offices placed concerned calls with similar reports. Campaign workers in Michigan and Pennsylvania, as well as Labor's Nonpartisan League, all phoned in panicked messages that Roosevelt had better act quickly to counter the dirty trick.[25]

The Saturday night before the election, in response to the pay-envelope tactic, President Roosevelt delivered a nationwide address.[26] He denounced what he called "the current pay-envelope campaign against America's working people." Calling the tactic an act of "desperate men with their backs to the wall," he roared, "It is an old strategy of tyrants to delude their victims into fighting their battles for them."

He pointed out, "Every message in a pay envelope, even if it is the truth, is a command to vote according to the will of the employer. But," he continued, "this propaganda is worse—it is deceit." He then catalogued all the misrepresentations in the Republican materials, misrepresentations that "[t]hey carefully conceal." He ended each point, "That omission is deceit." He concluded the litany of deceits with an observation that, like every other point he made, remains true today: "They do not tell him that the insurance policy that is bought for him is far more favorable to him than any policy that any private insurance company could afford to issue. That omission is deceit."

He finished with a most serious indictment: "But they are guilty of more than deceit. When they imply that the reserves thus created against both these policies will be stolen by some future Congress, diverted to some wholly foreign purpose, they attack the integrity and honor of American Government itself. Those who suggest that, are already aliens to the spirit of American democracy."

President Roosevelt was reelected on November 3, 1936, by a landslide. Nevertheless, the same charges can be heard today. Just as those pay inserts charged, today's opponents argue that Social Security reserves are just IOUs, that the money has already been spent – zombie charges refuted in chapter three. As opponents charged in 1936, they ominously warn that Congress could change the law, hinting implicitly what those pay inserts said explicitly: "Decide…whether or not you wish to take these chances."[27]

In an update of the old tactic of undermining confidence by warning that Congress could change the law, an arcane twist is occasionally used today. The new twist involves misrepresenting a Supreme Court case decided more than a half century ago, in 1960. Opponents of Social Security occasionally refer to the case to suggest that people may never see their benefits. The head Social Security researcher at the libertarian CATO Institute, has written, for example:[28]

> [I]n the 1960 case of Fleming [sic] v. Nestor, the U.S. Supreme Court ruled that workers have no legally binding contractual rights to their Social Security benefits, and that those benefits can be cut or even eliminated at any time.

That unqualified statement vastly overstates the holding of the case, which involved the rescission of Social Security benefits of a deported member of the Communist Party. Nestor was not the most sympathetic plaintiff in the late 1950s, when the case arose, though it is instructive to note, he did win in the lower court.

The rescission of the Social Security benefits of deported aliens who were communists had been enacted by Congress at the height of the anti-communist McCarthy era. The question before the Court was whether Congress had that power or had acted unconstitutionally.

The Court's exact holding reads:[29]

> We must conclude that a person covered by the [Social Security] Act has not such a right in benefit payments as would make every defeasance of "accrued" interests violative of the Due Process Clause of the Fifth Amendment. **This is not to say, however, that Congress may exercise its power to modify the statutory scheme free of all constitutional restraint.** [Emphasis added.]

There were three heated dissenting opinions (four of the nine justices dissented), and some legal scholars have criticized the opinion, as well. The Court's holding is a far cry from the claim of opponents that Congress has the power to cut benefits at any time for any reason. Moreover, Social Security contributors and beneficiaries have perhaps the most powerful safeguard of all: the ability to vote for leaders who honor Social Security's commitments and against those who do not.

Spreading Doubts About Social Security's Affordability

Along with arguing that Congress will act in bad faith and stop Social Security from paying earned benefits, Landon and other opponents of the newly-enacted Social Security program claimed that workers would not receive their benefits because Social Security was "unworkable."[30]

Obviously, the subsequent eighty years have proven that assessment wrong. Nevertheless, modern-day opponents warn of the same thing, only in slightly different terms. They assert that Social Security is in crisis, its collapse impending. Indeed, today's opponents have latched onto an unremarkable fact about pensions as part of their effort to undermine confidence in Social Security.

As explained in chapter two, the annuities provided by Social Security are insurance. Because insurers often face a substantial time lag between the receipt of premiums and the expenditure of benefits, they must, to be prudent, project their annual income and outgo over a substantial period of time into the future.

As a prudent insurer, the Social Security Administration employs more than forty actuaries whose job it is to make those projections. The law requires that Social Security's Board of Trustees (which oversees Social Security's finances) report to Congress about the financial status of Social Security. The Board submitted its first annual report in 1941, the first year after monthly benefits began. It has submitted annual reports every year ever since, in good economic times and bad, in times of war, and periods of peace.[31]

Over its history, Social Security's Board of Trustees has used valuation periods as short as thirty-five years and as long as eighty years. Since 1965, it has become routine to use 75-year valuation periods. It is important to understand that Social Security's 75-year valuation period is longer than private pensions use and, indeed, longer than most other countries use for their own Social Security programs. Germany, for example, relies on a fifteen-year valuation period, though it, like the other members of the European Union, is required to project out 45 years in reports to the EU.[32]

Such a long valuation period is a mark of how responsibly, carefully, prudently, and conservatively our American Social Security system is managed. Obviously the further one projects out, the less certain the projection. Whenever projections are made over such a long time horizon, they will rarely show perfect balance. Rather, they may show a surplus, or they may show a shortfall. That is unremarkable. The report comes out every year and employs such a lengthy valuation period in order that Congress always has plenty of time to act whenever there is a projected imbalance. That should ensure that promised benefits will always be paid on time and in full.

For a variety of reasons in the 1970s, Social Security started to project shortfalls. The primary reason was the result of events overseas. In the fall of 1973, Egypt and Syria attacked Israel, and the Organization of Petroleum Exporting Countries (OPEC) announced that its members would ship no oil to the United States or any other country supporting Israel in the war and would quadruple the price of oil worldwide.

An already-sluggish U.S. economy and already-high inflation intensified. Lines at gas stations grew long, sometimes snaking for miles, and prices on seemingly everything skyrocketed. The price of food jumped 20 percent. Overall inflation climbed to 11 percent, with some months reaching annualized rates of over 16 percent. At the same time, unemployment rates soared. By 1975, unemployment reached 8.5 percent, the highest it had been since before the nation's entry into World War II.

The economic conditions wreaked havoc on Social Security as the result of legislation enacted in 1972. In the 1950s and 1960s, Congress had increased Social Security's benefits on an ad hoc basis to offset their erosion as the result of rising standards of living and inflation. In 1972, Congress enacted automatic adjustments to take the place of those ad hoc enactments.

The unexpectedly high inflation caused benefit levels—outgo—to increase more rapidly than anticipated, and the unexpectedly high unemployment and slow wage growth caused Social Security income to be lower than projected. To make matters worse, the formula enacted in 1972 was extremely sensitive to the exact economic conditions the country was experiencing. The formula worked fine for adjusting the benefits of those already retired. It would have worked fine for workers just starting to retire had the same conditions that had existed over the life of the program continued. It did not work fine, though, in this period of rapid inflation and lethargic wage growth.

For those just applying for benefits, the formula produced larger and larger benefits as a percentage of final pay. If the formula were unchanged and the economic conditions had remained what they were, eventually it would have provided people more in monthly Social Security benefits than they took home in paychecks while working.

The impact of the economy's so-called stagflation and the problem with the formula became painfully obvious quite quickly. The annual Trustees Reports began showing higher costs and lower income each year. In the 1975 report, the trustees forecast that the funds would be exhausted by 1979.

Opponents of Social Security wasted no time seeking to capitalize on the projected deficit, caused by the flawed formula and the difficult economic conditions. Like today, in response to a projected deficit – today's much further away – critics of the program claimed that the program was going bankrupt and, as Landon had charged, was poorly designed and unworkable.

To its credit, the responsible press noted and criticized the opponents. An April 3, 1975 New York Times editorial entitled "Time-Tested Security," noted:[33]

> Thirty-five years after issuance of the first benefit checks by the Social Security system, critics of this widely and deservedly admired program are doing their utmost to undermine confidence in both its fairness and its actuarial soundness. The criticisms are of a kind Congress rightly rejected at the birth of Social Security, but recession-fed anxieties about every aspect of the economy tend to give them exaggerated credibility now.

The projected short-term deficit, as well as a long-term deficit projected to occur as a result of the aging of the post-war baby boom generation, was eliminated through legislation enacted in 1977 and 1983. As a result of the 1983 amendments that Reagan signed into law, to the dismay of self-proclaimed Leninist opponents, Social Security's annual Trustees Report projected that Social Security was in balance for its full 75-year valuation period, ending in 2057.

In the 1990s, when Social Security began to project a manageable shortfall, decades away, these same forces latched onto the news, proclaiming once again that Social Security was going bankrupt. The false claim was that the nation's aging population made Social Security unaffordable. Once more, an advisory council sought to set the record straight. The Report of the 1994-1996 Advisory Council on Social Security, using as its source the Social Security Administration's Office of the Actuary, stated in an appendix entitled "Developments since 1983":[34]

> The usual popular explanation of the present deficit has been to repeat the underlying reason why the Social Security system will be more expensive in the future than it is today. It is pointed out correctly that while today there are 3.3 active workers paying into the system for every beneficiary now drawing benefits, over time this ratio will change to two workers per

beneficiary and in the long run to perhaps 1.9 or 1.8. This is the main reason why Social Security will be more expensive in the future than it is today.

However, this has almost nothing to do with why there is a 2.17 percent of taxable payroll deficit. The estimate of the future relationship between beneficiaries and workers was just about the same in 1983 when the program was last in balance. In other words, the fundamental ratio of beneficiaries to workers was fully taken into account in the 1983 financing provisions and, as a matter of fact, was known and taken into account well before that. The current deficit has a different explanation, resulting from an accumulation of relatively small annual changes in the actuarial assumptions and in the method of making the estimates.

Nevertheless, once again, an advisory council's reassurance did not stop the fear-mongering. The careful monitoring contained in the annual reports should provide the American people with a sense of confidence that this vital program will always be adjusted to ensure that all benefits will always be paid, as they always have been.

Instead, the Leninist strategists have been able to spin the reports to an unquestioning press that the Social Security sky is falling. Like clockwork, once a year when the report came out, the press dutifully reported that Social Security was in imminent crisis. Absent from the scary headlines was any context: how distant and manageable in size the shortfall, and how unremarkable to forecast a mismatch in income and revenue when projecting so far into the future.

Then, in 2000, the Leninist strategists got a gift. A fellow-traveler, George W. Bush, was elected president. In 1978, when Social Security was projecting the shortfall that was eliminated in 1983, Bush was running for Congress in west Texas. Speaking to a group of real estate agents about Social Security in a campaign stop at Midland Country Club, he claimed, "[Social Security] will be bust in 10 years unless there are some changes." Failing to acknowledge that Social Security is insurance, Bush asserted, "The ideal solution would be for...people [to be] given the chance to invest the money the way they feel."[35]

Just a few months after becoming president, Bush established what he named – in true Orwellian fashion – the Commission to Strengthen Social Security. The president instructed the commission to recommend changes that "must include individually controlled, voluntary personal retirement accounts."[36]

The new president took other steps that certainly pleased the Leninist opponents. Two years into Bush's first term, Social Security's Board of Trustees, a majority of whom served in the Bush administration, included in its annual report a projection of Social Security's actuarial condition over an infinite time horizon – as if projecting out three-quarters of a century weren't long enough.

In a December 19, 2003 letter to Social Security's Board of Trustees and Advisory Board, the nonpartisan American Academy of Actuaries' Social Insurance Committee criticized the use of an infinite-time horizon as misleading, explaining:[37]

> [T]he new measures of OASDI's [i.e. Social Security's] unfunded obligations included in the 2003 report provide little if any useful information about the program's long-range finances and indeed **are likely to mislead** anyone lacking technical expertise in the demographic, economic and actuarial aspects of the program's finances into believing that the program is in far worse financial condition than is actually indicated. [Emphasis added.]

Indeed, the letter also urged caution with respect to the 75-year valuation period, stating:

> With regard to the infinite-time-period estimates, the Committee begins its analysis by noting that the results of the 75-year statutory valuation are themselves subject to extreme uncertainty. Consider the situation of actuaries or economists in the year 1928 attempting to project demographic and economic parameters 75 years into the future - to 2003. They likely would have missed the Great Depression, World War II, the baby boom, the influx of women into the labor force, etc. Nobody, no matter how

intelligent or educated, could have anticipated these very significant events.

From the Leninist strategists' point of view, though, the infinite time horizon had one large plus: It translated into huge scary-sounding numbers that made Social Security's projected shortfall sound impossibly large.

At the start of his administration, Bush empowered a commission to develop proposals to privatize Social Security and stacked his administration with Leninist strategists who added an infinite time horizon to Social Security's projections. He waited until after he was safely elected to a second term, though, to propose the radical overhauling of Social Security.

Two days after the 2004 election, Bush announced at a press conference that "reforming Social Security will be a priority of my Administration." He also said, "I earned capital in the campaign, political capital. And now I intend to spend it."[38]

At the February 2, 2005 State of the Union Address, Bush made his Social Security proposal the centerpiece of his discussion of domestic issues.[39] Apparently armed with the new tactic of seeming to support Social Security while undermining confidence in its future, he claimed that Social Security was a wonderful program, but unsustainable as the result of an aging population and therefore in need of "modernization" (i.e., replacement with what had been sought from the beginning, as described below).

His opening swipe was that Social Security was out of date. "Social Security was a great moral success in the 20th century," he said, subtly emphasizing that the program was outmoded by referring, in the very next phrase, to "this new century." He then asserted, to angry boos by the Democrats, that Social Security "is headed toward bankruptcy." To hammer home both points, President Bush continued: "Our society has changed in ways the founders of Social Security could not have foreseen. In today's world, people are living longer and, therefore, drawing benefits longer."

That, of course, was not only foreseeable, but foreseen. The actuaries working for the Committee on Economic Security, Roosevelt's interagency task force developing Social Security, knew that people in the twenty-first century would live longer and draw benefits longer. Specifically, in 1934, they projected that, in the year 2000, 12.7 percent of the population would be age 65 or older. According to the 2000 census figures, the percentage of those aged 65 and over was 12.4 percent of the population.[40]

Not content simply to rewrite history, Bush sought to prove the point that Social Security was unsustainable by citing a terribly deceptive and misleading factoid. The president announced, "And instead of sixteen workers paying in for every beneficiary, right now it's only about three workers."[41]

"Sixteen workers paying in for every beneficiary" is a meaningless statistic that never affected policy in the slightest. The 16-to-1 ratio is a figure plucked from 1950, the year that Social Security expanded to cover millions of theretofore uncovered workers: farm workers, domestic workers, and others. All pension programs, private as well as public, that require a period of employment for eligibility show similar ratios at the start. That happens because all newly covered workers are paying in, but no one in the newly covered group has yet qualified for benefits.

The president could just as accurately have said that in 1945, the ratio of workers to beneficiaries was 42 workers paying in for every beneficiary or the equally accurate but meaningless ratio from 1937: 26 million workers paying in for no monthly beneficiaries. Consistent with the meaninglessness and misleadingness of the 16-to-1 factoid, the worker-to-beneficiary ratio was halved to eight workers for every beneficiary within five years. By 1975, the ratio was where it is today.

The worker-to-beneficiary ratio, which compares the number of workers contributing to Social Security to the number of people drawing Social Security benefits, reveals virtually nothing about the affordability of Social Security. It sheds no light on whether other burdens on those workers are increasing or decreasing. The worker-to-beneficiary ratio does not reveal the burdens imposed on workers from support of all dependents, just of those receiving Social Security benefits. When children, not just Social Security beneficiaries, are counted, the ratio of workers to the so-called dependent population was greatest in 1965. Indeed, that ratio will not be greater, in the foreseeable future, than it was when baby boomers were children – not even when all surviving baby boomers are age 65 and over.

More importantly, the ratio reveals virtually nothing about the affordability of Social Security, because it sheds no light on how productive those workers are. Most importantly, Social Security's actuaries project that real compensation will increase by fifty percent over the next thirty years and double over the next half century.[42] (As a nation, we will be wealthier in the future, and therefore more able to shoulder the costs of a dependent population, though it may not feel that way, if income and wealth remain unfairly distributed and Social Security benefits are not increased.)

The ratio that Bush and other Social Security opponents have used to undermine confidence in the future of Social Security presents a one-sided, distorted picture. What is much more significant and informative is the percentage of the nation's Gross Domestic Product spent on Social Security. As the following graph shows, Social Security's costs are essentially a straight horizontal line, at around 6 percent of GDP:[43]

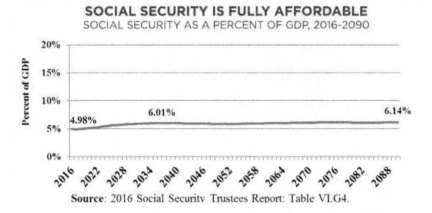

SOCIAL SECURITY IS FULLY AFFORDABLE
SOCIAL SECURITY AS A PERCENT OF GDP, 2016-2090

Source: 2016 Social Security Trustees Report: Table VI.G4.

That percentage is considerably lower than what other industrialized countries spend on their counterpart programs. It clearly reveals that our Social Security system is completely affordable, now and in the future. The question whether to expand its modest benefits, keep them where they are, cut them, or radically transform the program is a matter of values, not affordability.

But the myth that the aging baby boomers will wreck Social Security is such a good sound bite for the Leninist strategists. Despite the deceptiveness of the ratio, Bush, his vice president, his

Secretary of the Treasury, and every other member of the administration continually referenced the ratio in their quest to sell the need to radically change Social Security. Indeed, a pictograph showing 16 little men equaling 1 little man in 1950, $3\frac{1}{3}$ little men equaling 1 man today, and 2 men equaling 1, labeled "When Younger Workers Retire," was prominently displayed on the Bush White House website.

It was clear that the administration sought to make people believe that the traditional Social Security program was unworkable and fundamentally flawed, as Landon had tried to do in 1936. Callers to the Social Security Administration 800-number hotline were routinely placed on hold. While on hold, the captive listener was bombarded with a variety of "facts" designed to undermine confidence in the program.

Callers, of course, heard the 16-to-1, 3-to-1, 2-to-1 ratio factoid repeated. In addition, callers were subjected to rhetorical questions and answers, including, "Did you know that the 76 million-strong baby boom generation will begin to retire in about ten years? When that happens, changes will need to be made to Social Security." A few minutes later, a voice informed the person waiting on hold, "[T]he percentage of older Americans will about double between now and 2030....Long-run changes will need to be made." The selective facts pounding trapped callers were all aimed at undermining confidence. The subliminal message was that the program was broken and could not be easily repaired.[44]

All the talk about the unsustainability of Social Security and the president's desire to "strengthen" it hid the reality. Bush's desire for individual accounts was part of the same ideological battle, rooted in the same animosity toward the program, that had motivated Social Security's opponents from the beginning.

Illuminatingly, a memorandum from the president's director of strategic initiatives, dated January 3, 2005, and marked "not for attribution," put in writing what was patently obvious to anyone who knew much about the history of Social Security.[45] The memorandum concluded with a startling and refreshingly frank assessment: "For the first time in six decades, the Social Security battle is one we can win."

In emphasizing the importance of its conclusion, the memorandum stated that "this will be one of the most important conservative undertakings of modern times." As if written by true Leninists, the leaked memo explained that the first step was to convince the American people that "the current system is heading for an iceberg."

The Bush plan, of course, failed. And for good reason. It was a classic example of bait-and-switch. Bush and his allies used the need to maintain Social Security by closing its projected shortfall as a pretense for their ideological effort to radically transform Social Security.

Although President Bush was unsuccessful in converting the projected shortfall into a radical transformation of Social Security, he did succeed in popularizing the false claim that Social Security is unaffordable because the American population is aging.

The Truth About Our Aging Population

People, on average, are living somewhat longer. The invention of antibiotics as well as public investments in a variety of goods and services, including sanitation, public health, and education, have improved all of our lives. As a result of all of these investments, the United States, like virtually every other advanced industrial society, has reduced infant and childhood mortality substantially and increased longevity somewhat.

There are challenges that come with increased longevity, but it is undeniably good that more people are reaching old age, and once getting there are, on average, living somewhat longer than in the past. The fact that we are living somewhat longer at higher standards of living is a success, not a failure.

It is crucial to understand that opponents have exaggerated the gains and ignored the fact that those gains have not been equally distributed. Former Senator Alan Simpson, for example, has wrongly asserted that "[Social Security] was never intended as a retirement program. It was set up in '37 and '38....The [life expectancy] was 63. That's why they set retirement age at 65."[46]

Simpson's statement is not just incorrect; it is outrageous, as well as terribly misleading. At its most fundamental, it is both a disservice to Americans and an offensive slander of President Roosevelt to insinuate that he and the others who created Social

Security were taking workers' money while setting eligibility for benefits out of reach for most of them.

Simpson is able to make this contemptible claim by using figures that are misleading. He deceptively uses average life expectancy from birth at a time when infant and child mortality was high. To make his deceptive claim, he picked a year before medicine had conquered many lethal childhood diseases. Back in 1935, when Social Security was enacted, 55.7 of every thousand children died before their first birthdays; in 1940, the year that Simpson plucked his misleading statistic, infant mortality rates were 47.0 per thousand live births. In contrast, in 2010, the infant mortality rate was 6.15 per thousand.[47]

The age 63 that Simpson refers to is an average that includes all of those people who died in childhood. (To be precise, the average life expectancy for males at birth was 61.4; for females, 65.7, for a population average of around 63.) Those who survived childhood and made it to age 21 generally made it to age 65. In the very same table in the Social Security Trustees Report – indeed in the adjoining columns where you find Simpson's misleading fact – you also find life expectancies for those who made it to age 65. According to that very same table, men who made it to age 65 in 1940 lived, on average, an additional 11.9 years, to age 76.9, and women lived on average an additional 13.4 years, to age 78.4.[48]

Although people, on average, are living somewhat longer today, the increase is not the decades that Simpson implies. Rather, in 2013, the most recent year the trustees show actual data, men who reach age 65 are living, on average, 5.9 years longer than they were in 1940; women, on average, 6.9 years longer. Moreover, these are average increases across the population. Women in the bottom half of the income scale have actually seen their average life expectancy at age 65 decline over the last 25 years.

But focusing on increased average longevity and the so-called old-age dependency is used by opponents to scare people into the false, simplistic belief that an aging population makes Social Security unaffordable. The population is indeed aging. But that is primarily because birth rates are low, not because of rapidly increasing life expectancies. The Chief Actuary of the Social Security Administration has written:[49]

Adjusting birth rates to include only those children who survive to age 10 results in fairly flat total fertility rates near three children per woman from 1875 through 1925. From 1926 through 1965, this adjusted total fertility rate was still about 2.7 births per woman, on average, including both the temporary low-birth period of the Great Depression and World War II, and the temporary high-birth period after World War II. After 1965, however, the total fertility rate shifted to a new level around two children per woman. It is this apparently permanent shift to lower birth rates in the United States that is the principal cause of our changing age distribution between 2010 and 2030 and the resulting shift in the ratio of beneficiaries to workers.

It is important to recognize that the population is aging and to understand the causes. Because it is caused by lower birth rates, increased immigration is an obvious solution. Because immigrants into the U.S. are generally young, they increase the ratio of working age population to retirement age population in much the same way as do births. Those who immigrate tend to be younger and may, as a matter of culture, have larger families.

In Congressional testimony, the Chief Actuary of the Social Security Administration explained the benefit to Social Security of increased immigration:[50]

Immigration has played a fundamental role in the growth and evolution of the U.S. population and will continue to do so in the future. In the 2014 Trustees Report to Congress, we projected that net annual immigration will add about 1 million people annually to our population. With the number of annual births at about 4 million, the net immigration will have a substantial effect on population growth and on the age distribution of the population. Without this net immigration, the effects of the drop in birth rates after 1965 would be much more severe for the finances of Social Security, Medicare, and for retirement plans in general.

In addition to the population aging, causing a decrease in the worker-to-beneficiary ratio, wages have stagnated for most of the workforce, while income and wealth inequality has drastically increased. These facts suggest that revenue dedicated to Social Security from unearned income, where the worker-to-beneficiary ratio is immaterial, would be sound policy.

But, what the aging of the population absolutely does not call for is the scaling back of Social Security's already modest benefits or, worse, its radical transformation. Rather, it calls for the opposite. It seems perfectly appropriate that, in response to an aging population, more resources be directed toward the aged.

To repeat, the question of whether to expand, cut, or radically transform Social Security is a matter of values, not affordability. While recent Trustees Reports are projecting manageable shortfalls, still more than a decade away, those shortfalls – like those of the past – are neither surprising nor alarming.

To provide context, it is instructive to compare Social Security's projected shortfalls to those projected with respect to private pension plans. Out of concern about the financial well-being of so-called multiemployer plans, Congress enacted the Pension Protection Act of 2006, which established three categories of plans, based on the strength of their funding and ability to pay promised benefits.[51] Plans that are deemed in critical condition are said to be in the red zone; plans that are "endangered," in the yellow zone; and healthy plans, in the green zone. The law requires that each plan announce its status within the first ninety days of each plan year.

If Social Security had the same reporting requirement as those private sector multiemployer plans, it would announce that it is in the green zone. That standard finds plans are healthy if they are at least 80 percent funded over the next six years. Social Security is 100 percent funded over the next 17 years and 93 percent funded over the next 25 years.[52] The good news is that Social Security not only has substantial revenue coming in now, but will in the future, even without Congress doing anything whatsoever.

These projections should provide Americans with a sense of confidence, because Social Security is being so carefully monitored and managed. Instead, the annual Trustees Reports have been turned on their heads, giving the opponents the opportunity to trigger hysterical cries of bankruptcy every time a distant shortfall is projected.

The aging of the population does not mean that Social Security is in crisis or unaffordable. Nevertheless, the fact that the number of workers compared to beneficiaries is declining, together with the totally unremarkable fact that Social Security, from the beginning, has been primarily financed on a current-funded basis, has been used to undermine confidence in its future.

The aging of the population coupled with current funding certainly does not mean that the current system is a criminal enterprise. Nevertheless, these unsurprising facts have been exploited and sensationalized by Donald Trump, his OMB director, his Secretary of Energy and other Social Security opponents who have made the highly-charged slander that Social Security is a Ponzi scheme.

False Claim That Social Security is a Ponzi Scheme

Labeling Social Security as a Ponzi scheme is another effort to undermine confidence in the program. Donald Trump, Alan Simpson, and others who have used this phrase seek to suggest that Social Security's use of current or pay-as-you-go financing is somehow unsustainable in the same way that fraudulent criminal pyramid or Ponzi schemes are. As chapter three explains at length, while one can prefer advance funding, there are sound policy reasons not to fund Social Security that way.

Moreover, far from a Ponzi scheme, current funding could be seen as simply the age-old tradition of adult children caring for their aging parents. Social Security in some ways builds on that model but does so in such a way that ensures the dignity and independence of seniors and children. It also treats more equally and fairly those who have many children and those who have none, those whose children are prosperous and those whose children are struggling.

Whether to current-fund or advance-fund Social Security or use some combination of the two is a policy choice with advantages and disadvantages for all approaches. But none of them are Ponzi schemes, unsustainable over time, any more than adult children caring for aging parents – something that was done routinely throughout history – is a Ponzi scheme.

The use of the phrase "Ponzi scheme" to describe Social Security is an attempt to undermine confidence and weaken support for Social Security. The use of the phrase "Ponzi scheme" is contemptible. The slander is much more objectionable than calling Treasury bonds IOUs or arguing that the contributions have already been spent, or even that the program is in crisis, when it is not. Ponzi schemes are criminal undertakings.

Using the phrase to describe Social Security slanders President Roosevelt and his advisers who proposed partial current funding in 1935 and complete current funding in 1939. It slanders President Eisenhower and every other president who supported current funding. Also, every Congress. And also, all the actuaries and other expert advisers who understood that this form of funding is completely sound and legitimate.

Although it hardly seems necessary to dignify such slanderous name-calling with a response, Social Security is too important to the well-being of all of us to not address it. The now-retired Social Security Historian Larry DeWitt published the following detailed discussion of why Social Security is unquestionably not a Ponzi scheme:[53]

****

Larry DeWitt
Research Note #25, Special Studies by the
Social Security Administration Historian's Office
January 2009

PONZI SCHEMES VS. SOCIAL SECURITY

The Real Ponzi

Charles Ponzi was a Boston investor broker who in the early months of 1920 was momentarily famous as a purveyor of foreign postal coupons who promised fabulous rates of return for his investors. Ponzi issued bonds which offered 50% interest in 45 days, or a 100% profit if held for 90 days. The supposed source of this windfall was the differential earned on trading in postal coupons. The actual profit on the postal coupons never amounted to more than a fraction of a penny each, but it didn't matter to Ponzi since this was not the true source of his profits.

Ponzi opened his company, "The Securities Exchange Company," at 27 School Street in Boston the day after Christmas 1919. He was penniless at the time and had to borrow $200 from a furniture dealer in order to furnish his new office. Within days he was collecting money from his initial rounds of investors. He then expanded the circle of investors by collecting money from a larger round of investors. When the bonds of the first investors came due he paid them, with their miraculous profit, using the money collected from the second round of investors. The news of these extraordinary profits swept up and down the east coast and thousands of investors flocked to Ponzi's office for an opportunity to give him their money. Using the money from this new surge of investors he paid off the next round of bonds as they came due, with their full profit, which excited even more frenzy.

During the heady days of the spring and early summer of 1920 Ponzi was the toast of the northeast as people rushed to place their economic security in his capable hands. As Ponzi himself described the result:

"A huge line of investors, four abreast, stretched from the City Hall Annex . . . all the way to my office! . . . Hope and greed could be read in everybody's countenance. Guessed from the wads of money nervously clutched and waved by thousands of outstretched fists! Madness, money madness, was reflected in everybody's eyes! . . .To the crowd there assembled, I was the realization of their dreams . . . The 'wizard' who could turn a pauper into a millionaire overnight."

The Schemer Himself

The Problem With A Ponzi Deal

The problem with Ponzi's investment scheme is that it is difficult to sustain this game very long because to continue paying the promised profits to early investors you need an ever-larger pool of later investors. The idea behind this type of swindle is that the con-man collects his money from his second or third round of investors and then beats it out of town before anyone else comes around to collect. These schemes typically only last weeks, or months at most. There is of course always the temptation to stay around just a little longer to collect another round of investments—especially since each new round has to be bigger than the ones before. But Ponzi made another, equally fatal, error. He became a member of high society and once he had gotten the taste of this life, he couldn't give it up.

The Decline & Fall of the First Ponzi Scheme

Although he started his business as a penniless coupon clipper, by the end of May 1920 Ponzi was able to purchase a palatial home in the banker's colony of historic Lexington. He also acquired a

38% interest in Boston's Hanover Trust Bank and became an instant pillar of the community.

Ponzi started his scheme on December 26th. Precisely seven months later, on July 26th, at the insistence of the Massachusetts District Attorney, Ponzi quit accepting deposits from new investors. It was estimated that Ponzi had been taking in $200,000 a day of new investments prior to the halt. At that point he had already collected almost $10,000,000 from about 10,000 investors. As word got out about his legal troubles, worried investors swarmed his office. Ponzi confidently greeted them and assured them all was well. He announced he would continue to pay matured notes at face value. Unmatured notes would be refunded in the amount of the original investment for those not willing to wait. He assured investors and law enforcement personnel that he had millions in banks here and abroad, far in excess of his liabilities.

From July 26th until he was jailed on August 13th, Ponzi kept up this practice, appearing at the office each day and redeeming bonds from worried investors. During this time he actually redeemed $5,000,000 of his bonds in a futile attempt to convince the authorities that he was on the up and up. At his bankruptcy trial, it was discovered that Ponzi still had bonds outstanding in the amount of $7,000,000 and total assets of about $2,000,000. Indeed, the seemingly lucky investors who redeemed their bonds after July 26th had to return their windfalls to the bankruptcy court to be distributed among Ponzi's larger circle of creditors. Ultimately, after about seven years of litigation, Ponzi's disillusioned investors got back 37 cents on the dollar of their principal, with, of course, no whiff of any profits from the nation's first and most notorious Ponzi scheme.

During his trial Ponzi's attorneys considered a defense of "financial dementia." Ponzi's acquaintances testified that for more than twenty years he was obsessed with devising various grand plans for amassing immense wealth. Perhaps, after all, Charles Ponzi believed in his own scheme.

The Logic of Ponzi Schemes, Chain Letters & Pyramid Schemes

The essence of the **Ponzi scheme** was that Ponzi used the money he received from later investors to pay extravagant rates of return to early investors, thereby inducing more investors to place their money with him in the false hope of realizing this same extravagant rate of return themselves. This works only so long as there is an *ever-increasing number* of new investors coming into the scheme.

To pay a 100% profit to the first 1,000 investors you need the money from 1,000 new investors. Now there are 2,000 "investors" in the scheme, and in the second round of payouts to pay the same return to these 2,000 investors in the next round, you need the money from 2,000 new investors—bringing the number of participants to 4,000. And to pay these 4,000, you will end up with 8,000 "investors," then 16,000—and so on.

If all the investors stay in the scheme, the number of participants would double after every round of payouts. Even starting with only 1,000 "investors," by the 20th round of payouts you would need more new investors than the entire population of the U.S. Eventually, the number of new investors that would have to be found would exceed the population of the earth. Typically, however, Ponzi schemes collapse long before they reach their theoretical limit as an ever-increasing number of new participants cannot be found.

Ponzi Progression Starting with 1,000 "Investors"		
Payout Rounds		Number of Participants
Round	1	1,000
Round	2	2,000
Round	3	4,000
Round	4	8,000
Round	5	16,000
Round	6	32,000
Round	7	64,000
Round	8	128,000
Round	9	256,000
Round	10	512,000
Round	11	1,024,000
Round	12	2,048,000
Round	13	4,096,000
Round	14	8,192,000
Round	15	16,384,000
Round	16	32,768,000
Round	17	65,536,000
Round	18	131,072,000
Round	19	262,144,000
Round	20	524,288,000

In the classic chain-letter scheme 1 person gets, say, 10 people to make an investment and each in turn get 10 additional people to invest, who then in their turn must each get 10, and so on. The money for the first 10 "investors" comes from the 10 they enroll, and the money for the second group of 10 comes from the 10 investors that each of them enrolls, and so on. Diagrammatically, such a scheme looks like a pyramid—hence its alternative name.

```
              1
             10
            100
          1,000
         10,000
        100,000
      1,000,000
     10,000,000
    100,000,000
  1,000,000,000
 10,000,000,000
```

The reason that this is a scheme and not an investment strategy, is that the geometric progression it depends on is unsustainable. You must continually get more and more new people into the system to pay-off the promises to the earlier members. After a few rounds of this kind of increase, the number of new participants in the next round would be larger than the number of persons on the earth. That's why all pyramid schemes must inevitably come crashing down.

(The U.S. Securities and Exchange Commission has a one-page factsheet on their Web site explaining why pyramid schemes are not legitimate investments.)

The Logic of Pay-As-You-Go Systems

In contrast to a Ponzi scheme, dependent upon an unsustainable progression, a common financial arrangement is the so-called "pay-as-you-go" system. Some private pension systems, as well as Social Security, have used this design. A pay-as-you-go system can be visualized as a pipeline, with money from current contributors coming in the front end and money to current beneficiaries paid out the back end.

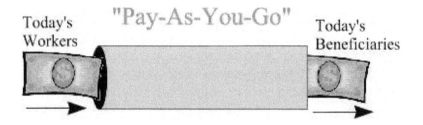

There is a superficial analogy between pyramid or Ponzi schemes and pay-as-you-go programs in that in both money from later participants goes to pay the benefits of earlier participants. But that is where the similarity ends.

....

The Start-Up Problem In Pension Programs

There is one other aspect of Social Security, and many private pension systems, that sometimes leads people to a mistaken analogy with Ponzi schemes, and that is the "bonus" paid to early participants in a pension system.

During the start-up of a new pension system the money paid to early participants is usually much in excess of their contributions and higher than the "return" to later participants. This is because people who are nearing the end of their working career will not have an opportunity to participate in the pension system long enough to accrue a significant benefit if computed strictly on an actuarial basis. There are three options: exclude such people from the system; leave them with an inadequate pension; or provide some kind of subsidy to early participants beyond what is justified by their contributions. In private pensions this differential is usually made up by subsidies from the employer. In public pensions this differential is funded by assessing higher taxes than would otherwise be necessary to pay a level benefit to all participants and using these additional taxes to pay higher benefits to early participants.

....

This type of "bonus" to early participants should not be confused with the mechanics of pyramid schemes. This type of benefit to early participants in a pension system has nothing to do with an investment scheme using Ponzi-like progressions to show false returns to early participants. In private pensions this bonus is simply an expression of the employer's beneficence. In public pensions it is an expression of public policy. In the context of the early years of the Social Security program it was an expression of a public policy which held that workers already old should not be turned away penniless. This spirit of public generosity has nothing to do with Ponzi schemes.

Ponzi vs. Social Security

Social Security is and always has been either a "pay-as-you-go" system or one that was partially advance-funded. Its structure, logic, and mode of operation have nothing in common with Ponzi schemes or chain letters or pyramid schemes.

The first modern social insurance program began in Germany in 1889 and has been in continuous operation for more than 100 years. The American Social Security system has been in continuous successful operation since 1935. Charles Ponzi's scheme lasted barely 200 days.

■■

False Claim About Social Security and the Debt

Related to the claim that Social Security is unaffordable because everyone is living longer is the claim that Social Security is gobbling up the budget and crowding out other priorities, such as spending on children. Nothing can be further from the truth.

Those making the claim focus only on spending and ignore the fact that Social Security has its own dedicated revenue. Their favorite trick is to use a pie chart, which misleadingly shows that Social Security, Medicare, Medicaid and defense spending account for most federal expenditures, supposedly leaving little room for other domestic spending. When the income and outgo are looked at together as they should be, however, the picture is quite different.

SOCIAL SECURITY DOES NOT ADD A SINGLE PENNY TO THE FEDERAL DEBT

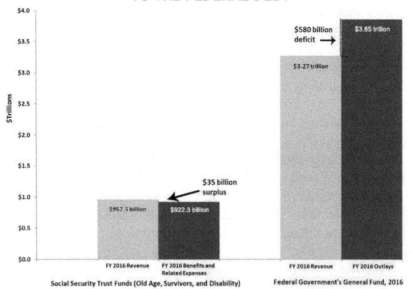

Sources: Data on Social Security Trust Funds from Social Security Administration, "Table II.B1.—Summary of 2016 Trust Fund Financial Operations," 2017 OASDI Trustees Report, accessed December 4, 2017. Data on General Fund from Office of Management and Budget, "Historical Tables, Table 1.4—Receipts, Outlays, and Surpluses or Deficits (—) by Fund Group: 1934-2022," accessed December 4, 2017.

The general operating fund has run a deficit every year but two, 1999 and 2000, since 1960.[54] In stark contrast, Social Security has always maintained an accumulated surplus.[55] Indeed, by law, it cannot pay benefits unless it has sufficient income and assets to cover all costs, including associated administrative costs. Moreover, it has no borrowing authority. Consequently, Social Security does not and cannot add a penny to the deficit.

Presidents sometimes try to argue that the deficit is lower than it really is by combining the general fund's income and receipts with those of Social Security. By that subterfuge, there were three other years, 1969, 1998, and 2001, in addition to 1999 and 2000, when the federal government supposedly ran a surplus. But that is misleading. In fact, the general operating fund can run a deficit, and almost always does. Social Security cannot and does not.

279

False Claim That Spending on Seniors is Hurting Children

A variant of the false claim that Social Security is a major contributor to the federal deficit is the particular charge that spending on seniors is imposing a crushing debt on children. Of course, Social Security does not add a penny to the debt. A related, false claim is that Social Security is crowding out spending on children.

It is catchy and apparently increases television ratings, newspaper readers, and website clicks to claim that there is an ongoing war between the generations. Indeed, the line is a regular staple in The Washington Post. In a 2013 column titled "America's Clash of Generations Is Inevitable," *Post* opinion writer Robert Samuelson claimed, "The elderly's well-being partly reflects Social Security and Medicare's success, but it also comes at the expense of younger Americans."[56]

One determined foe of Social Security, former Senator Alan Simpson, is fond of making this bogus point in a particularly insulting and crude way. He claims that "greedy geezers" – his favorite moniker for those who have spent their lives contributing to the nation – "don't care a whit about their grandchildren. Not a whit."[57]

The claim that Social Security somehow harms children fails to recognize that Social Security is the nation's largest children's program. It protects nearly all of the nation's children against the loss of earnings of a parent, grandparent, or other adult on whom those children depend for support. It provides benefits directly or indirectly to about 9 percent of the nation's children. It lifts more than a million children out of poverty and reduces the depth of poverty for millions more.[58]

The supposed generational warfare these critics of Social Security seem so eager to stoke has been accompanied by calls for generational "accounting"—analysis of government spending commitments and tax burdens distributed across generations, developed in part by Social Security opponent Laurence Kotlikoff. This misleading notion of generational equity even led to the introduction, in 2013, of a bill (The INFORM Act) which would require the Congressional Budget Office, the Government Accountability Office, and the Office of Management and Budget to prepare annual generational accounts and to use these accounting methods in their evaluation of proposed legislation.[59]

Though old versus young may sell newspapers, it makes no sense as a way to analyze government spending. The idea breaks down with even superficial analysis. Spending to prevent Alzheimer's sounds like spending on the old, but, if successful, it will not help today's old; it will benefit today's children, who will be tomorrow's old. So, which generation's account should that go in? Unlike many demographic identities, all of us are children at one time in our lives, and all of us hope to be old. Consequently, spending on one age group will likely help most of us at some point in our lives.

More fundamentally, the federal government spends money on many important concerns. These include the military, the environment, agriculture, infrastructure and other public concerns, expenditures which may disproportionately benefit a particular demographic but benefit us all, as well. Federal spending may go to defense contractors, farmers, business people, those of low income, and many other parts of the population. Of course, we should examine our priorities. But, in doing so, it makes absolutely no sense to pit just two subgroups of this spending against each other – unless your goal is to undermine support for Social Security.

Supposed Unfairness of Social Security

The false claim that Social Security is unfair to children is simply one of a number of current efforts to undermine support for Social Security by raising doubts about the program's fairness. Claims of Social Security's supposed unfairness are nothing new. They have been a part of the debate from the beginning.

At the start, Republicans legitimately complained that Social Security left many Americans out. As explained in chapter four, President Roosevelt's Treasury Secretary, Henry Morgenthau, was concerned about the administrability of the program and so argued that it should start with workers in industry and commerce, about half of the workforce. Moreover, because Social Security is insurance, those already old were ineligible for its benefits.

Gradually, and as intended, virtually the entire workforce participated, as coverage was expanded and the system matured. By

1952, three quarters of civilian workers were covered; five years later, the percentage was up to 85 percent. Today, 94 percent of the workforce is covered; nearly nine out of ten people aged sixty-five or older receive monthly Social Security benefits.[60]

At the start, opponents also argued that Social Security was unfair to business, supposedly imposing a crushing burden on employers struggling to escape the Great Depression. And, opponents argued that Social Security was unfair to enlightened businesses who offered their employees pensions, because the new Act would supposedly unfairly compete with those plans and, in opponents' words, "destroy" them.[61]

By the 1950s, though, experience made clear that Social Security was easier by far for employers than employer-sponsored retirement plans. The cost was completely manageable, especially with the conservative financing, where employers simply had to match what their workers paid and were able to deduct the payments as work expenses for income tax purposes. It is administratively easy, because earnings records are kept by and at the Social Security Administration.

It also became clear that, rather than compete with private retirement arrangements, Social Security made retirement with independence and dignity possible. Prior to the enactment of Social Security, most people, as they aged, were forced to move in with and be supported by adult children or other relatives. Because Social Security made retirement possible, it encouraged bargaining for employer-sponsored retirement arrangements to supplement Social Security.

Another early argument claimed that Social Security was unfair because it supposedly infringed freedom. Indeed, there were even rumors, during the 1936 election, when the program was not yet implemented, that Americans would be forced to be fingerprinted and wear dog tags.[62] More generally, the claim was – and is occasionally still heard today – that government, by enacting mandatory coverage, takes away freedom.

Once Social Security was up and operating, most Americans saw that Social Security increased freedom, rather than diminishing it. People who have independent income have more freedom, not less. They can choose where they want to live rather than going, hat in hand, to family members. Social Security beneficiaries have the freedom from worry that comes with a stable source of income. Independence and financial security in the aftermath of misfortune and in old age are blessings that exist today largely because of Social Security.

Because Social Security provides a foundation of economic security, it promotes entrepreneurship and professional risk-taking. It allows superannuated employees the ability to retire, rather than be fired when they no longer can perform the work required. Because Social Security is fully portable, carried from job to job, it frees people from being tied to a single employer. And, most importantly, it continues the progress of constraining work and allowing individuals to enjoy leisure after a lifetime of work.

New Claims of Unfairness to Replace the Old

As Social Security matured, the old claims of unfairness largely disappeared. But new bogus claims of unfairness cropped up. These new false claims are apparently part of the changed tactics of the Leninist revolutionaries who seek to chisel away support for Social Security, while hiding their ideological opposition. Today's opponents of Social Security have been creative in manufacturing arguments designed to question Social Security's fairness.

They claim that Social Security is unfair to poor Americans because it "wastes" benefits on those with higher incomes, despite the fact that Social Security is insurance, which is earned by rich and poor alike and, indeed, is the nation's most effective anti-poverty program. In addition to being supposedly unfair to poor Americans, it is also unfair to rich Americans because they could do better investing on their own – even though Social Security is insurance, not forced savings. The investment claim preys on the mistaken view that Social Security is forced savings. As chapter two explains, Social Security is insurance, not savings.

Outrageously, these opponents claim that Social Security is unfair to African Americans, despite its vital importance to that demographic group and others who have been discriminated against in the workplace and elsewhere. In short, opponents have argued that Social Security is unfair to every group for whom they could conjure up an ostensibly plausible argument.

The response to all the claims of unfairness by opponents of Social Security is that they are simply efforts to undermine support for the program. Social Security, of course, can be improved, but that is not the same as the accusation that it is inherently unfair.

A perfect example is the claim by President Bush and other opponents of Social Security that the program is unfair to African Americans because they, on average, have shorter life expectancies than European Americans.[63] The claim is false, though the underlying fact about longevity is true.

False Claim of Unfairness to African Americans

The shorter average life expectancies of African Americans is symptomatic of the nation's shameful history of discrimination. It results, at least in part, from a number of obvious social causes, including less reliable access to health care at every stage of life, higher rates of poverty, and disproportionate employment in physically demanding and dangerous jobs. The government should be investing aggressively to eliminate the causes of the disparities.

Obviously, Social Security is not the cause of these circumstances. Indeed, this claim of unfairness is a particularly cold-blooded, calculating charge. Those making the charge rarely, if ever, propose to address the underlying causes of shorter life expectancies. Rather, opponents of Social Security weaponize the fact in an effort simply to undermine support for Social Security by groups who, in fact, are most dependent on and benefit the most from Social Security.

Because Social Security provides disability and life insurance benefits, as well as retirement benefits, African Americans are not disadvantaged under Social Security. They disproportionately receive disability and survivor benefits for the same reasons they have, on average, shorter life expectancies.

Approximately 13 percent of the nation is African American, but 19 percent of those receiving disability insurance benefits are African Americans.[64] The numbers are even starker with respect to African American children. Approximately 14 percent of the nation's children are African American, but 22 percent of children receiving benefits as the result of a disabled or deceased parent are African American.[65]

Moreover, as explained in chapter two, Social Security's benefits are structured to provide a higher rate of return to those with lower earnings and those with more frequent periods of unemployment. Because African American workers, on average, disproportionately experience lower pay and higher unemployment, they benefit from that higher rate of return.

Rather than being unfair to African Americans, Social Security is vitally important to them. It is virtually the only source of retirement income for one out of two unmarried African Americans aged 65 and over.

False Claim of Unfairness to Women

Some supporters of Social Security have charged that the program is unfair to women. This charge, like the one about African Americans, is unfounded. Unfortunately, put forward generally by those who see themselves as supporters of Social Security, it unintentionally aids opponents trying to undercut support. The claim paints a false picture that Social Security has serious problems that require substantial modification.

As a group, women experience a serious pay gap, earning substantially less than men. Women more often take time out of the paid workforce to care for our families. For these reasons, women's Social Security benefits, on average, are lower than men's.

Like the shorter life expectancies of African Americans, Social Security does not cause those sexist outcomes, however. Indeed, as it does with African Americans, other people of color, and the LGBTQIA community, Social Security offsets these products of discrimination, to some extent.

As in the case of African Americans and other disadvantaged groups, women are advantaged by the fact that Social Security's benefits are structured to provide a higher rate of return to those with lower earnings and those with more frequent periods out of the paid workforce. But the degree to which women are advantaged is limited, because Social Security is insurance that replaces wages.

Moreover, women (and now, married same-sex partners) are advantaged in a way that other disadvantaged groups are not. Spouses, divorced spouses, and surviving spouses all may receive benefits based on their partners' work records. The provision is gender-neutral, but because one only receives those benefits if the spouse's earnings are substantially higher than those based on one's own work record, this structure disproportionately helps women, rather than men.

When the spousal and widowed benefits were first introduced in the law, in 1939, they were gendered: They were only available to wives and widows. The implicit assumption was that marriage consisted of a man and a woman who was a few years younger. The man was assumed to be the primary breadwinner. The woman either worked at home or, if she did work outside the home, earned considerably less than her husband. Although this was the norm, it did not fit every family. Rather, it was based on a predominant, yet sexist, stereotype.

As the nation became more self-aware of stereotypes based on gender and sexual orientation, the law changed. Over the years, as a result both of litigation and legislation, husbands were accorded the same benefits as wives, widowers as widows, and same-sex marriages, the same benefits as heterosexual marriages.

Even with the law as enacted in 1939, though, it is important to recognize that women were not financially disadvantaged; women were advantaged. Women received benefits identical to men with the same earnings records, if they earned cash compensation. But, they were eligible for higher benefits if they were married to men who earned considerably more than they did over their lifetimes.

Some have claimed that this structure is unfair, because those who are married and earn only relatively low wages contribute to Social Security but receive no more than those married who earn no wages and so contribute nothing. But, this is false logic. First, the former receive disability and life insurance protection. Moreover, it is perhaps impossible to structure Social Security to advantage both married women who work exclusively or primarily in the home for no cash wages, and married women who are paid for work outside the home.

The choice was made in 1939 to favor those who worked in the home for no wages. Indeed, the issue was debated during the deliberations of the 1937-38 Advisory Council, whose recommendations led to the 1939 amendments adding benefits payable to wives and widows. Walter D. Fuller, President of Curtis Publishing Company in Philadelphia, argued that "women who work all their lives should have a larger return than those who don't." In response, Paul H. Douglas, then a professor at the University of Chicago, and later a Democratic senator from Illinois, responded, "Of course, wives work too." That sentiment won the day.[66]

One member of the Advisory Council, Gerard Swope, President of General Electric Company, sought to address the difficulty; he proposed that, of the "total wages earned by any married person, one half would be credited to his (or her) account, and that the other half would be credited to the spouse's account."[67] This idea, known as earnings-sharing, has been explored from time to time over the history of the program. It has symbolic attractiveness and superficial appeal. However, serious analyses of the distributional effects reveal serious shortcomings.[68] The benefits generally would be lower for many beneficiaries, including widows, who, even under the current system, experience disproportionately high rates of poverty.[69]

A more limited proposal that has gained some traction recently is to impute income to those who take time out of the workforce to care for children or other family members. Although many caregivers would receive benefits that are no higher than they receive under current law, this change would nevertheless have value. Like the decision to make men eligible for spousal benefits, it would produce greater economic security for some. Moreover, it would explicitly recognize, at least to some extent, that unpaid work inside the home has value.

Because women, as a group, have been and continue to be discriminated against in the workplace, and because women live longer on average than men, Social Security is especially important to this demographic. Around two out of three Social Security beneficiaries aged 85 or older are women.[70] Of course, the older you are, the more likely you are to have exhausted your savings. You can outlive savings, but not Social Security's monthly income. Social Security is virtually the only income of nearly one out of two older women who are divorced, never married, or widowed.[71]

In short, rather than being unfair to women, Social Security is of vital importance to that demographic. Although the decision to provide wives and widows with add-on benefits in their own right was gendered, it is important to emphasize that the provision provided additional benefits, not lower benefits, to women.

Not dispositive, of course, it is instructive to recognize, in assessing women and Social Security, how many powerful women were architects of Social Security. Chairing the interagency task force that developed Social Security was Frances Perkins, the first female member of a presidential cabinet in the history of the country. Chairing the working group that put the idea of Social Security into concrete form was Barbara Nachtrieb Armstrong, the first tenured female law professor in the country.

Mary W. Dewson was a member of the three-person Social Security Board from 1937 until 1938, and Ellen S. Woodward was a member from 1938 until 1946, when the Board was replaced with a single Commissioner. Moreover, three members of the 1937-38 Advisory Council were women.[72] The Council's recommendations, including the addition of benefits for wives and widows, were largely enacted as part of the Social Security Act Amendments of 1939.

Most Outrageous Claims of Unfairness

Other claims that seek to chip away at confidence and support do not even have the veneer of truth that the claims about shorter life expectancies and lower benefits do. Another false claim, employed by the Trump campaign in the 2016 presidential election, is that undocumented workers are receiving Social Security benefits, which they have not earned.

The truth is quite the opposite. Millions of undocumented workers, working in jobs where Social Security is automatically deducted from paychecks, contribute billions of dollars to Social Security every year. Yet, by law, they cannot collect a penny of benefits. The actuaries of the Social Security Administration have estimated that undocumented workers have contributed over $100 billion to Social Security in the last decade alone.[73]

Not only is the claim of receipt of unearned benefits completely false, the truth is what is unfair. Social Security is earned. All working families that pay Social Security premiums should be eligible for its insurance payouts, if and when an insured event occurs. But that is not the law; undocumented workers do not receive their earned Social Security.

Like the lie about undocumented workers, opponents employ another outright lie, when they claim that Social Security is unfair to younger workers because it supposedly won't be around when it is time for them to collect. This lie ignores the fact that young workers' Social Security premiums are purchasing disability insurance and, if they have dependent children, life insurance. While young workers must wait until at least age 62 to begin receiving their earned retirement benefits, their earned disability and life insurance benefits are payable today, if tragedy should strike.

Moreover, even if Congress irresponsibly never increased Social Security's revenue by even a penny, the actuaries project that Social Security would still be able to pay 100 cents on the dollar until 2034 and 75 cents on the dollar for the rest of the century and beyond.[74] Indeed, it would take an act of Congress to make true the lie that future generations will receive nothing from Social Security.

Congress should expand Social Security's modest benefits and increase its dedicated revenue, so that future generations can count on receiving 100 cents on the dollar they have earned. Nevertheless, it is important to understand that Social Security provides insurance protection that cannot be found in the private sector at the same price or, indeed, for any price. Perhaps most important, in light of the disappearance of traditional private sector pensions and the failure of 401(k) retirement savings plans to fill in the gap, Social Security is likely to be even more important to today's younger workers.

All of these claims of unfairness falsely suggest that, rather than being of importance to the American people, Social Security is inherently unfair. The truth is that, with the one exception where undocumented workers are prevented from receiving their earned benefits, Social Security is extremely fair in its distribution. Though the program is neutral with respect to gender, race, age, and orientation, and though it, of course, cannot solve all the ills facing the nation, it does an enormous amount to offset the economic consequences of these ills.

There is a limit to what it can do when the nation fails to guarantee employment; provide everyone with decent, livable wages; ensure gender equality in pay and elsewhere; and provide universal, high quality health care as a matter of right to everyone. In expanding Social Security, it is important to work towards making the entire economy and society fairer.

Supporters of Social Security should be careful in the manner in which they argue for improvements to Social Security, such as caregiving credits or better returns for working women. They should be careful that their language does not inadvertently help the Leninist strategists seeking to undermine Social Security. Of course, Social Security can be improved, but claims of unfairness are unwarranted. They have been used throughout Social Security's history in an effort to undermine support.

The False Claim About Modernization

Related to the false claims that Social Security is unfair and to the fear-mongering claims of crisis and monies stolen either by undocumented workers or Congress, is the catch-all claim that Social Security needs to be "modernized." The 2016 Republican Platform, for example, makes this claim, asserting that Republicans promise "to preserve and modernize a system of retirement security forged in an old industrial era beyond the memory of most Americans."[75] (It is instructive to note that the promise to "modernize" Social Security is followed by the Leninist Strategy assurance, "Current retirees and those close to retirement can be assured of their benefits.")

The truth is that Social Security, at base, is thoroughly modern. Just as in the 1930s, people today are dependent on wages to purchase the necessities of life. Therefore, in order to be economically secure, today's workers need Social Security's time-tested wage insurance. That insurance is secure, fair in its distribution, and nearly universal. It is also incredibly efficient, spending less than a penny of every dollar on administration. And it is completely portable from job to job, with little administrative cost to employers. Their employees are required only to memorize their Social Security Number or retain their Social Security card.

Supporters and opponents of Social Security alike sometimes wrongly claim that the program needs to be modernized. That claim, like all the other false claims discussed in this chapter, is destructive. It subtly undermines confidence in and support for Social Security, a program that proves the effectiveness of government and provides such important economic security.

Subversive Language and Misleading Framing

In addition to seeking to undermine confidence that Social Security will be there in the future and undermine support with false claims that Social Security is unfair, today's Leninist strategists seek to undermine confidence and support in subtler, but nevertheless corrosive ways: using subtly subversive language and misleading framing to reinforce their lies.

The Social Security Act of 1935 created two insurance programs, Social Security and Unemployment Insurance, and three means-tested welfare programs, Aid to Dependent Children, Old Age Assistance, and Aid to the Blind. In the 1930s and 1940s, those who spoke about Social Security recognized it for the insurance that it is. Although, as described in chapter two, Landon might occasionally refer to Social Security as forced savings, he also accurately referred to it as insurance.

The basic features and structure described in chapters two and three are identical to the Social Security we know today. No one in the 1930s or 1940s mischaracterized Social Security as welfare. That changed in the 1950s and 1960s, when some started referring to Social Security as welfare. Senator Barry Goldwater (R-AZ) blurred the distinction between insurance and welfare. Ronald Reagan was even more explicit in asserting that Social Security was welfare, not insurance.

Chapter two explains why Social Security is indeed insurance and why opponents refuse to accept that insurance, not welfare or forced savings, is what it is. Today, opponents generally do not explicitly claim that Social Security is not insurance. Some unelected pundits sometimes claim it is welfare. Washington Post columnist Robert Samuelson, for example, wrote a column entitled, "Why Social Security is Welfare." But no one running for elective office makes such a bold, bald-faced claim.

To be clear, welfare is important, but it has never had the broad support that the universal programs of Social Security and Medicare enjoy. Founder Wilbur Cohen famously quipped that programs only for the poor make poor programs. In a debate against conservative economist and Goldwater adviser Milton Friedman, Cohen explained:[76]

I am convinced that, in the United States, a program that deals only with the poor will end up being a poor program. There is every evidence that this is true. Ever since the Elizabethan Poor Law of 1601, programs only for the poor have been lousy, no good, *poor* programs.

Social Security is so popular and successful precisely because it is earned. Need is irrelevant to its receipt.

It would be wonderful if all Americans generously supported welfare: government programs which involved all of us, through our tax dollars, assisting those among us who are most in need. Unfortunately, welfare programs and those who receive the benefits have been demonized throughout our history.

The attitude of many towards the most vulnerable among us is to stereotype them and try to control them. Take the example of Food Stamps, now called the Supplemental Nutrition Assistance Program, or SNAP, a means-tested program for those among us who cannot afford food and, presumably, the other necessities of life. The very idea of the program demonstrates the stereotyping and controlling of recipients. Rather, than simply giving food-insecure Americans cash benefits, Congress insists on giving them food vouchers, presumably fearing that the recipients are too irresponsible with the freedom and dignity of cash.

And even that degree of control isn't enough for some. A Republican New York State Senator recently introduced legislation prohibiting the use of Food Stamps for steak, lobster, and candy bars.[77] Similar measures have been pushed by the Republican Governors of Maine and Wisconsin, as well as by Republican members of Congress.[78] Measures requiring welfare recipients to be drug-tested are being advocated, as well.[79]

Conservatives have a long history of denigrating and demonizing welfare recipients. Long before President Ronald Reagan popularized the pejorative "Welfare Queen," those receiving Aid to Families with Dependent Children were stereotyped as lazy, sexually promiscuous, bearing children just to collect higher benefits, and the like.[80] It should be a warning to all Social Security supporters that the welfare program, enacted as part of the Social Security Act of 1935, was repealed in 1996.

Playing to these prejudices, the Leninist strategists have worked diligently to transform how we refer to Social Security. Through their use of subtly subversive language and veiled comments, they have succeeded in popularizing language that implies that Social Security is welfare, rather than insurance.

The purpose of the following discussions is to sensitize Social Security supporters to be on guard against the subversive language that opponents have succeeded in making commonplace. It is important to reclaim the language, so that the debate over Social Security is an honest one.

Social Security is Insurance, Not a Safety Net

One of those terms is "safety net." President Reagan may have been the first to call Social Security a safety net. Just a month after his Inauguration, in a February 18, 1981 speech before a joint session of Congress, he lumped Social Security and Medicare with means-tested welfare programs. In describing his program for economic recovery, he stated:[81]

> We will continue to fulfill the obligations that spring from our national conscience. **Those who, through no fault of their own, must depend on the rest of us—the poverty stricken, the disabled, the elderly, all those with true need—can rest assured that the social safety net of programs they depend on** are exempt from any cuts.

> **The full retirement benefits of the more than 31 million social security recipients will be continued, along with an annual cost-of-living increase. Medicare will not be cut,** nor will supplemental income for the blind, the aged, and the disabled. And funding will continue for [means-tested] veterans pensions. School breakfasts and lunches for the children of low-income families will continue, as will nutrition and other special services for the [low-income] aging. There will be no cut in [means-tested] Project Head Start or summer youth jobs. [Emphasis added.]

Note that Reagan lumped together, undifferentiated, the earned benefits of Social Security and Medicare, and a number of means-tested programs. He referred to all of them as part of the "social safety net."

Reagan may have been the first to use the phrase "safety net" to refer to Social Security, but today it is commonplace. This is not harmless. Words matter, because they can influence thought. "Safety net" subtly implies that Social Security is welfare, not insurance.

A safety net is something you fall into when you are in trouble. It catches you if you make a mistake on the high wire or trapeze and find yourself hurtling toward the ground. You are, of course, glad the safety net is there, but falling into it is to be avoided, if possible. It is the sign of a mistake.

Occasionally, the next step – transforming the image of a "safety net" into a "hammock" lulling able-bodied people to sleep – is made. House Speaker and former vice-presidential candidate Paul Ryan (R-WI), in the 2011 Republican response to President Obama's State of the Union Address, asserted:[82]

> We are at a moment, where if government's growth is left unchecked and unchallenged, America's best century will be considered our past century. This is a future in which we will **transform our social safety net into a hammock, which lulls able-bodied people into lives of complacency and dependency.** [Emphasis added.]

In contrast to a safety net, insurance is what prudent people purchase because they are aware of life's risks and are responsibly and admirably planning ahead to protect themselves and their families against economic loss. Those on the high wire do not want to fall into their safety net, even though they are glad that it is there. In contrast, insurance is an asset prudent people purchase to protect themselves. The distinction is subtle, but important.

The phrase "safety net" is generally used when talking about need. Today, proponents and opponents alike talk about increasing Social Security for those who "need" it, failing to recognize that it is an earned benefit. Social Security goes to those who earn its protection. Need is not a condition of receipt. Achieving insured status is.

A related term, which Reagan used in the above quote and has become commonplace, is "recipient" in connection with Social Security. Reagan referred to Social Security beneficiaries as "recipients" – a change of language that today even supporters of the program use. But the language is inaccurate.

"Beneficiaries" are the beneficial owners of funds held in trust – as Social Security beneficiaries are. Beneficiaries, along with the insured, are those who receive the proceeds of insurance, as Social Security beneficiaries do. "Recipients" is a term generally used for those who receive welfare. Referring to Social Security beneficiaries as recipients too is a subtle, but significant, change in language from earlier years.

Social Security is an Earned Benefit, Not a Government Handout

Another misleading change in language gained traction in the 1990s. Starting then, Social Security opponents popularized another welfare-sounding term for Social Security – "entitlement." Today, politicians and the media routinely refer to Social Security as an "entitlement."

"Entitlement" is a technical budgetary term that refers to programs where the right to a benefit is established under the law. Consequently, the spending is mandatory, not subject to the annual appropriations process. But the word "entitlement" has a subtle pejorative undertone to it. "Entitlement" sounds to the non-expert, not like an earned benefit, not like insurance, but like an undeserved government handout. A government handout that the undeserving nevertheless feel entitled to receive.

The widespread popularization of a technical budget term with a pejorative connotation to refer to Social Security and Medicare, two earned benefits, as well as Medicaid, was no accident. The popularization and promulgation of the terms "entitlement" and, with it, "entitlement crisis" did not happen by accident. They were, it appears, purposely advanced by the opponents of Social Security, with the aid of unwitting collaborators, to strengthen the hand of those wanting to undermine confidence in Social Security.

In 1993, President Bill Clinton established the Bipartisan Commission on Entitlement and Tax Reform. He named as members several people with long histories of opposition to Social Security. The membership included billionaire Pete Peterson, whose vendetta against Social Security stretched back at least to the early 1980s, when he penned "Social Security – The Coming Crash," for The New York Review of Books and funded a variety of anti-Social Security organizations.

Peterson-funded organizations are fixtures in Washington, D.C. today. All of them working to convince us that the federal deficit requires cutting "entitlements," their leaders are regularly quoted in The Washington Post and elsewhere. Not just a behind-the-scenes funder, Peterson, prior to his death, played a prominent role in the Peter G. Peterson Foundation's annual anti-Social Security fiscal summits.

Another prominent anti-Social Security member was former Senator Alan Simpson, whose misstatements about Social Security pepper this book. He has used the term "Greedy Geezers" so frequently to refer to older Americans, some believe he coined the phrase. Almost two decades later, Simpson would team up with another Social Security opponent, Erskine Bowles, to co-chair another commission that debated deep cuts to Social Security. As described later in this chapter, Bowles and Simpson offered a Social Security proposal whose ultimate impact closely resembles what Republicans have been advocating since 1936.

Though the entitlement commission never produced recommendations, it did succeed in popularizing the word "entitlement" as a synonym for Social Security, Medicare, and Medicaid. As a former staffer on the commission quipped, the commission turned an eleven-letter word – entitlement – into the proverbial four-letter "dirty" word.[83] Today, members of the media and politicians who may not see that they are undermining Social Security nevertheless frequently refer to Social Security, Medicare, and Medicaid as "entitlements."

To those seeking to undermine support for Social Security, this technical term with a pejorative sound serves three useful functions. First, it naturally lends itself to the false charge that there is an entitlement "crisis."

When the Entitlement Commission released an interim report identifying the size of the so-called problem of entitlements, front-page newspaper stories appeared and network news shows ran major segments on the problems supposedly caused by out-of-control entitlement spending. A headline in the Los Angeles Times alarmingly trumpeted, for example, "Entitlements Seen Taking Up Nearly All Taxes by 2012."[84]

In this way, the word obscures the fact that it is not spending on these programs, but out-of-control health care costs that is the problem. The nation is facing unsustainable health care costs, private as well as public. Medicare and Medicaid costs are symptoms – the canary in the coal mine – not the cause of these rapidly rising costs.

The truth is that Social Security, Medicare, and Medicaid are very different programs, with different structures and purposes. But lumping them together allows opponents to charge that Social Security is unaffordable and must be changed. As described at length in chapter three, Social Security does not add a penny to the federal debt or deficits of which the debt is comprised.

The use of the term "entitlement" obscures this fundamental and clarifying fact. As shown in the following graph – displayed earlier in this chapter but important to linger on here – Social Security's costs are essentially a straight horizontal line, at around 6 percent of GDP.[85]

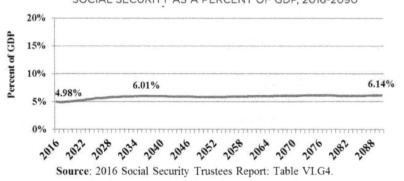

SOCIAL SECURITY IS FULLY AFFORDABLE
SOCIAL SECURITY AS A PERCENT OF GDP, 2016-2090

Source: 2016 Social Security Trustees Report: Table VI.G4.

In contrast, the following graph, produced in 2007 by the Congressional Budget Office, illustrates that if health care costs—private and public—were to continue to rise as they did from 1975 through 2005, these costs would consume a whopping 99 percent of GDP in seventy-five years.[86]

HISTORICAL GROWTH IN HEALTH CARE SPENDING IS UNSUSTAINABLE
(PROJECTED SPENDING ON HEALTH CARE AS PERCENTAGE OF GDP, ASSUMING COSTS CONTINUE TO RISE OVER THE LONG TERM AT THE HISTORICAL RATE)

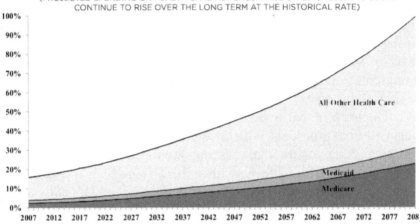

Source: Congressional Budget Office, "The Long-Term Outlook for Health Care Spending." November 2007

Recently, health care costs have slowed somewhat, but they continue to rise faster than overall inflation. The basic trend of Medicare, Medicaid and private sector health care costs remains the same: Medicare and Medicaid are merely symptoms of the real problem of rising health care costs, private as well as public, caused by an extremely inefficient and overly expensive health care system.

Market-based provision of health care, using for-profit corporations, is vastly inferior to universal, government-sponsored health insurance, which is the most effective and efficient way to cover everyone. Insurance is most cost-efficient and reliable when the risks can be spread across as broad a population as possible.

Only the national government has the power and ability to establish a nationwide, universal risk pool, with mandatory participation, making adverse selection impossible. And when the federal government administers the insurance, overhead is minimized. Instead of high-paid CEOs, hardworking civil servants are in charge. And other costs, like advertising and marketing, are unnecessary. The government can provide health care less expensively and more efficiently for everyone.

For these reasons, every other industrialized country provides universal coverage, spends less as a percentage of GDP, and produces better health outcomes. But we don't have to look to other countries to see the advantages.

Given the greater efficiency of government-sponsored wage and health insurance, it is not surprising that Social Security and Medicare are so efficient. More than 99 cents of every dollar Social Security spends is paid in benefits. Less than a penny goes to administration.[87] These are much lower administrative costs than can be found under Social Security's private sector counterparts.[88]

Similarly, Medicare covers seniors and people with disabilities, people who, on average, have the worst health and the most expensive medical conditions, requiring the largest numbers of doctor and hospital visits. Accordingly, they have the largest number of health care claims. Yet, Medicare is significantly more efficient than private health insurance.

According to the most recent Trustees Report, Medicare spends just 1.4 cents of every dollar on administrative costs. The rest is paid in benefits.[89] In contrast to administrative costs of just 1.4 percent, the administrative costs of private health insurance average around 11 to 17 percent. Indeed, the administrative costs of health insurance sponsored by very small firms or purchased by individuals can run as high as 30 percent.[90]

As a stark illustration of the greater efficiency and effectiveness of Medicare, a proposal floated a few years ago to raise Medicare's initial age of eligibility from 65 to 67 would have increased health care costs for the nation as a whole by $5.7 billion a year and increased premiums for Medicare and all other health insurance by about 3 percent.[91] Just as shrinking Medicare's coverage increases costs, expanding coverage would reduce our nation's overall health care costs.

Indeed, as just stated, Medicare's per capita administrative costs are substantially lower than those in the private sector. Strikingly, even Medicaid, despite its complicated administrative burden of means-testing those it covers, has lower per capita administrative costs than private health insurance, as well.[92]

If the United States had the same per capita health care cost as any other industrialized country, our nation would project long-term federal budget surpluses for the next seventy-five years and beyond. (The Center for Economic and Policy Research, a nonprofit think tank, based in Washington, D.C., has an online calculator that allows you to pick any of those other countries and see the effect on the U.S. budget. In every case, the federal budget is in surplus.)[93]

Focusing myopically on Medicare and Medicaid, rather than overall health care costs, points our attention in the wrong direction. It focuses us on the federal budget, rather than on rising health care costs, private as well as public. But misdirection is the point.

Lumping Medicare and Medicaid together with Social Security conveniently allows the Leninist strategists to argue that Social Security, as one of three "entitlements," is unaffordable. The framing shifts attention away from the real problem, out-of-control health care costs. Popularizing the concept of "entitlement" has fueled a new narrative – that Social Security, Medicare, and Medicaid are producing an entitlement crisis, the solution of which is to cut all three programs.

A second advantage of referring to Social Security as an "entitlement" is that many Americans do not understand the reference. Focus groups indicate that most people equate the word "entitlement" with a government handout—receiving something for nothing. Indeed, when told that the term "entitlement" includes Social Security, focus group members vigorously object. They assert that Social Security can't be an entitlement because they have earned those benefits, just as they earn their salaries, for work performed. When they are told that, in Washington, entitlement does indeed refer to Social Security, as well as to Medicare and Medicaid, they are often angry and insulted.

Because the word is not well understood by the general public, it supplies coded language to allow opaque discussions about cutting these programs. Those politically-explosive discussions can take place in plain view. Those who would vehemently object, if they understood what was being plotted, are left in the dark.

To the extent the connection to Social Security is understood, a third advantage to the use of the word entitlement is that it subtly implies that the benefits are a form of government handout. Like the phrase "safety net," the word "entitlement" obscures the reality that Social Security is earned.

Both the terms "safety net" and "entitlement" have become embedded in the language as ways to imply that Social Security is welfare, not insurance. Sometimes, the claim that Social Security is welfare is not subtle. As co-chair of President Obama's fiscal commission, former Senator Alan Simpson (R-WY) crudely asserted that Social Security is "a milk cow with 310 million tits [sic]!"[94] Less crudely, then Republican presidential standard bearer Mitt Romney stated at a private fundraiser, where he believed he was speaking off-the-record:[95]

> There are 47 percent of the people . . . who are dependent upon government, who believe that they are victims, who believe that government has a responsibility to care for them. . . . I'll never convince them that they should take personal responsibility and care for their lives.

The Romney 47 percent, inflated as it is, presumably includes Social Security, since its monthly benefits are received by one in four households. Two years before, Romney's vice-presidential running mate and now Speaker of the House, Paul Ryan, made the same point in public, and his percentage was even more inflated:[96]

> Right now about 60 percent of the American people get more benefits in dollar value from the federal government than they pay back in taxes. So we're going to a majority of takers versus makers in America and that will be tough to come back from that. They'll be dependent on the government for their livelihoods [rather] than themselves.

All of these comments conjure up a false image of Social Security. The false claim that Social Security is a government giveaway, that people are somehow receiving more than they have earned, has become a standard talking point of those who would dismantle the program. For example, on May 20, 2011, Fox Business launched a weeklong series, called *Entitlement Nation: Makers Vs. Takers*. The series pushed the idea that "the great divide in this country [is] between the folks who actually make things, and those who actually take what others make." Not surprisingly, those benefitting from Social Security, Medicare, and Medicaid were labeled as takers.

These are not new arguments. Those who are anti-government, who see themselves as having somehow made it on their own, generally are those who have been born with enormous privilege. Those who disregard the highways, military, court system, and all the other public expenditures without which they would be living in a state of nature, fit the quip that they were born on third base, but go through life thinking they hit a triple.

This mindset goes back well before the enactment of Social Security. Indeed, John Randolph, the son of a wealthy tobacco plantation owner in Virginia, served in both the House of Representatives and the Senate. In a speech at the Virginia Constitutional Convention of 1829-30, he explained his opposition to free public education, which he saw as giving those with children, what he believed was "a premium for idleness":[97]

> Among the strange notions that have been broached since I have been on the political theatre, there is one which has lately seized the minds of men, that all things must be done for them by the government, and that they are to do nothing for themselves. The government is not only to attend to the great concerns which are its province, but it must step in and ease individuals of their natural and moral obligations. A more pernicious notion cannot prevail.

Like Randolph about education, Leninist strategists seem to think that Social Security involves "things be[ing] done for" working families, "by the government," and working families doing "nothing for themselves." This malicious mischaracterization is deeply insulting. Social Security is part of our compensation for our hard work and contributions. People who receive the Social Security benefits they have earned are not takers. They are not helpless, pitiful individuals who have fallen onto hard times and into a safety net. They are not dependent on government any more than Representative Paul Ryan, who routinely uses the "takers" language, and other politicians, whose salaries are paid by the federal government.

Rather, those who contribute to and benefit from Social Security are responsible, contributing members of society. Insurance is what prudent people buy because they are aware of life's risks and plan ahead. People who are prudent do not need or want safety nets. It is why they purchase insurance. Just like fire insurance and car insurance, Social Security is insurance that each of us has purchased with our premiums. Just like private pensions, Social Security is a benefit we have earned.

The Eighty-Year-Old Plan to Repeal and Replace Social Security is With Us Still

From the beginning, opponents of Social Security have wanted to end it. Recognizing early on that it filled an important need of all workers dependent on wages, the tactic changed not just to repeal but to replace. Direct efforts to accomplish that end repeatedly failed, so opponents changed their approach: undermine confidence in and support for Social Security, while proposing "reforms" to "save" Social Security that all replace Social Security with the same basic ideological approach first proposed in 1936.

Then as now, Republicans recognized the popularity of the idea of Social Security. Consequently, in the lead-up to the presidential election of 1936, they wrote their Party Platform carefully. The platform appeared to support the idea of insurance. It acknowledged the role of government and the importance of collective responsibility, proclaiming "Society has an obligation to promote the security of the people, by affording some measure of protection against…dependency in old age."

At the same time, the platform claimed, "The New Deal policies, while purporting to provide social security, have, in fact, endangered it." In place of Social Security, it proposed, "Every American citizen over sixty-five should receive the supplementary payment necessary to provide a **minimum income sufficient to protect him or her from want.**"[98] [Emphasis added.]

On a superficial read, the alternative looked progressive. It covered all the elderly and was financed through a more progressive tax. It was immediately praised by newspaper editorials and liberal commentators.

However, the Social Security expert recognized that, notwithstanding its artful wording, the Republicans were not proposing insurance at all. The word "insurance" was never used in connection with the Republican proposal. It appeared only in the discussion of the Social Security Act, which the platform claimed was "unworkable."

Rather, the Republicans were proposing a benefit that focused on need, not insurance against the loss of wages. Eveline M. Burns, who taught economics and social work at Columbia University and had worked on the staff of Roosevelt's Committee on Economic Security, wrote a letter to the editor of The Nation. In the letter, she explained, "Careful study of the Republican plank reveals that...it nowhere suggests giving aged people security *as a right*." She continued, "Instead, there is to be a system of state-operated old-age pensions payable to people *in need*."[99]

The distinction that Burns insightfully pointed out has a very current ring. Today, Social Security opponents who put forth plans to "save" Social Security use the "need" language, just as the Republicans did in 1936 when advocating for their alternative to the newly-enacted Social Security. Senator Marco Rubio (R-FL), for example, has argued that "we should do more to protect seniors on the bottom of the income scale...by reducing the growth of benefits for upper income seniors while making the program even stronger for lower-income seniors."[100] Similarly, Jeb Bush, former Republican presidential candidate and brother of President George W. Bush, said in a 2015 Republican debate: "You have to reform Social Security, and the simple way to do it is to make sure that the wealthiest don't receive the same benefits as people that are lower-income."[101]

Even more drastically, former New Jersey Governor Chris Christie has proposed eliminating entirely the earned benefits of higher income Americans who don't "need" them. In defending his plan to means-test Social Security benefits, he said, "I quite frankly think that my friend Mark Zuckerberg doesn't need to collect Social Security, Warren Buffett doesn't need to collect Social Security. Their lives will not be materially changed by it."[102]

Landon and his fellow Republicans in 1936 were not quite as radical in what they proposed as Christie's proposal to replace Social Security with means-tested welfare. Nevertheless, their thinking aligned with his language as well as the language of others seeking radical change today. The 1936 Republican Party proposed replacing Social Security with a subsistence-level, universal payment to all, irrespective of prior earnings or contributions.

A subsistence-level payment, whether universal or means-tested, is a legitimate alternative, worthy of straightforward debate. Indeed, starting with the enactment of Social Security, we have had that straightforward debate a number of times. The American people have always sided with the advocates of Social Security, and consistently rejected the idea. Until the Leninist-strategist duplicitous approach, the debate was always candid and value-driven.

Representative Carl T. Curtis (R-NE), for example, was very frank in this matter. Joined by two of his Republican colleagues, he wrote his own minority view to the House Ways and Means Committee Report accompanying what would become the Social Security Act Amendments of 1950.

He clearly and openly argued that Social Security's wage insurance should be replaced with a universal, flat payment irrespective of prior wages or work history. His argument, just as those made today, was that this was a better use of limited resources:[103]

> The old-age and survivors insurance program is a grossly unsound and ineffective tool for the social-security purposes it attempts to accomplish. Because it is so unsound and ineffective, I cannot agree that the mere extension of its coverage or a mere numerical revision of its benefit formula, such as the majority of the committee proposes, can bring about significant improvement. Instead, the very fundamentals of the program should be objectively reexamined, and to the extent that such reexamination indicates the need for drastic overhauling of the program, that overhauling should be done, even though it proves necessary to abandon completely those concepts on which the present program rests.
>
> ....

Social-security funds are necessarily limited in amount...Because of this limitation, it is of the utmost importance that these funds be distributed wisely.

But the insurance program fails to make this wise distribution because it is tied down by the concept that benefit amounts should vary directly with the worker's former wage level....

It is my belief that benefits should be uniform in amount and independent of previous wage history.

Then, just a few years later, President Dwight D. Eisenhower was elected. This was the first Republican elected to the White House in twenty years. In that same election, Republicans gained control of both Houses of Congress. With that shift in power, Representative Curtis, backed by the Chamber of Commerce, advocated replacing Social Security with a minimal flat benefit paid to everyone 65 and older, irrespective of work history. Going back to 1936, many Republicans had proposed this plan to repeal and replace Social Security. However, President Eisenhower disagreed. To their apparent dismay, he proposed further expansion of Social Security.

Opponents of Social Security are still trying to achieve the end that conservatives in the 1930s, 1940s, and 1950s favored, but today they seek to accomplish it through deception. Conservative opponents of Social Security seek to slowly convert Social Security through seemingly technical, opaque proposals, such as price indexing and altering bend points, and describe their proposals as "progressive."

Today's opponents even claim disingenuously that their goal is to "save" rather than replace Social Security. In truth, these proposals would slowly but inexorably convert Social Security into a flat, subsistence-level benefit, unrelated to prior earnings or contributions. This is precisely what Landon, Curtis, and many other Republicans proposed over the years, as an alternative to Social Security.

Although President Bush's privatization proposal is best known for its provision allowing workers to divert a portion of their Social

Security contributions to private accounts, it also radically transformed Social Security's benefit structure. So did a proposal put forth by former Senator Alan Simpson (R-WY), together with Erskine Bowles, when they co-chaired a fiscal commission established by President Barack Obama to "address the growth in entitlement spending," among other goals. So did another put forward by Representative Sam Johnson (R-TX), the Republican chairman of the Social Security Subcommittee of the House Ways and Means Committee. And there are other, similar proposals advanced by Peterson-funded groups.

The proponents of those proposals all argue that they are seeking to "save" Social Security. In fact, they all reduce Social Security to a subsistence level benefit, irrespective of prior wages, just as the more honest opponents of Social Security proposed at its start. Though the details of the various proposals differ, the results are the same. As you see, current law provides benefits that remain at the same level over time, once the already-enacted cuts to benefits are fully phased in:[104]

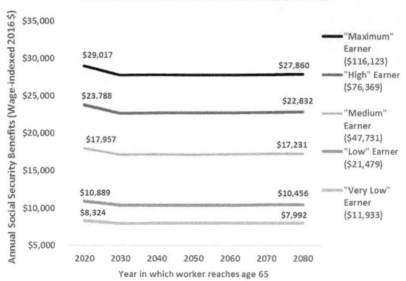

SOCIAL SECURITY'S WAGE RELATED BENEFIT STRUCTURE
ANNUAL BENEFIT'S FOR ILLUSTRATIVE WORKERS RETIRING AT AGE 65

Source: Office of the Chief Actuary, Social Security Administration, "Replacement Rates for Hypothetical Retired Workers," Actuarial Note no. 2016.9, June 2016.

In contrast, as the following three graphs reveal, the Bush proposal, the Simpson-Bowles proposal, and the Johnson proposal all cause benefits to converge toward a subsistence level benefit for all, largely unrelated to wages, just as opponents have proposed from the beginning:[105]

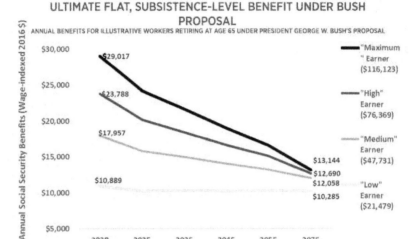

ULTIMATE FLAT, SUBSISTENCE-LEVEL BENEFIT UNDER BUSH PROPOSAL

ANNUAL BENEFITS FOR ILLUSTRATIVE WORKERS RETIRING AT AGE 65 UNDER PRESIDENT GEORGE W. BUSH'S PROPOSAL

Sources: Calculations by Social Security Works using estimated benefits under current law and estimated replacement rates from President Bush's proposal. Estimated benefits under current law & data for 2020: Office of the Chief Actuary, Social Security Administration, "Replacement Rates for Hypothetical Retired Workers," Actuarial Note no. 2016.9, June 2016. Replacement amounts from Bush Proposal: Stephen A. Goss, "Estimated Financial Effects of a Comprehensive Social Security Reform Proposal Including Progressive Price Indexing," Social Security Administration, February 10, 2005.

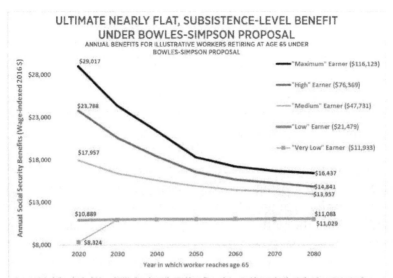

ULTIMATE NEARLY FLAT, SUBSISTENCE-LEVEL BENEFIT
UNDER BOWLES-SIMPSON PROPOSAL
ANNUAL BENEFITS FOR ILLUSTRATIVE WORKERS RETIRING AT AGE 65 UNDER
BOWLES-SIMPSON PROPOSAL

Source: Calculations by Social Security Works using estimated benefits under current law and estimated replacement rates from Bowles-Simpson proposal. Estimated benefits under current law and data for 2020: Office of the Chief Actuary, Social Security Administration, "Replacement Rates for Hypothetical Retired Workers," Actuarial Note no. 2016.9, June 2016. Replacement amounts from Bowles-Simpson Proposal: Stephen A. Goss, Memorandum to National Commission on Fiscal Responsibility and Reform, Social Security Administration, December 1, 2010.

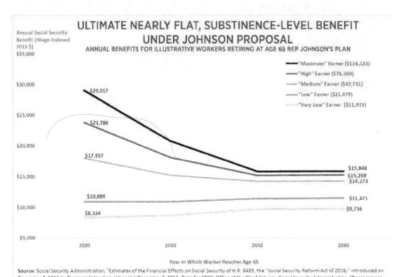

ULTIMATE NEARLY FLAT, SUBSTINENCE-LEVEL BENEFIT
UNDER JOHNSON PROPOSAL
ANNUAL BENEFITS FOR ILLUSTRATIVE WORKERS RETIRING AT AGE 65 REP JOHNSON'S PLAN

Source: Social Security Administration, "Estimates of the Financial Effects on Social Security of H.R. 6489, the 'Social Security Reform Act of 2016,' introduced on December 8, 2016 by Representative Sam Johnson," December 8, 2016. Data for 2020: Office of the Chief Actuary, Social Security Administration, "Replacement Rates for Hypothetical Retired Workers," Actuarial Note no. 2016.9, June 2016.

Although the details of the three proposals differ, all approximate what opponents of the past have proposed. The goal has remained unchanged: Essentially repeal Social Security and replace it with something more consistent with conservative ideology. Stealthily, these proposals are couched in technical changes to so-called bend points, percentage factors, and indexing methods, and are sold as efforts to "save" Social Security. Only those who are expert, who know the history, and who take the time to analyze the proposals carefully can see how similar these proposals are to past proposals to repeal and replace Social Security. Those proposals were advanced in the past by more honest adversaries.

Hiding the intent from view is the point of today's opponents. Indeed, those proposing the radical changes claim that they support Social Security. Though it requires vigilance, there is an easy way to cut through the obfuscation, as the concluding chapter explains. Clearly seeing what is going on is essential to an honest debate.

Americans deserve a debate over Social Security that is honest, free from misunderstandings, revisionist history, and zombie lies. A more honest debate will empower the American people, who overwhelmingly favor expanding, not cutting, Social Security. When the will of the people is respected by today's politicians, we will be able to move forward together in the step-by-step journey toward the greater economic security that the founders envisioned for us.

CHAPTER SIX: REMAINING VIGILANT AND MOVING FORWARD

As chapter one described, the vision of the architects of Social Security has still not, more than eighty years later, been completely realized. Yet it can be. The American people want greater economic security and deserve greater economic security.

The facts are on the side of the overwhelming majority of Americans. But the money is on the side of the tiny minority, outside the mainstream, who want our Social Security system cut and ultimately dismantled.

Money has provided access to policymakers and the media. That has allowed the zombie lies and distortions of fact told by the "tiny splinter group, whose number is negligible," as Eisenhower described them, to infiltrate far beyond the numbers of those who oppose Social Security.[1] The tiny splinter group includes anti-government ideologues and greedy plutocrats who have no interest in the common good, or, even worse, believe that money could be made if Social Security were not around. Enormous amounts of money flow through Social Security: dedicated revenue flowing in and benefit payments flowing out. None of it flows to the coffers of Wall Street.

That tiny splinter group used to have the courage of its convictions. Not anymore. Some of the most powerful and wealthy families in America considered President Roosevelt a traitor to his class because he championed Social Security and other progressive programs and policies – and they said so. In contrast, even those who today want to dismantle Social Security say they support Social Security. Their tactics are subtle but designed to be lethal.

Those who are determined to end Social Security are wily. To achieve their aim of ending Social Security, they resort to fearmongering and false claims. Many of the false claims are zombie lies; they have been made and answered from the start. Others are newer; indeed, new ones keep being invented.

One zombie lie, begun at the start, is that the trust funds are full of worthless IOUs, and the dead-beat Congress is stealing our money. A tactic of more recent vintage is to get the terms and phrases "safety net" and "entitlement" to be commonplace synonyms for Social Security, in order to change our basic understanding, and, in that way, erode our support for this vital program. The terms subtly imply that Social Security is something it is not – welfare or, more pejoratively, a government handout.

By never acknowledging that Social Security is insurance, and indeed asserting or implying that it is not, opponents never have to confront Social Security's striking superiority to private sector insurance. If Social Security is seen as welfare, simply a government transfer, not an earned benefit, that misperception leads easily to the charge that it is poor welfare because too many benefits go to those who don't "need" them.

A more obvious subversive use of language is the charge that Social Security is a Ponzi scheme. Seeking to cast doubt on Social Security's sustainability, opponents use the derogatory slur to imply that Social Security will one day collapse, just as all Ponzi schemes eventually do.

Cries of bankruptcy and crisis are another destructive use of language, intended to frighten and undermine confidence. Used the last time Social Security was projecting a shortfall, the language is being utilized again today, when Social Security is once more projecting a modest shortfall and consequently needs additional dedicated revenue. In response to the invented crisis, we once again hear that Social Security must be "saved."

In these ways, opponents have sought to convince the rest of us – and, unfortunately, have convinced too many of us – that Social Security is unaffordable and so, we must cut back the protections we already have.

None of the charges are likely to die. They are not honest, not about seeking truth, but simply intended to produce an outcome which the American people oppose. Having lost in their effort to win the ideological war against Social Security, opponents have instead turned to deception to undermine confidence and support.

Those seeking to "save" Social Security roll out plans that include technical changes, involving the jargon of bend points, percentage factors and indexing formulae. It is easy to be confused by these and other technical, eye-glazing proposals. But if we can emerge from the weeds and see the bigger picture, we see that the proposals gradually but inexorably transform Social Security into what the Republicans proposed in 1936.

Unlike those earlier days, however, today's opponents advocate their replacement in a much less transparent way. Indeed, today's opponents are totally opaque and claim that they are "saving" Social Security, but their solution is the same. The plan, then and now, is to replace Social Security with a uniform, subsistence-level benefit, unrelated to wages. Or even more radically, replace Social Security with means-tested welfare.

Today's opponents have been so effective that many elites who believe that they support Social Security have bought into the lie that it is unaffordable and must be scaled back. Today, some unwittingly propose to dismantle Social Security to "save" it. They may not even understand the implications of what they are proposing. They may simply be convinced that Social Security is unaffordable.

The truth is that Social Security, expanded as the founders intended, is fully affordable. The issue is one of values. Moreover, the values at stake are ones that unite us. It is these underlying values embodied in Social Security's very structure that make it so popular.

Social Security embodies basic American values. One value is reward for hard work. No one receives a penny of benefits if there has not been work. The more one works and contributes, the higher the benefit. Another value is fairness. In recognition that those of lower income have less discretionary income, the lower your average lifetime earnings, the larger the percentage of your pay that Social Security replaces.

Another value is family. Social Security is designed to protect the economic security of families. Another value is individual responsibility. Even the lowest-paid workers contribute to their own protection.

Another is shared risk. As President Obama so eloquently reminded us in his 2004 address before the Democratic National Convention, "We are one people, all of us pledging allegiance to the stars and stripes, all of us defending the United States of America."[2] Virtually all of us participate in Social Security, which protects each of us against risks to which we are all subject.

Another value is prudence and responsibility. As explained in chapter three, Social Security is prudently and responsibly managed. Through our work and contributions, we share common risks and responsibilities.

Social Security unites us. Moreover, it undergirds our economic security. The quintessential American values Social Security embodies and the vital protection it provides are what make Social Security so popular. They are also the reason that the Leninist strategists among us cannot allow an honest debate.

We Can Fully Afford an Expanded Social Security

Despite efforts to portray the future of Social Security in terms of affordability, the reality is that the debate over whether to expand or cut Social Security is about values and ideology. It is about what kind of society we want for ourselves and our children. The vision of the founders still has not been fully achieved. Whether this generation moves further in the direction those founders envisioned is a choice, plain and simple. Expansion is unquestionably affordable.

As the following chart shows, the United States is the wealthiest nation in the world, with the world's highest Gross Domestic Product ("GDP").[3]

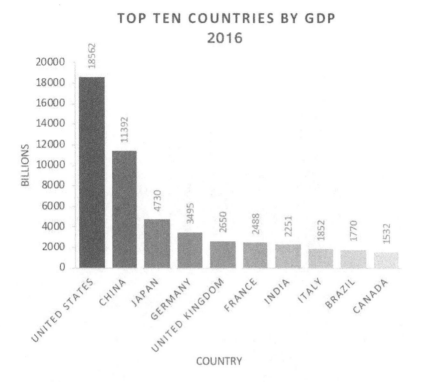

Source: IMF (Outlook October 2016), available at
http://statisticstimes.com/economy/projected-world-gdp-ranking.php.

Moreover, the United States is wealthier now than it has ever been in the past. Yet, our nation spends less on our Social Security system, as a percentage of its GDP, than other industrialized countries. As the following chart shows, the United States spends around half what many other industrialized countries spend on their counterpart programs. Indeed, the Social Security Administration actuaries have projected that, at the dawn of the 22nd century, Social Security will cost the nation only about six percent of GDP, considerably less than most other industrialized countries are spending on their counterpart Social Security programs today.[4]

MANY NATIONS SPEND MUCH MORE THAN THE UNITED STATES ON RETIREMENT, DISABILITY, AND SURVIVOR PROTECTION

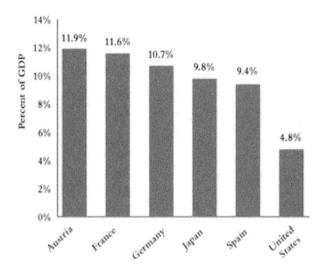

Note: All data are for 2009 (most recent comparative data available). All countries compared have similar, defined-benefit pension systems. Private systems are excluded, as are targeted social assistance programs. To increase data comparability, only half of spending was counted for program components in other countries that cover all government employees (and only a quarter of spending on those that cover a combination of government employees and members of the military/veterans), as only roughly half (a quarter) of such spending in United States is Social Security spending.

Source: Analysis by Social Security Works of OECD Social Expenditure Database

As the proportion of our population aged 65 and over is projected to grow from 15 percent to nearly 24 percent, Social Security's costs, as a percentage of GDP, remain basically a level, horizontal line.[5] As the proportion of the population which is older increases, it makes sense that a larger proportion of our common wealth is spent on that segment. That is just one reason that Social Security should be expanded.

Those who support Social Security must not be fooled. It is important to not be distracted by name calling, such as the schoolyard-like taunts of "Ponzi scheme!" "IOUs!" "Crisis!" and "Bankrupt!". Supporters must refute claims that are not based in fact; we must recognize and call out inconsistencies.

Opponents seek to have it both ways: On the one hand, they claim that Social Security is going bankrupt. On the other hand, they claim it is a major contributor to the federal deficit and debt. It can't be both. These are contradictory claims. If Social Security had a draw on general revenue and so was contributing to the deficit, it could not be in crisis and going bankrupt any more than the military is going bankrupt. The claim of crisis and bankruptcy rests on the fact that Social Security is self-financing and cannot contribute to the deficit!

Those who oppose Social Security are determined and persistent. They have tried to scare us with shouts of "bankruptcy" and "crisis." They have tried to convince us that young people would be better off with private accounts. They have sought to convince Congress to use undemocratic processes to enact anti-Social Security legislation, while shielding those who vote for it from accountability. They think that if action is taken behind closed doors, public debate is limited, no amendments are allowed, and action is taken speedily, the American people will be kept in the dark until it is too late and, then, will not know whom to blame.

They have tried to drive wedges between groups of Americans, in efforts to divide and conquer. They have sought to demonize the most vulnerable Social Security beneficiaries – those too disabled to support themselves through work. They have charged that these workers – who, but for good fortune, could be any of us – are fraudsters, lazy freeloaders who prefer to receive Social Security's modest benefits than work.[6]

And they are starting to try a carrot: sell the elimination of the Social Security premiums as tax relief. If successful, that tactic would undermine Social Security's structure and cut its funding stream, presumably as a first step to ending Social Security.

Some efforts to undermine Social Security are straightforward. With respect to others, it is more difficult to see what is really going on. Still others seek to complete the destruction before the American people know what is happening. These latter approaches involve undemocratic procedures to force through changes, such as working behind closed doors, and speeding changes through Congress, without the American people knowing what is being done until it is too late.

To prevent these efforts to weaken our security, all supporters of Social Security must be alert. We must know the facts. But that is not sufficient. Since everyone today claims to support Social

Security, it is imperative to have heightened vigilance. At base, it is crucial to understand that whether to expand or cut Social Security is an issue of values. It is an issue of what kind of country we want for ourselves and those who follow.

Pulling Back the Curtain and Seeing Clearly What is Really Going On

Unlike in the past, opponents of Social Security today claim that they support it. Fortunately, there are ways to determine who is truly a supporter and who is not. We should be skeptical of those who explain they are seeking to "save" Social Security. Supporters recognize that Social Security is a solution, not a problem.

Though the rhetoric is deceptive, the tactics change, and the precise proposals change, there is one fool-proof way to know what is going on. Indeed, it is a dead giveaway. The problem keeps changing, but the goal is always the same – cut Social Security's modest benefits or, worse, radically change its fundamental structure.

Those determined to end Social Security have their solution and are simply searching for a problem. Their description of the problem may vary. They may claim that their goal is middle class tax relief. They may say that they are forcing an intractable Congress to act. They may pretend that they are addressing an unfairness. They may state that they want to balance the budget or rein in the deficit.

But their solution is always the same: undermine Social Security's structure or simply cut it back, dismantling it brick by brick, in order to end Social Security as we know it. Indeed, the problem for which cutting Social Security is their solution sometimes actually contradicts another problem for which cutting Social Security is their solution. Take longevity.

Until recently, those determined to cut Social Security argued that everyone is living longer, so we must cut Social Security. In response, supporters of Social Security pointed out that not everyone is living longer. Okay, said those determined to cut Social Security. Not everyone is living longer. That is a problem. The solution? We must cut Social Security.

This is not an exaggeration. In 2005, President George W. Bush argued for cutting and privatizing Social Security because, "In today's world, people are living longer and therefore drawing benefits longer."[7] Supporters of Social Security dutifully pointed to research showing that this is not true. The wealthier are living longer but those without high school diplomas, for example, have experienced a decline in average life expectancy.[8]

Without missing a beat, those determined to cut Social Security simply pivoted to those new facts, arguing that Social Security must be cut because lower income people are not living as long, on average, as higher income people. Indeed, the Wall Street-funded Third Way think tank even went so far as to claim that Senator Bernie Sanders, a self-proclaimed socialist, favors the rich when he fights to expand Social Security![9]

Another solution in search of a problem is the claim that Social Security must be radically changed because African Americans have shorter average life expectancies than European Americans. The shorter life expectancies are, indeed, a natural disgrace. The nation should be doing all we can to eliminate the disparities.

The giveaway that this is, once again, simply a solution in search of a problem is that the solution is to dismantle Social Security. That, of course, will not increase anyone's life span. Worse, it hurts the very ones whom we are supposedly seeking to help.

The solution of those raising the problem is to make Social Security less valuable in the future. The "solution" fails to recognize how extremely important Social Security is to African Americans. Those employing the problem do not advocate solutions aimed at correcting the underlying causes of the problem of shorter life expectancies. When supporters of the Bush privatization scheme argued that Social Security was unfair to African Americans because of their shorter average life expectancies, their solution was to change Social Security in a way that would have hurt African Americans. By their logic, the solution to shorter life expectancies is to take resources away from those with shorter life expectancies.

A similar solution in search of a problem is the claim that spending on Social Security is hurting children. There is one clear giveaway that the concern is not about the wellbeing of children. The dead giveaway that the true motive is the dismantling of Social Security, that the charge is a solution in search of a problem, is that the problem and solution are a mismatch.

Adhering closely to the Leninist Strategy, those who claim they are concerned about children generally also say they will not cut the benefits of those close to retirement. Rather, the benefits they propose cutting most sharply are the benefits of those now children in whose interest they claim that they are acting. Let today's seniors keep their benefits but take them away from the very group supposedly aggrieved – today's children who will be tomorrow's retirees.

Once again, the "solution" proposed to address this concern would fall most heavily, or even entirely, on the supposed victims—today's young people and children. Like so many of the other claims, the apparent concern about children is simply a subterfuge.

As the wealthiest nation in the world at the wealthiest moment in our history, we can afford to spend more on seniors and on children. Indeed, countries that spend the most on seniors also spend the most on children, and those that spend the least on seniors also spend the least on children.[10]

Framing the policy discussion in terms of competition and fairness between generations ignores the fact that there is much more inequality within any given age group than there is between age groups. There is little "inequality" between rich old people and rich children. But there is substantial inequality and much to be concerned about when it comes to poverty and inequality that spans generations.

Focusing on generational equity points us in the wrong direction. So does a focus on a supposed entitlement crisis, which diverts our gaze from rising pharmaceutical and other health care costs. So does a focus on longevity, average life expectancies among different demographic groups, and all of the other problems used as explanations for why Social Security must be cut or, worse, dismantled. So, what gives?

In magic acts, it is called misdirection—focusing attention on one thing over here in order to distract from the real action over there. Linking the fact that the federal government should do more for children and young adults to the fact that seniors are benefited by Social Security is classic misdirection. The problem is not intergenerational; the problem is wealth inequality—which exists within every generation. The problem is not between races or genders or age groups, but between the bottom 99 percent and the top one percent.

The misdirection takes attention away from the fact that the wealthy are not being required to contribute their fair share toward the common good. Franklin Roosevelt understood this tactic extremely well. He laid it bare when he addressed the dirty pay-envelope trick on the eve of the 1936 election. He pulled back the curtain when, in response to misinformation being spread about Social Security in the 1936 campaign, he charged, "It is an old strategy of tyrants to delude their victims into fighting their battles for them."[11]

That is what is going on today. The tyrant is the same. Moneyed interests and ideologically driven groups are seeking to undermine confidence, undermine support, and get natural allies to fight with one another, in a longstanding effort to dismantle Social Security.

But a strong defense against those who want to tear Social Security apart is only part of the solution. We must work to expand Social Security, to further the goals and the vision of its founders.

The Time is Right for More Steps
Toward the Founders' Vision

Until recently, the idea of further expansion of Social Security was not part of the mainstream discussion. Having been swayed by the myth of unaffordability and the other zombie lies, both Democratic and Republican leaders seemed reluctant to speak boldly about Social Security. They recognized how popular Social Security is and, apparently, believed that to talk about it in anything but generalities was to anger the American people. Having successfully defeated the Bush plan to privatize Social Security, Democrats were more than happy to fight this old battle and declare their opposition to privatization. But neither side moved beyond generalities about "strengthening" and "saving" Social Security.

This timidity – and similarity – is captured in a comparison of the 2008 Democratic and Republican platforms.[12] The 2008 Democratic Party Platform, for example, promised in its preamble to "protect Social Security, and help Americans save for retirement." Despite the title of the plank, "Retirement and Social

Security," the phrase Social Security was not even mentioned until the 258th and 259th words of the 300-word section.

Its 53 words about Social Security offered only the vague promise to "fulfill our obligation to strengthen Social Security." The Social Security plank of the Republican Party Platform, like the Democratic plank, asserted vaguely, "We are committed to putting Social Security on a sound fiscal basis."

While the Democratic plank included the defensive promise, "We will not privatize Social Security," it asserted, near the outset, "In the 21st Century, Americans…need better ways to save for retirement." And, in contrast to its vague Social Security promise to "strengthen it," the plank followed the assertion about "better" ways for saving in the 21st century with the specific proposal: "We will automatically enroll every worker in a workplace pension plan that can be carried from job to job and we will match savings for working families who need the help."

Notwithstanding the Democratic line expressing opposition to privatization, the Republican plank did not use the words, "privatize Social Security." Muddying the distinction between what the two parties supported, the Republican plank deftly promised, "Comprehensive reform should include the opportunity to freely choose to create your own personal investment accounts which are distinct from and supplemental to the overall Social Security system."

To the careful reader, the two planks read very differently. The Republican plank engaged in fear-mongering and the tactics described in this book. It entitled its Social Security, Medicare, and Medicaid plank, "Entitlement Reform." It claimed, falsely, that "younger workers will not be able to depend on Social Security as part of their retirement plan." Following the Leninist strategy, it reassured, "No changes in the system should adversely affect any current or near-retiree." Moreover, it hinted at privatization, asserting, "We believe the solution should give workers control over, and a fair return on, their contributions." In contrast, the Democratic plank stated that it believed Social Security to be indispensable and promised "to make sure that it provides guaranteed benefits."

But on a quick read, the distinctions were easily overlooked. Though the Republicans devoted twice as many words to Social

Security, the specifics were similar. Vaguely promising to "strengthen" Social Security, in the case of the Democrats, or "putting Social Security on a sound fiscal basis," in the case of the Republicans, most of the focus of both was on saving for retirement.

The Social Security Debate is Becoming More Honest

The good news is that the conversation has begun to shift. No longer are calls for "saving" Social Security a disguised way of asking how much do we cut. No longer is a call for a bipartisan solution, a disguised way of expressing the need to cut. No longer is the question to be debated, how do we cut secretly, behind closed doors, and without accountability so the American people won't know whom to blame.

In the last few years, the Democratic Party has shaken free from the lie of unaffordability and has embraced expanding Social Security. Specific in its promise to expand this vital program, the Social Security plank of the 2016 Democratic Party Platform reads in its entirety:[13]

Protecting and Expanding Social Security
Democrats are proud to be the party that created Social Security, one of the nation's most successful and effective programs. Without Social Security, nearly half of America's seniors would be living in poverty. Social Security is more than just a retirement program. It also provides important life insurance to young survivors of deceased workers and provides disability insurance protection. We will fight every effort to cut, privatize, or weaken Social Security, including attempts to raise the retirement age, diminish benefits by cutting cost-of-living adjustments, or reducing earned benefits. Democrats will expand Social Security so that every American can retire with dignity and respect, including women who are widowed or took time out of the workforce to care for their children, aging parents, or ailing family members. The Democratic Party recognizes that the way Social Security cost-of-living adjustments are calculated may not always reflect the spending patterns of seniors, particularly the disproportionate amount they spend

on health care expenses. We are committed to exploring alternatives that could better and more equitably serve seniors.

We will make sure Social Security's guaranteed benefits continue for generations to come by asking those at the top to pay more, and will achieve this goal by taxing some of the income of people above $250,000. The Democratic Party is also committed to providing all necessary financial support for the Social Security Administration so that it can provide timely benefits and high-quality service for those it serves. Our plan contrasts starkly with Donald Trump. He has referred to Social Security as a "Ponzi scheme" and has called for privatizing it as well as increasing the retirement age.

Revealingly, the 2016 Republican Party Platform continued to employ deceptive tactics.[14] Under the alarmist title, "Saving Social Security," the plank falsely asserts that "everyone knows that [Social Security's] current course will lead to a financial and social disaster." Using the tactic of George W. Bush in his claim to be only "modernizing" the program, implying that it is outdated, the Republican Party promises "to preserve and modernize a system of retirement security forged in an old industrial era beyond the memory of most Americans."

Employing the Leninist strategy, the Republican plank immediately reassures older Americans: "Current retirees and those close to retirement can be assured of their benefits." It refuses to take a straightforward stance, though it takes another jab by implying that Social Security is in danger and needs saving, asserting, "Of the many reforms being proposed, all options should be considered to preserve Social Security."

Contradicting its all-options language, though, the next sentence takes it back: "As Republicans, we oppose tax increases and believe in the power of markets to create wealth and to help secure the future of our Social Security system."

Thanks to the Democratic Party awakening from its Leninist-strategist-induced slumber, the question has started to become more even-handed: Do we cut Social Security or expand it? And what is the fairest way, consistent with the program's fundamental structure, to pay for Social Security's earned benefits? When those are the questions, there is no need for secrecy, for fast tracks, for undemocratic processes, for gridlock. No need, because, as polarized as the American people are over many issues, we are united in our support for Social Security.

Expanding Social Security Represents the Will of the People

Support for Social Security expansion, and opposition to benefit reductions, cuts across ideological divides. Poll after poll shows that Americans are overwhelmingly united in our strong support for Social Security.[15] The overwhelming majority of us believe Social Security is more important than ever. We adamantly object to it being cut, and favor its expansion. These views are shared by Republicans, Independents, and Democrats. They are held by self-identified Tea Partiers and union households. All ages, genders, income levels, races, and ethnicities hold these views.

Consistent with the understanding by Democrats that the question of whether to expand or cut Social Security is a matter of values, not affordability, Democratic Senators and Representatives have introduced numerous bills expanding Social Security, while eliminating the program's modest shortfall.

The issue is how to enact expansion. The American people will carry the day, as we always have, if we are informed, get involved, and remember that politicians work for the American people, not the other way around.

Social Security should be expanded not only because it is the strong will of the people. Social Security expansion should become law because it is profoundly wise policy.

Expanding Social Security is Profoundly Wise Policy

Expanding Social Security is a solution. The nation is facing a looming retirement income crisis, where too many Americans fear they will never be able to stop work and maintain their standards of living for the remainder of their lives. Social Security is the most universal, secure, fair, portable, and efficient source of retirement income that we have, providing a guaranteed, inflation-protected source of income that one will never outlive. Expanding Social Security is a commonsense solution to that looming crisis.

Another challenge we face is rising income and wealth inequality. Not only is this unfair, it is deeply destabilizing. President Barack Obama has called it "the defining challenge of our time."[16] Expanding Social Security while requiring the wealthiest to pay more will begin to put the brakes on and perhaps begin to reverse the upward redistribution of wealth.

Another challenge of our time is the decline of the middle class. Among its other costs, it is, like income and wealth inequality more generally, highly destabilizing. Expanding Social Security can lessen the financial squeeze on working families.

Social Security is also an important solution to addressing racial disparities in wealth and incomes. People of color have lower incomes, less secure employment, and fewer savings, on average, than European Americans. Social Security, which replaces a higher proportion of earnings for workers with lower incomes and for those who have less regular paid employment, is especially important to people of color, women, and others who have faced discrimination in the employment market.

Next Steps to Expand Social Security and Move Forward Toward the Founders' Far-Reaching Vision

Expanding Social Security helps everyone. Increasing retirement benefits automatically increases disability and survivor benefits, because they are derived from the same benefit formula. Those benefits should be increased for current beneficiaries, current workers and their families who have not yet experienced an insured event, and all future workers and their families.

In addition to increasing the level of benefits, its protections should be expanded, as well. From the beginning, the founders spoke of temporary disability protection, as well as long-term disability insurance. Protection against long-term disability was added in 1956, but protection against short-term disability still is not part of our Social Security system. It is well past time to provide Social Security against that risk, as well. Under that protection, working families could receive paid family leave upon the birth or adoption of a child, and paid sick leave. Like Social Security's other insured events, these are generally times when wages disappear and costs increase.

Other Social Security benefits should be added. Other countries provide children's allowances, for example. In addition, at least one benefit should be restored. Social Security used to pay dependent benefits when children, who received benefits as the result of the death, disability or retirement of a worker, enrolled in college, university or vocational training after high school. The idea was that parents, if they are able, seek to support their children in obtaining this advanced training. When the parent is no longer earning a wage, all of us, through Social Security, are taking on that responsibility. That benefit should be restored.

It is important to recognize that these expansions are not efforts to "modernize" Social Security, a term which sometimes is used to imply that Social Security is out of date and past its usefulness. At a 2005 event in Montgomery, Alabama, President George W. Bush, for example, asserted, in his crusade to sell his privatization scheme:[17]

"…[T]his is a generational issue, it truly is. The system worked for the grandparents. The question is, will we be able to get something in place, modernize the system—not tear it apart, not destroy it—modernize it, reform it so it works for the grandkids."

Social Security is thoroughly modern in its goals. As long as people are dependent on wages, we need wage insurance against the loss of those wages.

As Social Security is increased, its companion program, the Supplemental Security Income program ("SSI") should be increased as well. SSI, which currently serves more than 8.3 million low-income aged and disabled Americans, is means-tested welfare that is an important complement to Social Security.[18] As described in chapter two, Social Security's goal, as wage insurance, is to prevent poverty and allow workers to maintain their standards of living when wages are lost. As long as there is poverty, however, welfare is essential.

Some talk about improving Social Security for the most vulnerable among us. While that is an important goal, it is crucial that the goal is not met by transforming Social Security into something it is not. As wage insurance, it is universal and requires a substantial attachment to the workforce. SSI, as a companion program, is the best way to help the most vulnerable among us without inadvertently undermining Social Security.

SSI's benefits are extremely low and in serious need of updating. In 2017, the maximum federal SSI payment was just $735 a month for individuals and just $1,103 for couples.[19] Those extremely modest benefit levels should be increased. In addition, SSI's very restrictive eligibility criteria are in desperate need of updating. The assets limit, $2,000 for individuals and $3,000 for couples, has only been updated once, in 1989. It should be updated and then increased automatically each year to offset changes in the cost of living. Same for the earnings limitations, which have not been increased since the program's enactment in 1972!

Note, too, that if Social Security is increased without changes to SSI, the inadvertent result could be that those whom policymakers are seeking to help would be no better off or even worse off. That is because Social Security benefits are deducted dollar-for-dollar from SSI benefits, after an initial disregard of just $20. Consequently, an increase in Social Security benefits could simply supplant a person's SSI benefits. Worse, if the increased benefits make the person ineligible for any SSI benefit, the recipient might lose Medicaid coverage, and thus be worse off!

Importantly, none of us can be economically secure, if we are one illness or accident away from bankruptcy. Medicare should be expanded until it covers everyone, just as the founders intended. Medicare for All is picking up support within the Democratic Party. Senator and 2016 presidential candidate Bernie Sanders (I-VT) has introduced a Medicare for All bill, co-sponsored by more than a third of the Senate Democrats.[20] The sixteen original co-sponsors include leaders of the party – Senators Elizabeth Warren (D-MA), Kamala Harris (D-CA), Cory Booker (D-NJ), and Kirsten Gillibrand (D-NY). The House counterpart has 120 cosponsors, more than 60 percent of the House Democrats![21]

If Medicare for All is not enacted soon, incremental steps can and should be taken. Medicare's initial age of eligibility should be reduced from 65 to 62, when beneficiaries can first start receiving Social Security. Even better would be to reduce the initial Medicare age to 50, when Americans begin to pay a so-called age tax for private insurance coverage. Lowering the Medicare age to 50 would not only eliminate the age tax, it would reduce the costs of both private insurance and Medicare. It would remove the most expensive private insurance enrollees – those aged 50 to 64 – and add them to Medicare, where they would be the youngest, healthiest and least expensive beneficiaries.

Consistent with the idea that Medicare was simply a first step, it is long past time to enact a universal counterpart to Medicare for the nation's children – a proposal that Social Security founders debated even before the enactment of Medicare. This would greatly benefit society by ensuring that our next generation has a healthy start in life, and it would save revenue that we currently spend determining eligibility for means-tested programs like the Children's Health Insurance Program (CHIP) and Medicaid.[22]

In addition to increasing Social Security's benefit amounts both across-the-board and in targeted ways, adding new protections, expanding Medicare, and updating Social Security's counterpart program, Supplemental Security Income, we must invest in education and ensure that everyone is guaranteed a good paying job. Education and guaranteed employment are essential elements to true and complete economic security,

The founders of Social Security and those who have followed worked tirelessly to create and improve our Social Security system. They fought for it, defended it, safeguarded it, expanded it, and passed it forward. Prior generations left Social Security stronger than before, as a legacy to all of us, young and old alike. Now it is our turn.

How do we successfully build on the legacy that has been bequeathed to us, leaving it even better for the generations that follow? At base, we must understand that the debate over Social Security is a debate over values. We must insist that the debate over Social Security be discussed in terms of values.

The Future of Social Security is a Question of Values

President Roosevelt saw this clearly. Fifteen months after his first inauguration, he sent a message to Congress, reviewing where they had come and where they were headed. In it, he spoke about values:[23]

****

Franklin Delano Roosevelt
Message to the Congress Reviewing the Broad Objectives and Accomplishments of the Administration
June 8, 1934

You are completing a work begun in March 1933, which will be regarded for a long time as a splendid justification of the vitality of representative government....

You and I, as the responsible directors of these policies and actions, may, with good reason, look to the future with confidence, just as we may look to the past fifteen months with reasonable satisfaction.

On the side of relief, we have extended material aid to millions of our fellow citizens.

On the side of recovery, we have helped to lift agriculture and industry from a condition of utter prostration.

But, in addition to these immediate tasks of relief and of recovery we have properly, necessarily and with overwhelming approval determined to safeguard these tasks by rebuilding many of the structures of our economic life and reorganizing it in order to prevent a recurrence of collapse.

It is childish to speak of recovery first and reconstruction afterward. In the very nature of the processes of recovery we must avoid the destructive influences of the past. We have shown the world that democracy has within it the elements necessary to its own salvation.

Less hopeful countries where the ways of democracy are very new may revert to the autocracy of yesterday. The American people can be trusted to decide wisely upon the measures taken by the

Government to eliminate the abuses of the past and to proceed in the direction of the greater good for the greater number.

Our task of reconstruction does not require the creation of new and strange values. It is rather the finding of the way once more to known, but to some degree forgotten, ideals and values. If the means and details are in some instances new, the objectives are as permanent as human nature.

Among our objectives I place the security of the men, women and children of the Nation first.

This security for the individual and for the family concerns itself primarily with three factors. People want decent homes to live in; they want to locate them where they can engage in productive work; and they want some safeguard against misfortunes which cannot be wholly eliminated in this man-made world of ours.

....

The third factor relates to security against the hazards and vicissitudes of life. Fear and worry based on unknown danger contribute to social unrest and economic demoralization. If, as our Constitution tells us, our Federal Government was established among other things, "to promote the general welfare," it is our plain duty to provide for that security upon which welfare depends.

....

These three great objectives the security of the home, the security of livelihood, and the security of social insurance—are, it seems to me, a minimum of the promise that we can offer to the American people. They constitute a right which belongs to every individual and every family willing to work. They are the essential fulfillment of measures already taken toward relief, recovery and reconstruction.

This seeking for a greater measure of welfare and happiness does not indicate a change in values. It is rather a return to values lost in the course of our economic development and expansion.

....

We must dedicate ourselves anew to a recovery of the old and sacred possessive rights for which mankind has constantly

struggled: homes, livelihood, and individual security. The road to these values is the way of progress. Neither you nor I will rest content until we have done our utmost to move further on that road. [Emphasis added.]

■■

A few weeks later, in one of his famous fireside chats, Roosevelt reiterated these points to the American people:[24]

> [W]e must still look to the larger future. I have pointed out to the Congress that we are seeking to find the way once more to well-known, long-established but to some degree forgotten ideals and values. We seek the security of the men, women and children of the Nation.

He explained that his goal was "to provide sound and adequate protection against the vicissitudes of modern life—in other words, social insurance." And he warned, as this book seeks to do, about those who would oppose this greater security:

> A few timid people, who fear progress, will try to give you new and strange names for what we are doing. Sometimes they will call it "Fascism," sometimes "Communism," sometimes "Regimentation," sometimes "Socialism." But, in so doing, they are trying to make very complex and theoretical something that is really very simple and very practical.
>
> I believe in practical explanations and in practical policies. I believe that what we are doing today is a necessary fulfillment of what Americans have always been doing—a fulfillment of old and tested American ideals.

Today, it is not enough to simply correct the misunderstandings, misinformation, and, in some cases, outright lies. It is not enough to know the truth. We must lead our leaders.

In the past, enlightened policymakers of both parties recognized the value of Social Security and worked hard to expand it, in accordance with the founders' vision. Enlightened business leaders of the past valued Social Security and worked to expand it, as well. Marion Folsom, for example, was an executive at Eastman Kodak Company for nearly forty years. In addition to championing employee benefits at Eastman Kodak, he helped to found Social Security. In 1934, he served as a business representative on the Advisory Council to the Committee on Economic Security and then on a number of other influential and important Social Security advisory councils in subsequent years. He was a key founder, fighting to improve the economic security of America's working families.

By vigorously fighting for Social Security, the American people can educate today's political and business leaders about the value of expanding this vital, well-designed program. Like their predecessors, today's enlightened political and business leaders can then become important champions themselves. They too can join the movement to expand Social Security.

Paying Social Security Forward

It has been more than four decades since the last major expansions of Social Security and Medicare. It was 1972 when Social Security was automatically indexed so that beneficiaries on fixed incomes would not have to wait for Congress to act to keep their modest benefits from eroding further with inflation. That was also the year that people with disabilities were covered under Medicare.

But that is where progress stopped. The reason for the stoppage was that opponents of Social Security and Medicare, who have opposed these programs from the start, convinced people that they were suddenly unaffordable.

So, how best to pay for the expansions, consistent with Social Security's basic structure?

Having most of Social Security's revenue come from highly visible deductions from employee compensation is valuable because it reinforces the earned benefit nature of the insurance. But the earned nature really comes from the fact that Social Security is compensation for work. Most employer pensions are financed completely by employers, but that doesn't make the benefits welfare or unearned. Even if Social Security's insurance contributions did not increase by a penny over current law, they would, at the end of the century, still cover three-quarters of the cost of Social Security.

Wage stagnation has cost Social Security an enormous amount of revenue over the last thirty years. The vast majority of workers contribute to Social Security with every paycheck, but when their wages are stagnant, so are their Social Security contributions. Moreover, the percentage of wages paid as current cash compensation has declined sharply because health insurance has accounted for a bigger and bigger portion of compensation. Social Security contributions are not assessed against that non-cash compensation. That has also resulted in a huge loss of revenue for Social Security.

Wage inequality is a major factor behind Social Security's projected modest funding shortfall.[25] The earnings of high-income workers have increased much more rapidly than the average in the last several decades. As a result, Social Security now covers only about 82 percent of all wages. In 2016 alone, those at the top paid $81.6 billion less to Social Security, simply because the cap has slipped from covering 90 percent of wages in past decades to 82 percent today. Those are billions of dollars that should have gone to Social Security but instead stayed in the pockets of the wealthiest among us.[26]

For all these reasons, it seems right, in order to expand Social Security and ensure that it remains self-financing and can continue to pay all benefits and related administrative costs, that Congress look to increasing Social Security's progressive revenue. Today, only about three percent of Social Security's revenue comes from a progressive source, the dedicated revenue derived from the taxation of benefits.

In light of today's income and wealth inequality, it seems appropriate to increase that percentage of progressive revenue somewhat by dedicating a new source of progressive revenue to Social Security. There are many possibilities. The estate tax could be dedicated to Social Security. A tax only on those with annual income over $1 million could be dedicated to Social Security. A tax on the purchase and sale by banks of stocks and exotic financial products, like derivatives and credit swaps, could be subject to taxation and dedicated to Social Security. Such a financial transactions tax has the added benefit of discouraging dangerous and wasteful speculation. Tax loopholes could be closed with the revenue dedicated to Social Security. A wealth tax could be created. Countless other possibilities exist.

Unquestionably, we can afford to greatly expand Social Security, while distributing the costs in a fair way without unduly burdening anyone. Both the expansions and the various potential revenue sources are consistent with the founders' vision and enacted structure.

It is long past time that Social Security and Medicare be expanded once again. The nation is far wealthier now than it was in 1972 and obviously wealthier than in 1935 when Social Security's founders envisioned its continual growth.

Within the fundamental structure discussed in detail in chapters two and three, Social Security has been updated and expanded throughout its history. Benefit levels have been increased, new protections added, and coverage broadened. Although benefits were initially extended in a gendered way, to wives and widows, husbands and widowers were added as gender roles became less stratified. In recognition that divorces were becoming more commonplace, benefits were added for divorced wives in 1965 and divorced husbands in 1976. More and more, society is recognizing the importance and value of uncompensated work providing caregiving. Proposals to expand Social Security to credit that uncompensated work are increasingly gaining traction.

The Social Security program should continue to expand in accordance with the vision and structure established by its founders. All of the expansions and revenue sources discussed in this chapter, together with many others, are consistent with the founders' vision. In that regard, it is instructive to read the words of founder Edwin Witte in the following conclusion of the remarks he delivered on the 20th Anniversary of the enactment of Social Security:[27]

****

Edwin Witte
Address Presented at the Observance of the
20th Anniversary of the Social Security Act
Department of Health, Education and Welfare
Washington, D.C
August 15, 1955

REFLECTIONS ON THE BEGINNINGS OF SOCIAL SECURITY

....

In conclusion, just a few words more specifically related to the progress made in the 20 years since the Social Security Act was enacted. As you know, many changes have been made in the American social security legislation....We today have a much more nearly adequate system of social security than we had in the original Act.

Even more have I been satisfied with the administration of social security. Billions of dollars have been expended by the Government of the United States for social security without a trace of scandal or corruption. Costs of administration have been far lower than anyone thought possible in 1935....

No confusion in keeping the records straight, which everybody feared in 1935, has developed...And the credit for good administration, of course, belongs to the administrators and to all of them who have so selflessly performed their task so well.

The Future

Of course, we have not attained the ideal. The possibility and need for continuous progress is one of the most distinctive features of the American way of life and our economic system of free enterprise. We cannot be satisfied with the social security protection now provided to Americans. Retirement benefits in our old-age and survivors insurance system supply only one-third as much income, or less, to the workers no longer able to work than is enjoyed by older people still in employment. While the benefits under State laws to unemployed and injured workers are greater, our unemployment insurance and workmen's compensation laws also are very much in need of liberalization and improvement. None of our social insurance programs are as broad in coverage as they should be. Great risks, like early disability and prolonged sickness, lack all Governmental protection; and the voluntary forms of insurance we have, although most valuable, do not protect many of those who most need protection. Even at this time of near full employment and unprecedented total and average incomes, there are millions of Americans who face a most uncertain economic future and many who barely have the minimum essentials of life. The great objective of social security—assurance of a minimum necessary income to all people in all personal contingencies of life, has not been attained even in this great country in which the common man fares better than in any other.

We have come a long way. Great tasks remain. But mindful of the progress that has been made and believing on the basis of their records that the people now in the driver's seat and their faithful and conscientious subordinates are sincere in their profession of belief in social security, I feel that we can view the future of social security in the United States with complete assurance. We have made great progress, and, in accordance with our American ideals, will do still better in the future.

∎∎∎

APPENDIX I: KEY FOUNDERS AND ADVISORY GROUPS

The list of Social Security founders is extremely long. The five-member cabinet-level Committee on Economic Security – the task force that developed the proposal that became the Social Security Act of 1935 – was assisted by staff and consultants as well as an Advisory Council, a Technical Board, and a number of advisory committees, consultants and their staff. All of those people are listed on the Social Security Administration History website,[1] which also features a list of Social Security pioneers.[2] At that same site, you can additionally find a complete list of members of the Social Security Board,[3] and a list of the Social Security Commissioners.[4] For most of Social Security's history, it was an agency within a Cabinet Department. A list of the heads of those Departments is likewise available at the Social Security Administration's website.[5]

The following are biographical sketches, in alphabetical order, of key Social Security founders mentioned in this book:

Arthur Altmeyer

Nicknamed "Mr. Social Security" by President Franklin Roosevelt who appointed Altmeyer to the first three-member Social Security Board when the Social Security Act of 1935 was enacted, Altmeyer was unquestionably the most important individual responsible for the creation, implementation, and development of Social Security over its first twenty years. As Assistant Secretary of Labor, he authored both the president's June 8 message to Congress and the June 29 executive order establishing the Committee on Economic Security, and served as Secretary Frances Perkins's liaison to the Committee Staff. Named Chairman of the Social Security Board in 1937, Altmeyer became the first Social Security Commissioner, when the Board was replaced by that position in 1946. He served as Commissioner until 1953. He remained active in Social Security policymaking as a consultant, author, and lecturer, until his death in 1972. His obituary in the New York Times accurately reported, "His death last week ended a life that brightened existence for millions who never heard his name."

Barbara Nachtrieb Armstrong

The first female law professor in the United States and a PhD economist, Armstrong spent most of her career teaching at the University of California at Berkeley. In 1932, she published a landmark treatise, *Insuring the Essentials: Minimum Wage Plus Social Insurance—A Living Wage Program* (NY: Macmillan Co., 1932). In 1934, she chaired the Committee on Economic Security's working group on old-age security. An infighter with highly attuned political instincts, she successfully convinced the Committee to propose a federal program, despite the deep misgivings of others that the arrangement made it more susceptible to be found unconstitutional. She, along with Douglas Brown, also may have saved it from being dropped from the administration proposal when they tipped off friendly reporters of that possibility. Unlike many founders, she returned to California after her brief but important tenure in Washington and did not participate in further policymaking, perhaps because she offended influential people. (She apparently openly referred to Witte as Half-Witte.)

Robert M. Ball

Still, today, the longest-serving Social Security commissioner in the history of the program, Ball began working on Social Security in 1939 in a Newark, New Jersey field office, where he started in the lowest-level job at the lowest pay given a college graduate. He worked himself up to the highest position in the agency, where he was essentially in charge in practice, though not in title, soon after Altmeyer left. He served as Social Security Commissioner under Presidents Kennedy, Johnson, and Nixon. Even after he left the government, he remained extremely active in Social Security policymaking. He was instrumental in every major set of Social Security amendments, including Medicare, until his death in 2008. At the time of his death, he was widely recognized as the world's foremost authority on the U.S. Social Security system.

Frank Bane

Founder of the American Public Welfare Association in 1930, Bane was the first executive director of the Social Security Board, serving from 1935 until 1938. For the next twenty years, he was executive director of the Council of State Governments. Over the course of his career, he held a number of other important government positions, and lectured at universities in the United States and abroad.

J. Douglas Brown

Economics professor, director of the Industrial Relations Section, and Dean of the Faculty of Princeton University, Brown was a key architect of Social Security. Together with Barbara Armstrong and Murray Latimer, he developed the old-age security proposals for the

Committee on Economic Security. After the passage of the legislation, he served on a number of highly influential Social Security advisory councils. Indeed, he chaired the 1937-38 Advisory Council, whose recommendations were largely enacted as the Social Security Act Amendments of 1939. He remained actively involved in Social Security policymaking until his death at age 87 in 1986.

Eveline M. Burns

A professor who taught economics and social work at Columbia University for nearly four decades, Burns was a member of the Employment Opportunities working group of the Committee on Economic Security. In that capacity, she authored three major research papers on employment security issues for the Committee. A leading expert on Social Security, she authored three major Social Security books and consulted frequently throughout her career with high-ranking officials in the Social Security Administration.

Wilbur J. Cohen

Senator Paul Douglas (D-IL) quipped that "an expert on Social Security is a person who knows Wilbur Cohen's phone number." A protégé of Edwin Witte and Arthur Altmeyer as a student at the University of Wisconsin, Cohen joined the staff of the Committee on Economic Security in 1934 as Witte's assistant. The first employee of the Social Security Board, employed as the assistant to Altmeyer, Cohen was involved in every development of the program until his death in 1987. He was particularly instrumental in the enactment of Medicare. President Kennedy named him the Assistant Secretary for Legislation at the Department of Health, Education, and Welfare, and President Johnson promoted him to the position of Under Secretary and then Secretary. After his government service, he became a professor at the University of Texas and the University of Michigan. He continued advocating for Social Security for the remainder of his life, helping to form and run the advocacy group Save Our Security.

Mary ("Molly") W. Dewson

An activist who was prominent in the women's suffrage movement and a longtime official in the Democratic Party, Dewson was appointed by President Roosevelt in 1934 to the Advisory Council to the Committee on Economic Security. Then, in 1937, the legislation now enacted, the president appointed her to the three-member Social Security Board (which was replaced by a single Social Security Commissioner in 1946).

Thomas H. Eliot

In 1934, Eliot served as Counsel to the Committee on Economic Security, and then became General Counsel for the Social Security Board (predecessor of the Social Security Administration).

Abraham Epstein

An economist, author, and progressive activist, Epstein fought hard for the enactment of social insurance in the United States. He founded the very influential American Association for Old Age Insurance, whose name was changed in 1933 to the American Association for Social Security. A tireless fighter for social justice, Epstein continued to work, after the enactment of Social Security, for improvements, including for the enactment of universal national health insurance.

Marion Folsom

An enlightened business leader, Folsom was an executive at Eastman Kodak where he championed employee benefits. In 1934, he served on the Advisory Council to the Committee on Economic Security. He also served on a number of other influential and important Social Security advisory councils. President Eisenhower named him Under Secretary of the Treasury and then Secretary of Health, Education, and Welfare. In both the private sector and government service, he was an unwavering proponent of Social Security.

Murray W. Latimer
(Pictured on the far left)

An expert on retirement income, Latimer was Chairman of the Railroad Retirement Board and one of three key staff, along with Barbara Armstrong and Douglas Brown, of the Committee on Economic Security's working group on old-age security. That was the group that developed the old age provisions of the Social Security Act.

Robert J. Myers

A lifelong Republican, Myers devoted his long life to Social Security and remains the longest serving chief actuary of Social Security in the history of the program. In 1934, he was a junior actuary on the staff of the Committee on Economic Security, and was assigned to work with the working group on old-age security. When the Social Security Act of 1935 was enacted, he was among the first hires of the Social Security Board. He served as Chief Actuary from 1947 until 1969. In 1981, he became the Deputy Commissioner for Programs and, in 1982, became the executive director of the bipartisan commission that was chaired by Alan Greenspan and developed the recommendations that were largely enacted as the Social Security Amendments of 1983. He remained involved in Social Security matters until his death in 2010.

Frances Perkins

The first female Secretary of Labor, Perkins spent her adult life as a social worker committed to improving the lives of the people of the United States. A close adviser to Franklin Roosevelt, she was a driving force behind the development and enactment of Social Security.

Franklin Delano Roosevelt

The 32nd President of the United States, Roosevelt championed the development, enactment, and early expansion of Social Security.

Edwin Witte

Often called the father of the Social Security Act, Witte was the executive director of the Committee on Economic Security. He was instrumental in the enactment of social insurance and other progressive legislation in Wisconsin and at the federal level. As a professor at the University of Wisconsin, he continued to remain active on Social Security issues through his service on key Social Security advisory councils, testimony before Congress, and writing.

Ellen S. Woodward

A strong advocate of women and children, Woodward held senior positions at the Federal Emergency Relief Administration under the leadership of Harry Hopkins, one of the five members of the Committee on Economic Security. In 1938, President Roosevelt appointed her to the three-member Social Security Board, where she served until 1946, when the Board was replaced by a single commissioner.

Key Advisory Groups Mentioned In This Book

Throughout the history of Social Security, advisory councils and commissions have played significant roles. In 1965, Congress enacted legislation providing for quadrennial advisory councils. Legislation enacted in 1994 established the Social Security Administration as an independent agency and replaced the quadrennial advisory councils with a permanently-standing advisory board.

The following, which all included founders among their members, are key advisory councils and commissions mentioned in this book:

Committee on Economic Security (CES)

On June 29, 1934, President Roosevelt promulgated Executive Order No. 6757, which established an interagency, cabinet-level task force, the Committee on Economic Security. CES, which developed the Social Security legislation, consisted of Secretary of Labor Frances Perkins (as chair), Secretary of the Treasury Henry Morgenthau, Secretary of Agriculture Henry A. Wallace, Attorney General Homer Cummings, and the Federal Emergency Relief administrator, Harry Hopkins.

The 1937-38 Advisory Council on Social Security

A number of founders were members of the council, whose recommendations led to the Social Security Act Amendments of 1939.

The 1948 Advisory Council on Social Security

Founder Robert M. Ball was the staff director and a number of other founders were members of the council, whose recommendations led to the Social Security Act Amendments of 1950.

The 1957-59 Advisory Council on Financing

A number of founders were members of the council, whose charge was to study and make recommendations regarding the financing of Social Security. This was the first advisory council that was established, not on an ad hoc basis, but on a quadrennial basis. Legislation enacted in 1994 established the Social Security Administration as an independent agency and replaced quadrennial advisory councils with a permanently-standing advisory board.

The 1982-83 National Commission on Social Security Reform

Colloquially known as the Greenspan commission, founder Robert J. Myers was executive director, founder Robert M. Ball was a key member, and founder Wilbur Cohen was influential through the

Save Our Security advocacy group. The commission's recommendations led to the Social Security Amendments of 1983. *

The 1994-96 Advisory Council on Social Security

Founder Robert M. Ball was a member, but so were a number of people antagonistic to Social Security. Its one contribution was an appendix, excerpted in this book. The appendix explains that, contrary to the widespread belief, the current projected shortfall is not primarily the result of an aging population.

APPENDIX II: KEY SPEECHES AND WRITINGS OF THE FOUNDERS

(Asterisks indicate excerpts that appear in this book.)

Arthur J. Altmeyer

The Formative Years of Social Security (Madison: University of Wisconsin Press, 1966)*

"Social Security—Yesterday and Tomorrow," An Address Presented at the 10th Anniversary Award Banquet, NASW, Honoring Wilbur J. Cohen, Under Secretary, HEW, Washington-Hilton Hotel, December 9, 1965*

Barbara Nachtrieb Armstrong

Compulsory health insurance (Oakland, CA: University of California, 1917)

Insuring the Essentials: Minimum Wage Plus Social Insurance—A Living Wage Program (NY: Macmillan Co., 1932)

Robert M. Ball

Social Security: Today and Tomorrow (NY: Columbia University Press, 1978)

Straight Talk about Social Security (NY: The Century Foundation Press, 1998)*

Insuring the Essentials: Bob Ball on Social Security (NY: The Century Foundation Press, 2001)

The Greenspan Commission: What Really Happened (NY: Century Foundation Books (The Century Foundation Press, 2010))

"What Medicare's Architects Had in Mind", *Health Affairs* (1995)*

Frank Bane

"A New American Reality," Social Security Bulletin, Volume 1, Number 8 (August, 1938)*

J. Douglas Brown

"The Idea of Social Security," An Address Before a General Staff Meeting of the Bureau of Old-Age and Survivors Insurance, Baltimore, MD, November 7, 1957*

"The American Philosophy of Social Insurance" (1957)

"The Birth of Old-Age Insurance" (1963)

"The Genesis of Social Security in America" (1969)

Essays on Social Security (Princeton, NJ: Industrial Relations Section, Princeton University, 1977)

Eveline M. Burns

The American social security system (Boston: Houghton, Mifflin, 1951)

Social Security and Public Policy (NY: McGraw-Hill, 1956)

"Health insurance: Not if or when, but what kind?" (An occasional paper - School of Social Work) (Madison: University of Wisconsin, 1971)

Wilbur Cohen

"Interview With Edwin Witte" (1955)

"Arthur J. Altmeyer: Mr. Social Security" (1973)

"Reflections on the enactment of Medicare and Medicaid," Health Care Financing Review (December 1985) (Supp.)*

Social Security: Universal or Selective? (with Milton Friedman) Rational Debate Seminars, American Enterprise Institute for Public Policy Research, (Washington, D.C., 1972)*

Mary W. Dewson

"This Social Security – What Is It?" An Address Before the Women's City Club of Boston, Mass, February 17, 1938*

Thomas H. Eliot

"The Social Security Bill — 25 Years After" (1960)*

"The Legal Background of the Social Security Act," February 3, 1961*

Abraham Epstein

The Challenge of the Aged (NY: The Vanguard Press, 1928)

Insecurity, a challenge to America; a study of social insurance in the United States and abroad (NY: H. Smith and R. Haas, 1933)

Marion Folsom

Kodak retirement annuity, life insurance and disability benefit plan (General management series) (NY: American Management Association, 1929)

Advances in social security (Washington, DC: Department of Health, Education, and Welfare, Social Security Administration, Bureau of Old-Age and Survivors Insurance, 1958)

Murray Latimer

Industrial pension systems in the United States and Canada (NY: Industrial Relations Counselors, 1932)

Industrial Pension Systems in the United States and Canada, Volume II (Part II: Financial, Actuarial and Administrative Aspects) (NY: Industrial Relations Counselors, Jan 1, 1933)

Robert J. Myers

Within the System: My Half Century in Social Security (New Hartford, CT: ACTEX Publications, 1992)*

Social Security (Fourth Edition), (Philadelphia: Pension Research Council, Wharton School of the University of Pennsylvania and University of Pennsylvania Press, 1993)*

Frances Perkins

The Roosevelt I Knew, Frances Perkins (NY: Viking Press, 1946)*

"Social Insurance For U.S." National Radio Address, February 25, 1935*

"Address at the 25th Anniversary Celebration of the Signing of the Social Security Act, Department of Health, Education, and Welfare," August 15, 1960*

Franklin D. Roosevelt

Message to Congress Reviewing the Broad Objectives and Accomplishments of the Administration — June 8, 1934*

Fireside Chat — June 28, 1934*

The Initiation of Studies to Achieve a Program of National Social and Economic Security— Executive Order No. 6757 — June 29, 1934

Fireside Chat — Sunday, September 30, 1934

Address to Advisory Council of the Committee on Economic Security on the Problems of Economic and Social Security — November 14, 1934

State of the Union Message to Congress, January 4, 1935*

Message to Congress on Social Security — January 17, 1935*

Presidential Statement Signing the Social Security Act — August 14, 1935*

Speech at Madison Square Garden, October 31, 1936*

A Recommendation for Legislation Amending the Social Security Act — December 14, 1937

A Recommendation for Liberalizing the Old-Age Insurance System — April 28, 1938

"A Social Security Program Must Include All Those Who Need Its Protection," Radio Address on the Third Anniversary of the Social Security Act, August 15, 1938*

A Message Transmitting to the Congress a Report of the Social Security Board Recommending Certain Improvements In the Law — January 16, 1939.

Message to Congress on the National Health Program — January 23, 1939

Presidential Statement on Signing Some Amendments to the Social Security Act — August 11, 1939*

State of the Union Message to Congress, January 7, 1943*

State of the Union Message to Congress, January 11, 1944*

Campaign Address on the "Economic Bill Of Rights" — October 28, 1944

State of the Union Message to Congress, January 6, 1945*

Oscar M. Sullivan

"Memorandum Concerning The Interests of the Physically Handicapped As Affected By Social Insurance Proposals, Particularly Old-Age Pensions with an Invalidity Corollary, and Unemployment Insurance"*

Edwin Witte

"Reflections on the Beginnings of Social Security," celebrating the twentieth anniversary of the enactment of Social Security Act, at the Department of Health, Education and Welfare, August 15, 1955*

The Development of the Social Security Act (Madison, WI: University of Wisconsin Press, 1962)*

Ellen S. Woodward

"Social Security in War and Peace," January 27, 1943

ACKNOWLEDGMENTS

First and foremost, I remember, with deep gratitude and affection, three Social Security founders: Robert M. Ball, Wilbur Cohen, and Robert J. Myers. Cohen and Myers started working on Social Security in 1934, the year before the legislation was enacted. Ball started in 1939. All three spent their long, productive lives fighting for Social Security.

I was extremely fortunate to meet all three when I was assistant to the chairman of the bipartisan commission that produced the 1983 Social Security amendments. Each of the three became my mentor and friend. All three were my most important and generous teachers in the field.

During the Summer and Fall of 1982, as staff work at the commission slowed in anticipation of the November election, I spent memorable afternoons in Bob Myers's office, where he regaled and enlightened me with anecdotes from Social Security's rich past. We talked regularly until his death at age 97.

As part of my commission work, I met frequently with Bob Ball, who was the informal head of the progressive Democrats on the commission. We became increasingly close over the years. Towards the end of his life, as I wrote my first book on Social Security, we talked daily, sometimes several times a day.

Wilbur died five years after our first meeting, and so I knew him less well and for a shorter period of time than I had the privilege to know Bob Ball and Bob Myers. Nevertheless, it was impossible to know Wilbur, and not feel like his best friend.

Although they have all passed away, I think about all three frequently. I am still guided and inspired by their compassion, wisdom, energy, and dedication to the economic security of the American people. This book would not have been written but for my friendship with all three.

In writing this book, considerations of space forced me to omit mention of many founders who made extremely important contributions to Social Security. I do not mean in any way to slight the significant role that they played in creating, building and sustaining America's most important social program. Many are left out completely. Others have only scant mention. In the biographical sketches, I gave different degrees of detail to them. None of this should be interpreted as ranking their contribution.

I thank The Century Foundation for granting copyright permission, quickly and enthusiastically, to reproduce the Bob Ball essay, which appears at the end of chapter two. Readers should know that some material that appears in this book builds on and was drawn from earlier publications of mine, as listed in the first endnote to chapter one.

This book became a reality thanks to the staff of Social Security Works and Strong Arm Press. I am especially grateful to Alex Abbott, whose close reading and copy editing was invaluable. He spent many, many hours finding sources and creating the endnotes. He worked meticulously, carefully, and tirelessly, reading the text from start to finish numerous times.

I am also deeply grateful to Ebonie Land, whose creativity and close attention to detail are superlative. She is responsible for the formatting and design of the book and its cover. Like Alex, she spent endless hours responding to edits, formatting and reformatting the text, modifying the charts and graphs, and helping in other ways, large and small.

I also am very appreciative to Stephanie Connolly, the former research director of Social Security Works, who read early drafts and helped with some early research. I also thank Alex Lawson, executive director of Social Security Works, Ryan Grim, co-publisher, with Alex Lawson, of Strong Arm Press, and Michael Phelan, deputy director of Social Security Works. Without them, this book would not be what it is.

I offer my warm thanks, as well, to my colleagues and friends, Edward Berkowitz, Professor of History and of Public Policy and Public Administration, George Washington University; Professor Max J. Skidmore, Curators' Professor of Political Science and Thomas Jefferson Fellow, University of Missouri-Kansas City; and Dr. Benjamin W. Veghte, Vice President for Policy, National Academy of Social Insurance, for their willingness to read an early draft of the manuscript and for their thoughtful comments. All mistakes and interpretations are, of course, mine.

Most importantly, I thank my extended family and friends, without whose love and support my work would be impossible. With everlasting gratitude and love, I offer special thanks to my husband, Chip Lupu. No one could ask for a more supportive partner.

I have dedicated this book to my grandchildren, Ezekiel Jackson, Kylie Conner-Sax, Beatrice Jackson, and Sadie David-Sax, as well as my grandnephews, Luke and Jake Trepanier, and Ryan and Jax Irwin. They are our future. I fight for economic justice so that the nation they inherit as adults will be better, fairer, and more secure.

NOTES

Some material that appears in this book builds on and was drawn from earlier publications of mine, including two books, *The Battle for Social Security* (Hoboken, NJ: John Wiley & Sons, 2005) and *Social Security Works! Why Social Security Isn't Going Broke and How Expanding It Will Help Us All* (New York, NY: The New Press, 2015) (co-authored with Eric R. Kingson); several law review articles, including "The Striking Superiority of Social Security in the Provision of Wage Insurance," 50 Harvard Journal on Legislation 109 (2013); Social Security and Intergenerational Justice," 77 George Washington Law Review 1383 (2009): and, "Social Security and the Low-Income Worker," 56 American University Law Review 1139 (June, 2007); articles in other publications, including "The War Against Social Security" (review of *The People's Pension: The Struggle to Defend Social Security Since Reagan*, by Eric Laursen), in Dissent (Fall 2012); as well as numerous blog posts over the years.

CHAPTER 1: THE FOUNDERS' VISION

[1] Frances Perkins, *The Roosevelt I Knew* (New York: Viking Press, 1946), p. 301.

[2] Michael Clingman, Kyle Burkhalter and Chris Chaplain, Social Security Administration, Memorandum (November 8, 2016), at *https://www.socialsecurityworks.org/wp-content/uploads/2017/09/23_Illustrative_Survivor_and_Disability_Case_2016.pdf.*

[3] Ibid.

[4] Kyle Burkhalter, Michael Clingman and Chris Chaplain, Social Security Administration, Memorandum (October 2, 2017), at *https://www.socialsecurityworks.org/wp-content/uploads/2017/09/illustrativeretiredworker_100217_FINAL-1.pdf.*

[5] Center for Global Policy Solutions, "Overlooked But Not Forgotten: Social Security Lifts Millions More Kids Out of Poverty" (Washington, DC: Center for Global Policy Solutions), at *http://globalpolicysolutions.org/report/overlooked-not-forgotten-social-security-lifts-millions-children-poverty/.*

[6] Michael Clingman, Kyle Burkhalter and Chris Chaplain, Social Security Administration, "Replacement Rates for Hypothetical Retired Workers," Actuarial Note Number 2017.9, Table A Scheduled and Payable Benefits and Replacement Rates for Hypothetical Retired Workers in their First Year of

Benefit Receipt at Age 62 (July 2017), at
https://www.ssa.gov/oact/NOTES/ran9/an2017-9.pdf.

[7] Ibid.

[8] National Academy of Social Insurance, "What is Social Security Disability Insurance?" at *https://www.nasi.org/learn/socialsecurity/disability-insurance.*

[9] Social Security Works, "Social Security, Medicare and Medicaid Work for the United States of America," (2015), at *http://www.socialsecurityworks.org/wp-content/uploads/2015/08/US20151.pdf*; "Policy Basics: Top Ten Facts About Social Security," Center on Budget and Policy Priorities (August 14, 2017), at *https://www.cbpp.org/research/social-security/policy-basics-top-ten-facts-about-social-security*; National Academy of Social Insurance, "What is Social Security Disability Insurance?" at *https://www.nasi.org/learn/socialsecurity/disability-insurance.*

[10] Christopher R. Tamborini, Emily Cupito and Dave Shoffner, "A Profile of Social Security Child Beneficiaries and their Families: Sociodemographic and Economic Characteristics," Social Security Bulletin, Vol. 71, No. 1 (2011), at *https://www.ssa.gov/policy/docs/ssb/v71n1/v71n1p1.html.*

[11] Kathleen Romig, Center on Budget and Policy Priorities, "Social Security Lifts 22 Million Americans Out of Poverty," (October 25, 2016), at *https://www.cbpp.org/blog/social-security-lifts-22-million-americans-out-of-poverty.*

[12] Economic Policy Institute, "401(k)s have left the overwhelming majority of Americans unprepared for retirement," (March 3, 2016), at *http://www.epi.org/press/401ks-have-left-the-overwhelming-majority-of-americans-unprepared-for-retirement-32-charts-show-how-the-retirement-system-has-exacerbated-inequality/.*

[13] Alicia H. Munnell, Wenliang Hou and Anthony Webb, Center for Retirement Research at Boston College, "NRRI Update Shows Half Still Falling Short," Number 14-20 (December 2014), at *http://crr.bc.edu/wp-content/uploads/2014/12/IB_14-20-508.pdf.*

[14] Sally R. Sherman, "Public Attitudes Toward Social Security," Social Security Bulletin, Vol. 52, No. 12 (December 1989), at *https://www.ssa.gov/policy/docs/ssb/v52n12/v52n12p2.pdf.*

[15] Ryan Grim, "Alan Simpson Attacks AARP, Says Social Security Is 'Not A Retirement Program' (VIDEO)," Huffington Post, May 9, 2011, at *https://www.huffingtonpost.com/2011/05/06/alan-simpson-aarp-social-security-retirement-program_n_858738.html.*

[16] Louis Jacobson, "George Will says Social Security was created in the 1930s 'as a way of getting people to quit working,'" PunditFact, February 11, 2014, at *http://www.politifact.com/punditfact/statements/2014/feb/11/george-will/george-will-says-social-security-was-created-1930s/.*

[17] Robert J. Samuelson, "Would Roosevelt recognize today's Social Security?," (Editorial), Washington Post, April 8, 2012, at *https://www.washingtonpost.com/opinions/would-roosevelt-recognize-todays-social-security/2012/04/08/gIQALChd4S_story.html?utm_term=.43a0612b6d54.*

[18] Franklin D. Roosevelt, State of the Union Message to Congress, January 11, 1944, at *http://www.fdrlibrary.marist.edu/archives/address_text.html.*

[19] Arthur J. Altmeyer, "Social Security— Yesterday and Tomorrow," December 9, 1965, on Social Security Administration History website: *https://www.ssa.gov/history/aja1265.html.*

[20] Franklin D. Roosevelt, State of the Union Message to Congress, January 7, 1943, at *http://www.presidency.ucsb.edu/ws/?pid=16386.*

[21] Mary "Molly" W. Dewson, "This Social Security - What Is It?," February 17, 1938, on Social Security Administration History website: *https://www.ssa.gov/history/dewsonspeech.html.*

[22] Franklin D. Roosevelt, "A Social Security Program Must Include All Those Who Need Its Protection," August 15, 1938, at Social Security Administration History website: *https://www.ssa.gov/history/fdrstmts.html#radio.*

[23] Dwight D. Eisenhower to Edgar Newton Eisenhower, Document #1147, The Papers of Dwight David Eisenhower, *Volume XV—The Presidency: The Middle Way,* at *http://web.archive.org/web/20051124190902/http://www.eisenhowermemorial.org/presidential-papers/first-term/documents/1147.cfm.*

CHAPTER 2: SOCIAL SECURITY'S UNCHANGING STRUCTURE

[1] Franklin D. Roosevelt, Message to Congress on the Objectives and Accomplishments of the Administration, June 8, 1934, at *http://www.presidency.ucsb.edu/ws/index.php?pid=14690.*

[2] Franklin D. Roosevelt, State of the Union Message to Congress, January 11, 1944, at *http://www.fdrlibrary.marist.edu/archives/address_text.html.*

[3] Franklin D. Roosevelt, State of the Union Message to Congress, January 7, 1943, at *http://www.presidency.ucsb.edu/ws/?pid=16386.*

[4] Frances Perkins, "Social Insurance for U.S.," National Radio Address, February 25, 1935, at Social Security Administration History website: *https://www.ssa.gov/history/perkinsradio.html.*

[5] Supra, note 3.

[6] "Landon Hits Social Security as 'Cruel Hoax' in Milwaukee Speech," THE DAY (Sept. 28, 1936), at *https://news.google.com/newspapers?nid=1915&dat=19360928&id=XqktAAAAIBAJ&sjid=Z3EFAAAAIBAJ&pg=999,2342658.*

[7] Thomas H. Eliot, "The Legal Background of the Social Security Act," Speech at Social Security Administration Headquarters, February 3, 1961, at Social Security Administration History website: *https://www.ssa.gov/history/eliot2.html.*

[8] Minority Views on the Social Security Bill of 1935, in House Committee Report no. 615, p. 42-43.

[9] Nancy J. Altman, *The Battle for Social Security: From FDR's Vision to Bush's Gamble,* (Hoboken, NJ: John Wiley & Sons, Inc., 2005), p. 124. See also: Gill Robert Geldreich, "Justice Owen Roberts's Revolution of 1937" (1997).

University of Tennessee Honors Thesis Projects, at *http://trace.tennessee.edu/cgi/viewcontent.cgi?article=1216&context=utk_cha nhonoproj.*

[10] Helvering v. Davis, 301 U.S. 619 (1937).

[11] Social Security Act Amendments of 1939, Pub. L. No. 76-379, at Social Security Administration History website: *https://www.ssa.gov/history/pdf/1939Act.pdf.*

[12] Gary Burtless, "Social Security Privatization and Financial Market Risk," Center on Social and Economic Dynamics, Working Paper No. 10, February 2000, at *https://www.brookings.edu/wp-content/uploads/2016/06/sspriv.pdf.*

[13] Barbara Nachtrieb Armstrong, J. Douglas Brown and Murray W. Latimer, et al., Committee on Economic Security, Part II Old Age Security, Chapter VII, The Economic Problems of Old Age, "Social Security in America," 1937, at Social Security Administration History website: *https://www.ssa.gov/history/reports/ces/cesbookc7.html.*

[14] Ronald Reagan, "A Time for Choosing" (1964), available at: *http://www.americanrhetoric.com/speeches/ronaldreaganatimeforchoosing.ht m.*

[15] Richard W. Stevenson, "For Bush, a Long Embrace of Social Security Plan," New York Times, February 27, 2005.

[16] George W. Bush, State of the Union Address, February 2, 2005.

[17] Barry Goldwater, *Conscience of a Conservative* (Shepherdsville, KY: Victor Publishing Company, 1960), p. 64.

[18] Ronald Reagan, "A Time for Choosing" (1964), available at: *http://www.americanrhetoric.com/speeches/ronaldreaganatimeforchoosing.ht m.*

[19] *Leviticus 19:9–10.* Bible, King James Version.

[20] Franklin D. Roosevelt, Public Papers of the Presidents of the United States, *The public papers and addresses of Franklin D. Roosevelt. Volume one, The genesis of the New Deal, 1928-1932: with a special introduction and explanatory notes by President Roosevelt. [Book 1],* "Annual Message to the Legislature, 1931," at *https://quod.lib.umich.edu/p/ppotpus/4925052.1928.001/155?page=root;rgn=f ull+text;size=100;view=image;q1=dole.*

[21] Frances Perkins, *The Roosevelt I Knew* (New York: Viking Press, 1946), p. 29.

[22] Report of the Committee on Economic Security, "Old-Age Security," at Social Security Administration history website, *https://www.ssa.gov/history/reports/ces/ces5.html.*

[23] Franklin D. Roosevelt, Fireside Chat, June 28, 1934, at Social Security Administration history website: *https://www.ssa.gov/history/fdrstmts.html#fireside1.*

[24] Franklin D. Roosevelt, State of the Union Message to Congress, January 4, 1935, at *http://www.presidency.ucsb.edu/ws/?pid=14890.*

[25] House Ways and Means Report on the Social Security Bill of 1935, in House Committee Report no. 615, at Social Security Administration history website: *https://www.ssa.gov/history/reports/35housereport.html.*

[26] "Social Security Lifts 22 Million Americans Out of Poverty," Kathleen Romig, Center on Budget and Policy Priorities, October 25, 2016, at *https://www.cbpp.org/blog/social-security-lifts-22-million-americans-out-of-poverty.*

[27] Michael Clingman, Kyle Burkhalter and Chris Chaplain, Social Security Administration, Actuarial Note Number 2017.9, July 2017, "Replacement Rates for Hypothetical Retired Workers," see Table A—Scheduled and Payable Benefits and Replacement Rates for Hypothetical Retired Workers in their First Year of Benefit Receipt at Age 62, at *https://www.ssa.gov/oact/NOTES/ran9/an2017-9.pdf.*

[28] Zach Carter, "Paul Ryan: 60 Percent of Americans Are 'Takers,' Not 'Makers'," *The Huffington Post,* October 5, 2012, *www.huffingtonpost.com/2012/10/05/paul-ryan-60-percent-of-a_n_1943073.html.*

[29] Frank Bane, "A New American Reality," Social Security Bulletin, Vol. 1, No. 8, August 1938, at Social Security Administration History website: *https://www.ssa.gov/history/bane838.html.*

[30] Social Security Administration, Program Operations Manual System (POMS), "RS 00301.101 Insured Status — Overview," at *https://secure.ssa.gov/poms.nsf/lnx/0300301101.*

[31] Dwight D. Eisenhower, "Special Message to the Congress Transmitting Proposed Changes in the Social Security Program," August 1, 1953, at Social Security Administration History website: *https://www.ssa.gov/history/ikestmts.html#special.*

[32] Social Security Administration, "Greenspan Commission: Report of the National Commission on Social Security Reform," January 1983, at Social Security Administration History website: *https://www.ssa.gov/history/reports/gspan5.html.*

[33] Supra, note 31.

[34] Stephen Goss, Michael Clingman, Alice Wade and Karen Glenn, Social Security Administration, Actuarial Note Number 155, July 2014, "Replacement Rates for Retirees: What Makes Sense for Planning and Evaluation?," at *https://www.ssa.gov/oact/NOTES/pdf_notes/note155.pdf.*

[35] Robert J. Myers, *Social Security* (Fourth Edition), (Philadelphia: Pension Research Council, Wharton School of the University of Pennsylvania and University of Pennsylvania Press, 1993), pp. 164-5.

[36] Supra, note 35.

[37] Supra, note 28.

[38] J. Douglas Brown, "The Idea of Social Security," November 7, 1957, at Social Security Administration History website: *https://www.ssa.gov/history/brown3.html.*

[39] Robert M. Ball, "The Nine Guiding Principles of Social Security: Where They Came From, What They Accomplish," *Straight Talk about Social Security: An*

Analysis of the Issues in the Current Debate, (New York: The Century Foundation, 1998), pp. 59-64, Appendix.

CHAPTER 3: SOCIAL SECURITY'S SOUND AND SECURE FINANCING

[1] Social Security Administration, "Social Security Income, Outgo, And Asset Reserves," at *https://www.ssa.gov/oact/progdata/assets.html*; Social Security Administration, "Trust Fund Financial Operations in 2015," 2016 Trustees Report, at *https://www.ssa.gov/oact/tr/2016/II_B_cyoper.html#96807*; Social Security Administration, Office of the Chief Actuary, "Old-Age, Survivors, and Disability Insurance Trust Funds, 1957-2016," at https://www.ssa.gov/oact/STATS/table4a3.html.

[2] Social Security Administration, 2017 OASDI Trustees Report, Table VI.A4—OASI Trust Fund Asset Reserves, End of Calendar Years 2015 and 2016, and Table VI.A5—DI Trust Fund Asset Reserves, End of Calendar Years 2015 and 2016, at *https://www.ssa.gov/OACT/TR/2017/VI_A_cyoper_hist.html#297482*.

[3] George W. Bush, "President Participates in Social Security Conversation in West Virginia," Parkersburg, West Virginia, April 5, 2005, at Social Security Administration History website: *https://www.ssa.gov/history/gwbushstmts5b.html#04052005b*.

[4] Public Law 103-296, "Social Security Independence and Program Improvements Act of 1994," at *https://www.gpo.gov/fdsys/pkg/STATUTE-108/pdf/STATUTE-108-Pg1464.pdf*.

[5] "Landon Hits Social Security as 'Cruel Hoax' in Milwaukee Speech," THE DAY (Sept. 28, 1936), at *https://news.google.com/newspapers?nid=1915&dat=19360928&id=XqktAAA AIBAJ&sjid=Z3EFAAAAIBAJ&pg=999,2342658*.

[6] Report of the 1937-38 Advisory Council on Social Security, Appendix, December 10, 1938, at Social Security Administration History website: *https://www.ssa.gov/history/reports/38advise.html*.

[7] Report of the 1948 Advisory Council on Social Security, Appendix 1-A, "The Old-Age and Survivors Insurance Trust Fund," at Social Security Administration History website: *https://www.ssa.gov/history/pdf/48advise5.pdf*.

[8] Report of the 1957-59 Advisory Council on Social Security Financing, January 1, 1959, at Social Security Administration History website: *https://www.ssa.gov/history/reports/58advise6.html*.

[9] Allen W. Smith, February 24, 2015, "Is the government able and willing to repay Social Security debt?," (Editorial), Florida Sun-Sentinel, at *http://www.sun-sentinel.com/opinion/commentary/fl-viewpoint-social2-20150224-story.html*.

[10] Ashley Parker, "'Corporations Are People,' Romney Tells Iowa Hecklers Angry Over His Tax Policy," New York Times, August 11, 2001, at *http://www.nytimes.com/2011/08/12/us/politics/12romney.html*.

[11] Civil Action No. 85-3466, First Amended Complaint for Declaratory Relief, Mandamus and Injunctive Relief, U.S. District Court for the District of Columbia, p. 14.

[12] Robert J. Myers, *Social Security* (Fourth Edition), (Philadelphia: Pension Research Council, Wharton School of the University of Pennsylvania and University of Pennsylvania Press, 1993), pp. 29-30.

[13] Id. at p. 386.

[14] Franklin D. Roosevelt, "Presidential Statement on Signing Some Amendments to the Social Security Act," August 11, 1939, at Social Security Administration History website: *https://www.ssa.gov/history/fdrstmts.html#1939b.*

[15] Supra, note 7.

[16] Supra, note 8.

[17] Omnibus Budget Reconciliation Act of 1990, Pub. L. 101-508, title XIII, Sec. 13301(a), Nov. 5, 1990, 104 Stat. 1388-623, at *https://www.ssa.gov/history/pdf/Downey%20PDFs/Omnibus%20Budget%20Re conciliation%20Act%20of%201990%20Vol%204.pdf.*

[18] *Economic Security Act: Hearings before the House Committee on Ways and Means,* 74th Congress, 897-911 (1935) (testimony of Henry Morgenthau), at Social Security Administration History website: *https://www.ssa.gov/history/pdf/hr35morgenaja.pdf.*

[19] Department of the Treasury/Federal Reserve Board, "Major Foreign Holders of Treasury Securities," last updated October 17, 2017, accessed on November 14, 2017, at *http://ticdata.treasury.gov/Publish/mfh.txt.*

[20] Ryan Grim, "Bernanke Channels Willie Sutton In Assault On Social Security: 'That's Where The Money Is'," Huffington Post, March 18, 2010, at *https://www.huffingtonpost.com/2009/12/03/bernanke-channels-willie_n_378963.html.*

[21] Alex M. Parker, "On the 'Super Committee's' Menu: Social Security Cuts and Tax Hikes," U.S. News & World Report, November 7, 2011, at *https://www.usnews.com/news/articles/2011/11/07/on-the-super-committees-menu-social-security-cuts-and-tax-hikes.*

[22] Laura Barrón-López and Arthur Delaney, "Senate Eyes Social Security 'Fugitives' to Pay For Highways," Huffington Post, July 20, 2015, at *https://www.huffingtonpost.com/entry/senate-eyes-social-security-fugitives-to-pay-for-highways_us_55ad401ee4b065dfe89ef26d.*

[23] *The Moment of Truth: Report of The National Commission on Fiscal Responsibility and Reform,* December 2010, at *http://momentoftruthproject.org/sites/default/files/TheMomentofTruth12_1_201 0.pdf.*

[24] Michael Hiltzik, "Has President Obama appointed a fox to guard the Social Security henhouse?," (Editorial), Los Angeles Times, May 10, 2016, at *http://www.latimes.com/business/hiltzik/la-fi-hiltzik-blahous-trustee-20160509-snap-story.html.*

[25] Paul Waldman, "Stop with the zombie lies: No, Social Security is not 'going broke'," (Editorial), Washington Post, March 11, 2016, at *https://www.washingtonpost.com/blogs/plum-line/wp/2016/03/11/stop-with-*

the-zombie-lies-no-social-security-is-not-going-broke/?utm_term=.e19ffe1811fa.

[26] Supra, note 1; Social Security Administration, 2017 OASDI Trustees Report, see Table IV.A3, at *https://www.ssa.gov/OACT/TR/2017/tr2017.pdf.*
[27] Social Security Works, "Fact Sheet on 2017 Social Security Trustees Report," July 13, 2017, at *https://www.socialsecurityworks.org/2017/07/13/fact-sheet-2017-social-security-trustees-report/.*
[28] 1957-59 Advisory Council on Social Security Financing, "Misunderstandings of Social Security Financing," at Social Security Administration History website: *https://www.ssa.gov/history/reports/58advise4.html.*
[29] "Grand Finale," Time magazine, November 9, 1938.
[30] Franklin D. Roosevelt, Address at Madison Square Garden, New York City, October 31, 1936, at *http://www.presidency.ucsb.edu/ws/?pid=15219.*

CHAPTER 4: BUILDING ON SOCIAL SECURITY'S STRONG, STABLE, TIMELESS FOUNDATION

[1] Franklin D. Roosevelt, Message to Congress on Social Security, January 17, 1935, at Social Security Administration History website: *https://www.ssa.gov/history/fdrstmts.html#message2.*
[2] Franklin D. Roosevelt, Presidential Statement Signing the Social Security Act, August 14, 1935, at Social Security Administration History website: *https://www.ssa.gov/history/fdrstmts.html#signing.*
[3] Frances Perkins, Address at the 25th Anniversary Celebration of the Signing of the Social Security Act, Department of Health, Education, and Welfare, August 15, 1960, at Social Security Administration History website: *https://www.ssa.gov/history/perkins6.html.*
[4] Franklin D. Roosevelt, State of the Union Message to Congress, January 7, 1943, at *http://www.presidency.ucsb.edu/ws/?pid=16386.*
[5] Franklin D. Roosevelt, State of the Union Message to Congress, January 6, 1945, at *http://www.presidency.ucsb.edu/ws/?pid=16595.*
[6] John Waggoner, "Social Security: 5 things you need to know," (Editorial), USA Today, February 26, 2013, at *https://www.usatoday.com/story/money/personalfinance/2013/02/26/social-security-myths-and-tips/1946975/.*
[7] Barbara Nachtrieb Armstrong, J. Douglas Brown and Murray W. Latimer, et al., Committee on Economic Security, Part II Old Age Security, Chapter VIII, Provisions for the Aged in the United States, "Social Security in America," 1937, at Social Security Administration History website: *https://www.ssa.gov/history/reports/ces/cesbookc8.html.*
[8] Thomas H. Eliot, Clark Amendment Added in Senate, "The Legal Background of the Social Security Act," Address at the Social Security Administration Headquarters, Baltimore, Maryland, February 3, 1961, at Social Security Administration History website: *https://www.ssa.gov/history/eliot2.html.*

[9] Arthur Schlesinger Jr., "Franklin Delano Roosevelt," TIME Magazine, April 13, 1998, at
http://content.time.com/time/world/article/0,8599,1652984,00.html.

[10] Tax Evasion and Avoidance: Hearings Before the Joint Committee on Tax Evasion and Avoidance, 75th Cong., 1st Sess. (1937), p. 296-98, statement of Hon. Charles T. Russell, Deputy Commissioner of Internal Revenue.

[11] Franklin D. Roosevelt, "Message to Congress on Tax Evasion Prevention," June 1, 1937, at *http://www.presidency.ucsb.edu/ws/?pid=15413.*

[12] Minority Views on Social Security Amendments of 1950, H.R. 6000, House Committee on Ways and Means, p. 157, at Social Security Administration History website:
https://www.ssa.gov/history/pdf/Downey%20PDFs/Social%20Security%20Ame ndments%20of%201950%20Vol%201.pdf.

[13] Historically, Social Security and private pensions have been considered by different subcommittees, often in different committees. Currently, the Subcommittee on Health, Employment, Labor, and Pensions of the Committee on Education and Workforce of the House of Representatives has jurisdiction, at least in part, over private pensions; while the Subcommittee on Social Security of the House Ways and Means Committee has jurisdiction over Social Security. In the Senate, the Subcommittee on Primary Health and Retirement Security of the Senate Health, Education, Labor and Pensions Committee has jurisdiction over private pensions, together with the Senate Finance Committee's Subcommittee on Social Security, Pensions, and Family Policy, which also has jurisdiction over Social Security. In the past, two different subcommittees of the Senate Finance Committee have had jurisdiction over private pensions and Social Security respectively. In the executive branch, the Treasury and Labor Departments each have some administrative responsibility for private pensions, as does the Pension Benefit Guaranty Corporation; the Social Security Administration administers Social Security.

[14] Franklin D. Roosevelt, Message to Congress on Social Security, January 17, 1935, at Social Security Administration History website:
https://www.ssa.gov/history/fdrstmts.html#message2.

[15] Social Security Administration Historian's Office, "Research Note #15: The Roosevelt Administration's Proposal for Voluntary Annuities," June 21, 2001, at Social Security Administration History website:
https://www.ssa.gov/history/voluntaryannuities.html. (Another purpose of the voluntary annuities was to supplement the pensions of those covered by the compulsory system. This is consistent with the view that benefits and related costs were kept low initially to not undermine the undertaking, in Roosevelt's words, "by extravagant action.")

[16] Robert J. Myers, *Social Security* (Fourth Edition), (Philadelphia: Pension Research Council, Wharton School of the University of Pennsylvania and University of Pennsylvania Press, 1993), pp. 361-2.

[17] Virginia P. Reno, Thomas N. Bethell and Elisa A. Walker, "Social Security Beneficiaries Face 19% Cut; New Revenue Can Restore Balance," Social

Security Brief No. 37, June 2011, National Academy of Social Insurance, at *https://www.nasi.org/sites/default/files/research/SS_Brief_037.pdf.*

[18] Edwin Witte, *The Development of the Social Security Act* (Madison, WI: University of Wisconsin Press, 1962) pp. 152-4.

[19] *Economic Security Act: Hearings before the House Committee on Ways and Means,* 74th Congress, 897-911 (1935) (testimony of Henry Morgenthau), at Social Security Administration History website: *https://www.ssa.gov/history/pdf/hr35morgenaja.pdf.*

[20] Frances Perkins, *The Roosevelt I Knew* (NY: Viking Press, 1946), pp. 297-8.

[21] *Economic Security Act: Hearings before the House Committee on Ways and Means,* 74th Congress, 552-577 (1935) (testimony of Abraham Epstein), at Social Security Administration History website: *https://www.ssa.gov/history/pdf/hr35epstein.pdf.*

[22] *Economic Security Act: Hearings before the Senate Committee on Finance,* 74th Congress, 504-505 (1935) (testimony of Abraham Epstein), at Social Security Administration History website: *https://www.ssa.gov/history/hquotes2.html.*

[23] Arthur Altmeyer, *The Formative Years of Social Security* (Madison: University of Wisconsin Press, 1966), p. 39.

[24] Edwin Witte, *The Development of the Social Security Act* (Madison: University of Wisconsin Press, 1962), pp. 143-145.

[25] Id. at p. 144

[26] *Economic Security Act: Hearings before the Senate Committee on Finance,* 74th Congress, 640-647 (1935) (testimony of Charles H. Houston), at Social Security Administration History website: *https://www.ssa.gov/history/pdf/hr35houston.pdf.*

[27] *Economic Security Act: Hearings before the House Committee on Ways and Means,* 74th Congress, 796-798 (1935) (testimony of Charles H. Houston), at Social Security Administration History website: *https://www.ssa.gov/history/pdf/hr35houston.pdf.*

[28] Supra, note 26.

[29] Larry DeWitt, "The Decision to Exclude Agricultural and Domestic Workers from the 1935 Social Security Act," Social Security Bulletin, Vol. 70, No. 4, 2010, at Social Security Administration Office of Retirement and Disability Policy website: *https://www.ssa.gov/policy/docs/ssb/v70n4/v70n4p49.html.*

[30] Oscar M. Sullivan, "Memorandum Concerning The Interests Of The Physically Handicapped As Affected By Social Insurance Proposals, Particularly Old-Age Pensions With An Invalidity Corollary, and Unemployment Insurance," November 3, 1934, at Social Security Administration History website: *https://www.ssa.gov/history/reports/ces/ces6handicap2.html.*

[31] Edwin Witte, "Reflections On The Beginnings of Social Security," Remarks Delivered in Observance of the 20th Anniversary of Social Security Act at Department of Health, Education, and Welfare, August 15, 1955, at Social Security Administration History website: *https://www.ssa.gov/history/witte4.html.*

[32] Arthur J. Altmeyer, "Social Security— Yesterday and Tomorrow," December 9, 1965, on Social Security Administration History website: *https://www.ssa.gov/history/aja1265.html.*

[33] Wilbur J. Cohen, "Reflections on the enactment of Medicare and Medicaid," Health Care Finance Review, December 1985; p. 3-11, at *https://www.ncbi.nlm.nih.gov/pmc/articles/PMC4195078/#fn7-hcfr-85-supp-003.*

[34] Robert M. Ball, "What Medicare's Architects Had In Mind," Health Affairs, Vol. 14, No. 4, Winter 1995, pp. 62-72, at *http://www.theinsidereport.org/FamilyHeritage/Arthur%20Hess/Perceptions%20on%20Medicare.pdf.*

[35] Franklin D. Roosevelt, Message to Congress on Social Security, January 17, 1935, at Social Security Administration History website: *https://www.ssa.gov/history/fdrstmts.html#message2.*

[36] WeAreSocialSecurity, "Ronald Reagan: Social Security has nothing to do with the deficit." *YouTube*, excerpt from the first Reagan-Mondale Presidential debate in 1984, November 5, 2012, *https://www.youtube.com/watch?v=ihUoRD4pYzI.*

[37] OECD (2015), Pensions at a Glance 2015: OECD and G20 indicators, OECD Publishing, Paris, at *http://dx.doi.org/10.1787/pension_glance-2015-en.* See, also, Presentation by Elaine Fultz to the National Academy of Social Insurance About International Comparisons of Benefit Levels, available at: *https://www.nasi.org/sites/default/files/events/182/Fultz_2015_NASI.pdf.*

CHAPTER 5: IN THE IMMORTAL WORDS OF YOGI BERRA, THIS IS DÉJÀ VU ALL OVER AGAIN

[1] Dwight D. Eisenhower to Edgar Newton Eisenhower, Document #1147, The Papers of Dwight David Eisenhower, *Volume XV—The Presidency: The Middle Way*, at *http://web.archive.org/web/20051124190902/http://www.eisenhowermemorial.org/presidential-papers/first-term/documents/1147.cfm.*

[2] Kitty Kelley, *The Family: The Real Story of the Bush Dynasty* (New York: Doubleday, 2004), p. 57.

[3] "Townsend to Burst," *Time* magazine, October 15, 1934.

[4] Representative Jenkins (OH). *Congressional Record - House* (1935), p. 5993, at Social Security Administration History website: *https://www.ssa.gov/history/pdf/h418.pdf.*

[5] Representative Reed (NY). *Congressional Record - House* (1935), p. 6051, at Social Security Administration History website: *https://www.ssa.gov/history/pdf/h419.pdf.*

[6] Representative Wadsworth (NY). *Congressional Record – House* (1935), p. 6061, at Social Security Administration History website: *https://www.ssa.gov/history/pdf/h419.pdf.*

[7] Frances Perkins, *The Roosevelt I Knew* (New York: Viking Press, 1946), p. 299.

[8] Max J. Skidmore, *Social Security and Its Enemies* (Boulder, CO: Westview Press, 1999), p. 43-44.

[9] "Landon Hits Social Security as 'Cruel Hoax' in Milwaukee Speech," THE DAY (Sept. 28, 1936), at *https://news.google.com/newspapers?nid=1915&dat=19360928&id=XqktAAA AIBAJ&sjid=Z3EFAAAAIBAJ&pg=999,2342658.*

[10] Supra, note 8.

[11] Harry S. Truman, "Veto of Bill to Exclude Vendors of Newspapers and Magazines From Social Security Coverage," April 5, 1948, at Social Security Administration History website: *https://www.ssa.gov/history/hststmts.html#veto.*

[12] "Veto of Resolution Excluding Certain Groups From Social Security Coverage," June 14, 1948, at Social Security Administration History website, at *https://www.ssa.gov/history/hststmts.html#4a.*

[13] Minority Views on Social Security Amendments of 1950, H.R. 6000, House Committee on Ways and Means, p. 157, at Social Security Administration History website: *https://www.ssa.gov/history/pdf/Downey%20PDFs/Social%20Security%20Ame ndments%20of%201950%20Vol%201.pdf.*

[14] Id., Additional Minority Views at, p. 173.

[15] Barry Goldwater, *Conscience of a Conservative* (Shepherdsville, KY: Victor Publishing Company, 1960), p. 64.

[16] Milton Friedman, *Capitalism and Freedom* (Chicago: University of Chicago Press, 2002), p. 182.

[17] Richard M. Nixon, "Statement on Signing a Bill Extending Temporary Ceiling on National Debt and Increasing Social Security Benefits," July 1, 1972, at *http://www.presidency.ucsb.edu/ws/index.php?pid=3487.*

[18] Ronald Reagan, "Second 1980 Presidential Debate," October 28, 1980, *www.debates.org/index.php?page=october-28-1980-debate-transcript.*

[19] David A. Stockman, The Triumph of Politics (New York: Harper & Row, 1986), p. 182; William Greider, The Education of David Stockman (New York: E. P. Dutton, 1982), p. 141.

[20] Ronald Reagan, Remarks on signing the Social Security Amendments of 1983, April 20, 1983, at: *www.ssa.gov/history/reaganstmts.html#letter.*

[21] Stuart Butler and Peter Germanis, "Achieving Social Security Reform: A 'Leninist' Strategy," Cato Journal (Fall 1983), pp. 547–556, at http://nwcitizen.com/images/fileuploads/CATO_Lenin_SS.pdf.

[22] George W. Bush, "Address Before a Joint Session of the Congress on the State of the Union," February 2, 2005, at *www.presidency.ucsb.edu/ws/index.php?pid=58746.*

[23] Supra, note 9.

[24] Arthur J. Altmeyer, The Formative Years of Social Security (Madison: University of Wisconsin Press, 1966), p. 69.

[25] Arthur M. Schlesinger, Jr., The Politics of Upheaval (Boston: Houghton Mifflin Co., 1960), p. 636.

[26] Franklin D. Roosevelt, Madison Square Garden address, New York City, (October 31, 1936) at *http://www.presidency.ucsb.edu/ws/index.php?pid=15219&st=Madison+Squa re+Garden&st1=.*

[27] Supra, note 24, at p. 69.

[28] Michael D. Tanner, "Is There a Right to Social Security?," Cato Institute, November 25, 1998, at *https://www.cato.org/publications/commentary/is-there-right-social-security.*

[29] Flemming v. Nestor, 363 U.S. 603 (1960), at *https://supreme.justia.com/cases/federal/us/363/603/.*

[30] Supra, note 9.

[31] Social Security Administration, "Letter of Transmittal," January 3, 1941. At Social Security Administration History website: *https://www.ssa.gov/history/reports/trust/tf1941.html#title-bar*; Social Security Administration, "Detailed reports on the financial outlook for Social Security's *Old-Age, Survivors, and Disability Insurance* (OASDI) Trust Funds," at Office of the Chief Actuary website: *https://www.ssa.gov/oact/TR/index.html.*

[32] Social Security Works, "Ensuring Social Security Is in Long-Term Actuarial Balance," July 15, 2015, at *http://www.socialsecurityworks.org/wp-content/uploads/2016/05/7-17-15-valuation-period-fact-sheet-7-16-15-1lc.pdf.*

[33] "Time-Tested Security, *New York Times*, April 3, 1975, p. A36.

[34] Report of the 1994-96 Advisory Council on Social Security, "Appendix I: Developments Since 1983," at Social Security Administration History website: *https://www.ssa.gov/history/reports/adcouncil/report/append1.htm.*

[35] Richard W. Stevenson, "For Bush, a Long Embrace of Social Security Plan," *New York Times*, February 27, 2005.

[36] Guiding Principles, the 2001 President's Commission to Strengthen Social Security, at Social Security Administration History website: *https://www.ssa.gov/history/reports/pcsss/pcsss.html.*

[37] Social Security Works, "Ensuring Social Security Is in Long-Term Actuarial Balance," July 15, 2015, at *http://www.socialsecurityworks.org/wp-content/uploads/2016/05/7-17-15-valuation-period-fact-sheet-7-16-15-1lc.pdf*; American Academy of Actuaries, Social Insurance Committee, letter to Social Security's Board of Trustees and Advisory Board (December 19, 2003), at http://www.actuary.org/pdf/socialsecurity/tech_dec03.pdf.

[38] George W. Bush, Transcript of news conference, November 4, 2004, at: *http://www.nytimes.com/2004/11/04/politics/transcript-of-president-bushs-news-conference.html?_r=1.*

[39] George W. Bush, "Address Before a Joint Session of the Congress on the State of the Union," February 2, 2005, at *www.presidency.ucsb.edu/ws/index.php?pid=58746.*

[40] Committee on Economic Security, Economic Security Act, January 1935, table 13, at Social Security Administration History website: *www.ssa.gov/history/reports/ces16.html*; US Census Bureau, "Census 2000 Brief, The 65 Years and Over Population: 2000" (October, 2001), at https://www.census.gov/prod/2001pubs/c2kbr01-10.pdf.

[41] Supra, note 39.

[42] Social Security Administration, 2017 OASDI Trustees Report, Program-Specific Assumptions and Methods, "Covered and Taxable Earnings, Taxable Payroll, and Payroll Tax Contributions," at *https://www.ssa.gov/OACT/TR/2017/V_C_prog.html#989891*.

[43] Social Security Administration, 2016 OASDI Trustees Report, Table VI.G4, "OASDI and HI Annual and Summarized Income, Cost, and Balance as a Percentage of GDP, Calendar Years 2016-2090," at *https://www.ssa.gov/oact/tr/2016/VI_G2_OASDHI_GDP.html#200732*.

[44] Nancy J. Altman, *The Battle for Social Security: From FDR's Vision to Bush's Gamble*, (Hoboken, NJ: John Wiley & Sons, Inc., 2005), pp. 275-6.

[45] Id., at p. 277L. Randall Wray, "Manufacturing A Crisis: The Neocon Attack on Social Security," The Levy Economics Institute of Bard College, Policy Note, 2005, No. 2, at *http://www.levyinstitute.org/pubs/pn05_2.pdf*.

[46] Ryan Grim, "Alan Simpson Attacks AARP, Says Social Security Is 'Not a Retirement Program'," Huffington Post, July 6, 2011, at *https://www.huffingtonpost.com/2011/05/06/alan-simpson-aarp-social-security-retirement-program_n_858738.html*.

[47] Robert D. Grove and Alice Hetzel, "Vital Statistics Rates in the United States, 1940–1960," U.S. Department of Health, Education and Welfare, Public Health Service, table 38, p. 206 (1968) at https://www.cdc.gov/nchs/data/vsus/vsrates1940_60.pdf; Marian F. MacDorman et al., "Recent Declines in Infant Mortality in the United States, 2005–2011," *NCHS Data Brief*, no. 120 (April 2013) U.S. Department of Health and Human Services, Centers for Disease Control and Prevention, at www.cdc.gov/nchs/data/databriefs/db120.pdf.

[48] Social Security Administration, 2017 OASDI Trustees Report, Table V.A4., "Period Life Expectancy," at *https://www.ssa.gov/OACT/TR/2017/V_A_demo.html#226697*.

[49] Stephen C. Goss, "The Future Financial Status of the Social Security Program," *Social Security Bulletin*, Vol. 70, No. 3, 2010, at *https://www.ssa.gov/policy/docs/ssb/v70n3/v70n3p111.html*.

[50] *Testimony to the Senate Committee on Homeland Security and Governmental Affairs: "Financial Implications for the Social Security Trust Funds of the President's Executive Actions on Immigration, Announced November 20, 2014*, 114th Congress, February 4, 2015 (testimony of Stephen C. Goss), at *https://www.ssa.gov/oact/testimony/SenateHomeSec_20150204.pdf*.

[51] Pension Protection Act of 2006, Pub. L. No. 109-280, 120 Stat. 280 (2006), at *www.gpo.gov/fdsys/pkg/PLAW-109publ280/pdf/PLAW-109 publ280.pdf*.

[52] Elliot Schreur and Benjamin W. Veghte, "Social Security Finances: Findings of the 2017 Trustees Report," National Academy of Social Insurance, July 2017, No. 50, at *https://www.nasi.org/sites/default/files/research/SS_Brief_50_lowres.pdf*.

[53] Larry DeWitt, "Ponzi Schemes vs. Social Security," Research Note #25, Special Studies by the Social Security Administration Historian's Office, January 2009, at

https://web.archive.org/web/20121031144750/http:/www.ssa.gov/history/ponzi. htm.

[54] *Historical Tables*, Fiscal Year 2017 Budget of the U.S. Government, Office of Management and Budget, Table 1.4—Receipts, Outlays, and Surpluses or Deficits (—) by Fund Group: 1934-2022," at *https://www.govinfo.gov/content/pkg/BUDGET-2017-TAB/pdf/BUDGET-2017-TAB.pdf.*

[55] Office of Research, Statistics, and Policy Analysis, Social Security Administration, Annual Statistical Supplement 2017, Table 4.A1—Old-Age and Survivors Insurance, 1937–2016, and Table 4.A2 2—Disability Insurance, 1957–2016, at https://www.ssa.gov/policy/docs/statcomps/supplement/

[56] Robert J. Samuelson, "Robert Samuelson: America's clash of generations is inevitable," (Editorial), Washington Post, December 8, 2013, at *https://www.washingtonpost.com/opinions/robert-samuelson-americas-clash-of-generations-is-inevitable/2013/12/08/e4810416-5ea0-11e3-be07-006c776266ed_story.html?utm_term=.16fb8202ee48.*

[57] Nancy Altman and Eric Kingson, "Has Obama Created a Social Security 'Death Panel'?" Nieman Watchdog (May 21, 2010) at http://www.niemanwatchdog.org/index.cfm?fuseaction=ask_this.view&askthisi d=456; Kim Geiger, "Alan Simpson Pens Scathing Letter to 'Greedy Geezers' Retiree Group," *Los Angeles Times*, May 23, 2012, at *http://articles.latimes.com/2012/may/23/news/la-pn-alan-simpson-pens-scathing-letter-to-greedy-geezers-retiree-group-20120523.*

[58] Center for Global Policy Solutions. (2016). "Overlooked But Not Forgotten: Social Security Lifts Millions More Kids Out of Poverty." Washington, DC: Center for Global Policy Solutions. at *http://globalpolicysolutions.org/report/overlooked-not-forgotten-social-security-lifts-millions-children-poverty/.*

[59] S. 1351, "Intergenerational Financial Obligations Reform (INFORM) Act," 113th Congress, introduced by Sen. John Thune (R-SD), July 24, 2013, at *https://www.congress.gov/bill/113th-congress/senate-bill/1351/related-bills.*

[60] Social Security Administration, Office of Retirement and Disability Policy, *Annual Statistical Supplement, 2017* "Social Security (Old-Age, Survivors, and Disability Insurance) Program Description and Legislative History," at https://www.ssa.gov/policy/docs/statcomps/supplement/2017/oasdi.html; Social Security Administration, Fact Sheet, at *https://www.ssa.gov/news/press/factsheets/basicfact-alt.pdf.*

[61] Thomas H. Eliot, Speech at General Staff Meeting of the Social Security Administration: The Legal Background of the Social Security Act (Feb. 3, 1961), available at *http://www.ssa.gov/history/eliot2.html.*

[62] Nancy J. Altman, *The Battle for Social Security: From FDR's Vision to Bush's Gamble*, (Hoboken, NJ: John Wiley & Sons, Inc., 2005), p. 104.

[63] William E. Spriggs, "African Americans and Social Security: Why the Privatization Advocates Are Wrong," *Dollars & Sense*, November/December 2004, at *http://www.dollarsandsense.org/archives/2004/1104spriggs.html.*

[64] United States Census Bureau, QuickFacts, United States, "Population estimates, July 1, 2016, (V2016)," at https://www.census.gov/quickfacts/fact/table/US/PST045216; Social Security Administration, *Annual Statistical Supplement, 2010 – OASDI Current-Pay Benefits: Summary (5.A),* "Table 5.A1—Number and average monthly benefit, by type of benefit and race, December 2009," at https://www.ssa.gov/policy/docs/statcomps/supplement/2010/5a.pdf. (The 19 percent was calculated by dividing 1,838,933 (the number of Blacks receiving Disability Insurance benefits) by 9,694,114 (the total number of all races receiving those benefits), which equals 18.9 percent.)

[65] Kids COUNT Data Center, Annie E. Casey Foundation, "Child population by race," at *http://datacenter.kidscount.org/data/tables/103-child-population-by-race#detailed/1/any/false/870,573,869,36,868/68,69,67,12,70,66,71,72/423,424*; Social Security Administration, *Annual Statistical Supplement, 2010 – OASDI Current-Pay Benefits: Summary (5.A),* "Table 5.A1—Number and average monthly benefit, by type of benefit and race, December 2009," at https://www.ssa.gov/policy/docs/statcomps/supplement/2010/5a.pdf. (The 22 percent was calculated by dividing 384,003 (the number of African-American children receiving Disability Insurance benefits) by 1,747,979 (the total number of children of all races receiving those benefits), which equals 21.9 percent; and by dividing 426,761 (the number of Black children receiving Survivor Insurance benefits) by 1,921,148 (the total number of children of all races receiving those benefits), which equals 22.2 percent.

[66] Alice Kessler-Harris, Chapter 4: "Designing Women and Old Fools: The Construction of the Social Security Amendments of 1939," in *U.S. History as Women's History: Key Feminist Issues,* edited by Linda K. Kerber, Alice Kessler-Harris, and Kathryn Kish Sklar, The University of North Carolina Press, Chapel Hill & London, 1995, citing Advisory Council Minutes from February 18-19, 1938. The materials from the Council's work are at the National Archives, Washington, D.C., p. 101.

[67] Id. p. 97, citing Chairman's Files.

[68] Howard M. Iams, Gayle L. Reznik and Christopher R. Tamborini, "Earnings Sharing in Social Security: Projected Impacts of Alternative Proposals Using the MINT Model," *Social Security Bulletin,* Vol. 69, No. 1, 2009, at *https://www.ssa.gov/policy/docs/ssb/v69n1/v69n1p1.html.*

[69] Ellen O'Brien, Ke Bin Wu and David Baer, AARP Public Policy Institute, "Older Americans in Poverty: A Snapshot," April 2010, at *https://assets.aarp.org/rgcenter/ppi/econ-sec/2010-03-poverty.pdf.*

[70] Social Security Administration, Office of the Chief Actuary, Beneficiary Data, "Number of Beneficiaries By Age," at *https://www.ssa.gov/oact/progdata/byage.html.*

[71] Social Security Administration, Fact Sheet, "Social Security is Important to Women," (November, 2016) (The fact sheet states: "In 2014, 46 percent of all elderly unmarried females receiving Social Security benefits relied on Social Security for 90 percent or more of their income.") at https://www.ssa.gov/news/press/factsheets/ss-customer/women-ret.pdf.

[72] At the start of the Advisory Council, the women named as members representing the public were: Lucy R. Mason, General Secretary, National Consumers' League, New York, N.Y.; Theresa Mcmahon, University of Washington, Seattle, WA; and Elizabeth Wisner, Past-President of the Association of Schools of Social Work, New Orleans, LA. Part way through, Mason had to resign and was replaced by Josephine Roche, who was head of The Rocky Mountain Fuel Company, Denver, CO, and a progressive activist who worked, among other things, for national health insurance. See the Social Security Administration History website at: *https://www.ssa.gov/history/reports/38advise.html.*

[73] Stephen Goss, Alice Wade, J. Patrick Skirvin, et al., "Effects of Unauthorized Immigration on the Actuarial Status of the Social Security Trust Funds," Actuarial Note Number 151, April 2013, Social Security Administration Office of the Chief Actuary, at *https://www.ssa.gov/oact/NOTES/pdf_notes/note151.pdf.*

[74] Social Security Administration, 2017 OASDI Trustees Report, at *https://www.ssa.gov/OACT/TR/2017/tr2017.pdf.*

[75] *2016 Republican Platform*, Government Reform, "Saving Social Security," pp. 24-5, at *https://prod-static-ngop-pbl.s3.amazonaws.com/media/documents/DRAFT_12_FINAL%5b1%5d-ben_1468872234.pdf.*

[76] Wilbur J. Cohen and Milton Friedman, *Social Security: Universal or Selective?* Rational Debate Seminars, American Enterprise Institute for Public Policy Research, Washington, D.C., 1972, p. 55.

[77] Peter Holley, "Republican lawmaker wants to ban welfare recipients from buying steak and lobster," *Washington Post*, February 23, 2016, at *https://www.washingtonpost.com/news/wonk/wp/2016/02/23/republican-lawmaker-wants-to-ban-welfare-recipients-from-buying-steak-and-lobster/?utm_term=.858680911efe.*

[78] Arthur Delaney and Alissa Scheller, "Think People on Food Stamps Are Eating More Lobster Than You? Think Again," The Huffington Post (December 6, 2017), at https://www.huffingtonpost.com/2015/05/16/food-stamps-lobster_n_7293630.html

[79] National Conference of State Legislatures, "Drug Testing for Welfare Recipients and Public Assistance," (March 24, 2017), at http://www.ncsl.org/research/human-services/drug-testing-and-public-assistance.aspx.

[80] Josh Levin, "The Welfare Queen," *Slate*, December 19, 2013, at *www.slate.com/articles/news_and_politics/history/2013/12/linda_taylor_welfare_queen_ronald_reagan_made_her_a_notorious_american_villain.html.*

[81] Ronald Reagan, "Address Before a Joint Session of the Congress on the Program for Economic Recovery," February 18, 1981, at *http://www.presidency.ucsb.edu/ws/index.php?pid=43425.*

[82] CBS News, "GOP State of the Union Response: Full Paul Ryan Text," (Transcript), January 26, 2011, at *https://www.cbsnews.com/news/gop-state-of-the-union-response-full-paul-ryan-text/.*

[83] Nancy J. Altman and Eric R. Kingson, *Social Security Works!*, (New York, NY: The New Press, 2014), p 150. (Kingson was the staff person who made the quip.)

[84] Robert A. Rosenblatt, "Entitlements Seen Taking Up Nearly All Taxes by 2012," *Los Angeles Times*, August 9, 1994, at *https://articles.latimes.com/1994-08-09/news/mn-25181_1_entitlement-programs.*

[85] Social Security Administration, 2016 OASDI Trustees Report, Table VI.G4, "OASDI and HI Annual and Summarized Income, Cost, and Balance as a Percentage of GDP, Calendar Years 2016-2090," at *https://www.ssa.gov/oact/tr/2016/VI_G2_OASDHI_GDP.html#200732.*

[86] Congressional Budget Office, "The Long-Term Outlook for Health Care Spending," November 2007, at *https://www.cbo.gov/sites/default/files/110th-congress-2007-2008/reports/11-13-lt-health.pdf.*

[87] Social Security Administration, 2017 OASDI Trustees Report, p. 7, "Table II.B1.—Summary of 2016 Trust Fund Financial Operations," at *https://www.ssa.gov/oact/tr/2017/tr2017.pdf.*

[88] Nancy J. Altman, "The Striking Superiority of Social Security in the Provision of Wage Insurance," Harvard Journal on Legislation, Vol. 50, No. 1 (2013) at pp. 155-6 at http://harvardjol.com/wp-content/uploads/2013/09/Altman_Article1.pdf.

[89] Centers for Medicare & Medicaid Services, 2017 Medicare Trustees Report, p. 45, Table III.BI.—Statement of Operations of the HI Trust Fund during Calendar Year 2016," at *https://www.cms.gov/Research-Statistics-Data-and-Systems/Statistics-Trends-and-Reports/ReportsTrustFunds/Downloads/TR2017.pdf.*

[90] Congressional Budget Office, "Key Issues in Analyzing Major Health Insurance Proposals," December 2008, at *https://www.cbo.gov/sites/default/files/110th-congress-2007-2008/reports/12-18-keyissues.pdf.*

[91] Paul N. Van de Water, "Raising Medicare's Eligibility Age Would Increase Overall Health Spending and Shift Costs to Seniors, States, and Employers," Center on Budget and Policy Priorities, August 23, 2011, at *https://www.cbpp.org/research/raising-medicares-eligibility-age-would-increase-overall-health-spending-and-shift-costs-to*; Kaiser Family Foundation, "Raising the Age of Medicare Eligibility: A Fresh Look Following Implementation of Health Reform," July 18, 2011, at *https://www.kff.org/medicare/report/raising-the-age-of-medicare-eligibility/.*

[92] Tim H. Henderson, "State-By-State Comparisons Administrative Costs," American Academy of Family Physicians, December 2005, at *http://www.aafp.org/dam/AAFP/documents/advocacy/coverage/medicaid/ES-MedicaidAdministrativeCosts-121305.pdf.*

[93] Center for Economic and Policy Research, "CEPR Health Care Budget Deficit Calculator," at *http://cepr.net/calculators/hc/hc-calculator.html.*

[94] Stephanie Condon, "Alan Simpson: Social Security Is Like a 'Milk Cow with 310 Million Tits!'" CBS News, August 25, 2010,

www.cbsnews.com/news/alan-simpson-social-security-is-like-a-milk-cow-with-310-million-tits.

[95] David Corn, "SECRET VIDEO: Romney Tells Millionaire Donors What He REALLY Thinks of Obama Voters," *Mother Jones*, September 17, 2012, at *http://www.motherjones.com/politics/2012/09/secret-video-romney-private-fundraiser/.*

[96] Ben Craw and Zach Carter, "Paul Ryan: 60 Percent of Americans Are 'Takers,' Not 'Makers,'" *Huffington Post*, October 5, 2012, at *https://www.huffingtonpost.com/2012/10/05/paul-ryan-60-percent-of-a_n_1943073.html.*

[97] Frank Bane, "A New American Reality," Social Security Bulletin, Vol. 1, No. 8, August 1938, at Social Security Administration History website: *https://www.ssa.gov/history/bane838.html.*

[98] *Political Party Platforms: Parties Receiving Electoral Votes: 1840-2016,* "Republican Party Platform of 1936," June 9, 1936, at *http://www.presidency.ucsb.edu/ws/?pid=29639.*

[99] Eveline M. Burns, "Letters to the Editor," *The Nation*, July 11, 1936.

[100] Marco Rubio, "Saving Social Security in the 21st Century," *National Review*, August 15th, 2015, at *http://www.nationalreview.com/article/422581/saving-social-security-21st-century-marco-rubio.*

[101] *New York Times*, "Transcript: Republican Presidential Debate," (Transcript), October 28, 2015, at *https://www.nytimes.com/2015/10/29/us/politics/transcript-republican-presidential-debate.html?_r=0.*

[102] Melissa Hayes, "Chris Christie Pitches Overhauling Social Security and Health Care," *Tribune News Service (Governing)*, April 15, 2015, at *http://www.governing.com/topics/politics/tns-chris-christie-social-secutiry.html.*

[103] Additional Minority Views, House Report 1300 on H.R. 6000, Social Security Act Amendments of 1950, 81st Cong, 1st Sess., p. 173.

[104] Social Security Administration, Office of the Chief Actuary, "Replacement Rates for Hypothetical Retired Workers," Actuarial Note No. 2016.9, June 2016.

[105] Calculations were made by Social Security Works using estimates developed by the Office of the Chief Actuary, Social Security Administration. For the Bush proposal, we used "Estimated Financial Effects of a Comprehensive Social Security Reform Proposal Including Progressive Price Indexing--INFORMATION," Social Security Administration, February 10, 2005, at https://www.ssa.gov/oact/solvency/RPozen_20050210.pdf; for Bowles-Simpson: Chief Actuary's December 1, 2010 letter to Bowles and Simpson, co-chairs, National Commission on Fiscal Responsibility and Reform, Social Security Administration, December 1, 2010, at https://www.ssa.gov/OACT/solvency/FiscalCommission_20101201.pdf; for Rep. Sam Johnson: Chief Actuary's December 8, 2016 letter estimating the financial effects on Social Security of H.R. 6489, at https://www.ssa.gov/oact/solvency/SJohnson_20161208.pdf.

CHAPTER 6: REMAINING VIGILANT AND MOVING FORWARD

[1] Dwight D. Eisenhower to Edgar Newton Eisenhower, Document #1147, The Papers of Dwight David Eisenhower, *Volume XV—The Presidency: The Middle Way*, at *http://web.archive.org/web/20051124190902/http://www.eisenhowermemorial.org/presidential-papers/first-term/documents/1147.cfm.*

[2] Barack Obama, "Keynote Address at the 2004 Democratic National Convention," July 27, 2004, at *http://www.presidency.ucsb.edu/ws/?pid=76988.*

[3] StatisticsTimes, "Projected GDP Ranking (2016-2020)," Top 10 countries by GDP (Nominal) 2016, (Chart) at http://statisticstimes.com/economy/projected-world-gdp-ranking.php.

[4] Social Security Administration, 2016 OASDI Trustees Report, Table VI.G4, "OASDI and HI Annual and Summarized Income, Cost, and Balance as a Percentage of GDP, Calendar Years 2016-2090," at *https://www.ssa.gov/oact/tr/2016/VI_G2_OASDHI_GDP.html#200732*; Analysis by Social Security Works of OECD Social Expenditure Database. (All data are for 2009 (most recent comparative data available). All countries compared have similar, defined-benefit pension systems. Private systems are excluded, as are targeted social assistance programs. To increase data comparability, only half of spending was counted for program components in other countries that cover all government employees (and only a quarter of spending on those that cover a combination of government employees and members of the military/veterans), as only roughly half (a quarter) of such spending in United States is Social Security spending.)

[5] Mark Mather, "Fact Sheet: Aging in the United States," Population Reference Bureau, January 2016, at *http://www.prb.org/Publications/Media-Guides/2016/aging-unitedstates-fact-sheet.aspx.*

[6] Nancy J. Altman and Eric R. Kingson, Social Security Works! (New York, NY: The New Press, 2015), pp.185-196. See also, Matt Shuham, "WH Budget Chief: 'I Hope' Fewer People Get Social Security Disability Insurance," *Talking Points Memo*, May 23, 2017, at *http://talkingpointsmemo.com/livewire/mick-mulvaney-i-hope-fewer-people-social-security-disability-insurance.*

[7] George W. Bush, "Address Before a Joint Session of the Congress on the State of the Union," February 2, 2005, at *http://www.presidency.ucsb.edu/ws/index.php?pid=58746.*

[8] Debra B. Whitman, Ph.D., "Not Everyone Is Living Longer," *Huffington Post*, May 30, 2014, at *https://www.huffingtonpost.com/debra-b-whitman-phd/not-everyone-is-living-longer_b_5418329.html.*

[9] Nancy Altman, "Wall Street's Third Way Absurdly Wrong About Sanders' Social Security Plan," *Huffington Post*, January 31, 2016, at *https://www.huffingtonpost.com/nancy-altman/wall-streets-third-way-ab_b_9125786.html.*

[10] Center for Economic and Policy Research, "Contra the Crowd-Out Thesis: Countries that Spent More on Seniors Also Spend More on Children," March 18, 2013, at *http://cepr.net/blogs/cepr-blog/contra-the-crowd-out-thesis-countries-that-spent-more-on-seniors-also-spend-more-on-children.*

[11] Franklin D. Roosevelt, "Address at Madison Square Garden, New York City," October 31, 1936, at *http://www.presidency.ucsb.edu/ws/?pid=15219.*

[12] *Political Party Platforms: Parties Receiving Electoral Votes: 1840-2016,* "2008 Democratic Party Platform," August 25, 2008, at *http://www.presidency.ucsb.edu/ws/?pid=78283*; "2008 Republican Party Platform," September 1, 2008, at *http://www.presidency.ucsb.edu/ws/?pid=78545.*

[13] 2016 Democratic Party Platform, at *http://www.presidency.ucsb.edu/papers_pdf/117717.pdf.*

[14] 2016 Republican Party Platform, at *https://prod-cdn-static.gop.com/media/documents/DRAFT_12_FINAL%5B1%5D-ben_1468872234.pdf.*

[15] Social Security Works, "Polling Memo: Americans' Views on Social Security," (March, 2018), at https://www.socialsecurityworks.org/wp-content/uploads/2018/03/Social-Security-Polling-Memo-March-2018.pdf.

[16] "Full transcript: President Obama's December 4 remarks on the economy," *Washington Post,* (Transcript), December 4, 2013, at *https://www.washingtonpost.com/politics/running-transcript-president-obamas-december-4-remarks-on-the-economy/2013/12/04/7cec31ba-5cff-11e3-be07-006c776266ed_story.html?utm_term=.b8b33daeebfb.*

[17] "President Participates in Social Security Conversation in Alabama, March 10, 2005, Auburn University, Montgomery, Alabama," at Social Security Administration History website: *https://www.ssa.gov/history/gwbushstmts5.html#03102005.*

[18] Social Security Administration, "Recipients (by type of payment), total payments, and average monthly payment, October 2016–October 2017," at *https://www.ssa.gov/policy/docs/statcomps/ssi_monthly/2017-10/table01.pdf.*

[19] Social Security Administration, "SSI Federal Payment Amounts For 2018," at *https://www.ssa.gov/oact/cola/SSI.html.*

[20] Medicare for All Act of 2017, S. 1804, 115th Cong. (2017), at *https://www.congress.gov/bill/115th-congress/senate-bill/1804.*

[21] Expanded & Improved Medicare For All Act, H.R. 676, 115th Cong. (2017), at *https://www.congress.gov/bill/115th-congress/house-bill/676.*

[22] Nancy Altman and Merton Bernstein, "Medikids: A Proposal to Improve Children's Health Care, Reduce Public Program Non-Benefit Costs and Shrink Adult Health Care Outlays," *Huffington Post,* February 1, 2015, at *https://www.huffingtonpost.com/nancy-altman/merton-bernstein-medikids-childrens-health-care-proposal_b_6591024.html.*

[23] Franklin D. Roosevelt, "Message to Congress Reviewing the Broad Objectives and Accomplishments of the Administration," June 8, 1934, at Social Security Administration History website: *https://www.ssa.gov/history/fdrstmts.html#message1.*

[24] Franklin D. Roosevelt, "Fireside Chat," June 28, 1934, at Social Security Administration History website: *https://www.ssa.gov/history/fdrstmts.html#fireside1*.

[25] Benjamin W. Veghte, Ph.D., "What are the Implications of Rising Inequality for Social Security Policy?," February 25, 2015, at *https://www.socialsecurityworks.org/wp-content/uploads/2015/02/What-are-the-Implications-of-Rising-Inequality-for-Social-Security-Policy-2.pdf*.

[26] Nancy Altman, "The GOP wants to eliminate the estate tax. Let's use it to expand Social Security instead," The Hill (November 15, 2017), at http://thehill.com/blogs/congress-blog/politics/360376-the-gop-wants-to-eliminate-the-estate-tax-lets-use-it-to-expand. Page 339: "those at the top paid $81.6 billion less" (For the 82% figure: Congressional Budget Office, "Increase the Maximum Taxable Earnings for the Social Security Payroll Tax," Options for Reducing the Deficit: 2017 to 2026, December 8, 2016, at *https://www.cbo.gov/budget-options/2016/52266*. For $81.6 billion figure: see Table II.B1 of 2017 OASDI Trustees Report, at *https://www.ssa.gov/oact/tr/2017/tr2017.pdf*. The author calculated the amount the following ratio: 82% produced $836.2 billion, so 90% would have produced $917.8 billion, for a difference of $81.58 billion.)

[27] Edwin Witte, "Reflections On The Beginnings of Social Security," Remarks Delivered in Observance of the 20th Anniversary of Social Security Act at Department of Health, Education, and Welfare, August 15, 1955, at Social Security Administration History website: *https://www.ssa.gov/history/witte4.html*.

APPENDIX I: KEY FOUNDERS AND ADVISORY GROUPS

[1] "CES Report," Social Security Administration, at Social Security Administration History website: *https://www.ssa.gov/history/reports/ces6.html*.

[2] "Social Security Pioneers," Social Security Administration, at Social Security Administration History website: *https://www.ssa.gov/history/pioneers.html*.

[3] "Social Security Board," Social Security Administration, at Social Security Administration History website: *https://www.ssa.gov/history/boardmembers.html*.

[4] "Social Security Commissioners," Social Security Administration, at Social Security Administration History website: *https://www.ssa.gov/history/commissioners.html*.

[5] "Cabinet Officers," Social Security Administration, at Social Security Administration History website: *https://www.ssa.gov/history/cabinet.html*.

INDEX

A

Adams, Albert C., 134
administrative difficulties, exclusions and, 222–25
advance funding, 116, 118–21, 269
Advisory Council, 81, 104–9, 117–20, 132–48, 258–59, 286, 288
affordability, opposition spreading doubt about, 255–65, 268, 314, 325
African Americans, 170–71, 186–90, 193–203, 208, 217–18, 222, 283–85, 319
aging population, 265–69. See also life expectancy
agricultural workers, 170–85, 188–228
Alston, Lee. J., 194, 204, 211–12, 215
Altmeyer, Arthur, 10–12, 14, 24–25, 178, 185–87, 206, 209–11, 215, 220, 226, 230–32
American Farm Bureau, 206. See also agricultural workers
annuities, 1–3, 33, 42, 46–48, 53, 65, 69, 153, 164, 167, 169, 174–75, 189–91, 211–12, 220–21, 241–42
Armstrong, Barbara Nachtrieb, 49, 58–59, 80, 209, 210., 288

B

Baby Boomers, 120, 258, 260, 262–64
Baird, Zoe, 208
Baker, James, 113–14
Ball, Robert M., 85–92, 151, 225, 233–36
Bane, Frank, 71–72, 74
beneficiary, recipient vs., 295
benefit formula, 68–69, 77–80, 83–84, 146–48, 236–37, 305, 326
benefits
    envisioned size and role of, 156–64
    fear-mongering on loss of, 252–55
Bipartisan Commission on Entitlement and Tax Reform, 296–97
bonds. See Treasury bonds
Booker, Cory, 328
Bowles, Erskine, 296, 307–9
Bozell, L. Brent, 57

ABOUT THE AUTHOR

Nancy J. Altman has a forty-year background in the areas of Social Security and private pensions. She is president of Social Security Works and chair of the Strengthen Social Security coalition.

Democratic House Leader Nancy Pelosi appointed Altman to a six-year term, starting October 1, 2017, on the Social Security Advisory Board. The seven-person Board is a bipartisan, independent federal government agency established in 1994 to advise the President, Congress, and the Commissioner of Social Security.

Altman is the author of *The Battle for Social Security: From FDR's Vision to Bush's Gamble* (John Wiley & Sons, 2005), and co-author of *Social Security Works! Why Social Security Isn't Going Broke and How Expanding It Will Help Us All* (The New Press, 2015). She has shared her Social Security expertise on numerous television and radio shows, including PBS NewsHour, MSNBC, and FOX News. She has published op-eds in dozens of newspapers including the New York Times, Wall Street Journal and USA Today.

From 1983 to 1989, Altman was on the faculty of Harvard University's Kennedy School of Government and taught courses on private pensions and Social Security at the Harvard Law School. In 1982, she was Alan Greenspan's assistant in his position as chairman of the bipartisan commission that developed the 1983 Social Security amendments.

From 1977 to 1981, she was a legislative assistant to Senator John C. Danforth (R-MO) and advised the Senator with respect to Social Security issues. From 1974 to 1977, she was a tax lawyer with Covington & Burling, where she handled a variety of private pension matters.

Altman chairs the Board of Directors of the Pension Rights Center, a nonprofit organization dedicated to the protection of beneficiary rights. She is a member of the Board of Directors of the Alliance for Retired Americans Educational Fund and the Economic Opportunity Institute. In the mid-1980's, she was on the organizing committee and the first board of directors of the National Academy of Social Insurance.

Altman has an A.B. from Harvard University and a J.D. from the University of Pennsylvania Law School.

CPSIA information can be obtained
at www.ICGtesting.com
Printed in the USA
LVHW06s1212150818
587050LV00014BA/372/P

9 781947 492165